D1516576

Career Decision Making

CONTEMPORARY TOPICS IN VOCATIONAL PSYCHOLOGY

A series of books edited by
W. Bruce Walsh and Samuel H. Osipow

WALSH and OSIPOW • *Career Decision Making, 1988*

CAREER
DECISION MAKING

Edited by
W. Bruce Walsh
Samuel H. Osipow
The Ohio State University

LAWRENCE ERLBAUM ASSOCIATES, PUBLISHERS
1988   Hillsdale, New Jersey   Hove and London

Lawrence Erlbaum Associates, Inc., Publishers
365 Broadway
Hillsdale, New Jersey 07642

Library of Congress Cataloging-in-Publication Data
Career decision making / edited by W. Bruce Walsh, Samuel H. Osipow.
       p.   cm.—(Contemporary topics in vocational psychology)
   Includes bibliographies and indexes.
   ISBN 0-89859-756-0
   1. Career development—Decision making.   2. Career changes-
-Decision making.   I. Walsh, W. Bruce, 1936–   .   II. Osipow,
Samuel H.   III. Series.
HF5549.5.C35C36 1988
158.6—dc19   88-283
                                                                               CIP

Printed in the United States of America
10 9 8 7 6 5 4 3 2 1

Contents

Preface   **xi**

Chapter 1   **History and Theory of the Assessment of Career Development and Decision Making**
Susan D. Phillips and Nicholas J. Pazienza   **1**

Prior to Developmental Theory   *1*
Career Developmental Theory
   and Assessment   *3*
Formulations of Vocational Development   *4*
Summary   *12*
Decision-Making Theory and Assessment   *13*
Summary   *26*
Retrospect and Prospect   *26*

Chapter 2   **The Assessment of Career Decision Making**
Robert B. Slaney   **33**

Introduction   *33*
Approaches to Career Indecision   *37*
The Developmental Perspective   *38*
The Measurement of Career Indecision   *45*
The Career Decision Scale   *46*
Manual for the Career Decision Scale   *47*

v

Research on the Career Decision Scale   48
My Vocational Situation Scale   51
Research on the My Vocational
    Situation Scale   54
The Vocational Decision Scale   58
The Occupational Alternatives Question   60
Career Decision-Making   65
Summary   70

**Chapter 3   The Assessment of Career Development
and Maturity**
Nancy E. Betz   **77**

Introduction   77
Measures of Career Maturity   81
Career Development Inventory   92
Cognitive Vocational Maturity Test   99
Additional Measures of Career Maturity   101
Career Maturity and Adjustment   109
Issues in Career Maturity Assessment   117
Summary and Recommendations   128

Chapter 4   Advances in Career-Planning Systems
Karen M. Taylor   **137**

Introduction   137
Paper-Pencil Programs   142
Career Occupational Preference System
    (COPSystem)   143
Computer-Assisted Career Guidance
    Systems   184
Curricular Career Planning Systems   205
Summary   205

**Chapter 5   An Expanded Context for the Study
of Career Decision Making, Development,
and Maturity**
Howard E. A. Tinsley and Diane J. Tinsley   **213**

Historical Foundations   214
A Theory of Leisure Experience   218

Research on Need-Satisfying Properties
     of Leisure Activities   *234*
Measurement of Leisure Constructs   *248*
Thoughts about Future Priorities   *256*

Author Index   265
Subject Index   273

List of Contributors

Nancy E. Betz
  The Ohio State University
Nicholas J. Pazienza
  State University of New York at Albany
Susan D. Phillips
  State University of New York at Albany
Robert B. Slaney
  The Pennsylvania State University
Karen M. Taylor
  The Ohio State University
Diane J. Tinsley
  Southern Illinois University at Carbondale
Howard E. A. Tinsley
  Southern Illinois University at Carbondale

Preface

Keeping up with new developments in Vocational Psychology is important to both psychological practitioners and researchers. This title (*Career Decision Making*) is the first volume in a new series called *Contemporary Topics in Vocational Psychology*. The aim of the series is to identify, report, and evaluate significant contemporary developments in Vocational Psychology and thus to provide both professional workers and students with an informed understanding of the progress taking place in the field. The plan of the series calls for a new volume containing six to seven chapters in relevant contemporary topics every two to three years.

W. Bruce Walsh
Samuel H. Osipow

1 History and Theory of the Assessment of Career Development and Decision Making

Susan D. Phillips
Nicholas J. Pazienza
State University of New York at Albany

The business of assessment—of any variety—is essentially directed toward collecting observations on some dimension of interest. The dimension of interest is often drawn from a theory or model that has been offered to explain a given phenomenon, and the various phenomena that have been selected for explanation reflect the questions that have been posed about human behavior. In the domain of vocational behavior, a variety of questions have been posed, each of which has been pursued by an array of theoretical perspectives, which, in turn, have dictated the dimensions to be observed and assessed. The focus of this chapter is on the assessment of career development and decision making, and in the review that follows, our purpose is to trace the origins of the questions that have been asked, to outline the theoretical models that have pursued those questions, and to identify the assessment devices generated by those models.

PRIOR TO DEVELOPMENTAL THEORY

It is clear that questions related to career decisions were asked long before "career development" became an area of interest. As is evident in Zytowski's (1967) notes on the history of vocational guidance, plans for assessment and recommendations about vocational choice were discussed as early as the time of Plato. In the more recent era, reflected in early vocational literature, there is evidence that individuals engaged in a variety of methods of searching for vocational direction, and that they relied heavily on the identification of significant individual differences. The primary questions of this period appeared to be, "What shall I do?" and "How wise is this choice?" and such questions were placed before a variety of experts, including graphologists, palmists, phrenologists, and other diviners of predetermined forces. Richards (1881), for example, pointed to the need to form a system that would identify the most fitting pursuit for a person, and recommended, among other methods, phrenological analysis.

As the vocational guidance movement gained momentum in the early 20th century, however, these methods of identifying a "good fit" were apparently sufficiently widespread to warrant criticism and warning from more prudently minded writers. Parr (1937), for example, provided an amusing account of the failure of astrological predictions about vocational choice when put to an empirical test. Further, while reinforcing the necessity of identifying one's talents, Kitson (1929) warned against the efforts of individuals engaged in such pseudosciences. Instead, he argued, thoughtful information gathering and analysis were necessary.

The search for a "wise choice" and for a more systematic method of vocational assessment was dramatically altered when Parsons (1909) offered his famous dictum:

> In a wise choice of a vocation, there are three broad factors: (1) a clear understanding of yourself, your aptitudes, abilities, interests, ambitions, resources, limitations, and their causes; (2) a knowledge of the requirements and conditions of success, advantages and disadvantages, compensation, opportunities, and prospects in different lines of work; (3) true reasoning on the relations of these two groups of facts. [p. 5]

From his social and moral guidance origins, Parsons attempted to abandon the "pseudosciences" in favor of applying the scientific method to social problems, and his classic prescription became the model for occupational decision making and assessment.

Although Parsons's prescription was more scientific than many of the less respected methods of the time, even he made reference to inferring individual differences in mental development from observing the shape of the head. Advances in the assessment of individual differences were clearly needed. The work of Binet, Otis, and Terman in the assessment of intelligence are often cited as critical beginnings, and in the vocational domain the work at Minnesota (e.g., Patterson & Darley, 1936) stands out as the major effort in developing assessment methods that would supply the data for a logical, empirical analysis as the basis for responding to the question, "How wise is this choice?"

While methods for assessing individual differences and assisting career decision making benefitted from increasing technological and theoretical sophistication in differential psychology, this perspective on career decision making was characterized by a strongly deterministic view of individuals and by reliance on expert analysis either to divine or identify empirically the individual differences that would be critical in determining an individual's best occupational direction. Vocational decision making was regarded as a discrete event, and limited attention was directed to antecedents and consequences of a given decision, to changes over time, or to the decision-making process. In this tradition (still in evidence today in the models of Holland, 1973, 1985; and Dawis & Lofquist, 1984), there has been clearly more emphasis on the content and outcome of a decision—on the question of *what* to choose—than on the process by which the decision is made, and, consequently, the focus of the assessment efforts has been on the nature of the decider and his or her alternatives, with the goal of achieving a maximally congruent match between person and occupation.

CAREER DEVELOPMENTAL THEORY
AND ASSESSMENT

Emergence of Vocational Development as a Concept

While the initial systematic efforts associated with the problem of vocational decision making and choice were primarily those of identifying individual and occupational differences, a movement away from concern about the *content of a choice* and toward the *process of choosing* was evident as early as 1919. In the years prior to Super's (1953) introduction of "vocational development" as a concept, several trends in the psychological and sociological literature can be identified as influential in introducing questions related to time, evolution, and change into conceptions of vocational behavior.

The first of these was in the vocational domain, where increased attention was being directed to the antecedents and consequences of decisions. Brewer (1919) offered an expansion of Parsonian notions into the educational system, arguing against choice as a point-in-time phenomenon, and for an emphasis on vocational preparation, choice, entry, and adjustment. Similarly, Kitson (1925, 1938) argued that choices are not just the unfolding of a preordained future, but rather are actively shaped by the decider. By 1929, Kitson was already warning against the misconceptions underlying the attempt to "find out what I am cut out for," and he made a strong case for the adaptability of individuals in terms of their suitability for a number of occupations and their capacity for developing new interests and abilities as a function of their life experiences.

A second precursor to notions of vocational development emerged in both the sociological and the psychological literature in the study of life histories. In the sociological domain, attempts were being made to analyze changes in work status over time. For example, Davidson and Anderson (1937) studied occupational mobility in social and economic terms, tracing careers from parental occupation through the child's schooling, initial workforce entry, and eventual adult occupation. Hollingshead (1949) studied the social status determinants of opportunities and progress in both educational and occupational endeavors. Additionally, Miller and Form (1951) offered an analysis of career patterns: the sequence of work periods and the succession of jobs held by individuals over the course of several years.

The study of life histories in the psychological literature yielded a picture of the normal problems and evolution of an individual over time. Beuhler's (1933) classic analysis of life histories revealed that distinct types of problems emerged as predominant at different ages. Such authors as Terman (1925), White (1954), and Erikson (1950) also provided a view of the individual as subject to predictable developmental changes, and Lazarsfeld's (1931) study of the determinants of choice suggested that it was possible to examine the history of a process of choosing.

While advances in the vocational domain and in sociological and psychological study of life histories both offered a view of the effects of age and time on an individual's behavior, and on predictable changes over time, a third influential trend stemmed from changes in the assumptions underlying applied psychology. Aubrey (1977) noted that a major factor in the evolution of guidance and counseling activities during the 1940s was the issue of freedom and self-determination. Rogers's (1942) classic work, in particular, illustrated the trend away from structural analysis and predetermination and toward self-awareness, acceptance, and growth.

In sum, the trends leading to developmental conceptualizations of career behavior, derived from a variety of domains, suggested that individuals change over time, often in predictable ways, and that visions of a preordained future could be challenged by the recognition that self-determination and participation in constructing one's future were possible, and, perhaps, necessary. Given these observations, new questions about career decisions—"How does a career progress?" and "What happens prior to and following an implemented vocational choice?"—were warranted.

FORMULATIONS OF VOCATIONAL DEVELOPMENT

The first formally presented model of vocational development was that of Ginzberg, Ginsburg, Axelrad, and Herma (1951). Observing that occupational choice actually appeared to be a series of decisions, they sought to address the question "How do individuals make decisions about their occupations?" Drawing on Lazarsfeld's (1931) suggestion that it was possible to examine how the person came to make the series of decisions that led to a particular choice, Ginzberg et al. identified the progressive development of factors involved in vocational choices. The product of their efforts was the delineation of three predictable stages: The *fantasy* stage, in which the process of choosing is conducted without attention to rational considerations; the *tentative* stage, characterized by advances in self-knowledge, time perspective, and reality orientation; and the *realistic* stage, in which both subjective considerations and a greater awareness of external reality serve as the basis for choice.

Although Ginzberg et al. provided a clearly articulated view of expectable developmental changes in vocational decision making, their view prompted quick response—and the emergence of the most widely known career development model. Super (1953) criticized the Ginzberg model for its failure to build on previous literature, for its focus on preferences rather than actual choice, for its arbitrary distinction between choice and adjustment, and for its failure to articulate the nature of the process of compromise between self and reality.

In proposing a more adequate alternative, Super (1953) detailed a continuous process of development characterized by a lifelong succession of stages. This process, he asserted, was one of developing and implementing a self-concept, and of compromise through role play between self-concept and reality. Observing that vocational psychologists had relied more heavily on the contributions of differential psychology than on those of developmental psychology, Super (1957) argued that the term "occupational choice" conveyed a misleading sense of precision and uniqueness. While individual and occupational differences were important, an array of occupations might be suitable for a given person, and there was enough intra-occupational variability to tolerate a variety of individuals.

Further, choosing an occupation was clearly not a point-in-time phenomenon. Rather, it was a process, a whole sequence of choices that evolved over time. Vocational development was seen to be an orderly, ongoing process that was marked by an evolving interchange between developmental tasks and individual repertoires (Super, Crites, Hummel, Moser, Overstreet, & Warnath, 1957). Similarly, "occupational adjustment" was not that which occurred after choice, but rather was the set of consequences associated with how developmental problems were addressed. In articulating his theory, Super (1953) deliberately selected the term "vocational development" because it encompassed the concepts of preference, choice, entry, and adjustment. "Vocational development" was used "to denote the process of growth and learning that underlies the sequence of vocational behavior" [Super et al., 1957, p. vii].

Drawing on the work of Beuhler (1933), Super (1953) proposed five vocational life stages that encompassed the entire life span. In these stages—*growth, exploration, establishment, maintenance,* and *decline*—characteristic undertakings and problems are described (Jordaan, 1974; Super, 1957; Super, Starishevsky, Matlin, & Jordaan, 1963). During the *growth* stage (birth to approximately age 14), the central activity is one of forming a picture of the self and an orientation to the world of work. *Exploration* (approximately ages 14 to 24) is characterized by increasing examination of self and of self-in-context. Various roles are tried out in fantasy and in reality, and provisional commitment to a particular occupational alternative is made. In the *establishment* stage (ages 25 to 44), effort is directed first toward any adjustment necessitated by the result of trial, and second toward gaining a permanent position within the chosen occupation and advancing within that occupation. *Maintenance* (ages 45–64) is characterized by a shift from seeking to improve one's position to preserving that status which has been achieved. Finally, in the *decline* stage (age 65 and on), the individual is concerned with gradual disengagement from former work activities, and with seeking new roles to replace those formerly available in work.

As evident in the forgoing description, the life stages present predictable vocational developmental tasks. The tasks of one stage differ from the tasks of another, and different kinds of attitudes and behaviors are necessary to address the various developmental tasks. Thus, for example, the tasks associated with the exploration stage include crystallizing and specifying a vocational preference. In order to accomplish these tasks successfully, the individual must be aware of the need to crystallize and specify preferences, be able to use appropriate resources, and be aware of present–future relationships. In the establishment stage, however, developmental tasks include consolidation of status and advancement in an occupation, which require the individual to be aware of the need to consolidate, to acquire information about advancement, and to make and execute plans related to securing and improving one's position in a given field of work (Super et al., 1963). Drawing on the work of Havighurst (1953), Super further argued that success in coping with the set of tasks encountered in a particular life stage was essential for coping well with the tasks of the next life stage, and that the degree of vocational adjustment experienced by an individual at any given life stage was determined by the adequacy of his or her previous task-related coping (Super et al., 1957).

Vocational and Psychosocial Development of Adults

While a majority of the predevelopmental views of vocational choice and decision making focused on youth, Super's life-span perspective on careers served to highlight the existence of continued change, growth, and learning in adulthood.

As is evident in Super's (1953) formulations, important elements of vocational behavior occur after initial occupational selection and implementation. In addition, while Super (1957) detailed the nature of adult stages of career development (establishment, maintenance, and decline) in the context of life-span stages, other authors have offered a more specific focus on developmental phenomena associated with adulthood. From a psychosocial perspective, for example, Erikson (1950) detailed the series of issues addressed by the developing individual. In adulthood, these issues include developing intimacy as opposed to isolation and alienation (early adulthood, approximately 20 to 40), establishing patterns of generativity and guidance versus self-indulgence and stagnation (40 to 60), and achieving a sense of satisfaction and fulfillment with past life versus meaninglessness and dispair (60 and older). Havighurst (1953) also outlined a sequence of life tasks that confront the developing individual. Similar to the sequence outlined by Erikson, his formulation included the necessity of leaving one's family of origin, establishing an independent role with respect to marriage, family, occupation, and social and civic involvement, maintaining achievements in these domains, and adjusting to changes in social, familial and occupational roles, as well as to changes in one's own capacities.

Also drawing on a psychosocial perspective, Levinson, Darrow, Klein, Levinson, and McKee (1978) focused on critical transition points in development. Beginning with the early adult transition (ages 18–20), in which the individual develops an adult identity that is independent of family of origin, Levinson et al. described the critical turning points encountered at decade intervals, in which the individual re-evaluates existing life structures and plans, and sets the foundation for subsequent years. Similar to other models of adult development, an age 30 transition marks the shift from exploration to more stable commitments, a mid-life transition (age 40) signals a readjustment of personal and vocational goals, given the increasing recognition of inevitable physical decline, and a late adult transition (age 60) is marked by the change in roles that accompanies retirement.

Formulations of development with more explicit implications for the vocational behavior of adults have been offered recently by Schein (1978) and Super (1980). Schein's model details the specific vocational tasks facing an individual from birth to retirement. Beyond the growth, fantasy, and exploratory tasks of youth and young adulthood, Schein outlined tasks associated with entering the world of work and undertaking basic training (ages 16 to 25), with assuming full membership in early (17–30) and midcareer (25 and up), with negotiating leadership and nonleadership roles in later career phases (age 40 to retirement), and with disengagement from the workforce and retirement.

Super's (1980) life-span–life-space model of career development highlighted the continuous interplay among the variety of roles played by an individual in different arenas of life. Defining a career as "a sequence of positions held during the course of a lifetime," Super argued that the positions included in a career can be both occupational and nonoccupational (1980, p. 286). In detailing the nine major roles of child, student, leisurite, citizen, worker, spouse, homemaker, parent, and pensioner, and the four primary theaters in which these roles are enacted (home, community, school, and workplace), Super (1980) sought to describe the typical life space of an individual and to demonstrate how the combination, and sometime overlapping, of various roles and theaters may have conflictual or enriching effects. Further, he argued that roles vary in terms of temporal importance and emotional involvement at different life stages, and that significant role shifts are preceded and accompanied by decision points that should be approached in a rational manner.

Indexes of Development

From the developmental view, vocational behavior was one aspect of more general development, and could be marked by progress through a series of life stages. Each of the stages imposed certain tasks which must be addressed in order to pass through the current stage adequately and progress to the next stage. Stages and tasks reflected social and biological realities, and advancement through the stages and tasks was evident in the individual's increasingly realistic, independent, and goal-directed behavior (Super et al., 1957).

Having detailed this predictable developmental process, an index by which one could evaluate development was needed, and it was argued that the extent to which an individual has progressed through the developmental sequence may be considered to be the extent to which the individual has matured. *Vocational maturity*, thus, represented "the place reached on the continuum of vocational development from exploration to decline" [Super, 1957, p. 186], and the concept of a "vocational maturity quotient" was proposed as a ratio of vocational to chronological age (Super, 1957).

Following this initial conceptualization of vocational maturity as the yardstick by which vocational development could be measured, a variety of different definitions were offered. In considering criteria for maturity, Super et al. (1957) suggested that the normality of behavior be considered. However, "in reference to what or whom?" was a significant question. If one used adults as the reference group when evaluating the behavior of a child—one method of inferring maturity—then one must assume that adulthood is a mature and stable state. Arguing that growth, change, and learning continues in adulthood, Super et al. (1957) proposed two alternate reference points for evaluating an individual's vocational maturity. In the first, VM I, the individual's chronological age may be used to establish the expected life stage. This expected life stage may then be compared with the actual life stage as evident in the developmental tasks with which the individual is engaged. In the second, VM II, the focus is on the comparative adequacy of methods of dealing with developmental tasks. Using this reference point, the repertoire available to an individual for coping with a given developmental task is evaluated against the repertoires of others coping with that same task, whether or not the task in question is appropriate for the individual's age or life stage.

In order to establish standards for evaluating vocational maturity, the developmental tasks characteristic of each life stage had to be detailed, and the variations in behavior used in addressing these tasks had to be identified. Hence, using the VM II definition, Super et al. (1957) initially proposed five dimensions of vocational maturity associated with the behaviors required by the developmental tasks of the exploratory life stage. These dimensions included orientation to vocational choice, information, and planning about preferred occupations, consistency of vocational preferences, crystallization of traits, and wisdom of vocational preferences.

This a priori identification of the dimensions of vocational maturity was put to empirical test in the Career Pattern Study—a longitudinal examination of vocational behavior in the exploration and establishment stages of development. The

Career Pattern Study began in 1951, and its results have been reported in a series of monographs (Jordaan & Heyde, 1979; Super et al., 1957; Super, Kowalski, & Gotkin, 1967; Super & Overstreet, 1960). Initial methods used to measure these dimensions of vocational maturity included semistructured interviews, tests, and questionnaires, and required extensive coding and scoring efforts. Based on the results of the Career Pattern Study, several refinements in and variations on the concept of vocational maturity and its measurement were offered. These efforts are evident in the four lines of research and the resulting measures outlined herein.

Super and Colleagues: The Career Development Inventory

The first efforts were undertaken by Super and his colleagues in the context of the emerging results of the Career Pattern Study. Based on factorial analysis of the data for ninth-grade boys, Super and Overstreet (1960) offered a refined view of vocational maturity. One major dimension—planfulness—was identified, together with interpretable factors representing evidence of planning orientation, independence of work experience, and short-, intermediate-, and long-term time perspectives. Jordaan and Heyde's (1979) subsequent comparison of data drawn from 9th and 12th grades revealed some differences between the two grade levels. For example, the 9th-grade factors of independence of work experience and agreement between expressed and measured interests had no 12th-grade counterpart, and the 12th-grade factors of commitment to and acceptance of responsibility for vocational choices, and weighing of alternatives and contingencies had no 9th-grade counterpart. However, some commonalities (specification of a vocational preference, planning, occupational information, and steps in implementation) were also identified as worthy of attention in assessing vocational maturity.

The Career Development Inventory (Super, Thompson, Lindeman, Jordaan, & Myers, 1981) evolved from these results. In an effort to refine the indexes used in the longitudinal study, which were cumbersome and impractical for field use, Forrest (1971), Super and Forrest (1972), and Forrest and Thompson (1974) distilled from Career Pattern Study findings four components of vocational maturity (planning, exploration, information, and decision making) for abbreviated measurement. Subsequent revisions in the CDI yielded a six-scale, two-factor measure (an attitudinal factor, composed of planfulness and use of resources in exploration, and a cognitive factor, composed of career decision making, career development information, knowledge of the world of work, and information about preferred occupation; Super & Thompson, 1979). More recently, a measure with five dimensions containing indexes of career planning, career exploration, decision making, work information, and knowledge of preferred occupational group was developed (Super et al., 1981).

Crites: The Career Maturity Inventory

A second line of research directed toward improving the concept and measurement of vocational maturity was undertaken by John Crites. In response to the increasing array of conceptions and definitions related to vocational maturity, Crites (1961) offered an analysis and critique of definitions of vocational maturity. He argued that existing formulations of vocational maturity that were based on typical behaviors or developmental tasks as criteria yielded absolute or relative indexes with potentially conflicting interpretations. That is, an individual could be judged as immature on one and mature on another. Given that the evaluation of vocational maturity is based on the responses of an individual to a given stimulus (in this case, a developmental task), reliable measurement is only possible if the stimulus remains constant for all individuals, and individuals' responses differ in a reliable manner. Given that the stimulus (developmental tasks) does not remain constant—that is, by definition, different developmental stages impose different tasks—Crites argued that those definitions which only examined behavior (e.g., VM II) were flawed. Similarly, attempts to classify an individual by life stage (e.g., VM I) failed to allow for examination of variation in individual responses. Furthermore, those definitions that relied on age scales (that is, scales based on the "percentage passing" in a certain age group) would yield incomparable scores for different age levels. Point scale methods (those that are constructed according to successive levels of difficulty) require the construction of a theoretically based scoring key which may or may not correspond with practical reality.

Based on his critique, Crites suggested that vocational maturity would be best evaluated if the definition included both behavior and developmental tasks. That is, the age-expectable stage would be identified, and an individual's behavior in relation to addressing the tasks of that stage would be evaluated. Further, by combining the best features of age and point scale methods of assessment, he proposed that a scoring key could be constructed that differentiated older and younger individuals within a given life stage, and norms could be generated for each age level. The product of these propositions was the formulation of two measurable variables: the *degree* of vocational development (maturity as indicated by comparison between an individual's behavior and that of the oldest in his or her life stage), and the *rate* of vocational development (maturity as indicated by comparison of the individual's behavior and that of his or her age peers).

In addition to the critique and analysis of measurement methods, Crites (1965) proposed a model of the structure of vocational maturity. Using a hierarchical approach, he argued that the degree of career development was composed of two group factors: career-choice content and career-choice process. These two factors reflect a critical distinction between *what* is chosen and *how* it is chosen. Career-choice content included consistency and realism of career choices, while career-choice process included career-choice competencies and attitudes. Drawing on his critique of measurement models, and his subsequent analysis of the structure of career maturity, Crites designed the Career Maturity Inventory (Crites, 1973, 1978; formerly the Vocational Development Inventory), a paper-and-pencil measure of variables associated with the process factor. The CMI contains indexes of competencies (including self-appraisal, occupational information, goal selection, planning, and problem solving) as well as attitudes (including decisiveness, involvement, independence, orientation, and compromise).

Gribbons & Lohnes: Readiness for Vocational Planning

The third line of research related to the concept of vocational maturity and its measurement is reflected in the work of Gribbons and Lohnes (1968, 1982). These researchers initiated a longitudinal study in which they attempted to establish, among other things, measurable evidence of "early vocational maturity." Assessed through a semistructured interview, the evaluation of an individual's readiness for vocational planning is based on the logic and consistency of his or her use of self-knowledge regarding interests, abilities, and values. Eight variables are examined: (1) awareness of relevant factors in curriculum and (2) occupational choice, (3) ability to verbalize strengths and weaknesses in relation to choice, (4) accuracy of self-appraisal, (5) quality of evidence on which self-appraisal is based, awareness of (6) interests and (7) values and their relation to choice, and (8) extent to which the individual is prepared to assume independent responsibility for choice.

Westbrook: The Cognitive Vocational Maturity Test

The fourth line of research on vocational maturity was undertaken by Westbook and his colleagues. Arguing that assessment of attitudinal maturity provided an incomplete view of an individual's development, Westbrook's work focused on the cognitive, competency domain. Noting the importance of accurate information in mature vocational behavior, Westbrook (1970), and Westbrook, Parry–Hill, and Woodbury (1971) sought to develop an instrument to measure the acquisition and use of occupational knowledge. The Cognitive Vocational Maturity Test (Westbrook, 1970) was constructed to provide indexes of six cognitive areas of vocational maturity: field of work, job selection, work conditions, education required, attributes required, and duties.

Indexes of Adult Vocational Development

The majority of work in developing indexes of vocational development has clearly been directed toward youth and younger adults. However, consistent with the view that development occurs over the course of the life span, and, therefore, that maturity is a relevant concept at ages and stages beyond adolescence, several authors have presented indexes of vocational maturity geared toward the developmental tasks of adults. For example, Sheppard (1971) constructed a measure of adult career maturity using Crites's (1965) five attitudinal dimensions. Based on the idea that current vocational coping is predicated on the manner in which previous tasks were addressed, his is an indirect measure of readiness to cope with present and future adult career tasks.

A second example is that of Crites (1975, 1982). Drawing on his 1976 model of the elements of career adjustment, Crites constructed the Career Adjustment and Development Inventory to measure coping strategies and accomplishment of career development tasks during the establishment stage. A third index of adult vocational maturity was suggested by Super and Kidd (1979). The resulting Adult Career Concerns Inventory (Super, Thompson, & Lindeman, 1984) measures the extent to which an individual is concerned with exploration, establishment, maintenance, and disengagement tasks. Finally, Manuele (1983) drew on LoCascio's (1964, 1974) classification of individuals with late, delayed, or impaired career development to construct a measure of what developmental tasks were being addressed by such adults, and with what degree of competence.

SUMMARY

The observation that important phenomena occur both before and after a vocational decision is made served to expand the questions that were asked regarding career decisions and vocational behavior. Initially focusing on vocational choice as a relatively isolated event, and on the individual differences relevant to that choice, vocational psychologists began to inquire about the preparation for and consequences of career decisions. While not abandoning the important role of individual differences in suggesting decisional content, developmentalists posed questions about the process of choosing and about the evolution of vocational behavior. In contrast to the strongly deterministic emphasis of earlier views, the developmental perspective suggested that individuals can and do change over time. As it was observed that advancing age presents a series of new social and biological realities with which to cope, predictable sequences of change were identified and the process of career development was detailed. The developmental view of vocational behavior necessitated an assessment tool that would reveal an individual's status in the developmental process. Initially conceptualized as an index of developmental location, vocational maturity came to be viewed as an index of developmental preparedness, suggesting how well equipped an individual was to address the tasks of any given life stage.

DECISION-MAKING THEORY AND ASSESSMENT

While the developmental perspective on vocational behavior highlighted questions of process, available models generally portrayed a global, life-span view and offered little information about the process by which vocational decisions are made on the more specific, molecular level. Given the emerging view that career development is reflected in a series of decisions, a closer examination of the question "How are vocational decisions made?" was necessary. Two perspectives on this question were taken. In the first, models of a generic, decision-making process were offered, and in the second, individual differences in decision-making behavior were examined. Theoretical models and associated indexes from each perspective are reviewed next.

Formulations of the Career Decision-making Process

The advent of modern theories of the decision-making process can be seen as early as in Aristotle's development of the rules of logic, which involved the use of a reasoning process to determine consistency between premises and conclusions (Bross, 1953). The use of reasoning as a basis and method for individual decision making was more recently advocated by Benjamin Franklin in his description of "moral algebra" [Horan, 1979], a process by which one formally evaluates alternatives by systematically weighing the pros and cons of each (in written form) and choosing the one alternative which maximizes personal gain. Parsons's (1909) model of "true reasoning" between one's own characteristics and those of various occupations represents the modern application of the reasoning process to vocational decision making.

More recently, during the period between 1950 and 1970, a variety of theorists sought to elaborate the process by which vocational decisions are made. The models that have been advanced can be usefully distinguished in terms of those that attempt to describe career decision-making processes as they naturally occur, and those that attempt to prescribe how career decision making should proceed (Jepsen & Dilley, 1974). This distinction provides the basis for the following review of those models most influential in the theory and assessment of career decision-making process.

Descriptive Models. The descriptive models of the decision making process address the question, "How *are* decisions made?" and represent a variety of theoretical perspectives. Probably the most comprehensive is that proposed by Tiedeman (1961) and Tiedeman and O'Hara (1963), who described the complete sequential process of career decision making. Their conceptualization of the career decision-making process involved the notion of progress through a series of stages.

The first major stage—anticipation—is divided into a number of substages, including exploration (a period of awareness and information gathering), crystallization (emergence of particular alternatives), choice (selection of and commitment to one alternative) and clarification (specification of the manner in which the chosen alternative will be implemented). The second major stage—implementation and adjustment—contains substages of induction (initial reception of the consequences of implementing a given alternative), reformation (active effort to affect some of those consequences), and maintenance (balance between one's own assertive efforts and the demands of the environment). In general, progress through these stages represents a sequential expanding and narrowing process which eventually results in one alternative being chosen, implemented, and adjusted to. However, choice is not viewed as final, and a decision maker might recycle to an earlier stage or substage. Drawing on the Tiedeman–O'Hara model, Harren (1979) provided a more recent sequential model of the decision-making process that entailed stages of awareness, planning, commitment, and implementation. Harren also detailed the individual and contextual factors that might affect how a decision progresses.

In a more focused description of the decision-making process, Hilton (1962) sought to identify factors which precede and thus stimulate career decision making. The key elements of this model are premises (one's beliefs about the world) and plans (one's projected means of entry into an occupation). Hilton drew from Festinger's (1957) theory of cognitive dissonance in suggesting that career decision making occurs when premises and plans become inconsistent with one another, thus creating cognitive dissonance. As a means of reducing this dissonance, the decider must revise either plans or premises, and the process is terminated when plans again appear satisfactory.

While Hilton (1962) focused on the initial stages of the decision-making process, other models have been offered which focused on a later stage, that of evaluating alternatives. Vroom (1964), for example, drew on previous theoretical efforts to describe animal behavior in mathematical terms in suggesting how alternatives are evaluated in human decision making. Based on the work of Lewin (1951), he suggested that the force, or preference for a certain alternative, was a function of the valence (attraction) multiplied by the expectancy of success. In a second model of decision making that emphasized the evaluation of alternatives, Fletcher (1966) suggested that the process of evaluating alternatives is based almost exclusively on the affect associated with various alternatives at the time of choice.

Prescriptive Models. While the descriptive models vary in the extent to which they portray the decider as having a natural tendency toward rationality, assumptions about the value of rationality are far more explicit in prescriptive decision-making models. Each of those detailed herein address the question "How are decisions *best* made?" These models tend to portray the ideal decision maker as a scientist, seeking out information and using it to arrive at a choice that maximizes the chance for successful implementation.

Gelatt (1962), for example, prescribed a method of decision making which represented an application of the scientific method. Drawing on the work of Bross (1953), Gelatt suggested that decision making should involve the collection and utilization of relevant and reliable information. Quality decision making was seen as dependent on the acquisition of information, and it was recommended that the decider assume responsibility for choice and proceed in a rational, self-aware fashion. The possibility for recycling through the decision-making process was recognized in the notion of investigatory versus terminal decisions (e.g., a decision to gather more information versus a satisfactory appraisal of one's information search and choice).

Katz's (1963) prescription of how to reach the best career decision is quite similar to Gelatt's, but represents the added influence of statistical/mathematical models of decision making. His model focused on the importance of subjective values as the basis for establishing the desirability of various alternatives. Expectations, or the objective probabilities, were also considered, and a good decision was defined as one in which the alternative with the greatest expected value (in mathematical terms) was chosen.

Kaldor and Zytowski (1969) presented another prescriptive model which reflected the general influence of statistical decision theory and the particular influence of economic models. They suggested that individuals process informational input about themselves and the world of work in terms of costs and potential gains. Their prescription for quality decision making was to choose the alternative with the highest net value in terms of input costs versus output gains.

Descriptive Models with Prescriptive Implications. While the decision-making models outlined in the preceding section explicitly prescribe the basis for quality career decision making, there have also been a number of theoretical developments in relation to the more general constructs of career development and human decision making which have implications for the best ways to proceed in career decision making.

The first of these is directly related to the vocational domain. Krumboltz, Mitchell, and Jones (1976) provided a comprehensive theoretical formulation of career development and decision making as derived from the tenets of social-learning theory. These authors portrayed the decision-making process as consisting of several component skills that are learned through various means, such as observation of reinforced models, and direct reinforcement for the practice of certain behaviors. Drawing from classical decision theory, Krumboltz and Baker (1973) defined the behaviors and skills necessary for quality career decision making, and Krumboltz and Hamel (1977) later outlined the DECIDES model, which advocated the use of a rational decision-making process composed of the following skills: *D*efining the problem, *E*stablishing an action plan, *C*larifying values, *I*dentifying alternatives, *D*iscovering probable outcomes, *E*liminating alternatives systematically, and *S*tarting action.

A second model which presents implications for quality decision making was detailed by Janis and Mann (1977) in their "conflict model." Using cognitive dissonance and information-processing theories, seven criteria were detailed as necessary for "vigilant" (e.g., quality) decision making. Specifically, Janis and Mann suggested that vigilant decision making depended on the decider having (1) reviewed a wide range of alternatives, (2) surveyed values and objectives met by alternatives, (3) carefully weighed the pros and cons of each, (4) searched for relevant information, (5) assimilated any new information obtained, (6) re-examined options prior to choice, and (7) made provisions for implementing the chosen alternative. As evident from these criteria, Janis and Mann considered cognitive avoidance or distortion of information as the primary threat to quality decision making.

A third area of theory and research which has implications for career decision making is in the domain of problem solving. As detailed by D'Zurilla and Goldfried (1971), the process of problem solving involves a progression through (1) a general orientation to the problem situation, (2) problem definition and formulation, (3) generation of alternatives, (4) evaluation of alternatives, and (5) verification of choice. Using this model, Heppner (1978) maintained that quality problem solving was a function of adequate skills in terms of gathering information, assessing probabilities, assessing utilities and preferences, and assessing the consequences of several alternatives.

Indexes of the Career Decision-making Process

Differential views of vocational behavior provided the basis for evaluating decision making from the perspective of *what* is chosen. However, models of career development in general, and the proliferation of decision-making process models in particular, suggested that decision making could also be evaluated on the basis of *how* the decision is made. That is, assessment of career decision making could include not only measures of decisional outcomes (e.g., wisdom or congruence of the alternative chosen), but also measures of decisional process. In the review that follows, it should be noted that unlike the basic uniformity among measures of career development, the different perspectives on career decision-making processes necessitated a variety of different methods and targets of assessment.

Assessment from the Descriptive Perspective. Descriptive models have offered two basic avenues for assessment of decisional processes. The first of these was derived from the comprehensive stage models of Tiedeman (1961), Tiedeman and O'Hara (1963), and Harren (1979) which prompted the notion of assessing progress through the described decision-making process (decision-making process "maturity" or "location," as it were). Harren (1966) initiated the operationalization of this notion by designing a Q-sort of statements that were rationally constructed to reflect the stages in the Tiedeman–O'Hara model. The initial Q-sort was later converted into a checklist form (Harren, 1972), and eventually, with theoretical changes reviewed earlier, into the Assessment of Career Decision Making (Harren, 1979, 1984). Designed for high school and college students, the progress portions of the ACDM reflect the decision maker's degree of progress in the pre-implementation stages of decisions related to major and occupation, and in the postimplementation stages of the school or college decision.

The second form of assessment which arose from the descriptive models of decision-making processes follows from the influence of cognitive dissonance theory as evident in the Hilton (1962) and Janis and Mann (1977) models. In these models, dissonance was viewed as the impetus for decision making. Thus, simple measures of satisfaction with choice (e.g., Harren, Kass, Tinsley, & Moreland, 1978; Holland & Holland, 1977; Lunneborg, 1978), or regret (Mann, 1972) were developed, which provide a description of the decider's satisfaction with efforts at progressing toward a choice. Given that satisfaction, or lack of dissonance, signals the termination of decision-making processes, such measures also indicate whether or not futher decision making is forthcoming.

Assessment from the Prescriptive Perspective.   The various formulations of how career decision making should proceed each imply a basis for determining the extent to which the prescribed process has been followed. Those models that focused on the process of evaluating alternatives from a rational perspective (e.g., Katz, 1963; Kaldor & Zytowski, 1969) resulted in a number of assessment devices designed to measure the capacity of a decider to perform the recommended evaluation. One such device, developed by Dilley (1965), requires respondents to consider several alternative solutions to a variety of educational and vocational problems. Expected outcomes, and the associated probability, value, and preference ratings for each alternative are elicited. Assessment of decision-making ability involves comparing the calculated expected utility (probability $\times$ value) of the highest ranked alternative for each problem with that of the remaining alternatives. Higher quality decisions are defined as those in which the first-ranked alternative also has the highest expected utility.

There are also a number of other assessment devices that reflect the influence of prescriptive models, but that are less formal in that they do not rely on the use of mathematical evaluation to determine the best alternative. Examples of these are the various multiple-choice format tests that assess the decision maker's ability to process information about a fictitious other and about the world of work, and to choose an alternative that is objectively correct based on available information. The decision-making scales of the CMI (Crites, 1978) and CDI (Super et al., 1981) are measures of this type.

Other assessment devices have been derived from the view of career decision making as a complex skill composed of several component behaviors (e.g., Krumboltz et al., 1976). The identification of a number of behavioral components which are relevant to career decision making served as the basis for assessment. Information-seeking behavior is one such component that has achieved prominence as an indicator of competence in career decision making. Information-seeking behavior has been assessed by self-report, paper-and-pencil measures (e.g., Jones & Krumboltz, 1970; Stumpf, Collarelli, & Hartman, 1983), and also more directly by unobtrusive observation of the decider's use of various sources of information (e.g., Cooper, 1976). The ability to generate a range of alternatives is another behavioral component that has been used as a basis for assessing decision making (e.g., Dixon, Heppner, Petersen, & Ronning, 1979).

Decision-making ability or competence has also been assessed by less objective means. For example, Katz (1966) initially advocated the use of trained interviewers using a semistructured format to assess the degree to which a decider (1) knew which information it was important to obtain, (2) was able to access needed information, and (3) could systematically process information which was obtained. Janis and Mann (1977) also proposed the use of an interview format as a means of assessing decision-maker competence in terms of their seven vigilance criteria.

Assessment of Process: A Critique. In general, the assessment of career decision-making processes drawn from descriptive models is limited by its nature. That is, it does little more than describe or categorize the decider. In contrast, those assessment efforts drawn from the prescriptive models are potentially more useful in that the factors necessary for competent decision making are detailed. However, prescriptive assessment has been criticized in terms of both conceptual basis and methods of measurement. For example, semistructured interviews by raters trained to assess various aspects of decision-making competency are limited in terms of overreliance on rater judgment. In reference to those attempts to measure decision making more objectively from a statistical model, Katz (1966) noted the difficulty of assigning probability values with any degree of accuracy. While some prescriptive models advocated the use of subjective probability estimates (e.g., Gelatt & Clarke, 1967), existing assessment devices have not been notably influenced by this perspective.

A second criticism concerns the general overreliance on paper-and-pencil methods of assessment. Katz (1979) maintained that the competencies involved in processing information as a means of making the "best" occupational choice for a fictitious other are too far removed from the competencies involved in real-life career decision making. Drawing on Tiedeman's (1967) distinction between data and information, Katz noted that since the decider does not use constructs and plans which are relevant to him or herself, test performance cannot define real-life career decision-making competencies. Furthermore, he argued that the multiple-choice measures, such as those found in the CMI, imply the trait-and-factor assumption that there is one right occupation for any given individual's characteristics. Thus, Katz argued that, at best, such test scores should be viewed as representations of potential career decision-making competency. This view is echoed in Pitz and Harren's (1980) comment that even those scales which assess component skills believed to be necessary to competent career decision making (e.g., the World of Work Information Scale on the CDI) are too far removed from actual behavior, and, in the case of possession of information, are based on the tenuous assumption that a decider can appropriately utilize the information that he or she possesses.

In reference to the attempts to measure the component skills and behaviors involved in career decision making, Katz (1979) advanced the criticism that measures of specific behaviors (such as information seeking) are often too trivial to be tied meaningfully to the larger construct of career decision making. Pitz and Harren (1980) cautioned against the use of measures of information seeking in which it is assumed that "more is better." Given that all information is obtained at some cost, it is difficult to determine how much information is optimal, and, further, which sources are likely to contain the most relevant information. Even the assessment of the range of alternatives generated may be criticized on similar grounds: The assumed value of considering a wide range of alternatives also fails to take into account the degree of progress through the decision-making process (Oliver, 1979; Pitz & Harren, 1980). More specifically, while a wide range of alternatives may be beneficial early in the process, as one moves toward commitment to one alternative, it may be more advantageous to have narrowed the range of alternatives for consideration.

Alternate Forms of Process Assessment.   In response to the several criticisms noted, a number of alternative forms of assessing career decision making through simulation have been proposed. These alternatives generally stem from the desire to obtain, as nearly as possible, a sample of "real" career decision-making behavior which spans a large part, if not the entire, career decision-making process.

The Life Career Game (Boocock, 1967) was the first widely used career decision-making simulation. In this game, players are involved in making decisions that affect the life of a fictitious person about whom they are given information. Consequences of decisions are fed back to players in terms of objective national probability statistics. Good decision making is evidenced when players make decisions that closely meet the values of the fictitious person. While not designed as a means of formally assessing career decision-making competence, the Life Career Game revealed the potential for simulating complex life tasks.

Katz, Norris, and Pears (1978) developed the Simulated Occupational Choice in an effort to assess career decision-making competency more accurately in terms of the ability to recognize, obtain, and use necessary information (Katz, 1966). This three-phase simulation requires the decision maker to prepare questions that he or she considers important to ask in making a choice, to choose from available sources the most useful additional information, and to use appropriately final sources of information that are provided. Through comparing a respondent's pre-endorsed work values with those met by the occupation selected following each phase of the simulation, it is possible to determine (1) if the decider initially asked questions in line with his or her later endorsed values, (2) if the decider was able to ask for the most relevant information when presented with the total universe of information, and (3) if the decider was able to use the information provided to make a choice which was logically consistent with his or her values.

Following the work of Katz, Norris, and Pears (1978), Krumboltz, Scherba, Hamel, Mitchell, Rude, and Kinnier (1979) developed the Career Decision Simulation. In the initial use of this device, Krumboltz et al. were interested in determining if rational decision-making training could improve career decision-making competence (defined as the ability to make an occupational choice that was consistent with one's values). This simulation involves choosing from among 12 fictitious occupations, each of which satisfies a specific array of work values. At the beginning of the simulation, the decision maker is asked to rank order nine work values and is informed that he or she will have up to 2 hours to gather information from nine prepared sources. The information contained in the sources concerns the values satisfied by the various occupations. The final choice is scored in terms of its consistency with the prespecified work values of the decider, and process behaviors such as amount of information gathered, number of sources consulted, range of alternatives considered, and time spent in the process are recorded.

Formulations of Individual Differences

Virtually all of the theoretical formulations of decision-making process that we have reviewed were characterized by their portrayal of one typical (descriptive) or one best (prescriptive) process of career decision making. While Jepsen and Dilley (1974) noted that decision-making theorists typically acknowledged individual differences, it is clear that the focus of early decision-making models was on defining some generic type of career decision-making structure. As these models and their related measures were developed, and deviations from described or prescribed processes were noted, a critical appraisal of their shortcomings led to a renewed interest in individual differences in decision making (Edwards, 1961). That is, understanding how vocational decisions are made could be facilitated by examining such questions as "What accounts for observed differences in decision-making behavior?" and "Why do some deciders have more difficulty than others?"

The study of individual differences in career decision making has been conducted from two perspectives. The first of these focuses on the manner in which decisions are approached (decision-making styles or strategies), while the second focuses on sources and types of decisional difficulty.

Decision-making Styles and Strategies.   The study of individual differences in the manner in which decisions are approached, responded to, and engaged in has been primarily descriptive, with the product being a variety of taxonomies of decision-making styles or strategies. These taxonomies are characterized by two distinct theoretical perspectives. The first of these assumes that people possess "relatively stable, but pervasive, approaches to solving problems" [Jepsen, 1974a, p. 33]. This notion of traits, or core personality characteristics, is familiar in vocational theory. Having achieved prominence in the early matching models of vocational guidance, the concept of characteriological individual differences in vocational behavior has remained active in more recent models of vocational choice (e.g., Holland, 1973, 1985), and is evident in those conceptualizations of individual differences in decision making described herein.

One of the initial attempts to identify individual trait-like differences with respect to decision making was undertaken by Dinklage (1968). Based on interview data, she categorized decision-making behavior into eight trait-like ways of approaching decisions. These "decision-making styles" were defined as follows. The *planning* style is one in which the decision maker consciously plans a method for carrying out a decision. The *agonizing* decider spends much time and thought in gathering information and evaluating alternatives, only to be overwhelmed by the data accumulated. With the *delaying* style there is a recognition of the need to decide, but an inability to do so at present. The *paralysis* style is characterized by an acceptance of responsibility for decision making opposed by an inability to act. The *impulsive* decider tends to take the first available alternative without consideration of others. The *intuitive* decision maker tends to base choices on what "feels right." With the *fatalistic* style, the decider tends to relegate choice to fate or chance. Finally, the *compliant* decider allows another individual or agency to choose. Dinklage's initial analysis supported the notion that decision-making behavior thus classified was largely consistent across types of decisions, thus giving credence to the trait concept and stimulating further exploration of decision-making styles.

Jepsen (1974a) also derived a taxonomy of decision-making styles and provided descriptions based on interview data. While he identified a number of styles, two in particular emerged as most distinct and reliable. The *active planning* style was characterized as one in which the decider is well informed as a result of being actively and consciously involved in the decision-making process. In contrast, the *singular fatalist* type of decider is generally quite passive in relation to decision-making tasks.

Johnson's (1978) taxonomy of decision-making styles was based on his observation of students involved in vocational decision making at a college counseling center. Through what he termed a "mental factor analysis," he derived four styles of career decision making that represented the ways that individuals gather and process information. Johnson suggested that individuals gather information either systematically or spontaneously, and that they process information either internally or externally. Specifically, systematic gatherers are methodical and deliberate in their information search, with a cautious attitude toward commitment. Spontaneous gatherers, in contrast, tend to react holistically to whatever information they encounter, often resulting in quick psychological commitment. Regarding individual differences in information processing, Johnson described internal processers as tending to think about alternatives and reach a decision before discussing it with others. External processors tend to discuss alternatives with others before deciding how they feel. The four decision-making styles which result from crossing these two dimensions, thus, were *internal-systematic, internal-spontaneous, external-systematic,* and *external-spontaneous.*

In one of the most recent attempts to categorize styles of career decision making, Harren (1979) drew from earlier work (particularly that of Dinklage, 1968) and presented what appear to be the three least redundant and most reliable style categories: The *rational* style involves an awareness of the effect of prior actions on subsequent ones such that the decider accepts responsibility for choice and is active, deliberate, and logical. The *intuitive* style also involves acceptance of responsibility for decision making, but with little anticipation of the future, and little information seeking or logical weighing of alternatives. Rather, the intuitive style involves a focus on emotional self-awareness as the basis for choice. The *dependent* style is one in which responsibility is projected outside of the self, such that choice is based on the expectations or advice of others.

While the taxonomies of decision-making styles that have been detailed presumed that individual differences in decision making were pervasive and stable across situations, a second set of taxonomies were drawn from theoretical perspective that behavior is situationally determined. Similar to the so-called "state-versus-trait" debate, the trait assumption was called into question by theorists who referred to the individual's possession of a repertoire of decision-making strategies. Expressing this position, Arroba (1977) asserted that "each individual will possess a repertoire of decision making styles and . . . the styles he uses will vary across situations [p. 150].

Early reference to strategies of decision making is evident in the work of Simon (1957). His notion of "satisficing," or choosing the first alternative that is acceptable, implied that different strategies of decision making may be more or less appropriate, depending on the decision-making situation.

In more recent work, Arroba (1977) defined six strategies of decision making (*logical, hesitant, no-thought, intuitive, emotional,* and *compliant*) that correspond closely to the styles described by Dinklage (1968). The primary distinction is Arroba's contention that an individual may utilize a variety of decision-making strategies, depending on the decision-making situation.

Finally, Krumboltz et al. (1979) focused on inter- and intra-individual differences in decision making in their description of five primary decision-making strategies. Drawing upon prior taxonomies, their classification included *rational, impulsive, intuitive, dependent,* and *fatalistic.* These authors suggested that an individual would use similar strategies in similar types of situations, but, in general, the strategy selected would be influenced by the decision-making situation.

As is evident in the taxonomies we have detailed, the primary ways in which individuals are thought to differ in their approach to decision making are quite similar across taxonomies. The notion of an active, involved style, as compared with a more dependent, passive style is particularly evident, as is the notion of a logical, deliberate versus an impulsive, emotional style. Further, although the classifications that have been offered have been primarily descriptive, it is clear that some styles or strategies are thought to result in higher quality decisions than others. For example, the planning style of Dinklage (1968) and Jepsen (1974a), along with the systematic style of Johnson (1978), the logical strategy of Arroba (1977), and the rational approach detailed by Harren (1979) and Krumboltz et al. (1979) would be expected to result in ''better'' decisions than those styles or strategies that are less active or more impulsive.

Sources of Decisional Difficulty. Descriptions of decision-making styles and strategies imply that certain individuals should produce higher quality decisions and encounter less decisional difficulty than others. However, the ability to engage successfully in career decision making has been addressed more directly by those theorists and researchers who have focused on vocational indecision. Although reference to ''undecidedness'' has been pervasive in the vocational literature, the increasing recognition of individual differences among those who are undecided prompted several authors to inquire about the cause or causes of decisional difficulty.

Based on an analysis of vocationally undecided individuals, Holland and Holland (1977) classified types or levels of vocational indecision that reflected possible causes ranging from the fairly superficial (e.g., lack of information) to the more pervasive and deep-rooted. They hypothesized that the most debilitating cause of vocational indecision, the indecisive personality, is the result of a life history of conflicting learning experiences which prevent the formation of a clear sense of self, and, consequently, the ability to proceed in any type of decision-making task.

Social learning and cognitive behavioral theorists have also contributed to an understanding of vocational decision-making difficulty. For example, drawing primarily from Bandura's (1977) presentation of the construct of self-efficacy, Taylor and Betz (1983) suggested that individual differences in perceived ability to perform a task successfully may explain why some individuals have more difficulty in career decision making than others. Heppner's (1978) work also reflected the potential effect of cognition on decision-making difficulty. His analysis of the problem-solving literature yielded a view of the effective problem solver as one who is characterized by attitudes of control (ability to maintain self-control in problem situations), confidence (trust in one's ability to solve new problems), and approach toward (rather than avoidance of) problem situations. Individual perceptions on these dimensions would be expected to affect one's ability to engage in and successfully complete the career decision-making process.

Indexes of Individual Differences in Decision Making

Following the recognition of individual differences in how decisions were made, and in the extent to which difficulty was experienced by the decider, a variety of assessment devices were developed. In contrast to the process indexes that monitored an individual's overall progress or the adequacy of specific decisional skills, indexes of individual differences were largely directed toward classification of an individual's decisional behavior. These recent contributions to the assessment of career decision making are outlined herein.

Decision-making Styles and Strategies.   Efforts to assess decision-making styles or strategies have been generated from several of the taxonomies just outlined. Measurement generally entails self-report of behavior in past decision-making situations, although the available indexes vary in how those behaviors are evaluated and scored.

Jepsen's (1974b) effort represented one of the first attempts to measure individual differences in decision-making behavior. Based on a review of the decision-making literature, he derived 32 indexes that were representative of career decision-making processes. These indexes were subsumed under five primary dimensions on which vocational choice alternatives could be defined (range, specificity, level, heterogeneity, and consistency), and measured on an open-ended, paper-and-pencil questionnaire in which respondents report their thoughts and behaviors associated with various types of decisions. Trained scorers rate responses on each of the five dimensions.

More easily conceptualized and more objectively scored measures of stylistic individual differences have been provided by Harren (1984) and Johnson, Coscarelli, and Johnson (1978). Harren's (1984) Assessment of Career Decision Making contains three 10-item scales to measure the extent to which an individual engages in the rational, intuitive, and dependent decision-making behaviors that were detailed by Harren (1979). Johnson's (1978) taxonomy provided the basis for Johnson et al.'s (1978) Decision Making Inventory. This measure contains 20 Likert-type items, 12 of which form subscales that tap preferred style of information gathering (spontaneous and systematic), and information analyzing (internal and external).

Measures of decision-making strategies have been offered by Krumboltz et al. (1979) and Hesketh (1982). Consistent with their notion that strategies vary with situations, the Decision Making Questionnaire developed by Krumboltz et al. (1979) requires respondents to report their thoughts and actions in various types of decision-making situations. This questionnaire is scored by trained judges, who, using a detailed scoring manual, rate the degree to which each of the five strategies in the Krumboltz et al. taxonomy (outlined heretofore) is evident in each of the decision-making situations. Hesketh (1982) designed an instrument to measure the use of the six decision-making strategies proposed by Arroba (1977). Her measure involves having the respondents rate their degree of similarity to brief case descriptions of each strategy.

Decisional Difficulty and Indecision. A range of assessment devices have been developed to measure individual differences in decisional difficulty. While all are paper-and-pencil, self-report devices, the available measures vary in terms of theoretical sophistication.

Exemplifying the simpler forms of assessment are those scales that ask the respondent to rate the certainty of his or her choice (e.g., Lunneborg, 1978), with the implication being that the less certain, the more undecided. Other devices simply require the respondent to categorize him- or herself as definitely decided, tentatively decided, undecided with alternatives under consideration, or completely undecided (e.g., Yaegel, 1978; Zener & Schneulle, 1972).

More sophisticated are those devices that attempt to assess various causes of vocational indecision. The Career Decision Scale (Osipow, Carney, & Barak, 1976), for example, assesses both level and cause of indecision. This instrument contains 2 items that assess level of educational and vocational decidedness, and 16 items that reflect four potential causes of indecision: (1) lack of structure; (2) external barriers to preferred choice; (3) "approach-approach" conflict between equally attractive alternatives, and (4) personal conflict regarding career decision making.

Also attempting to assess both level and cause of indecision, Holland, Daiger, and Power (1980) developed My Vocational Situation. This instrument is derived from the work of Holland and Holland (1977), and contains three separate scales that measure previously identified causes of indecision. The scales include identity (the degree of certainty about one's strengths, weaknesses, and goals), information (extent to which the individual believes he or she has sufficient information), and barriers (perceptions about the ability to succeed in career decision making).

Other instruments relevant to indecision and sources of decisional difficulty are measures of attitudes or cognitions associated with the task of decision making. Taylor and Betz (1983), for example, devised the Career Decision Making Self Efficacy scale which yields an index of overall self-efficacy rating as well as individual ratings with respect to the five career choice competencies detailed by Crites (1965, 1978). Heppner and Petersen's (1982) Problem Solving

Inventory, while not explicitly related to career decision making, provides a self-appraisal on the dimensions of confidence, approach–avoidance, and personal control in problem-solving situations.

SUMMARY

Stimulated by developmental views of vocational behavior, several theorists sought to detail how career decisions are, or should be, made. While each selected a different focus or emphasis in this effort, the decider was typically described as proceeding, with varying degrees of self-awareness and rationality, from an initial state in which information is gathered and organized, to an eventual state in which information is evaluated as the basis for choice. A variety of assessment devices were developed, using both self-report and direct observational methods, from which it was possible to identify an individual's location in the decision-making process as well as the adequacy of his or her behavior in selected aspects of the process. Evidence that differences could be observed in decision-making process behavior prompted what may be a return to a differentialist view of vocational behavior. Several classification systems were offered to describe decisional styles and strategies, and to detail sources of decisional difficulty. The assessment of individual differences in career decision making represents the most recent contribution in this domain, and provides a view of the characteristic or situational factors that impinge on the process by which vocational decisions are made.

RETROSPECT AND PROSPECT

In reviewing the questions, theories, and measures associated with the history of career development and decision making, several observations can be made. First, it is clear that the kinds of questions that have been posed have shifted over time. From the initial inquiries regarding vocational choice content, questions about developmental and decisional processes emerged. Further, while early developmental process models focused on broad, life-span phenomena, subsequent decisional process models addressed more detailed questions about specific, molecular phenomena, and the inquiries about generic, uniform processes gave way to examination of individual and situational differences in career decision-making behavior.

A second observation is that while it is not possible to forecast what kind of questions will be forthcoming, several directions are suggested by this review. For those who would extend this historical account into the future, the recent trend toward identifying and explaining those characteristic and situational factors that affect the quality and ease of decision making seems particularly promising. However, pursuit of such questions as "What is the impact of various decision-making behaviors on decisional outcomes?," "Does competent decision making at the molecular level lead to positive lifespan developmental outcomes?," and "How are differential (content) and developmental (process) phenomena related?" would also seem useful to consolidate available perspectives and knowledge. Finally, from an applied standpoint, inquiry about how best to facilitate decision making and development is needed.

A third observation is that the theoretical models that have pursued these questions represent a rich array of intellectual perspectives. The models that have been detailed have been informed by a variety of psychological perspectives as well as by models drawn from other disciplines. Reviewing the array of theoretical models, it is evident that both differential and developmental contributions have been used to understand vocational behavior. Additionally, social learning and cognitive models of human behavior, as well as sociological, economic, and mathematical models, have been used. The wealth of perspectives has been both admirable and fruitful, and it is to be hoped that future theorizing about career development and decision making continues to be so informed.

In considering the assessment devices that have been generated by these models, a final observation is that several useful tools are now available. It is possible not only to estimate the likely satisfactoriness of choosing a given alternative, but also to place that decision in a developmental context which suggests what problems and competencies have previously occurred and what may be expected to follow. Further, behavior associated with any single decision may be used to monitor decisional progress, specific decision-making skills can be evaluated for adequacy, and individual and situational factors that may impede or facilitate decisional and developmental progress can be identified. The array of devices available to counselors and researchers is an invaluable resource for better understanding and assisting those who are confronted with the tasks of career development and decision making.

REFERENCES

Arroba, T. (1977). Styles of decision making and their use: An empirical study. *British Journal of Guidance & Counselling, 5,* 149–158.

Aubrey, R. F. (1977). Historical development of guidance and counseling and implications for the future. *Personnel & Guidance Journal, 55,* 288–295.

Bandura, A. (1977). Self-efficacy: Toward a unifying theory of behavioral change. *Psychological Reports, 84,* 191–215.

Buehler, C. (1933). *Der Menschliche Lebenslauf als Psychologisches Problem.* Leipzig: Hirzel.

Boocock, S. S. (1967). The life career game. *Personnel & Guidance Journal, 45,* 8–17.

Brewer, J. M. (1919). *The vocational guidance movement.* New York: Macmillan.

Bross, I. D. (1953). *Design for decisions.* New York: Macmillan.

Cooper, J. F. (1976). Comparative impact of the SCII and the Vocational Card Sort on career salience and career exploration of women. *Journal of Counseling Psychology, 23,* 348–352.

Crites, J. O. (1961). A model for the measurement of vocational maturity. *Journal of Counseling Psychology, 8,* 255–259.

Crites, J. O. (1965). Measurement of vocational maturity in adolescence: I. Attitude test of the vocational development inventory. *Psychological Monographs, 79*(2, Whole No. 595).

Crites, J. O. (1973). *Theory and research handbook for the career maturity inventory.* Monterey, CA: CTB/McGraw–Hill.

Crites, J. O. (1975). *The career adjustment and development inventory.* College Park, MD: Gumpert.

Crites, J. O. (1976). A comprehensive model of career development in early adulthood. *Journal of Vocational Behavior, 9,* 105–118.

Crites, J. O. (1978). *The career maturity inventory.* Monterey, CA: CTB/McGraw–Hill.

Crites, J. O. (1982). Testing for career adjustment and development. *Training & Development Journal, 36*(2), 20–24.

Davidson, P. E., & Anderson, H. D. (1937). *Occupational mobility in an American community.* Stanford, CA: Stanford University Press.

Dawis, R. V., & Lofquist, L. H. (1984). *A psychological theory of work adjustment.* Minneapolis, MN: University of Minnesota Press.

Dilley, J. S. (1965). Decision making ability and vocational maturity. *Personnel & Guidance Journal, 44,* 423–427.

Dinklage, L. B. (1968). *Decision strategies of adolescents.* Unpublished doctoral dissertation, Harvard University, Cambridge, MA.

Dixon, D. N., Heppner, P. P., Petersen, C. H., & Ronning, R. R. (1979). Problem solving workshop training. *Journal of Counseling Psychology, 26,* 133/139.

D'Zurilla, T. J., & Goldfried, M. R. (1971). Problem solving and behavior modification. *Journal of Abnormal Psychology, 78,* 107–126.

Edwards, W. (1961). Behavioral decision theory. *Annual Review of Psychology, 12,* 473–498.

Erikson, E. H. (1950). Childhood and society. New York: Norton.

Festinger, L. (1957). *A theory of cognitive dissonance.* Stanford, CA: Stanford University Press.

Fletcher, F. M. (1966). Concepts, curiosity, and careers. *Journal of Counseling Psychology, 13,* 131–138.

Forrest, D. J. (1971). *The construction and validation of an objective measure of vocational maturity for adolescents.* Unpublished doctoral dissertation, Teachers College, New York.

Forrest, D. J., & Thompson, A. S. (1974). The career development inventory. In D. E. Super (Ed.), *Measuring vocational maturity for counseling and evaluation* (pp. 53–66). Washington, DC: National Vocational Guidance Association.

Gelatt, H. B. (1962). Decision making. A conceptual frame of reference for counseling. *Journal of Counseling Psychology, 9,* 240–245.

Gelatt, H. B., & Clark, R. B. (1967). Role of subjective probabilities in the decision process. *Journal of Counseling Psychology, 14,* 332–341.

Ginzberg, E., Ginsburg, S. W., Axelrad, S., & Herma, J. L. (1951). *Occupational choice.* New York: Columbia University Press.

Gribbons, W. D., & Lohnes, P. (1968). *Emerging careers.* New York: Teachers College Press.

Gribbons, W. D., & Lohnes, P. (1982). *Careers in theory and experience.* Albany: State University of New York Press.

Harren, V. A. (1966). The vocational decision-making process among college males. *Journal of Counseling Psychology, 13,* 271–277.

Harren, V. A. (1972). *Preliminary manual for the vocational decision making checklist.* Unpublished manuscript, Southern Illinois University, Carbondale, IL.

Harren, V. A. (1979). A model of career decision making for college students. *Journal of Vocational Behavior, 14,* 119–133.

Harren, V. A. (1984). *Assessment of Career Decision Making*. Los Angeles: Western Psychological Services.

Harren, V. A., Kass, R. A., Tinsley, H. E. A., & Moreland, J. R. (1978). Influence of sex role attitudes and cognitive styles on career decision making. *Journal of Counseling Psychology, 25*, 390–398.

Havighurst, R. J. (1953). *Human development and education*. New York: Longmans Green.

Heppner, P. P. (1978). A review of the problem solving literature and its relationship to the counseling process. *Journal of Counseling Psychology, 25*, 366–375.

Heppner, P. P., & Petersen, C. H. (1982). The development and implications of a personal problem solving inventory. *Journal of Counseling Psychology, 29*, 66–75.

Hesketh, B. (1982). Decision-making style and career decision-making behaviors among school leavers. *Journal of Vocational Behavior, 20*, 223–234.

Hilton, T. L. (1962). Career decision making. *Journal of Counseling Psychology, 9*, 291–298.

Holland, J. L. (1973). *Making vocational choices*. Englewood Cliffs, NJ: Prentice–Hall.

Holland, J. L. (1985). *Making vocational choices*. (2nd ed.) Englewood Cliffs, NJ: Prentice–Hall.

Holland, J. L., Daiger, D. C., & Power, P. G. (1980). *My vocational situation*. Palo Alto, CA: Consulting Psychologists Press.

Holland, J. L., & Holland, J. E. (1977). Vocational indecision: More evidence and speculation. *Journal of Counseling Psychology, 24*, 404–414.

Hollingshead, A. B. (1949). *Elmstown's youth*. New York: Wiley.

Horan, J. J. (1979). *Counseling for effective decision making*. North Sciutate, MA: Doxbury Press.

Janis, I. L., & Mann, L. (1977). *Decision making*. New York: Free Press.

Jepsen, D. A. (1974a). Vocational decision-making strategy types. *Vocational Guidance Quarterly, 23*, 17–23.

Jepsen, D. A. (1974b). Vocational decision-making patterns among noncollege-aspiring adolescents. *Journal of Vocational Behavior, 4*, 283–297.

Jepsen, D. A., & Dilley, J. S. (1974). Vocational decision-making models: A review and comparative analysis. *Review of Educational Research, 44*, 331–349.

Johnson, R. (1978). Individual styles of decision making: A theoretical model for counseling. *Personnel & Guidance Journal, 56*, 530–536.

Johnson, R., Coscarelli, W., & Johnson, J. (1978). *Decision making inventory*. Columbus, OH: Marathon Consulting & Press.

Jones, G. B., & Krumboltz, J. D. (1970). Stimulating occupational exploration through film-mediated problems. *Journal of Counseling Psychology, 17*, 107–114.

Jordaan, J. P. (1974). Life stages as organizing modes of career development. In E. L. Herr (Ed.), *Vocational guidance & human development* (pp. 263–295). Boston: Houghton Mifflin.

Jordaan, J. P., & Heyde, M. B. (1979). *Vocational maturity during the high-school years*. New York: Teachers College Press.

Kaldor, D. B., & Zytowski, D. G. (1969). A maximizing model of occupational decision making. *Personnel & Guidance Journal, 47*, 781–788.

Katz, M. R. (1963). *Decisions and values: A rationale for secondary school guidance*. New York: College Entrance Examination Board.

Katz, M. R. (1966). A model of guidance for career decision-making. *Vocational Guidance Quarterly, 15*, 2–10.

Katz, M. R. (1979). Assessment of career decision making: Process and outcome. In A. M. Mitchell, G. B. Jones, & J. D. Krumboltz (Eds.), *Social learning and career decision making* (pp. 81–101). Cranston, RI: Carroll Press.

Katz, M. R., Norris, L., & Pears, L. (1978). Simulated occupational choice: A diagnostic measure of competencies in career decision making. *Measurement & Evaluation in Guidance, 10*, 222–232.

Kitson, H. D. (1925). *The psychology of vocational adjustment.* Philadelphia: Lippincott.

Kitson, H. D. (1929). *How to find the right vocation.* New York: Harper.

Kitson, H. D. (1938). *How to find the right vocation.* (rev. ed.). New York: Harper.

Krumboltz, J. D., & Baker, R. D. (1973). Behavioral counseling for vocational decisions. In H. Borow (Ed.), *Career guidance for a new age* (pp. 235–284). Boston: Houghton Mifflin.

Krumboltz, J. D., & Hamel, D. A. (1977). *Guide to career decision making skills.* New York: College Entrance Examination Board.

Krumboltz, J. D., Mitchell, A. M., & Jones, G. B. (1976). A social learning theory of career selection. *Counseling Psychologist, 6,* 71–80.

Krumboltz, J. D., Scherba, D. S., Hamel, D. A., Mitchell, L., Rude, S., & Kinnier, R. (1979). *The effect of alternate career decision making strategies on the quality of resulting decisions.* Final report. Stanford, CA: Stanford University. (ERIC Document Reproduction Service No. 195 824)

Lazarsfeld, P. (1931). *Jugend und Beruf.* Germany: Gustav Fischer Verlag.

Levinson, D. J., Darrow, C. N., Klein, E. B., Levinson, M. H., & McKee, B. (1978). *The seasons of a man's life.* New York: Knopf.

Lewin, K. (1951). *Field theory in social science.* New York: Harper & Row.

LoCascio, R. (1964). Delayed and impaired vocational development: A neglected aspect of vocational development theory. *Personnel & Guidance Journal, 42,* 885–887.

LoCascio, R. (1974). The vocational maturity of diverse groups: Theory and measurement. In D. E. Super (Ed.), *Measuring vocational maturity for counseling and evaluation* (pp. 123–133). Washington, DC: National Vocational Guidance Association.

Lunneborg, P. W. (1978). Sex and career decision-making styles. *Journal of Counseling Psychology, 25,* 299–305.

Mann, L. (1972). Use of a "balance sheet" procedure to improve the quality of personal decision making: A field experiment with college applicants. *Journal of Vocational Behavior, 2,* 291–300.

Manuele, C. A. (1983). The development of a measure to assess vocational maturity in adults with delayed career development. *Journal of Vocational Behavior, 23,* 45–63.

Miller, D. C., & Form, W. E. (1951). *Industrial sociology.* New York: Harper.

Oliver, L. W. (1979). Outcome measurement in career counseling research. *Journal of Counseling Psychology, 26,* 217–226.

Osipow, S. H., Carney, C. G., & Barak, A. (1976). A scale of educational-vocational undecidedness: A typological approach. *Journal of Vocational Behavior, 9,* 233–243.

Parr, F. W. (1937). How's your horoscope? *Occupations, 16*(3), 236–238.

Parsons, F. (1909). *Choosing a vocation.* Boston: Houghton Mifflin.

Patterson, D. G., & Darley, J. G. (1936). *Men, women, and jobs.* Minneapolis: University of Minnesota Press.

Pitz, G. F., & Harren, V. A. (1980). An analysis of career decision making from the point of view of information processing and decision theory. *Journal of Vocational Behavior, 16,* 320–346.

Richards, L. S. (1881). *Vocophy.* Marlboro, MA: Pratt Brothers.

Rogers, C. R. (1942). *Counseling and psychotherapy.* Boston: Houghton Mifflin.

Schein, E. H. (1978). *Career dynamics: Matching individual and organizational needs.* Reading, MA: Addison–Wesley.

Sheppard, D. I. (1971). The measurement of vocational maturity in adults. *Journal of Vocational Behavior, 1,* 399–406.

Simon, H. A. (1957). *Models of man.* New York: Wiley.

Stumpf, S. A., & Collarelli, S. M., & Hartman, K. (1983). Development of the Career Exploration Survey (CES). *Journal of Vocational Behavior, 22,* 191–226.

Super, D. E. (1953). A theory of vocational development. *American Psychologist, 8,* 185–190.

Super, D. E. (1957). *The psychology of careers.* New York: Harper & Row.

Super, D. E. (1980). A life-span, life-space, approach to career development. *Journal of Vocational Behavior, 13,* 282–298.

Super, D. E., Crites, J. O., Hummel, R. C., Moser, H. P., Overstreet, P. L., & Warnath, C. F. (1957). *Vocational development: A framework for research.* New York: Teachers College Press.

Super, D. E., & Forrest, D. J. (1972). *Preliminary manual for the Career Development Inventory, Form I.* Unpublished manuscript, Teachers College, Columbia University, New York.

Super, D. E., & Kidd, J. M. (1979). Vocational maturity in adulthood: Turning a model into a measure. *Journal of Vocational Behavior, 14,* 255–270.

Super, D. E., Kowalski, R. S., & Gotkin, E. H. (1967). *Floundering and trial after high school.* Unpublished manuscript, Teachers College, Columbia University, New York.

Super, D. E., & Overstreet, P. L. (1960). *The vocational maturity of ninth-grade boys.* New York: Teachers College Press.

Super, D. E., Starishevsky, R., Matlin, N., & Jordaan, J. P. (1963). *Career development: Self concept theory.* New York: College Entrance Examination Board.

Super, D. E., & Thompson, A. S. (1979). A six-scale, two-factor measure of adolescent career or vocational maturity. *Vocational Guidance Quarterly, 28,* 6–15.

Super, D. E., Thompson, A. S., & Lindeman, R. H. (1984). *The Adult career concerns inventory.* Palo Alto, CA: Consulting Psychologists Press.

Super, D. E., Thompson, A. S., Lindeman, R. H., Jordaan, J. P., & Myers, R. A. (1981). *The Career Development Inventory.* Palo Alto, CA: Consulting Psychologists Press.

Taylor, K. M., & Betz, N. E. (1983). Applications of self-efficacy theory to the understanding and treatment of career indecision. *Journal of Vocational Behavior, 22,* 63–81.

Terman, L. M. (1925). *Genetic studies of genius.* Stanford, CA: Stanford University Press.

Tiedeman, D. V. (1961). Decisions and vocational development: A paradigm and its implications. *Personnel & Guidance Journal, 40,* 15–21.

Tiedeman, D. V. (1967). Predicament, problem, and psychology: The case for paradox in life and counseling. *Journal of Counseling Psychology, 14,* 1–8.

Tiedeman, D. V., & O'Hara, R. P. (1963). *Career development: Choice and adjustment.* New York: College Entrance Examination Board.

Vroom, V. (1964). *Work and motivation.* New York: Wiley.

Westbrook, B. W. (1970). *The cognitive vocational maturity test.* Unpublished test, Department of Psychology, North Carolina State University, Raleigh.

Westbrook, B. W., Parry–Hill, J. W., & Woodbury, R. W. (1971). The development of a measure of vocational maturity. *Educational & Psychological Measurement, 31,* 541–543.

White, R. W. (1954). *Lives in progress.* New York: Dryden.

Yaegel, J. S. (1978). Certainty of vocational choice and the persistence and achievement of liberal arts community college freshmen. *Dissertation Abstract International, 38,* 118A. (University Microfilms No. 77–14, 882)

Zener, T. B., & Schneulle, L. (1972). *An evaluation of the Self-Directed Search* (Report No. 124). Baltimore: Johns Hopkins University, Center for Social Organization of Schools.

Zytowski, D. G. (1967). Some notes on the history of vocational counseling. *Vocational Guidance Quarterly, 16,* 53–55.

2 The Assessment of Career Decision Making

Robert B. Slaney
Pennsylvania State University

INTRODUCTION

Theories and research concerning career choice and career development have historically played a central and established role in the specialty of counseling psychology. Similarly, the concept of career indecision has occupied a central position in the theoretical and empirical literatures on career choice and development (Crites, 1969; Osipow, 1983). In light of the apparent importance of career indecision it seems surprising that until approximately 10 years ago the assessment of career decision making was characterized by either neglect or what, at least in retrospect, appear to be extremely simplistic approaches to its conceptualization and measurement. Little interest was shown until very recently in the actual process of decision making. Instead, the early focus was on career indecision. The research that was done usually classified subjects, who were most frequently college students, as either decided or undecided about their career choices or college majors. Occasionally other terms were used or the possibility of being tentatively decided was raised, but for the most part, subjects were classified as either decided or undecided.

Two questions about career indecision were dominant in the early research. The first question asked what percentage of college students were undecided. Although estimates vary widely across different samples using different measures, estimates of 20–30% seem representative (Astin, 1977; Crites, 1969; Lunneborg, 1975). Gordon (1984) suggested that these estimates may be conservative because they were based on only those who were willing to identify themselves as undecided. The estimates, whether conservative or not, do provide a clear substantive basis for concluding that career indecision is a common concern for young adults and thus deserves attention. More relevant here, the second, and perhaps more interesting question, asked how career-decided and -undecided subjects differed.

An early study by Williamson (1937) on the differences between decided and undecided subjects is revealing not only because of its results but also because of the questions that were raised and the assumptions behind the questions. Williamson questioned what he believed was a tendency for educators to assume that students who had made a career decision worked harder, performed better, and had less need for guidance and counseling because they had a definite vocational goal. His results indicated that men with career choices did not get higher grades than men who were undecided. However, he also found that women who were undecided got higher grades than women who were decided. This study is sometimes cited as an early example of a study that demonstrated the absence of differences between career-decided and -undecided subjects or, for women, the absence of the type of differences that were expected. The study is interesting in this sense but it is also historically interesting because the source of Williamson's skepticism about differences between decided and undecided subjects was his general skepticism about the ability of college students to choose careers for themselves without the aid of a counselor.

If Williamson was skeptical about the career choices of decided students, he was even more skeptical about the status of undecided students. In his book *How to counsel students* (Williamson, 1939), he wrote "The causes of vocational choice uncertainty are many, usually consisting of fear and lack of aptitude, fear of displeasing parents and friends, and fear of failure in the chosen occupation . . . . Frequently the cause lies in the student's general emotional instability." This statement, quoted by Baird (1969), was used to illustrate a perspective that Baird believed was widely held by counselors and guidance workers. Baird (1969) conducted two studies that used extremely large numbers of subjects (12,432, and 59,618), as well as an impressive number of dependent variables. For the first study, Baird found that undecided male students were "slightly less interested in science" and that undecided males and females were "not vocationally oriented." In summary, however, he wrote that "the overwhelming conclusion is that there is no real difference between the student who has decided upon a vocation and the student who has not [p. 432]." For the second study, Baird found no differences in academic aptitude and concluded that the only differences that occurred concerned college goals. Undecided students more frequently emphasized "the college goal of developing their minds and intellectual abilities and chose the goal of vocational or professional training less frequently [p. 432]." Overall it is clear that Baird considered his studies important primarily because they demonstrated a lack of differences between decided and undecided students. In fact, in discussing his results, Baird recommended that undecided students should be told that being undecided about their career goals did not make them different from other students.

Baird's paper was significant for a number of reasons: (1) his samples were not only extremely large but they were representative of relevant populations, (2) he used an impressive array of dependent variables, and (3) he derived and interpreted his results in a very reasonable manner. (Lunneborg [1975] has noted the tendency in this literature to emphasize the differences found between decided and undecided students even though the bulk of the results may suggest a lack of differences.) The overall importance of Baird's paper was that it made the negative perspective held by Williamson and others toward students who were experiencing career indecision virtually untenable. If Baird was correct that the negative perspective held by Williamson was widely shared, then the results of Baird's studies provided a sharp challenge to that perspective. In essence, Baird's studies, seriously considered, provided an empirical basis for challenging previously held assumptions about undecided students.

Another extremely important aspect of Baird's results was that they were consistent with major theoretical perspectives which were exerting a major influence on the thinking of vocational psychologists. Theories by Super (1957), Ginzberg, Ginsburg, Axelrad, and Herma (1951), Tiedeman and O'Hara (1963), and, most importantly, Erikson (1957), all shared a common developmental perspective. This perspective placed career indecision in the context of normal development for young adults. From this perspective it was expected that young adults would experience some career indecision which would then be followed by a developmental progression that would lead to the selection of a career. Simply stated, most young adults who were undecided at one point would, in the course of normal development, become career-decided. Viewed in this manner, career-undecided students would not be expected to differ in major ways from decided students, as Baird had found.

Other studies also exist which suggest that there are few clear differences between students who are decided about their career plans and those who are undecided. Examples of studies that are cited in the literature to support this point are (Abel, 1966; Bohn, 1968; Elton & Rose, 1970, 1971; Hall, 1963; Harman, 1973; Miller, 1956; Nelson & Nelson, 1940; Watley, 1965). In fact some studies seemed to suggest that undecided students, rather than being nearly pathological, were actually lower attrition risks (Abel, 1966), more achievement oriented (Holland & Nichols, 1964; Watley, 1965; Williamson, 1937) and more creative (Holland & Nichols, 1964) than decided students.

In contrast, other studies are cited as finding differences that were more in line with the negative expectations held for career-undecided students. In these studies undecided students are described as having lower academic achievement (Lunneborg, 1975, 1976), lower satisfaction with college (Hecklinger, 1972), lower career salience (Greenhaus & Simon, 1977), lower career decision-making self-efficacy expectations (Taylor & Betz, 1983) and higher attrition rates (Astin, 1975; Elton & Rose, 1970; Foote, 1980; Rose & Elton, 1971; Thompson, 1966). Relative to personality characteristics, undecided students have been described as being lower in self-esteem (Barrett & Tinsley, 1977; Resnick, Fauble, & Osipow, 1970), both lower in self-esteem and higher in dogmatism (Maier & Herman, 1974), overly sensitive, compulsive, and withdrawn (Watley, 1965), more external and fearful of success (Taylor, 1982), anxious (Galinsky & Fast, 1966; Hawkins, Bradley, & White, 1977; Kimes & Troth, 1974; Walsh & Lewis, 1972), less inclined to take risks (Ziller, 1957), less self-directive (Marr, 1965), and more dependent (Ashby, Wall, & Osipow, 1966).

In considering these studies, Lunneborg's comments about the tendency to exaggerate differences and ignore or minimize the lack of differences deserve to be repeated. An example of the need for such concern is provided by the widely cited study by Ashby, Wall, and Osipow (1966). These investigators studied decided, undecided, and tentatively decided undergraduates, using 23 dependent variables. They found that the decided and undecided groups were generally academically superior to the tentative group. There were significant differences between the decided and undecided students on only two of the variables. The decided students had better high school grades and lower dependence scores on the Bernreuter Personality Inventory. However, when this study is cited, it is sometimes merely noted that the results indicated that undecided students were higher on dependence than decided students (Hecklinger, 1972; Maier & Herman, 1974). Although this is technically correct, it also seems incomplete as a description of the overall results.

A number of observations seem directly relevant to the number and variety of studies that have been cited. First, it does appear that a sizable number of studies seem to suggest that personality differences do exist that reflect more favorably on the career-decided student. It also seems readily apparent that the results of these studies as a whole are often inconsistent with and at times contradictory to the studies where no differences were found. In reviewing these studies it was interesting to note that some studies cited in one review as evidence for differences between decided and undecided students were cited in other reviews as evidence for a lack of differences, e.g., Elton and Rose (1970), Harman (1973), Watley (1965), and even Baird (1969). Interestingly, although the citations occasionally seemed inaccurate, most often they were technically correct but less than complete in their descriptions of the cited studies. At times it appeared that bits and pieces of studies were selected to provide support for whatever contention the authors supported.

This confusing state of affairs does not indicate that researchers in the area of career indecision are necessarily careless, capricious, or cavalier in their reviews of previous research. Rather it seems true that this literature presents reviewers with unwieldy, inconsistent, and confusing results that are difficult to understand, conceptualize, categorize, and particularly difficult to summarize accurately. The studies are marked by sample sizes ranging from less than 10 to almost 60,000 subjects. Multiple dependent variables are used frequently, often without being subjected to appropriate multivariate analyses to control for false positives. The results are often difficult to summarize briefly, especially in the few words that are often used in the introductory sections of research papers. The studies have also taken place in a shifting historical and intellectual context where career indecision has been viewed differently over time by both students and researchers. Finally, as noted initially, the research has been characterized by the simplicity of the approaches to the measurement of career indecision or, more accurately perhaps, the categorization of career-decided and career-un-decided students.

In summary, it appears that the diverse and numerous studies comparing career-decided and career-undecided students have not yielded what appears to be a readily recognizable body of coherent findings. This seems true primarily because the studies reviewed here do seem to lead to two general conclusions which seem inconsistent with each other. The first group of studies, e.g., Baird, seem to suggest that there are no clear or very important differences between career-decided and career-undecided students. In contrast, another group of studies seems to suggest that there are differences, especially personality differences, between decided and undecided students that generally favor the decided students.

APPROACHES TO CAREER INDECISION

The tension between these two apparently contradictory bodies of research has had high heuristic value. Two significant developments in the more recent research on the assessment of career indecision appear to be related to attempts to make sense of the apparent inconsistencies in the research findings. The first approach accepted a developmental perspective that suggested that for most students or young adults being undecided about a career choice was not a sign of personality problems. Instead, being undecided was seen as a part of normal development. Most young adults, according to this view, resolve their indecision with relative ease, either by themselves or with some assistance, professional or otherwise. However, for a minority, career indecision is not easily resolved and a problem, usually referred to as indecisiveness, is said to exist. These students are experiencing something that is seen as different from and more difficult to resolve than "normal, developmental" career indecision.

Because most people pass, without major difficulties, from being undecided to being decided, pronounced differences between these shifting groups may not generally be expected. At the same time it may also be reasonable to expect that those who experience a substantial amount of difficulty in deciding on a career may be different from both career-decided and "developmentally" undecided persons. The central point is that by hypothesizing two types of career indecision it is possible to conclude that the research that suggests there are no differences between career-decided and -undecided students is correct for most people. It is, however, also possible to conclude that the research that suggests there are differences is also correct when the minority experiencing indecisiveness is considered.

The second major approach to making sense of the apparently contradictory findings on career indecision has been to suggest that the lack of clarity in the previous research results is caused by the extremely simplistic approaches to the measurement of career indecision that are found in the research cited. According to this approach, what is needed is the development of instruments that approach the measurement of career indecision with appropriate psychometric sophistication. The research and thought on the differences between career indecision and indecisiveness and the research on the development of measures of career indecision will be examined in subsequent sections.

THE DEVELOPMENTAL PERSPECTIVE

The need to delineate between career indecision and indecisiveness can be seen as beginning where Baird's studies left off. Baird's findings and others like his, along with the theories that placed career indecision in a developmental context exerted a strong influence on the perceptions of career indecision. This influence is still present and currently vocational psychologists generally accept career indecision as a normal developmental phenomenon. However, even in this developmental context, some people appear to have particular difficulty in choosing a career. Although the definitions and terms vary, a number of studies and theoretical papers have hypothesized that there are two general types of problems that occur in deciding on a career choice. The first is normal or developmental career indecision, which over time or in response to information or appropriate interventions, is resolved. The second problem has been most frequently called indecisiveness and is usually described as being more difficult to treat and longer lasting.

Tyler (1961) appears to have been the first to attempt to draw a clear distinction between career indecision, which involves the inability to specify a career choice or a career direction, and general indecisiveness. For Tyler the latter concept referred to a more generalized problem in making decisions, regardless of their nature or importance. Tyler also hypothesized that there would be a positive relationship between indecisiveness and the presence of personal problems. Goodstein (1965), who is more frequently cited for the distinction between career indecision and indecisiveness, actually wrote about two kinds of career indecision. To illustrate his first type, Goodstein used an example of a client who was anxious about not having made a career decision but who, when given relevant information, made a decision which alleviated the anxiety. In his second example, Goodstein described a client who also found decision making anxiety arousing. However, providing information for this client was not helpful. According to Goodstein in the second client avoided experiencing anxiety by avoiding making a decision.

Obviously, Goodstein placed a great deal of importance on anxiety and for him the central diagnostic distinction between two types of indecision was whether the anxiety was a consequence (the first example) or an antecedent (the second example) of the indecision. The similarities between Tyler and Goodstein seem clear with both perceiving indecisiveness as more general, intractable, and problematic. When Crites (1969) wrote about the distinctions between career indecision and indecisiveness his definitions also seemed to be clearly in agreement with major aspects of Tyler and Goodstein. Crites wrote that

> indecision is specific to vocational choice and can usually be resolved by changing the conditions for decision making, i.e., information about choice supply, incentive to choose, and freedom to choose, whereas indecisiveness is a more generalized personality attribute and persists even when the conditions for choice are optimal. [p. 576]

Although Crites's definition of indecisiveness did not specifically mention anxiety, the small number of studies that are cited as relevant to the distinction between career indecision and indecisiveness have often involved anxiety in accordance with the emphasis of Goodstein. For example, Kimes and Troth (1974) measured trait anxiety using the State-Trait Anxiety Inventory by Spielberger, Gorsuch, and Lushene (1970). The 829 male and female college students were divided into five levels of "career decisiveness" and five levels of satisfaction with career decision, based on their responses to two questionnaire items. The authors found a clear inverse relationship between career decisiveness and "anxiety-proneness." A similar but even more pronounced inverse relationship was found between anxiety and the satisfaction with career decision items. The authors concluded that career indecision and anxiety were related.

A study by Hawkins, Bradley, and White (1977) contained data on 127 female and 300 male undergraduates. They had 10 independent variables, including measures of general anxiety, major choice anxiety, and vocational choice anxiety. There were 4 dependent variables: yes and no responses were used to measure major choice and vocational choice; 7-point scales were used to measure major certainty and vocational certainty. Using stepwise multiple regression the authors found that 9 of the 10 variables were significantly related to at least 1 of the dependent variables. Major choice anxiety accounted for a greater total amount of change in variance in "decidedness" (32.4%) than any other variable. General anxiety contributed nothing significant to predicting vocational decidedness but made small contributions to predicting major choice and major certainty. This study, similar to Kimes and Troth, found evidence for a relationship between anxiety and career indecision. Although both studies are cited in the literature on indecision/indecisiveness, neither actually investigated this distinction.

Mendonca and Siess (1976) randomized college students to one of five groups: (1) an anxiety management group, $n = 7$; (2) a problem-solving group, $n = 5$; (3) a combination of (1) and (2), $n = 5$; (4) a discussion placebo group, $n = 7$; and (5) a no treatment control group, $n = 5$. The authors used a variety of outcome measures, including measures of state and trait anxiety as well as self-report measures and laboratory tasks to assess problem solving. There were no statistically significant treatment effects on the anxiety measures. The main finding was that combined training in anxiety management and problem solving was more effective than either method alone and more effective than control conditions in increasing exploratory behavior and problem-solving behavior. Problem-solving training was second to the combination training in improving performance on problem solving.

This study is relevant because the authors interpret their results as suggesting that they were tapping Goodstein's ''antecedent'' anxiety because subjects increased their exploratory behavior when they were trained to resist the distracting effects of anxiety. This interpretation does not explain why there were not significant changes on anxiety for these treatment groups. There are also other possible reasons why the minimal treatment effects may have occurred. Given the preceding findings and the extremely small number of subjects in each group, the interpretation of these results in terms of Goodstein's ideas about anxiety seems speculative.

McGowan (1977) devised a study that had as one of its central purposes the goal of testing the validity of Goodstein's (1965) hypothesis ''that career indecision and career indecisiveness are differentially related to anxiety.'' McGowan used two criteria that had been suggested by Crites (1969) as a basis for discriminating career indecision and indecisiveness. First, the number of vocational choices had to be greater on the posttest in the experimental groups than in the control groups. Second, with the experimental group, there had to be some individuals who were able to make a vocational choice and some who were still undecided after receiving Holland's Self-Directed Search. McGowan wrote:

> The experimental subjects who were able to make a vocational choice were those who were previously undecided but were able to solve their problems after the informational experience; the experimental subjects who were still unable to make a vocational choice were considered to be those with problems of indecisiveness since they still could not make an occupational choice even after they were given the information needed to make a decision. [p. 198]

It was expected, in accordance with Goodstein, that the group that became decided would show less anxiety on the Taylor Manifest Anxiety Scale than would the indecisive group, i.e., the group that remained undecided. This hypothesis was not supported by an analysis of variance or an analysis of covariance using the anxiety scores gathered at pretest as the covariate.

Although McGowan's study was carefully conceived and carried out along the lines suggested by Crites (1969), the results do not, as is sometimes suggested, necessarily indicate that Goodstein's ideas about the dichotomy between indecision and indecisiveness are incorrect. McGowan noted that Goodstein would have assigned subjects who failed to respond to the treatments to the indecisive category. This assumes that the treatment chosen is or should be effective for all of the undecided subjects and that the residual subjects are indecisive. This assumption, as McGowan appropriately noted in his discussion section, is highly questionable. It also seems reminiscent of the uniformity myths of psychotherapy described by Kiesler (1966). This important problem with Goodstein's definitions of indecision and indecisiveness points to the desirability of developing methods for categorizing subjects based on a priori instead of a posteriori approaches so that less equivocal hypotheses can be developed.

These studies, though often cited in discussions of the career indecision, indecisiveness delineation, can be seen to be only marginally related. Only McGowan's study seems directly relevant. His results, though not supportive of Goodstein's speculations, cannot be considered as evidence against Goodstein's ideas. The other studies are simply not informative. Despite the lack of research support, or for that matter, research attention, the idea that there are career clients or high school and college students who can be described as indecisive seems to have persevered and even flourished. In an important paper on career indecision, Holland and Holland (1977) collected a great deal of data on the career concerns of high school and college students. In a speculative discussion that appears at the end of their empirical article, the authors described a syndrome that they call the indecisive disposition. They described this disposition as

> the outcome of a life history in which a person has failed to acquire the necessary cultural involvement, self-confidence, tolerance for ambiguity, sense of identity, self- and environmental knowledge to cope with vocational decision making as well as with other common problems. [p. 413]

This sounds reminiscent of Tyler's expectation that indecisiveness was related to the presence of personality problems. Holland and Holland also sounded similar to Goodstein when they suggested that most students expressing indecision will respond to one of a variety of career interventions and that those who do not "are more likely to have some or many of the personal characteristics associated with the indecisive disposition" [p. 413].

Holland and Holland suggested that only a small percentage of undecided students possess an indecisive disposition. They also seemed in agreement with Tyler, Goodstein, and Crites when they suggested that "the personal histories of undecided students with special problems (i.e., an indecisive disposition) should be characterized by a general failure to make decisions at culturally approved times." In closing, the authors suggested a number of scales, including the one that they presented in their article, that could be used to identify career clients with indecisive dispositions.

The forgoing seems to suggest that the same scales used to measure career indecision can also be used to measure the indecisive disposition. This suggestion seems curiously at odds with the general direction of the thought in this area, including Holland and Holland's, that seems to suggest qualitative rather than quantitative differences between career-undecided and indecisive students. It is also noticeable that the Holland and Holland scale does not contain items that seem sensitive to personality disturbances, or that attend to anxiety or to a general difficulty in making decisions. Unfortunately, no attention is given to the specifics of using the suggested scales in identifying students who possess indecisive dispositions. Salomone (1982), in a theoretical paper on the indecisive client, seemed to agree with the basic delineation between indecision and indecisiveness, although he used different terms. In his description of the indecisive client, Salomone suggested that the issues of concern are emotional-psychological, rather than rational-cognitive issues with a developmental aspect as in the case of indecision. Indecisive clients may have serious identity confusion, be anxious about decision making, and unable to "make a vocational choice no matter how carefully they are led through a decision making process" [p. 498]. It is not clear, however, how Salomone would operationalize the treatment that constitutes the litmus test that separates undecided from indecisive career clients. In addition, what is "serious" confusion about identity or how much anxiety discriminates? It is hoped that Salomone will clarify these issues in future work.

Salomone concludes that labeling young adults (under 25) as indecisive is "potentially a very serious mistake " [p. 498]. However, it is not clear whether letting these students "stumble and flounder" without trying to identify and treat them is not potentially an even more serious mistake. If, as it appears, Salomone fears the possible repercussions of the labeling process, there may be other possible options in addition to his controversial suggestion that "the study of indecisiveness should, in large measure, be confined to adults, not to high school or college students" [p. 498].

More directly relevant, Salomone presented two examples of rehabilitation clients who were ultimately labeled as having indecisive dispositions. He then derived 12 conclusions about the characteristics of indecisive adults based on these clients. It is not clear whether Salomone expected these characteristics to generalize to all indecisive clients (over 25) or whether all of these characteristics were necessary or whether some were more important or diagnostically meaningful than others. No specific mention of anxiety was made although difficulty in making decisions was mentioned first. The composite picture of indecisiveness that was portrayed conveys the suggestion of very real difficulties in adjustment if not a marginal adjustment in general.

Van Matre and Cooper (1984) suggested that indecision should be considered a trait while indecisiveness should be thought of as a state. They developed a four-category (2 × 2) diagnostic quadrant and describe the characteristics of clients in each quadrant and the appropriate treatments. The authors referred to indecision in Salomone's terms, i.e., decidedness–undecidedness and described it as a state that "refers to the transitory level of indecision that accompanies all decision-making tasks" [p. 637]. In contrast "the trait of decisiveness–indecisiveness refers to a more enduring and consistent proneness when encountered by any decision-making task" [p. 637]. This article is interesting because it ends with "four distinct diagnostic categories" and suggestions for treatment based on a delineation between indecision and indecisiveness which no data support.

More recently, several empirical studies have attempted to investigate the proposed delineation between career indecision and indecisiveness. Hartman, Fuqua, and Hartman (1983) investigated the usefulness of the Career Decision Scale (CDS; Osipow, Carney, Winer, Yanico, & Koschier, 1976) in identifying chronic career indecision in high school seniors. Hartman, Fuqua, and Hartman (1983) appear to use the term chronic career indecision as the equivalent of indecisiveness. The CDS was administered to 205 high school seniors whose career decisions were followed up 3 years after graduation. Two groups of students were studied: those whose choices remained unchanged over 3 years (always decided) and those who remained undecided (always undecided). The results indicated that the always undecided students had higher scores on Factor I of the CDS than did the always decided group. It was unfortunate, as the authors noted, that there were 57 decided versus 10 undecided students in the study. This study did indicate that the scores of career-undecided high school seniors were higher (more undecided) on Factor I of the CDS than were the scores of career-decided high school seniors. These results are supportive of the validity of the CDS but otherwise seem unremarkable. The study does not actually address the delineation between career indecision and indecisiveness.

In Hartman, Fuqua, Blum, and Hartman (1985) the sample used in Hartman, Fuqua, and Hartman (1983) was followed up by telephone for a fourth year. Remarkably, only one subject, who refused to participate, was lost ($N = 204$). Again the study was "designed to examine the ability of the Career Decision Scale to discriminate among the career indecision types" [p. 203]. In this study three groups were formed as follows: ". . . those who responded no change in each of the 4 yearly follow-ups were labeled decided. Those who changed one or two times were labeled developmentally undecided, while those who changed three or more times were labeled chronically undecided" [p. 204]. Again, the term chronically undecided is used as the equivalent of indecisive. A discriminant analysis was performed, using the factors scores for three factors derived from a factor analysis conducted by the authors. Two statistically significant functions resulted. The first suggested that the decided students had lower Factor I scores than did the two undecided groups, suggesting that the undecided groups had a lack of structure and confidence relative to making a career decision. The second statistically significant function separated the developmentally undecided from the chronically undecided students. The authors viewed the developmentally undecided students as perceiving an external barrier and, to a lesser degree, a lack of knowledge about their abilities. The authors speculated that the chronically undecided students had psychological barriers that inhibited their choices. However, the basis for this speculation is unclear. Overall, the criteria for the assignment of subjects to either the developmentally undecided or the chronically undecided groups seemed somewhat arbitrary. In addition, the criteria were not conceptually linked to the qualitative differences that might be expected between undecided and indecisive students. Still, this study represents a clear advance in the right direction and is a tribute to the perseverance of these authors in pursuing these issues as well as these subjects.

A study by Hartman, Fuqua, and Blum (1985) was more closely related to the theorizing about the dichotomy between career indecision and indecisiveness. The authors developed a model based on Goodstein and his emphasis on anxiety. They used path analysis to examine the relationships between trait and state anxiety, identity, locus of control, and career indecision. Hartman et al. (1985) tested their proposed model, using 164 graduate students and 155 high school students. They found some support for their proposed model especially in the relationships between state and trait anxiety and career indecision. However, the study is weakened by the lack of a measure of indecisiveness. The authors noted that a considerable amount of the total variance in career indecision was not accounted for by the model and that the model needs to be tested using samples of career undecided and indecisive students.

Finally, a study by Cooper, Fuqua, and Hartman (1984) developed an eight-item measure of indecisiveness entitled the Trait Indecisiveness Scale. This scale used a yes/no response format and the items were adapted from Salomone (1982), apparently from his description of the characteristics of the two rehabilitation clients. The respondents were first-year college students, 268 males and 57 females, who responded to the Trait Indecisiveness Scale, a measure of interpersonal characteristics, and to an item concerning the respondents' certainty of career choice (yes–no). It was found that self-reported vocational uncertainty was positively related to indecisiveness and that there were several differences on personality characteristics when subjects were divided by using a median split on the indecisiveness measure.

Although the Trait Indecisiveness Scale represents a somewhat primitive beginning, the study at least gives overt recognition to the need to develop a measure of indecisiveness. The scale, however, lacks careful development and a compelling theoretical or empirical basis for its items. As in most of the studies reviewed, it simply does not address the need to attend seriously to delineating career indecision and indecisiveness. This delineation will be central to establishing the validity of any measure purporting to measure indecisiveness.

The distinction between career indecision and indecisiveness has a considerable history. The ideas behind the distinction seem reasonable; however, very little clear progress has been made thus far in demonstrating that the two constructs are valid and discriminable. Despite this lack of empirical support, there is a notable trend in the literature to discuss the constructs as if they were clearly defined, measured, delineated and useful for prescribing career interventions. If progress is to occur in this area, clear operational definitions must lead to the development of scales, rationally or empirically derived, that are then subjected to empirical investigation of their reliability and especially their validity. Studies that identify persons who have general problems in making decisions might be a starting point.

A cautionary note relative to the suggestions that indecisive persons may have personal problems seems appropriate. If the term *indecisive* is to be useful, its measurement should be clearly related to its operational definition. To indicate that chronic schizophrenics, for example, are indecisive will only be useful if it is possible to discriminate indecisiveness from schizophrenia or any other personal problems. Simply stated, it will not be enough to demonstrate that persons with personal problems are indecisive if it cannot be demonstrated that indecisiveness contributes some unique variance. Clearly, it is time to develop a measure of indecisiveness and to gather data that are truly relevant to demonstrating the reasonable sounding but otherwise almost entirely speculative delineation between career indecision and indecisiveness.

THE MEASUREMENT OF CAREER INDECISION

It was suggested that the second major approach to unraveling the apparently inconsistent and at times contradictory research on career indecision involved the position that the cause of these confusing results was a measurement problem. The earlier research results were seen as severely limited by the primitive approaches to the categorization of career-undecided students. In fact, the early literature did repeatedly suggest that students were either career-decided or -undecided and that the meanings attached to these terms were clear and consistent. Little apparent consideration was given to the possibility that one person's career-decidedness might equal another's indecision. For example, one person might consider herself decided based on her awareness that she wanted to be a physician. Another might consider herself undecided because, despite knowing that she wanted to be a physician she might be undecided about an area of specialization. Other obvious examples can be easily developed that illustrate that it may be more productive to think of career indecision and decidedness as continuous rather than dichotomous variables. For example, one may be undecided because one has no clear idea of what career to follow or because one is undecided between two closely related careers or between specializations within a career area.

From this perspective, it seems obvious that scales that would examine different degrees of indecision would be a clear advance over the early categorizations used in the research on career indecision. It also makes sense that without clearly specifying the components or antecedents of career indecision, the research would be inconsistent, contradictory, and confusing.

A second and related incentive behind the development of measures of career indecision was also based on the recognition that career indecision could represent a range of concerns. This incentive concerned the possibility of delineating the various components of career indecision in the hope that more specific and individually relevant career interventions might be developed. Both of the incentives noted are discernible in the development of measures of career indecision. These measures will be examined in some detail.

THE CAREER DECISION SCALE

The Career Decision Scale[1] by Osipow, Carney, Winer, Yanico, and Koschier (1976) represents the earliest published attempt to develop an instrument that measured the antecedents of career indecision. This scale consists of 19 items that measure the degree to which respondents report that the individual career-related items describe them and their particular circumstances. There are 16 items that describe the components of vocational and/or educational indecision, 2 that describe career-decidedness and a final item that has a free response format so respondents can insert descriptions of their unique circumstances relative to career indecision.

The original development of the scale apparently began in a graduate seminar directed by Osipow. The overall plan was to determine the basic components or antecedents of career indecision and then develop items that represented them. The next step was to develop self-administered, audio-cassette interventions that, together with accompanying workbook exercises, would be responsive to each of the specified antecedents. The antecedents and their items were based on the authors' experience with career clients. An article by Osipow, Winer, Koschier, and Yanico (1975) contains the plan, an early version of the Career Decision Scale, and an example of a script for one of the audio-cassettes.

The evolution of the scale from its original 14 items to the 19 items contained in the current edition is not clearly explained in the article in which the scale originally appears (Osipow, Carney, & Barak, 1976) or the manual for the Career Decision Scale (Osipow, 1980). However, Osipow (personal communication) recently noted that Clarke Carney had suggested that adding the first 2 items on career-decidedness gave respondents who were decided an opportunity to say so. The rationale was that this would make them feel better about the

instrument. Osipow also noted that these first 2 items formed an informal validation check because they should be negatively correlated with items 3–18.

The entire scale is contained on a four-page, 7″ × 8½″ sheet with detailed,
clear instructions on the front page for responding to the simple format. A sample
question and answer are then followed by the 19 items. Opposite each item are
the numbers, 4, 3, 2, and 1 (4 = "exactly like me"; 3 = "very much like me";
2 = "only slightly like me"; 1 = "not at all like me"). Respondents are asked
to circle the number which most accurately describes their situation in relation to
each of the items.

This scale is potentially useful to career counselors, researchers, and teachers
of a variety of courses relevant to educational and vocational exploration and/or
career decision making. The scale provides an estimate of career indecision and
its antecedents as well as an outcome measure for determining the effects of a
variety of interventions relevant to career choice or career development. It can be
administered in classes or large groups as well as individually. The measure was
designed for high school and college students. Although no reading level is noted
in the manual, the language is clear and simple and seems appropriate for the
intended audience. It is unusual to have questions raised about how to respond.
There is no specified time limit but 10 to 15 minutes is usually enough time to
complete the scale. The instructions for scoring are clear and simply involve
summing the numerical values that were circled for Items 3–18. This yields an
objective overall score for career indecision with higher numerical values representing higher degrees of career indecision. Items 1 and 2, which indicate decidedness about the choice of a career or college major, are not included in the
career indecision score and are scored in the opposite direction, i.e., high scores
on these items indicate greater decidedness. This is a possible source of confusion although the manual is clear on this point. Item 19 is not scored and may
offer clues to issues that are of concern to respondents but are not covered by the
other items. There is some room perhaps, for counselor interpretations using
Item 19, although the published studies on the scale thus far have simply dis-
regarded it.

MANUAL FOR THE CAREER DECISION SCALE

The current edition of the manual provides succinct, articulate, and accurate
summaries of the published and unpublished research that has been conducted on
the scale. It is nicely produced and includes, in addition to the research summary, a table of contents, 39 references, a copy of the Career Decision Scale and 53
pages of tabular data. It is a rich source of data for potential users but perhaps
even more so for researchers. There is, of course, a certain irony in the fact that
because the scale has been well received and used with increasing frequency in
recent years, the manual is already dated and, as a matter of fact, is currently

being revised. The need for revision is likely to recur because the measure seems likely to become even more widely used in future studies on career indecision and career interventions. Given the alternatives, the authors may consider the need for frequent revision a tolerable problem.

RESEARCH ON THE CAREER DECISION SCALE

The Osipow, Carney, and Barak article (1976) was the first published paper focusing on the current version of the Career Decision Scale. The article contains an impressive amount of data on the scale. Seven undergraduate samples ($N = 737$) were involved in an elaborate plan to gather data on relevant groups. The hypothesis that students requesting help on career decision making would score higher on the scale than students not requesting such help was supported. Students requesting career counseling had significantly higher scores on the scale than students who did not request career counseling. The results were mixed for students in courses on educational-vocational exploration. It was also found, as expected, that the career indecision scores for two groups of students in courses on education-vocational exploration declined significantly while the scores for introductory students and two groups of students in a course on personal effectiveness did not change significantly. Items 3–18, as expected, were almost all negatively correlated with Items 1 and 2. The above results provide clear support for the construct and concurrent validity of the scale and its individual items.

Test-retest reliabilities calculated over 2-week intervals on the summary scores yielded values of .90 for 56 introductory students and .82 for 59 students in a course on personal effectiveness. For the individual items, the reliabilities varied considerably. Osipow, Carney, and Barak (1976) also conducted a factor analysis on the 16 indecision items using the Principal Factors solution with test-retest reliability coefficients used as the principal diagonal estimates. Using the Varimax method, four factors were rotated that accounted for more than 81% of the variance. The factor structure raised the possibility that instead of 16 basic antecedents of career indecision, perhaps there were just 4. The authors said the first factor seemed to have two basic elements that involved a lack of structure and confidence in approaching decision making and choice anxiety. Both led to avoiding a choice. The second factor was seen as suggesting a perceived or actual external barrier to a preferred choice and questions about alternative possibilities. The third factor was interpreted as representing an approach-approach conflict where the difficulty involved choosing from a number of attractive alternatives. The fourth and final factor seemed to indicate the presence of some kind of personal conflict over making the decision. One of the implications of the factor analysis was that perhaps interventions could be devised to respond to the factors that were found.

No studies were located that developed specific interventions that would be differentially responsive to the factors found by Osipow, Carney, and Barak (1976). However, Barak and Friedkes (1982) did divide students who had been referred for counseling services into different problem-type categories based on matching their CDS scores with the Osipow, Carney, and Barak factors. They found clear evidence that (1) the initial decidedness levels differed among the four problem groups, and (2) the effectiveness of the counseling intervention was mediated by the type of problems the clients had, according to the CDS. Although this study and its results seem promising no other studies were located that looked for differential treatment effects based on CDS scores.

However, other studies have added to the initial support for the validity of the Career Decision Scale. Slaney, Palko–Nonemaker, and Alexander (1981), using a large sample ($N = 857$), divided subjects into career-decided and -undecided groups based on their responses to a six-item scale on career decidedness that appeared in a study by Holland and Holland (1977). There were statistically significant differences in the expected direction for the summary scores, the factor scores, and all of the individual items. A factor analysis using Principal Factors and Varimax rotation replicated Osipow, Carney, and Barak's first factor but otherwise the factor structure was unclear.

Rogers and Westbrook (1983) found clear support for the construct and concurrent validity of the scale. They factor analyzed the responses of 175 students to the Career Decision Scale using a varimax rotation. They found four factors, two of which coincided with the second and third factors found by Osipow. They concluded that the factor analysis generally supported the contention that career indecision is multidimensional in nature. More specifically, they noted that the match of two factors obtained by using different methods of analysis and different subjects indicated "some degree of convergent validity for the CDS" [p. 84]. Williams–Phillips (1983) conducted a factor analysis of the responses of 75 male and 45 female college students to the CDS. Her results also failed to replicate the original four-factor solution of Osipow, Carney, and Barak (1976). Overall, the failure of subsequent studies to replicate the original factor structure raises questions about the usefulness of factor scores and, in turn, the development of treatments based on these factor scores. This point is noted in reviews by Harmon (1985), Herman (1985), Slaney (1985) and, reassuringly, by Osipow (1980). Clarification of the factor structure of the CDS is one area where additional research is needed.

Other recent studies have provided additional support for the construct and concurrent validity of the CDS (Graef, Wells, Hyland & Muchinsky, 1985; Niece & Bradley, 1979; Slaney, 1980; Slaney, Stafford & Russell, 1981; Williams–Phillips, 1983). Slaney (1984) found that the Career Decision Scale scores of undergraduate women who changed their career choices over a 2-year period were significantly higher originally (more undecided) than were the scores for women whose career choices remained stable. This result not only supports the construct validity of the scale, it also attests to its potential pragmatic usefulness for career counselors. A study by Taylor (cited in Harmon, 1985) provided evidence that the CDS is sensitive to the changes that may result from career counseling.

Finally, the CDS is beginning to appear as an outcome measure in an increasing number of studies (Cesari, Winer, & Piper, 1984; Cesari, Winer, Zychlinksi, & Laird, 1982; Glaize & Myrick, 1984; Larson & Heppner, 1985; Lowe, 1981; Neimeyer, Nevill, Probert, & Fukuyama, 1985; Osipow & Reed, 1985; Pinder & Fitzgerald, 1984; Taylor & Betz, 1983). Additional signs of the growing popularity of the CDS are found in its adaptations for use with high school students (Hartman & Hartman, 1982), graduate students (Hartman, Utz, & Farnum, 1979), physicians (Savickas, 1984) and professional and graduate students (Savickas, Alexander, Osipow, & Wolf, 1985).

For the Career Decision Scale, a number of issues, mostly minor, remain unclear or in need of additional investigation. For example, the amount of information available on the initial stages of the development of the scale is minimal. How was it determined that there were 16 antecedents of career indecision? Why not more or less? What revisions took place at what points and for what reasons?

A more important issue concerns the lack of clarity of the factor structure, which may be related to the lack of clarity that exists in some of the items. Several consist of two or three sentences that make it unclear which aspect subjects are responding to. For example, Item 11 requires subjects to give one response to the following statements: "Having to make a career decision bothers me. I'd like to make a decision quickly and get it over with. I wish I could take a test that would tell me what kind of a career I should pursue." These three statements seem at least potentially independent of each other. The need for clarifying the factor structure does seem important, especially if the future development of the scale is to involve the development of career interventions that are based on this structure. The development of such interventions was, of course, part of the original plan and the idea still seems imaginative despite numerous difficulties. One of the major difficulties is that developing this plan will involve an extended effort in performing complex and time-consuming intervention studies. Whether that effort will occur remains to be seen.

On the other hand, if the research done thus far on the scale is predictive, there may be less need to be concerned about clarifying the individual items or the factor structure. Almost all of the studies have used the scale as a unidimensional measure of career indecision by deriving a scale score by summing items 3–18. Used in this way, the scale has received an impressive amount of research attention since its initial development. The fact that this research has provided substantial support for the test-retest reliability of the instrument and for its construct and concurrent validity is even more impressive. This seems particularly true in an area where so many of the measures do not have adequate research, or for that matter, any research at all on their reliability or validity. It can be concluded that the Career Decision Scale is a brief, easily administered, valid, and reliable measure of career indecision that is also capable of measuring changes that occur over time. The early development of this measure has been promising and recommends its use by researchers and counselors as a measure of career indecision.

MY VOCATIONAL SITUATION SCALE

Another scale that was developed initially with a focus on vocational indecision is the My Vocation Situation Scale by Holland, Daiger, and Power (1980a).[2] The scale was developed to provide a diagnostic scheme for career decision making that could be used in career counseling and research to "increase the likelihood of selecting and following an effective treatment" [Holland, Daiger, & Power, 1980b, p. 1].

More specifically, the manual states that the:

diagnostic scheme is based on the assumption that most difficulties in vocational decision making fall into one or more of the following categories: (a) problems of vocational identity, (b) lack of information about jobs or training, or (c) environmental or personal barriers. [Holland, Daiger & Power, 1980b, p. 1]

Vocational Identity is defined as:

the possession of a clear and stable picture of one's goals, interests, personality, and talents. This characteristic leads to relatively untroubled decision-making and confidence in one's ability to make good decisions in the face of inevitable environmental ambiguities. [p.1]

The My Vocational Situation Scale is used to measure (1) Vocational Identity, as just defined, (2) the need for occupational information, and (3) the presence of barriers to making a choice. Based on the responses to the scale, the authors suggest that career clients may be assigned to:

two or three kind of treatments: (1) those for clients with a poor sense of identity who need experience, career seminars, personal counseling, (2) those for clients with a clear sense of identity who need only information and reassurance, and (3) those for clients who exhibit a combination of these needs. [Holland, Daiger, & Power, 1980b, p. 7]

---

[2]Material from the manual of the My Vocational Situation Scale is reproduced by special permission of the publisher, Consulting Psychologists Press, Palo Alto, CA 94306. Further reproduction is prohibited without the publisher's consent.

The overall goal, simply stated, was to develop an instrument that would provide a diagnostic schema that could be used as the basis for differential treatment for career-counseling clients or others in need of assistance in career decision making.

Three subscales make up the essential core of the My Vocational Situation Scale. The 18-item Vocational Identity Scale is presented on the front side. Two 4-item scales, the Occupational Information Scale and the Barriers Scale are presented on the reverse side. In addition, space is provided on the front side for demographic data (name, date, sex, age, education completed, other). Respondents are also provided with 12 blank lines and instructed to "list all the occupations you are considering right now." On the reverse side, beneath the Occupational Information Scale, 2 lines are provided for responding to the question, "other." Under the Barriers Scale, space is provided for free responses to two additional questions. For the first question, "anything else?" 3 lines are provided. Five blank lines are provided for presenting "other comments and questions."

The entire scale is contained on two sides of an 8½" by 11" sheet of paper. The instructions are brief and clear. For the Vocational Identity Scale items, respondents are given the following instructions: "Try to answer all of the following statements as mostly TRUE or mostly FALSE. Circle the answer that "best represents your present opinion." Then the following stem precedes the 18 Vocational Identity Scale items; "In thinking about your present job or in planning for an occupation or career:". To the right of each of the items appear the capital letters T and F. At the bottom of the Vocational Identity Scale is a box for summing the number of F or false responses. The higher the number the greater the degree of decidedness. For the Occupational Information and the Barriers scales, respondents circle either a Y for yes or an N for no to indicate that they need information or are experiencing certain barriers. Boxes are provided for summing the number of Ys circled for each scale.

The development of the scale is somewhat complex. Conceptually, the authors reported that they reviewed previous attempts to develop diagnostic schemes. In doing this they tried to reduce the difficulties found in the older schemes. The main difference, according to Holland, Daiger, and Power (1980b), was that they ". . . assigned intra-psychic problems to a single category of vocational identity" [p. 2]. The empirical roots of the instrument can be ultimately traced to Holland's early research but its more immediate empirical origins can be found in Holland and Holland (1977). This study involved a multitude of measures and large samples of high school and college students in research that examined the correlates of career indecision. As part of this study, a 13-item scale was developed based on "students explanations for being unsure, dissatisfied, or undecided about a vocational choice" [p. 408]. The procedure behind the derivation of these specific items is not clearly explained in the article although the items are referred to as "potential explanations of their [the students] indecision or dissatisfaction" [p. 408]. This 13-item scale was later referred to as the Vocational Decision-Making Difficulty Scale (VDMD) in Holland, Gottfredson, and Power (1980) although this name was not used in the Holland and Holland article where the scale first appeared.

Holland and Holland (1977), in addition to developing the VDMD, found that the Identity Scale developed by Holland, Gottfredson, and Nafziger (1975) differentiated decided and undecided male and female high school and college students with clarity while most of the numerous other instruments did not. To keep things straight, it may be helpful to note that this Identity Scale is different from the Vocational Identity Scale that is a major subscale of the My Vocational Situation Scale. Lest this seem too easy it can also be noted that the earlier Identity Scale became a source of items for the later Vocational Identity Scale when Holland, Gottfredson, and Power (1980) reported that the Vocational Decision-Making Difficulty Scale and the Identity Scale were found to be substantially but negatively correlated. They stated, "We also noted that the ID (Identity) and VDMD scales might actually be the same scale stated in different kinds of contents" [p. 1193].

The next reported step was to lengthen the ID and VDMD scales to increase their reliability. This was accomplished by "reviewing the old scales and examining similar scales" [Holland, Gottfredson, & Power, 1980, p. 1193]. They lengthened the Identity Scale to 20 items and the VDMD from "12 to 41 items." (Here it appears that even the authors lost track, i.e., the VDMD scale had 13 items, not 12.) Regardless, at this point a factor analysis was conducted and the first version of the Vocational Identity Scale, a combination of the Identity Scale and the Vocational Decision-Making Difficulty Scale, emerged. Any item that correlated .35 or less with either the ID scale or the VDMD scale was omitted. The factor structure was also the basis for forming the Occupational Information Scale although precisely how this was accomplished is unclear. The Barriers Scale was formed by using "items whose content appeared to be a sign of an environmental barrier or a clear psychological limitation" [Holland, Gottfredson, & Power, 1980, p. 1194].

This version of the Vocational Identity Scale contained 23 items. However, when the current published version of the MVS (Holland, Daiger, & Power, 1980a) appeared, the Vocational Identity Scale contained 18 items. The manual simply states that "five redundant items were omitted from the original 23-item scale" [Holland, Daiger, & Power, 1980b, p. 6]. No additional information is provided on the deletion of the 5 items. The rest of the measure was unchanged from the description in Holland, Gottfredson, and Power (1980). Finally, those who have followed the development of the MVS this far may be interested to know that the second author of the *Journal of Personality and Social Psychology* article, Denise C. Gottfredson, is actually the married name of Denise C. Daiger (Holland, 1986, personal communication).

The primary use the authors seem to have in mind for the scale appears to be with career counseling. The authors also suggested that the scale could be used to screen larger groups to locate those most in need of additional assistance. Precisely how this would be done is unclear but once those in need of assistance are located the MVS could be used for self-exploration by going over the items with individuals or groups. It is reported that the scale can be filled out by most people in 10 minutes or less, perhaps while they are waiting to see a career counselor.

The instrument is self-administered and it can be given individually or in groups. Developed on and for high school and college students, the items certainly appear appropriate for these groups although no reading level is mentioned in the manual. The scale is hand scored. No machine scoring is available but it hardly seems necessary given the simplicity and ease of scoring. Beyond the simple summing of the false or yes responses, it is suggested in the manual that the free response questions may "help the counselor judge the level of help required" [p. 2]. It is also suggested that the number, occupational level and relatedness of the occupations listed on the scale by the respondents be examined. In concluding the manual's section on administration and scoring, Holland, Daiger, and Power (1980b) state that, "For most clients, the MVS will elicit some responses that can quickly lead into discussions of problem areas and thus the device will often shorten the time required to identify the clients' major needs" [p. 2].

Manual for the My Vocational Situation Scale

The current edition of the manual is an extremely brief, eight-page, distillation of the larger and more complete Holland, Gottfredson, and Power (1980) article. It is particularly brief on the development of the scale although it does refer the reader to the longer article which was apparently in press when the manual was being produced. In addition to a reference section that contains nine references, the manual consists of six sections: (1) Introduction, (2) Administration and Scoring, (3) Development, (4) Reliability, (5) Construct Validity, and (6) Discussion. Three tables provide: (1) reliability data that are actually based on an earlier, though highly related, version of the Vocational Identity Scale, (2) a table of intercorrelations, and, (3) a table of normative data. Clearly the manual needs to be updated, revised and expanded.

RESEARCH ON THE MY VOCATIONAL SITUATION SCALE

The manual presents Kuder–Richardson 20 values for samples used to devise the scales and for an accidental sample of college students and workers. Values for the Vocational Identity Scale ranged from .86 to .89. For the Occupational Information Scale values ranged from .39 to .79. The values were substantially higher for the college students and workers than the scores for high school students. For the Barriers Scale, the values ranged from .23 to .65 with the lower values again found for high school students. Later in the manual (p. 6), it is noted that the tabled values were for the 23-item Vocational Identity Scale and the value for the 18-item scale was around .85. Holland, Daiger, and Power (1980b) conclude that the Vocational Identity Scale seems internally consistent while the Occupational Information and Barrier scales are not and probably resemble checklists more than scales.

The validity data were gathered on a sample of 824 persons in high schools, colleges, and businesses. These data are largely based on how well the scales of the My Vocational Situation Scale correlate with a variety of other variables. The authors hypothesized that the V.I. and O.I. scales would be positively correlated with age. They concluded that they were. The correlations ranged from .06 to .32. For women, especially, the relationships seem tenuous indeed, and it is not immediately clear why the Barrier items were not expected to correlate with age although, in fact, they did for males. The three scales were expected to be negatively correlated with the variety and number of vocational aspirations listed and the V.I. scale was expected to be most negatively correlated. This was not found. The V.I. and O.I. scales were similarly related. The correlations overall were rather modest, ranging from −.04 to a high of −.25. The amount of variance accounted for seems minimal.

Correlations between the Vocational Identity Scale and ratings of a subsample of 245 subjects by student experimenters were performed. The student experimenters used a 5-point rating scale (strongly agree = 5, to strongly disagree = 1) to rate subjects on whether they seemed: (1) well organized, (2) at loose ends, (3) self-confident, (4) tense and uncomfortable, and (5) competent to handle life well. The authors reported that the expected relationships between the ratings and the V.I. scale occurred except for the "tense and uncomfortable" rating. Although no real information is provided on the circumstances surrounding the rating or on the background and training of the student experimenters, these correlations, especially for the males, were at least moderate generally.

Finally, normative data were provided for male and female samples over four educational levels. Holland, Daiger, and Power (1980b) concluded that for the V.I. scale, the sums generally increased with age. This did appear to be the case although no tests of statistical significance were performed. For the Occupational Information and Barrier scales the authors wrote that they "vary with age in more complex ways but the haphazard sampling makes any conclusion premature" [p. 6]. It is, of course, not clear why the haphazard sampling would affect some scales and not others. Surely lack of reliability is another possible influencing factor for both of the scales. The authors finally suggest that local norms should be developed.

Holland, Gottfredson, and Power (1980) after reviewing the data on construct validity note that "the evidence for the construct validity of the Vocational Identity scale is substantial" [p. 1198]. This judgment does not seem to be strongly supported by the data and, in fact, the three previous reviews of the measure are consistent in voicing reservations about the validity data (Lunneborg, 1985; Tinsley, 1985; Westbrook, 1985). Other concerns that were raised concerned the haphazard sampling, the heavy reliance on correlations, and the interpretation, at times, of quite modest relationships as supportive of the measure. All of the reviews recommended additional research on the MVS, especially additional data on validity.

More recently, additional studies on the validity of the Vocational Identity Scale have appeared. These studies have been particularly revealing because they illustrate an inherently interesting question about this variable. Simply stated, the question is whether the scale is primarily a measure of career indecision or whether it encompasses broader aspects of personality that include but are not limited to career indecision. The answer to this question, of course, has extremely important implications for approaching the study of validity for this scale. For example, two studies were located that focused on career indecision. Williams–Phillips (1983) studied the responses of 45 females and 75 males to both the CDS and V.I. scales and found a correlation of −.73. Grotevant and Thorbecke (1982) found that scores on the V.I. scale (the earlier 23-item version) were moderately correlated with occupational commitment (.42 for females and .49 for males) using their revised and, expanded version of Marcia's identity interview. Both studies offer support for the concurrent validity of the V.I. scale and career indecision variables.

Two additional studies explored both career indecision and personality variables. Graef, Wells, Hyland, and Muchinsky (1985) studied the ability of life history information to predict career decidedness, vocational identity, and vocational maturity in 103 male and 97 female undergraduates. The Biographical Questionnaire, a 118-item multiple-choice, self-report measure (Owens, 1976), was used to gather life history information. The Career Decision Scale was used to measure decidedness. The Vocational Identity Scale measured identity and the subscales and composite scores of the Career Development Inventory (Super, Thompson, Lindeman, Jordaan, & Myers, 1981) measured vocational maturity. The authors found that males high on the Vocational Identity Scale were upperclassmen who were socially extroverted, socially well adjusted, not strongly independent or dominant, who possessed strong scientific interests. Males low on these factors were expected to lack a clear vocational identity. Females low on Vocational Identity had poor GPAs, cold paternal relationships, few high school and cultural activities, a negative academic attitude and had not declared a major. These findings can be seen as offering general, though somewhat vague, support for Holland's identity construct. For both males and females, correlations between the Career Decision Scale and the Vocational Identity Scale were .63 and .67 respectively, indicating a substantial overlap for these scales.

Savickas (1985) examined the relationships between the Vocational Identity Scale of the MVS, the Ego Identity scale, a 12-item instrument designed to measure Erikson's conceptualization of ego identity achievement, and the Medical Career Development Inventory, a measure of vocational development designed especially for medical students (Savickas, 1984). The sample consisted of 83 males and 60 females who were in the first 2 years of a 6-year combined bachelor of science and doctor of medicine program. Savickas found that Vocational Identity was moderately related to both vocational development ($r = .40$) and ego identity ($r = .44$). Ego identity and career development were correlated .26. Savickas interpreted these relationships as supporting Holland's construct of vocational identity because it "includes both vocational and identity components which themselves are distinct" [p. 335]. Although it is perhaps arguable whether variables that correlate .26 are distinct, overall this carefully done study does provide support for the construct validity of the Vocational Identity Scale, at least for this somewhat unique sample. Both studies offer support for the concurrent and construct validity of the Vocational Identity Scale as a measure of career indecision and personality.

Only one study was located that focused on the relationship of the Vocational Identity Scale to personality variables. Henkels, Spokane, and Hoffman (1981) found that subjects who had high V.I. scores ($N = 16$) differed from subjects with low V.I. scores ($N = 18$) on two scales of the California Psychological Inventory. High V.I. subjects had higher scores on the Sense of Well-Being scale and on the Capacity for Status scale. Differences on the Achievement via Independence scale and the Achievement via Conformance scale were not statistically significant. This study offers some modest support for the Vocational Identity Scale as a measure of personality.

Other studies were located that suggest the MVS may be useful in measuring the effects of interventions. Rayman, Bernard, Holland, and Barnett (1983) found that the Vocational Identity Scale and the Occupational Information Scale of the MVS showed changes in the expected direction for college students enrolled in a career course. The students were 255 male and female undergraduates at Iowa State, who were in 22 sections of a career course taught by academic advisers. The course met for 1 hour per week for 11 weeks. For the entire sample, the Vocational Identity Scale scores went from 6.47 to 9.52. This difference was statistically significant using a t-test. A second t-test found that changes on the Occupational Information Scale from .77 to 1.83 were also statistically significant. Changes on the Barriers Scale were not statistically significant nor were any of the interaction effects for instructor or student characteristics. These results suggest that the V.I. and O.I. scales are sensitive to treatment effects and may be useful for measuring changes. Other recent studies were also located that suggest the MVS, especially the Vocational Identity Scale, is beginning to be used as an outcome measure (MacKinnon–Slaney, 1986; MacKinnon–Slaney, Barber & Slaney, 1986; Slaney & Lewis, 1986; Slaney & MacKinnon–Slaney, 1986).

One additional and extremely important issue that suggests that the Vocational Identity Scale will be used with increasing frequency in the future is the emphasis that Holland (1985) has given to this construct in his recent revision of his theory. This emphasis is illustrated by Holland's statement that identity as measured by the Vocational Identity Scale "is intended to provide an alternate assessment that may be more useful than either consistency or differentiation" [Holland, 1985, p. 28].

These latter constructs both had important roles in Holland's earlier statement of his theory (1973). In fact, in a recent APA address about the revision of his theory, Holland noted that he had considered eliminating the constructs of consistency and differentiation in favor of identity at one point. He did not, of course, but in reading Holland's statements about identity it becomes clear that he sees the construct as a measure of potentially major aspects of personality beyond career indecision. For example, Holland, Gottfredson, and Power (1980) stated that "A poor sense of identity would be expected to affect vocational and nonvocational tasks and our clinical experience suggests that the V.I. scale might also be a general adjustment scale" [p. 1197]. In a similar vein, Holland (1985) wrote, "My speculation is that identity and integration [Seeman, 1983] are similar concepts and that neuroticism may be the opposite pole of both concepts" [p. 201]. Curiously, no specific reference is made to indecisiveness although it sounds like low Vocational Identity scores might be related to this construct.

Clearly one important implication of Holland's speculation about the Vocational Identity construct is that it may lead to the establishment of clearer ties between vocational psychology and the study of personality and quite possibly psychopathology. With his construct of Vocational Identity, Holland continues his consistent tendency of clearly stating ideas that are both interesting and testable and providing instruments, such as the Vocational Identity Scale, that operationalize the central constructs. This formula has been at least one central factor behind the impressive amount of research that has been generated by Holland's ideas in the past. It seems reasonable to expect that this formula will also operate successfully for the construct of Vocational Identity in the future.

THE VOCATIONAL DECISION SCALE

Jones and Chenery (1980), in an attempt to specify the subtypes of career indecision, developed a model of vocational decision status and an instrument to assess its dimensions. The model was based on the authors' judgment that there were three essential questions that should be asked to determine the vocational decision status of respondents. The questions were: (1) How decided are you about your choice of an occupation? (2) How comfortable are you with where you are in the process of making this choice, and (3) For what reasons are you decided or undecided? These questions were the basis for the three dimensions that were hypothesized as constituting a model of vocational decision status, i.e., decidedness, comfort, and reasons.

The instrument that was developed to measure the three dimensions of vocational decision status was called the Vocational Decision Scale. The original scale consisted of 38 items; 1 assessed decidedness, 1 comfort, and 36 assessed the reasons for being vocationally undecided. These latter items were developed by examining incidents from counseling mentioned by counseling center staff and "a comprehensive review of the literature" [p. 471]. Six-point Likert scales (from completely agree to disagree completely) were used for recording the responses to all of the items.

The authors reported that test-retest correlations for the items ranged from .36 to .64, with 74% having correlations of .50 or greater. The time between administrations for one sample was apparently 2 weeks but unspecified for a second sample. As predicted, positive relationships were found between the decidedness item and (1) scores on the Decision-Making Task-Occupation scale of Harren's (1978) Assessment of Career Decision Making, (2) scores on the Identity Scale of Holland, Gottfredson, and Nafziger (1975), and (3) scores on the short form of the Career Salience Questionnaire by Greenhaus and Simon (1977). The prediction that students in a career exploration course would be more decided after the course was not supported. Similarly, the prediction of a negative relation between trait anxiety and vocational decidedness was not supported.

The decidedness and comfort dimensions were found to be positively related and it was found, as expected, that decided, comfortable students had higher scores on the Identity Scale than did students who were decided but uncomfortable.

To examine the reasons dimension, the items that were not correlated with the decidedness item at .10 or better were eliminated as were the responses of students who completely agreed with the decidedness item. Thirteen items were eliminated and the remaining 23 were factor analyzed using the Principal-Axis solution with test-retest reliability coefficients as principal-diagonal estimates. These factors were rotated using the Varimax method and three factors accounted for 64.7% of the total variance. Factor 1 was labeled as "self-uncertainty" and was composed of items indicating indecisiveness, lack of self-confidence about decision-making ability, and lack of clarity about self. Factor 2, labeled "choice/work salience," indicated that respondents had not related their interests and abilities to occupational areas and were not strongly inclined to do so. Factor 3, "transitional self," suggested indecision whose origin was perceived as being external to the person, deriving from either a lack of educational or occupational information or a conflict with significant others.

Three scales, four items long, were derived based on the interpreted factor structure and it was found that after a brief course (10 class hours) that provided educational and vocational information. the Transitional Self Scale declined, as expected by the authors. The Self Uncertainty and Choice/Work Salience scales did not decline significantly. For the three scales, test-retest correlations ranged from .61 to .77.

Two studies were located that used the VDS. Larson and Heppner (1985) used the VDS as a dependent variable in exploring possible differences between 32 female and 32 male college students who rated themselves as either positive or negative on problem-solving skills. Problem-solving skills were assessed by the Problem Solving Inventory (Heppner & Petersen, 1982). The dependent variables were the decidedness and comfort items, the 36-item Reasons Scale, and the three 4-item scales that Jones and Chenery had proposed, based on their factor analysis results. No statistically significant differences were found for the decidedness and comfort items. There were statistically significant differences for the Reasons scale and for the three shorter scales with positive problem solvers scoring lower (the positive direction) on all the scales. There were no statistically significant sex or interaction effects. These results seem reasonable and were similar to the results found for the Career Decision Scale which was also used as a dependent variable. Together these results offer some support for the concurrent validity of the VDS.

A study by Williams–Phillips (1983) offers more direct support for the test-retest reliability and the concurrent validity of the instrument. Using 117 male and female college students, Williams–Phillips found a 3-week test-retest reliability of .86, using the 36-item Reasons Scale. She also found that this scale correlated .69 with the Career Decision Scale and $-.73$ with the Vocational Identity Scale of the MVS. These results offer substantial support for the reliability and concurrent validity of the VDS.

The initial development of this scale and the two subsequent studies seem to offer support for continued research on this instrument. The idea of looking at the degree of comfort that is expressed approaches an important motivational aspect of career indecision. Some students may be undecided but perfectly comfortable or at least relatively unconcerned about their indecision. Also, the three four-item scales that were based on the factor analyses, if replicated, seem to offer a promising approach to exploring the differential needs of career clients in relation to differential interventions and their effects. Though the initial development seems promising, the VDS presently appears to be overshadowed by both the CDS and the MVS. It seems questionable that this scale will receive the research attention it will need to become widely used. With the greater research attention and support the two other scales have received, potential researchers may not have an adequate basis for choosing the VDS in preference to the MVS or the CDS. If future studies were found in support of the brief scales based on the factor structure, especially if these scales could be related to different interventions, such a basis for preference might emerge. However, at present, it seems questionable whether the VDS will receive this needed research attention.

THE OCCUPATIONAL ALTERNATIVES QUESTION

One different approach to the study of career indecision appears to be somewhat responsive to the difficulty of assigning meaning to the different degrees of career indecision and potentially responsive to assigning differential treatments based on these meanings. Slaney (1980) approached the study of career indecision via a brief measure of expressed vocational interests. Expressed interests were relevant because they have been found, repeatedly and consistently, to have predictive validity relative to chosen college majors or actual career choices that equals or exceeds the predictive validity of very widely used inventoried vocational interests (Bartling & Hood, 1981; Borgen & Seling, 1978; Cairo, 1982; Dolliver, 1969; Dolliver & Will, 1977; Holland & Lutz, 1968). However, given this resilient finding on the predictive validity of expressed vocational interests, it appears that (1) Most college students have expressed vocational interests (Slaney, 1978, 1983, 1984; Slaney & Dickson, 1985; Slaney & MacKinnon–Slaney, 1986; Slaney & Russell, 1981), but (2) Many college students are unsure of these choices, seek career counseling relative to these choices, and change their choices during their undergraduate years (Gordon, 1984; Osipow, 1983).

Based on these findings it can be assumed with some assurance that some expressed vocational interests are likely to be more stable and predictive than others. To explore this aspect of expressed interests, Slaney (1980) used the Occupational Alternatives Question (Zener & Schnuelle, 1976). The OAQ consists of two parts: (a) "list all the occupations you are considering right now," and (b) "which occupation is your first choice? (if undecided, write undecided)." The two parts of the question provide at least four possibilities in responding: (a) A first choice is listed with no alternatives; (b) A first choice is listed with alternatives; (c) Alternatives are listed without a first choice, (d) No first choice and no alternatives are listed. Numerical values were attached to the above possibilities so that a = 1, b = 2, c = 3, and d = 4. Using these values, Slaney divided 232 college students into eight equal groups based on sex and their OAQ scores. Using a number of vocationally relevant variables as dependent measures, it was found that there were clear relationships between the OAQ, as scored, and (1) brief scales by Holland and Holland (1977) measuring decidedness with college major and career choice, (2) the summary score of the Vocational Decision-Making Difficulty Scale (Holland & Holland, 1977), and the summary score of the Career Decision Scale (Osipow, Carney, Winer, Yanico, & Koschier, 1976).

Other studies, using the 4-point scoring system, have also found support for the concurrent validity of the OAQ as a measure of career indecision. Burkey–Flanagan (1981) divided 75 male and 75 female subjects into groups based on their OAQ scores. Because of the generally low percentage of 4s in the college population, she combined 3s and 4s into one group for both sexes and had three groups for each sex with 25 subjects in each group. Using the Vocational Identity Scale of the MVS as a dependent variable, Burkey–Flanagan found a statistically significant main effect for OAQ level and that for both sexes all the groups were significantly different from each other in the expected direction. More specifically, OAQ 1s had higher V.I. scores than 2s who had higher scores than 3s and 4s. The correlation of the OAQ score and the V.I. scores was −.48. Slaney,

Stafford, and Russell (1981) compared high school, college, and re-entry women on several measures of career indecision, including the OAQ, a short indecision scale by Holland and Holland (1977) as well as their longer Vocational Decision-making Difficulty scale and the Career Decision Scale. The group differences for the OAQ were consistent with the differences found for the other scales which, in turn, were consistent with each other. Correlations of the OAQ with the other measures range from the skewed low of .08 (re-entry women on the CDS) to a high of .58 (college women on the CDS). The average correlation over groups and instruments was a modest .33.

Slaney (1983) used the OAQ as a subject attribute in a study that included an initial survey and a later treatment study. An examination of differences between survey subjects who were willing to participate and those who were not, over the four OAQ levels, yielded a statistically significant OAQ effect on the brief Holland and Holland Career Indecision Scale. *Post hoc* analyses revealed three subsets made up of Levels 1 and 2, Level 3, and Level 4 which were significantly different from each other in the expected direction. None of these survey subjects were in the treatment study, which used only three OAQ levels because of the difficulty in locating OAQ 4 subjects. For this sample there were statistically significant differences according to OAQ levels using the same Holland and Holland scale. All groups were significantly different from each other in the expected directions. Finally, Williams–Phillips (1983) divided her subjects according to OAQ levels (combining Levels 3 and 4). Using five measures of career indecision, she found statistically significant differences in the expected direction for all the measures except the CDS where the means were in the expected direction but were not significantly different. Correlations ranged from .20 to a high of .44 but were mostly in the 20s, indicating low to modest common variance.

Overall, these studies lend support to the OAQ as a brief, easily administered measure of expressed vocational interests that, when scored as a 4-point scale, has a modest but generally consistent level of concurrent validity with other measures of career indecision. Given its primitive scaling and the modest amount of variance it appears to share with other more extensive measures of career indecision, it is probably more reasonable to view the OAQ as a rough estimate of career indecision rather than as a scale, per se. Clearly, it is not competitive with the longer scales already reviewed as a measure of the antecedents of career indecision. Nor would the OAQ seem appropriate as a measure of change where the longer scales are more likely to be sensitive to change and more likely to be informative about the nature of the changes that occur. Still the OAQ has some merit as a brief and relevant estimate of career indecision. Relative to the longer scales, where reactivity of the instruments may be an issue when measuring treatment effects, it is not immediately obvious that the OAQ is a measure of career indecision. It does seem clear, however, that as a measure of career indecision the OAQ is limited in usefulness and less sensitive and informative for use in counseling or research.

However, it should be recalled that the measures of career indecision developed by Jones and Chenery, Holland and his colleagues, and Osipow et al. were all developed to examine the antecedents of career indecision. Having done this, the next step was to develop differential treatments based on these antecedents. One irony in the research reviewed on these scales is that, despite the common goal of differential treatments, no studies were located that examined the effects of such treatments based on the antecedents measured. Perhaps it is simply too early in this process to expect such studies. One problem that needs to be solved, or at least addressed, is how the scales can be used, in a pragmatic sense, to divide subjects into different groups. What scores on which subscales or factor scales indicate which treatment or treatments clients should optimally receive? Ultimately decisions on these issues, which are basically diagnostic issues, need to be made and studied. Based on these decisions then, the difficult treatment studies can be done. Not only are these studies difficult, time consuming, and expensive to conduct, but previous studies on treatment effects are not generally encouraging relative to finding differential effects (Holland, Magoon, & Spokane, 1981).

In addition, the tendency for researchers to use the CDS and V.I. scales as unidimensional measures glosses over the issue of developing differential treatments based on the antecedents of career indecision. Rather, the emphasis is on career indecision as a single dimension with higher scores indicating quantitative rather than qualitative differences. The implications for differential treatments based on quantitative differences are, of course, quite different. Given a particular career intervention, it follows that more treatment is needed if clients have high scores on the quantitative dimension, i.e., are highly undecided; less of the treatment is needed for lower scores. Or, stated another way, the same career intervention will have differential effects on clients who differ to some meaningful degree on the quantitative dimension. It can be argued that this approach, as vague and primitive as it sounds, is not unrepresentative of the present state of the research on career interventions. In fact, only a few studies exist that have explored different degrees of career decidedness relative to differential treatment effects.

One study that did look for differential treatment effects was done by Slaney and Dickson (1985). They studied re-entry women who represented extreme differences on the Vocational Identity Scale of the MVS. They had two treatment groups and a control group. Their results confirmed the expectation that the decided women would be less responsive to career interventions than would the highly undecided women. This study, though useful, avoided one practical difficulty raised by the unidimensional V.I. scale. The difficulty is in determining which scale scores are different from each other or, stated another way, how meaningful group differences are determined based on a unidimensional scale. One solution is to examine the scores of known groups, e.g., career clients or students who choose to take courses on career choice or career development. A difficulty is that the scores of these subjects may vary within groups and from one location to another. This often leads to the suggestion that local norms should be developed. This suggestion, however, appears to be made more frequently than it is followed. A different type of solution is provided by the OAQ which, although it can be used as a quantitative scale, has only four levels which form four natural categories.

Slaney (1983) used the OAQ as a unidimensional scale and randomly assigned equal numbers of OAQ 1s, 2s, and 3s to two separate treatment groups or to a control group. The treatments did not differ according to the OAQ level. He found, consistent with expectations, that OAQ 1s changed their career choices as a result of treatment far less frequently than did the OAQ 3s. In a more recent study, Slaney and Lewis (1986) chose women who were all at OAQ Level 3 for an intervention study, based on previous findings that these subjects were more likely to respond to career interventions and were similar to actual career clients (Slaney & MacKinnon–Slaney, 1986). Whether future studies will also find that Level 3 on the OAQ is a useful benchmark remains to be seen.

Besides providing benchmarks for career indecision as a unidimensional variable, the OAQ may also raise some possibilities relative to the qualitative aspects of potential differential treatments. For example, at Level 1 the concurrent validity studies suggest that clients are relatively decided about their career choices. This makes intuitive sense because persons who have a first choice and are not considering alternatives probably are decided about that choice because they are not seeking alternatives. Although these students do not appear to seek career counseling frequently, (Slaney & MacKinnon–Slaney, 1986) when they do, they may be seeking confirmation of that first choice. In contrast, clients who are unable to list any alternatives may not only need more career counseling but counseling that provides more basic information on the world of work in general and, more specifically, how these clients may relate to that world. Other aspects may, of course, be involved. At OAQ Level 2 it might be reasonable to expect that clients are giving some thought to a first choice but that they also have some other alternatives they are still considering. It might be relevant to compare their first choices with the alternatives that are being considered. Similarly, for Level 3, it would seem logical to help the client compare the alternatives being considered, using an array of relevant dimensions for the comparisons.

When the suggestions made herein are combined with the data on expressed vocational interests and the OAQ, it appears that there are few college students who do not have any expressed vocational interests at all and few college students at OAQ Level 1 who feel the need for or request career counseling (Slaney, 1983; Slaney & MacKinnon–Slaney, 1986). In fact, Slaney and MacKinnon–Slaney (1986) found only 1 woman, out of 54 undergraduate women who requested and received career counseling, who was a 4 on the OAQ. There were no women clients at OAQ Level 1. Although the results for men were not included in the study, they were similar. Of 50 male clients, two were at Level 4 on the OAQ. The rest were 2s and 3s. If results like these are replicated to any degree,

the implication is that most of the clients who request ca
alternative choices that they are considering. For Levels 2 ·
differential treatment that naturally comes to mind is o..
alternatives that are being considered across a common set of dimc..
relevant to the clients. Simply stated, these findings raise the possibu..
interventions focusing on decision making as a process may be extremely relevant for large numbers of career clients. The next section will examine the
current work on career decision making.

CAREER DECISION-MAKING

There is a sizable and developing literature on decision making that, according to
a recent review, is part of the larger field of cognitive psychology although this
association is not always clearly recognized (Pitz & Sachs, 1984). The origins of
the study of decision making are in mathematical and classical or statistical
decision theory. These areas, although perhaps somewhat unfamiliar to many
vocational psychologists, provide the background for a related array of approaches to assisting or aiding the process of decision making. These approaches
have relevance for decision making in general and career decision making in
particular. These approaches and their background will be discussed here only in
a brief and general sense. Those who wish to read more extended treatments are
referred to Mitchell and Krumboltz (1984) for a particularly clear and literate
presentation of these issues relative to career decision making and to Pitz and
Harren (1980) for an earlier attempt at exploring the implications of decision
theory for career decision making. Earlier papers by Gelatt (1962), Jepsen and
Dilley (1974), and Katz (1966, 1973) are also extremely relevant.

In considering decision making, it is clear that there is a need to have at least
one alternative choice or course of action available. Without alternatives no
choice is possible and no decision is necessary. Less obvious perhaps in the
literature on decision making is the assumption that the alternatives, (e.g., think
of choosing between three possible careers), can be divided or decomposed into
component parts or aspects, e.g., salary, variety of activities, time spent alone,
etc. These components can then be analyzed or considered across the three
possible careers e.g., the salaries and other components of careers *a, b,* and *c* are
analyzed and considered before the component parts are reintegrated to constitute
a judgment about the alternatives.

The analysis of the components is often aided by a process of subjective
evaluation that relates the respondents' values, often referred to as utilities, to the
component parts of each alternative with a numerical scaling system. Here there
is a good deal of room for differences between systems. The numerical system
considers, with varying degrees of exactness, the relative importance of the
values and then looks at the alternatives to see whether or to what degree these

alues are represented in each alternative. The values are usually presented in a manner that allows for individual differences.

An example may help. If I am trying to decide whether to pursue a career as a brain surgeon or a beef splitter (D.O.T. 525.684–018) and I value economic return highly, I will attach a numerical rating to economic return that is higher than the rating given to other values. Then I'll consider the possible economic return I might receive as a brain surgeon and as a beef splitter. Note that economic return may be a somewhat special, though frequently relevant, dimension because it is often possible to quantify it with some degree of accuracy. Other values, such as prestige, leisure time, freedom from stress relative to the threat of malpractice suits, may be difficult or impossible to quantify in any other than a relatively primitive and highly subjective manner. In any event, the idea is that through figuring in the strength of the value and its presence or strength in each alternative and then summing these numbers for each alternative one gets a clearer overall idea of which alternative is preferred and why. (See Zakay & Barak [1984] for a related approach that uses a subjects' ''ideal alternative'' as a basis for comparing alternatives. The alternative closer to the ideal is the one to be chosen.)

Basic to the process described is the assumption that the consideration given to the component parts of each alternative leads to more careful overall consideration of the alternatives themselves than would occur without the decomposition process. It is also assumed that this more careful consideration leads to better decisions. For example, Pitz and McKillip (1984) reasoned that the decomposition procedure yields better decisions because judgments of single events are more reliable and sensitive to relevant information than global judgments about complex alternatives. Although this assertion seems reasonable, as does the process that is involved, there is little available support for the contention that the process leads to better decisions.

In fact, one of the more difficult problems with the area of decision making is dealing with the problem of establishing criteria by which a decision can be judged. It is one thing to believe that, for example, more careful consideration of the components of the available alternatives leads to better decisions. Providing empirical support for this reasonable sounding belief has, however, proven to be a difficult task. Those familiar with the problem of developing adequate outcome measures for career interventions (Oliver, 1979) or for counseling outcomes are somewhat familiar with the litany of woe that Gelso refers to dispassionately as the ''perennial criterion problem'' [Gelso, 1979].

Although this problem involves the general inadequacy of individual lives as experimental studies, an issue more specific to career decision making involves the difficulty of knowing a good decision when one is encountered. One may, for example, be happy as a brain surgeon. But the same person may have been ecstatic as a beef splitter. It is impossible to measure the outcome of the alternatives that were not selected. It is also possible that a bad decision can lead to a good outcome and vice versa. Consider the plight of the ecstatic beef splitter in a society that decides that cattle should be raised as pets and soybeans given a more prominent role at McDonald's. A similar, less exotic example, concerns the person, who in response to the prediction of a high probability of rain, carries an umbrella though it doesn't rain. Was this a good decision? The point, of course, is that outcomes may not necessarily be indicative of the adequacy of the decision-making process. Still Krumboltz, Scherba, Hamel, and Mitchell (1982) argue that no matter how reasonable the process may appear, that no process can be justified without some reference to data indicating that the process leads to better outcomes. This conclusion, however, takes us back full circle to where this paragraph started and only touches on a few of the problems in establishing criteria for decisions.

However, if there are difficulties in agreeing on how to measure the outcome of decision making, there does appear to be a consensus or a near consensus that says that the evaluation process utilized in considering the components of the alternative choices is a subjective process. If the process is subjective then it also seems reasonable to assume that the outcome may be subjective. In addition, there is also an apparent consensus that states that the values a person holds are centrally important to the evaluation process and ultimately to the career chosen. This contention seems consistent with a great deal of the explicit and implicit theorizing on career choice and career development. If this seems reasonable, then it seems to follow that a good career decision should generally lead to a career choice which has component parts that overall have a value structure that is consistent with the values espoused by the respondent.

Recently, Krumboltz and his colleagues (Krumboltz, Scherba, Hamel, & Mitchell, 1982) published an ingenious study that also reasoned that a "good" career decision should lead to a career choice where the values represented in the career choice would be consistent with the values of the respondents. Krumboltz and his colleagues developed a 90-minute curriculum based on the DECIDES decision-making model of Krumboltz and Hamel (1977). This model consists of seven steps: (a) defining the problem, (b) establishing an action plan, (c) clarifying values, (d) identifying alternatives, (e) discovering probable outcomes, (f) eliminating alternatives systematically, and (g) starting action. The subjects were 99 female and 48 male community college students ranging in age from 16 to 50. The subjects were randomized to either the decision-making curriculum or to a control curriculum where interviewing skills were taught.

Of primary interest here, Krumboltz et al. developed the Career Decision Simulation to measure whether subjects made a career decision that was consistent with their values. The simulation task had subjects begin by rating nine values, taken from Katz (1963), into three equal groups, high, medium, or low. Subjects were then allowed to gather information on 12 fictitious occupations, e. g., plinder, zampic, kralician. The information was contained on 324 index cards distributed through various information sources. The items of information were developed to indicate or infer where the particular occupations ranked on a specific value. A maximum of 2 hours was allowed for subjects to choose a career.

For the analyses, subjects were divided into two age groups, 16–21 and 22–50. A computer program was developed to determine the consistency of the values ratings and the career chosen. The results of the study indicated that there was a three-way interaction between sex, treatment, and age. For females the training in rational decision making produced better (more value-consistent) career decisions than occurred for the control group. The same effect held for the younger males but for the older males the rational group made poorer decisions than did the control group. These generally promising results were followed up by Hamel (1980), reported in Mitchell and Krumboltz (1984). Hamel attempted to improve on the original study by using a modified simulation instrument and a more extensive treatment with a sample of high school students but found no significant effects on the quality of the students' career decisions.

A study by Krumboltz, Rude, Mitchell, Hamel, and Kinnier (1982) attempted to identify behaviors that differentiated subjects who made "good" decisions (defined, as before, on the basis of consistency with values) and subjects who made "bad" decisions. Seven dependent variables were based on behaviors performed in responding to the Career Decision Simulation. Good decision makers were those 40 of 148 total subjects whose choices were most consistent with their values. Poor decision makers were the 40 who made choices that were least consistent with their values. Only one difference was statistically significant. Good decision makers were more persistent in immediately continuing to explore an occupation that they had just found to be consistent with one of their highest values.

There are many questions that can be raised about the studies that have been described, especially questions relative to generalizability. It also seems clear that the results for the latter two studies were somewhat disappointing. Still these studies represent a creative and carefully reasoned approach to the criterion problem in career decision making. If it seems Krumboltz and his colleagues have approached the problem in a reasonable manner, then the first study reviewed provides general, though not unanimous, support for the decision-making model of Krumboltz and Hamel (1977) and suggests that it leads to "better decisions" operationally defined. It can be noted that the Krumboltz and Hamel model has similarities to an array of approaches to decision making that are mentioned in Mitchell and Krumboltz (1984). If the initial results can be replicated (as they were not in Hamel, 1980) especially with real clients and actual career choices, then this study by Krumboltz et al. (1982) will have been extremely important in validating a process that appears reasonable but has been difficult to support empirically.

The general approach to decision making that has been discussed seems most applicable when the number of alternatives has been reduced to around three or four. It is possible to use more but if many more than four are used the task quickly becomes cumbersome and laborious. Although the research on the OAQ suggests that the decision-making tasks described may be relevant for large numbers of career clients, it may also be the case that the OAQ artificially limits the number of alternatives because of the small number of lines that are provided for alternatives. If it is true that at least some career clients have a larger number of alternatives under consideration, then it may be necessary for counselors to help reduce this number before a decision-making approach is relevant. A recent paper by Gati is extremely relevant to this specific issue.

Gati (1986) describes what is referred to as the sequential elimination model (SEM) which is an adaptation for career decisions of Tversky's (1972) elimination by-aspects theory of choice. SEM can handle a sizable array of occupational alternatives and each alternative is seen as being made up of components or aspects which have quantitative or qualitative dimensions, e.g., salary. As before, values are often central in considering the aspects of the career alternatives.

In the elimination process an aspect or component is selected based on its overall importance to the respondent. Based on the presence or absence or the degree to which this aspect is present, alternatives are selected or eliminated from further consideration. Either desirable or undesirable aspects may be used and elimination (based on the presence, absence, or degree of presence of the chosen aspects) leads to the sequential elimination of all of the alternatives that are not acceptable. Clearly this process places a central emphasis on the identification and subjective ordering of the aspects of careers that are important to the individual respondents and Gati discusses a number of approaches to these tasks.

Gati also contrasts the sequential elimination model to the decision models which are based on a limited number of alternatives. The SEM model, instead of beginning with a restricted list of alternatives which are given relatively intense consideration, selects an aspect and identifies alternatives that are acceptable, based on some quantitative or qualitative criterion, e.g., these occupations pay above or below an acceptable amount of salary or they emphasize close human interactions (or solitary brooding) to an acceptable or unacceptable degree. After the first and most important aspect is considered, the second aspect is considered with the remaining alternatives. While some of the decision-making models ordered the aspects or components of the alternatives, it did not make much difference how they were approached in the task. For the SEM the sequencing of the aspects is extremely important because once an alternative is eliminated it receives no further consideration.

Although Gati gives much more extensive consideration to the advantages and theoretical relevance of the SEM, the essential elements have been described. Gati does not miss the similarity of his approach to the recent theorizing of Gottfredson (1985) nor does Gati fail to note what is of particular relevance here, that the SEM approach may be useful for reducing a large number of options to a number of alternatives that can then be subjected to the more intense decision-making analyses described earlier. Clearly Gati raises a number of possibilities relative to career decision making that have theoretical and applied implications for future work.

SUMMARY

In summary, this chapter has attempted to examine carefully the research and writing on the assessment of career indecision and career decision making. In this examination it was found that earlier studies looking for differences between career-decided and -undecided students seemed to produce inconsistent and, at times, contradictory results. Attempts at resolving these inconsistencies were seen to lead in two general directions. The first direction was mainly theoretical and speculative and concluded that for most people career indecision is a part of normal development and is generally resolved without great difficulty. When resolution proves difficult, it is concluded that the cause is actually indecisiveness. The concept of indecisiveness was found to be ingrained in the literature but in clear need of adequate scaling and empirical support.

The second direction that was explored in resolving the contradictory early findings on career indecision concluded that these early results were due to the overly simplistic approaches to the measurement of career indecision that were used. The development of carefully constructed scales measuring the components or antecedents of career indecision was seen as the direction to take if progress were to be made. The scales that were developed and the research in this area were reviewed and signs of real progress in measuring this variable seem evident. Progress in identifying clear and reliable factors or subcomponents of career indecision that could serve as the basis for differential career interventions has proven more elusive. This does seem to be a direction for future research. Finally, the research and thought on career decision making were related to the need for differential treatments. The available literature in this general area was examined. This literature and research are just beginning to be recognized and incorporated into the work of vocational psychologists. The possibilities for future research into the uses of decision-making aids in career decision making are intriguing if not exciting. Overall, after what appeared to be a relatively slow and at times sporadic period of early development, the last 10 years have been a period of accelerating growth and progress for assessing career indecision and decision making. It appears that the future may be an even more intense period of development with real possibilities for progress in theoretical as well as applied research into career indecision and career decision making.

ACKNOWLEDGMENT

The author expresses appreciation to Professor Paul R. Salomone for his thoughtful comments on an earlier version of this chapter and to Karen J. Rains for her preparation of the manuscript.

REFERENCES

Abel, W. H. (1966). Attrition and the student who is certain. *Personnel & Guidance Journal, 44*, 1042–1045.

Ashby, J. D., Wall, H. W., & Osipow, S. H. (1966). Vocational certainty and indecision in college freshmen. *Personnel & Guidance Journal, 44*, 1037–1041.

Astin, A. W. (1975). *Preventing students from dropping out*. San Francisco: Jossey–Bass.

Astin, A. W. (1977). *Four critical years*. San Francisco: Jossey–Bass.

Baird, L. L. (1969). The undecided student: How different is he? *Personnel & Guidance Journal, 47*, 429–434.

Barak, A., & Friedkes, R. (1982). The mediating effects of career indecision and subtypes on career-counseling effectiveness. *Journal of Vocational Behavior, 20*, 120–128.

Barrett, T. C., & Tinsley, H. E. A. (1977). Vocational self-concept crystallization and vocational indecision. *Journal of Counseling Psychology, 24*, 301–307.

Bartling, H. C., & Hood, A. B. (1981). An 11-year follow-up of measured interest and vocational choice. *Journal of Counseling Psychology, 28*, 27–35.

Bohn, M. (1968). Vocational indecision and interest development in college freshmen. *Journal of College Student Personnel, 9*, 393–395.

Borgen, F. H., & Seling, M. J. (1978). Expressed and inventoried interests revisited: Perspicacity in the person. *Journal of Counseling Psychology, 25*, 536–543.

Burkey–Flanagan, R. J. (1981). *Relationships among vocational indecision, vocational identity, self-concept and assertiveness*. Unpublished master's thesis, University of Akron, Ohio.

Cairo, P. C. (1982). Measured interests versus expressed interests as predictors of long-term occupational membership. *Journal of Vocational Behavior, 20*, 343–353.

Cesari, J. P., Winer, J. L., & Piper, K. R. (1984). Vocational decision status and the effect of four types of occupational information on cognitive complexity. *Journal of Vocational Behavior, 25*, 215–224.

Cesari, J. P., Winer, J. L., Zychlinski, F., & Laird, I. O. (1982). Influence of occupational information giving on cognitive complexity in decided versus undecided students. *Journal of Vocational Behavior, 21*, 224–230.

Cooper, S. E., Fuqua, D. R., & Hartman, B. W. (1984). The relationship of trait indecisiveness to vocational uncertainty, career indecision, and interpersonal characteristics. *Journal of College Student Personnel, 25*, 353–356.

Crites, J. O. (1969). *Vocational psychology*. New York: McGraw–Hill.

Dolliver, R. H. (1969). Strong vocational interest blank versus expressed vocational interests: A review. *Psychological Bulletin, 72*, 95–107.

Dolliver, R. H., & Will, J. A. (1977). Ten-year follow-up of the Tyler vocational card sort and the Strong Vocational Interest Blank. *Journal of Counseling Psychology, 24*, 48–54.

Elton, C. F., & Rose, H. A. (1970). Male occupational constancy and change: Its prediction according to Holland's theory. *Journal of Counseling Psychology*, Monograph 17, part 2, 1–19.

Elton, C. F., & Rose, H. A. (1971). A longitudinal study of the vocationally undecided male student. *Journal of Vocational Behavior, 1*, 85–92.

Erikson, E. (1957). Childhood and society, (rev. ed.). New York: Norton.

Foote, B. (1980). Determined—and undetermined—major students: How different are they? *Journal of College Student Personnel, 21*, 29–34.

Galinsky, D. A., & Fast, S. (1966). Vocational choice as a focus of the identity search. *Journal of Counseling Psychology, 13*, 89–93.

Gati, I. (1986). Making career decisions: A sequential elimination approach. *Journal of Counseling Psychology, 33*, 408–417.

Gelatt, H. B. (1962). Decision making: A conceptual frame of reference for counseling. *Journal of Counseling Psychology, 9*, 240–245.

Gelso, C. J. (1979). Research in counseling: Methodological and professional issues. *Counseling Psychologist, 8*(3), 7–35.

Ginzberg, E., Ginsburg, S. W., Axelrad, S., & Herma, J. L. (1951). *Occupational choice: An approach to a general theory.* New York: Columbia University Press.

Glaize, D. L., & Myrick, R. D. (1984). Interpersonal groups or computers? A study of career maturity and career decidedness. *Vocational Guidance Quarterly, 32,* 168–176.

Goodstein, L. D. (1965). Behavior theoretical views of counseling. In B. Steffire (Ed.), *Theories of counseling.* New York: McGraw–Hill.

Gordon, V. N. (1984). *The undecided college student: An academic and career advising challenge.* Springfield, IL: C. C. Thomas.

Gottfredson, L. S. (1985). Circumscription and compromise: A developmental theory of occupational aspirations. *Journal of Counseling Psychology, 28,* 545–579.

Graef, M. I., Wells, D. L., Hyland, A. M., & Muchinsky, P. M. (1985). Life history antecedents of vocational indecision. *Journal of Vocational Behavior, 27,* 276–297.

Greenhaus, J. H., & Simon, W. E. (1977). Career salience, work values, and vocational indecision. *Journal of Vocational Behavior, 10,* 104–110.

Grotevant, H. D., & Thorbecke, W. L. (1982). Sex differences in styles of occupational identity formation in late adolescence. *Developmental Psychology, 18,* 396–405.

Hall, D. W. (1963). *A study of the interrelationships among manifest anxiety, vocational choice certainty, and choice behavior.* Doctoral Dissertation, University of Iowa. (Ann Arbor, MI: University Microfilms, 1963, No. 63–8006.)

Hamel, D. (1980). *The effect of decision training on selected measures of career decision-making competence.* Unpublished dissertation, Stanford University, California.

Harman, R. L. (1973). Students who lack vocational identity. *Vocational Guidance Quarterly, 21,* 169–173.

Harmon, L. W. (1985). Review of S. H. Osipow, C. G. Carney, J. L. Winer, B. Yanico, & M. Koschier, Career Decision Scale. In J. V. Mitchell, Jr. (Ed.), *Ninth mental measurements yearbook, Vol. 2* (p. 270). Lincoln: University of Nebraska Press.

Harren, V. A. (1978). *Assessment of career decision making: Counselor/instructor guide.* Unpublished manuscript. Southern Illinois University, Carbondale, IL.

Hartman, B. W., Fuqua, D. R., & Blum, C. R. (1985). A path-analytic model of career indecision. *Vocational Guidance Quarterly, 33,* 231–240.

Hartman, B. W., Fuqua, D. R., Blum, C. R., & Hartman, P. T. (1985). A study of the predictive validity of the career decision scale in identifying longitudinal patterns of career indecision. *Journal of Vocational Behavior, 27,* 202–209.

Hartman, B. W., Fuqua, D. R., & Hartman, P. T. (1983). The predictive potential of the career decision scale in identifying chronic career indecision. *Vocational Guidance Quarterly, 32,* 103–108.

Hartman, B. W., & Hartman, P. T. (1982). The concurrent and predictive validity of the career decision scale adapted for high school students. *Journal of Vocational Behavior, 20,* 244–252.

Hartman, B. W., Utz, P. W., & Farnum, S. O. (1979). Examining the reliability and validity of an adapted scale of educational/vocational undecidedness in a sample of graduate students. *Journal of Vocational Behavior, 15,* 224–230.

Hawkins, J. G., Bradley, R. W., & White, G. W. (1977). Anxiety and the process of deciding about a major and vocation. *Journal of Counseling Psychology, 24,* 398–403.

Hecklinger, F. J. (1972). The undecided student: Is he less satisfied with college? *Journal of College Student Personnel, 13,* 247–251.

Henkels, M. T., Spokane, A. R., & Hoffman, M. A. (1981). Vocational identity, personality, and preferred mode of interest inventory feedback. *Measurement & Evaluation in Guidance, 14,* 71–76.

Heppner, P. P., & Petersen, C. H. (1982). The development and implications of a personal problem solving inventory. *Journal of Counseling Psychology, 29,* 66–75.

Herman, D. O. (1985). Review of S. H. Osipow, C. G. Carney, J. L. Winer, B. Yanico, & M.

Koschier, Career Decision Scale. In J. V. Mitchell, Jr. (Ed.), *The ninth mental measurement yearbook: Vol. 1* (pp. 270–271). Lincoln: University of Nebraska Press.

Holland, J. L. (1973). *Making Vocational Choices.* Englewood Cliffs, NJ: Prentice–Hall.

Holland, J. L. (1985). *Making Vocational Choices (2nd Ed.).* Englewood Cliffs, NJ: Prentice–Hall.

Holland, J. L., Daiger, D. C., & Power, P. G. (1980a). *My vocational situation.* Palo Alto, CA: Consulting Psychologists Press.

Holland, J. L., Daiger, D. C., & Power, P. G. (1980b). *Manual for my vocational situation.* Palo Alto, CA: Consulting Psychologists Press.

Holland, J. L., Gottfredson, G. D., & Nafziger, D. H. (1975). Testing the validity of some theoretical signs of vocational decision-making ability. *Journal of Counseling Psychology, 22,* 411–422.

Holland, J. L., Gottfredson, D. C., & Power, P. G. (1980). Some diagnostic scales for research in decision making and personality: Identity, information, and barriers. *Journal of Personality & Social Psychology, 39,* 1191–1200.

Holland, J. L., & Holland, J. E. (1977). Vocational indecision: More evidence and speculation. *Journal of Counseling Psychology, 24,* 404–414.

Holland, J. L., & Lutz, S. W. (1968). The predictive value of a student's choice of vocation. *Personnel & Guidance Journal, 46,* 428–434.

Holland, J. L., Magoon, T. M., & Spokane, A. R. (1981). Counseling psychology: Career interventions, research and theory. *Annual Review of Psychology, 32,* 279–305.

Holland, J. L., & Nichols, R. C. (1964). The development and validation of an indecision scale: The natural history of a problem in basic research. *Journal of Counseling Psychology, 11,* 27–34.

Jepsen, D. A., & Dilley, J. S. (1974). Vocational decision-making models: A review and comparative analysis. *Review of Educational Research, 44,* 331–349.

Jones, L. K., & Chenery, M. F. (1980). Multiple subtypes among vocationally undecided college students: A model and assessment instrument. *Journal of Counseling Psychology, 27,* 469–477.

Katz, M. R. (1963). Decisions and values. New York: College Entrance Examination Board.

Katz, M. R. (1966). A model for guidance for career decision making. *Vocational Guidance Quarterly, 15,* 2–10.

Katz, M. R. (1973). Career decision making: A computer based system of interactive guidance and information (SIGI). *Proceedings of the 1973 conference on testing problems: Measurement for self-understanding and personal development.* Princeton, NJ: Educational Testing Service.

Kiesler, D. J. (1966). Some myths of psychotherapy research and the search for a paradigm. *Psychological Bulletin, 65,* 110–136.

Kimes, H. G., & Troth, W. A. (1974). Relationship of trait anxiety to career decisiveness. *Journal of Counseling Psychology, 21,* 277–280.

Krumboltz, J. D., & Hamel, D. A. (1977). *Guide to career decision making skills.* New York: College Entrance Examination Board.

Krumboltz, J. D., Rude, S. S., Mitchell, L. K., Hamel, D. A., & Kinnier, R. T. (1982). Behaviors associated with "good" and "poor" outcomes in a simulated career decision. *Journal of Vocational Behavior, 21,* 349–358.

Krumboltz, J. D., Scherba, D. S., Hamel, D. A., & Mitchell, L. K. (1982). Effect of training in rational decision making on the quality of simulated career decisions. *Journal of Counseling Psychology, 29,* 618–625.

Larson, L. M., & Heppner, P. P. (1985). The relationship of problem-solving appraisal to career decision and career indecision. *Journal of Vocational Behavior, 26,* 55–65.

Lowe, B. (1981). The relationship between vocational interest differentiation and career undecidedness. *Journal of Vocational Behavior, 19,* 346–349.

Lunneborg, P. W. (1975). Interest differentiation in high school and vocational indecision in college. *Journal of Vocational Behavior, 7,* 297–303.

Lunneborg, P. W. (1976). Vocational indecision in college graduates.*Journal of Counseling Psychology, 23*, 402–404.

Lunneborg, P. W. (1985). Review of J. L. Holland, D. C. Daiger, & P. G. Power, My Vocational Situation. In J. V. Mitchell, Jr. (Ed.), *The ninth mental measurements yearbook: Vol. 2* (pp. 1026–1027). Lincoln: University of Nebraska Press.

MacKinnon–Slaney, F. (1986). Career indecision in reentry and undergraduate women. *Journal of College Student Personnel, 27*, 114–119.

MacKinnon–Slaney, F., Barber, S., & Slaney, R. B. (1986). *The effects of marital status on career decisions of reentry women.* Unpublished manuscript. Southern Illinois University, Carbondale, IL.

Maier, D., & Herman, A. (1974). The relationship of vocational decidedness and satisfaction with dogmatism and self-esteem. *Journal of Vocational Behavior, 5*, 95–102.

Marr, E. (1965). Some behaviors and attitudes relating to vocational choice. *Journal of Counseling Psychology, 12*, 404–408.

McGowan, A. S. (1977). Vocational maturity and anxiety among vocationally undecided and indecisive students. *Journal of Vocational Behavior, 10*, 196–204.

Mendonca, J. D., & Siess, T. F. (1976). Counseling for indecisiveness: Problem-solving and anxiety-management training. *Journal of Counseling Psychology, 23*, 339–347.

Miller, C. H. (1956). Occupational choice and values. *Personnel & Guidance Journal, 35*, 244–246.

Mitchell, L. K., & Krumboltz, J. D. (1984). Research on human decision making: Implications for career decision making and counseling. In S. D. Brown & R. W. Lent (Eds.), *Handbook of counseling psychology.* New York: Wiley.

Neimeyer, G. J., Nevill, D. D., Probert, B., & Fukuyama, M. (1985). Cognitive structures in vocational development. *Journal of Vocational Behavior, 27*, 191–201.

Nelson, E., & Nelson, N. (1940). Student attitudes and vocational choices. *Journal of Abnormal & Social Psychology, 35*, 279–282.

Niece, D., & Bradley, R. W. (1979). Relationship of age, sex, and educational groups to career decisiveness. *Journal of Vocational Behavior, 14*, 271–278.

Oliver, L. W. (1979). Outcome measurement in career counseling research. *Journal of Counseling Psychology, 26*,217–236.

Osipow, S. H. (1980). *Manual for the career decision scale.* Odessa, FL: Psychological Assessment Resources.

Osipow, S. H. (1983). *Theories of career development* (3rd ed.). Englewood Cliffs, NJ: Prentice–Hall.

Osipow, S. H., Carney, C. G., & Barak, A. (1976). A scale of education-vocational undecidedness: A typological approach. *Journal of Vocational Behavior, 9*, 233–243.

Osipow, S. H., Carney, C. G., Winer, J. L., Yanico, B., & Koschier, M. (1976). *The Career Decision Scale* (3rd rev. ed). Columbus, OH: Marathon Consulting and Press.

Osipow, S. H., & Reed, R. (1985). Decision making style and career indecision in college students. *Journal of Vocational Behavior, 27*, 368–373.

Osipow, S. H., Winer, J., Koschier, M., & Yanico, B. (1975). A modular approach to self-counseling for vocational indecision using audio-cassettes. In Simpson, L. (Ed.), *Audio-visual media in career development.* Bethlehem, PA: College Placement Council.

Owens, W. A. (1976). Background data. In M. D. Dunnette (Ed.), *Handbook of industrial and organizational psychology.* Chicago: Rand McNally.

Pinder, F. A., & Fitzgerald, P. W. (1984). The effectiveness of a computerized guidance system in promoting career decision making. *Journal of Vocational Behavior, 24*, 123–131.

Pitz, G., & Harren, V. A. (1980). An analysis of career decision making from the point of view of information processing and decision theory. *Journal of Vocational Behavior, 16*, 320–346.

Pitz, G. F., & McKillip, J. (1984). *Decision analysis for program evaluators.* Beverly Hills, CA: Sage

Pitz, G. F., & Sachs, N. J. (1984). Judgment and decision: Theory and application. *Annual Review of Psychology, 35,* 139–163.

Rayman, J. R., Bernard, C. B., Holland, J. L., & Barnett, D. C. (1983). The effects of a career course on undecided college students. *Journal of Vocational Behavior, 23,* 346–355.

Resnick, H., Fauble, M. L., & Osipow, S. H. (1970). Vocational crystallization and self-esteem in college students. *Journal of Counseling Psychology, 17,* 465–467.

Rogers, W. B., & Westbrook, B. W. (1983). Measuring career indecision among college students: Toward a valid approach for counseling practitioners and researchers. *Measurement & Evaluation in Guidance, 16,* 78–85.

Rose, H. A., & Elton, C. F. (1971). Attrition and the vocationally undecided student. *Journal of Vocational Behavior, 1,* 99–103.

Salomone, P. R. (1982). Difficult cases in career counseling: II—the indecisive client. *Personnel & Guidance Journal, 60,* 496–500.

Savickas, M. L. (1984). Construction and validation of a physician career development inventory. *Journal of Vocational Behavior, 25,* 106–123.

Savickas, M. L. (1985). Identity in vocational development. *Journal of Vocational Behavior, 27,* 329–337.

Savickas, M. L., Alexander, D. E., Osipow, S. H., & Wolf, F. M. (1985). Measuring specialty indecision among career-decided students. *Journal of Vocational Behavior, 27,* 356–367.

Seeman, J. (1983). *Personality integration.* New York: Human Sciences.

Slaney, R. B. (1978). Expressed and inventoried vocational interests: A comparison of instruments. *Journal of Counseling Psychology, 25,* 520–529.

Slaney, R. B. (1980). Expressed vocational choice and vocational indecision. *Journal of Counseling Psychology, 27,* 122–129.

Slaney, R. B. (1983). Influence of career indecision on treatments exploring the vocational interests of college women. *Journal of Counseling Psychology, 30,* 55–63.

Slaney, R. B. (1984). Relation of career indecision to changes in expressed vocational interests. *Journal of Counseling Psychology, 31,* 349–355.

Slaney, R. B. (1985). Review of S. H. Osipow, C. G. Carney, J. L. Winer, B. Yanico, & M. Koschier, Career decision scale. In D. J. Keyser & R. C. Sweetland (Eds.), *Test critiques: Vol. 2.* (pp. 138–143). Kansas City, MO: Test Corporation of America.

Slaney, R. B., & Dickson, R. D. (1985). Relation of career indecision to career exploration with re-entry women: A treatment and follow-up study. *Journal of Counseling Psychology, 32,* 355–362.

Slaney, R. B., & Lewis, E. T. (1986). Effects of career exploration on career undecided reentry women: An intervention and follow-up study. *Journal of Vocational Behavior, 28,* 97–109.

Slaney, R. B., & MacKinnon–Slaney, F. (1986). Relation of expressed and inventoried vocational interests in women career counseling clients. *Career Development Quarterly, 35,* 24–33.

Slaney, R. B., Palko–Nonemaker, D., & Alexander, R. (1981). An investigation of two measures of career indecision. *Journal of Vocational Behavior, 18,* 92–103.

Slaney, R. B., Russell, J. E. A. (1981). An investigation of different levels of agreement between expressed and inventoried vocational interests among college women. *Journal of Counseling Psychology, 28,* 221–228.

Slaney, R. B., Stafford, M. J., & Russell, J. E. A. (1981). Career indecision in adult women: A comparative and descriptive study. *Journal of Vocational Behavior, 19,* 335–345.

Spielberger, C. D., Gorsuch, R. L., & Lushene, R. E. (1970). *Manual for the state-trait anxiety inventory.* Palo Alto, CA: Consulting Psychologists Press.

Super, D. E. (1957). *The psychology of careers.* New York: Harper.

Super, D. E., Thompson, A. S., Lindeman, R. H., Jordaan, J. P., & Myers, R. A. (1981). *Career Development Inventory,* College and University Form. Palo Alto, CA: Consulting Psychologists Press.

Taylor, K. M. (1982). An investigation of vocational indecision in college students: Correlates and moderators. *Journal of Vocational Behavior, 21,* 318–329.

Taylor, K. M., & Betz, N. E. (1983). Applications of self-efficacy theory to the understanding and treatment of career indecision. *Journal of Vocational Behavior, 22,* 63–81.

Thompson, O. (1966). Impact of commitment upon performance of college students. *Personnel & Guidance Journal, 44,* 503–506.

Tiedeman, D. V., & O'Hara, R. P. (1963). Career development: Choice and adjustment. New York: College Entrance Examination Board.

Tinsley, H. E. A. (1985). Review of J. L. Holland, D. C. Daiger, & P. G. Power, My Vocational Situation. In D. J. Keyser & R. C. Sweetland (Eds.), *Test Critiques: Vol. 2* (pp. 509–516). Kansas City, MO: Test Corporation of America.

Tversky, A. (1972). Elimination by aspects: A theory of choice. *Psychological Review, 72,* 281–299.

Tyler, L. E. (1961). Research explorations in the realm of choice. *Journal of Counseling Psychology, 8,* 195–201.

Van Matre, G., & Cooper, S. (1984). Concurrent evaluation of career indecision and indecisiveness. *Personnel & Guidance Journal, 62,* 637–639.

Walsh, W. B., & Lewis, R. O. (1972). Consistent, inconsistent, and undecided career preferences and personality. *Journal of Vocational Behavior, 2,* 309–316.

Watley, D. (1965). Performance and characteristics of the confident student. *Personnel & Guidance Journal, 43,* 591–596.

Westbrook, B. W. (1985). Review of J. L. Holland, D. C. Daiger, & P. G. Power, My Vocational Situation. In J. V. Mitchell, Jr. (Ed.), *The ninth mental measurements yearbook: Vol. 2* (pp. 1027–1029). Lincoln: University of Nebraska Press.

Williams–Phillips, L. J. (1983). *Five career decidedness scales: Reliability, validity, and factors.* Unpublished master's thesis, North Carolina State University at Raleigh.

Williamson, E. (1937). Scholastic motivation and the choice of a vocation. *School & Society, 46,* 353–357.

Williamson, E. G. (1939). *How to counsel students.* New York: McGraw–Hill.

Zakay, D., & Barak, A. (1984). Meaning and career decision-making. *Journal of Vocational Behavior, 24,* 1–14.

Zener, T. B., & Schnuelle, L. (1976). Effects of the self-directed search on high school students. *Journal of Counseling Psychology, 23,* 353–359.

Ziller, R. C. (1957). Vocational choice and utility for risk. *Journal of Counseling Psychology, 4,* 61–64.

3 The Assessment of Career Development and Maturity

Nancy E. Betz
Ohio State University

INTRODUCTION

This chapter will begin with a brief overview of the history and initial conceptualization of the constructs of career development and maturity. The review, like the research, will focus on the measurement of career maturity in adolescence and young adulthood but will also include discussion of the related but more recently elaborated ideas of career adjustment and adaptability in adulthood. Next, the major measures of the constructs will be reviewed; measures of career maturity in adolescence and young adulthood will be addressed first, followed by those of career development in adulthood. The discussion of each instrument will highlight recent developments regarding that instrument in the area of psychometric data, extensions to new populations, and recent critical reviews. New instruments will be presented and their current status summarized. Finally, current issues in the conceptualization and measurement of career maturity will be discussed, as will the implications of these for theory and research. The last chapter of this book, by Howard E. A. Tinsley and Diane J. Tinsley, will provide an expanded context for the study of career development and maturity, as well as career decision making.

Historical Overview and Definition of the Concept

The current theories and measures of career development and maturity may be said to have begun with the work of Donald Super (1957), along with Ginzberg, Ginsburg, Axelrad, and Herma (1951) and Tiedeman and his colleague Robert O'Hara (1963). These writers can be credited with the development of the

77

theoretical underpinnings for both measures of career development and career maturity and for the extensive emphasis on career education in the schools and a variety of other settings. Although the reader should consult the many excellent resources on career development theory, including Chapter 1 of this volume (by Susan Phillips) and S. H. Osipow's (1983) *Theories of career development,* a brief overview of Super's theory will serve as a basis from which to proceed.

The major tenet of Super's theory for the purposes of this chapter was the idea that vocational development could be conceived as following the same stages as did other life tasks. Super followed Charlotte Buehler (1933) in the use of the stages of growth, exploration, establishment, maintenance, and decline to describe vocational development.

Most significantly for the concept of vocational maturity was Super's postulate that each of the vocational life stages presented one or more vocational tasks or challenges which the individual needed to successfully negotiate or master in order to progress in his or her career development. For example, tasks important in the exploration stage were crystallization, specification, and implementation. Crystallization, usually occurring between the ages of 14 and 18, included such subtasks as the formation of an occupational self-concept and the ability to relate that self-concept to educational and occupational possibilities.

The view of career development as a continuous, lifelong process, involving the acquisition of successively more advanced vocationally relevant knowledge and skill led to the emphasis on the assessment of the individual's progress in that process.

Super (1955) first defined the concept of vocational maturity as "the place reached on the continuum of vocational development from exploration to decline" [p. 153]. In his 1955 article, Super defined five dimensions of career maturity: (1) Orientation to vocational choice (concern with choice, use of resources); (2) Information and planning about preferred occupation; (3) Consistency of vocational preferences (over time and within fields, levels, and occupational families); (4) Crystallization of traits (e.g., interest maturity, realism of attitudes toward work); and (5) Wisdom of vocational preferences (primarily a "fit" construct).

Super also developed the idea that, just as the Intelligence Quotient—IQ— had originally been defined as the ratio of *mental age* (degree of actual intellectual development) to *chronological age,* a Vocational Maturity Quotient could be developed to indicate degree of vocational development relative to individuals of the same chronological age. Although this idea was not operationalized explicitly, it serves to illustrate the close relationship of the idea of career maturity to other developmental concepts.

In 1957, Super, Crites, Hummel, Moser, Overstreet, and Warnath first described their work on the Career Pattern Study. This study was designed as a long-term, follow-up study of the vocational development of 142 eighth-grade and 134 ninth-grade boys. In a report of results after the first year of research, Super and Overstreet (1960) further defined vocational maturity as a general trait (at least in ninth-grade boys) of an "orientation to the need to make educational and vocational choices including acceptance of responsibility for choosing and planning, and a planning and information-getting approach to the orientation and choice process: it is, essentially, planfulness" [p. 150].

About 10 years later, Super and his colleagues developed the Career Development Inventory. In the preliminary manual (Super & Forrest, 1972), vocational maturity is further defined as including planning orientation, resources for exploration, and information and decision making. In 1979, Super and Thompson reported that research with Form III of the CDI had led to the conclusion that vocational maturity could be defined as consisting of six meaningful dimensions: (1) extent of planning, (2) use and evaluation of resources in exploration, (3) career decision making, (4) career development information, (5) world of work information, and (6) information about the preferred occupation. Since 1979, Super and his colleagues have produced a revised and expanded model of career maturity and a revised version of the CDI. These will be described in more detail in the section to follow.

While Super and his colleagues were continuing work on the CDI, John O. Crites was elaborating his own theory of career maturity. In a 1961 paper Crites critiqued available definitions of vocational maturity and revised the definition to describe two independent measurable constructs, degree and rate of vocational development. Degree was defined as the similarity of one's vocational behavior to that of the oldest individuals in his or her vocational life stage, and rate was degree of maturity relative to one's own age group. In 1965, Crites's Model of Vocational Maturity appeared, organizing vocational maturity into two major factors, career-choice content and career-choice process. The maturity of content choice was defined by the dimensions of *consistency* of vocational choice and *realism* of choice; the maturity of the career-choice process was defined by *competencies* (cognitive factors) and *attitudes* (conative factors).

In 1965, the first practical measure of career maturity, Crites's Vocational Development Inventory, was published. The VDI assessed five aspects of vocational choice attitudes. In 1973 the first version of the Career Maturity Inventory, measuring both competencies and attitudes, was published. The current revision of this instrument appeared in 1978 and will be discussed in detail.

A final contributor early in the development of measures of career maturity was Bert Westbrook, whose Cognitive Vocational Maturity Test was somewhat similar in conception to Crites's competency group factor. The CVMT was never published commercially, but elements of the scales have been incorporated into two broader-scale testing programs—ACT's Assessment of Career Development (now no longer available) and CEEB's Career Skills Assessment Program. Westbrook himself is now developing a new set of career maturity indexes, the Career Planning Questionnaire, to be discussed later.

Since 1974, when both an NVGA monograph (Super, 1974) and a review by Westbrook and Mastie (1973) on the topic of measuring vocational maturity described the CMI, CDI, and CVMT as the three major instruments for this purpose (Super, 1974), there have been several additional measures developed to assess career maturity in adolecence and young adulthood. Specifically, Fadale's Career Awareness Inventory, ACT's Assessment of Career Development, the College Entrance Examination Board's Career Skills Assessment Program, Healy and Klein's New Mexico Career Education Test Series, and Westbrook's Career Planning Questionaire are among the instruments that will be described in the next section.

At least as important as advances in the assessment of career maturity in adolescence and young adulthood are advances in the conceptualization and measurement of career development in the adult years. Most existing measures of career maturity have focused on Super's exploration and early establishment stages of career development, but Crites, Super, and others have recently extended their work to assess mastery of developmental tasks in the establishment, maintenance, and disengagement/retirement (formerly decline) stages. As will be discussed subsequently, Crites's career ADI assesses mastery of tasks in the establishment stage, while Super's Adult Career Concerns Inventory assesses concerns about tasks in the stages from exploration to disengagement, including the tasks of retirement planning and retirement living. Other writers (e.g., Johnson, 1982) have focused on tasks of preretirement and retirement. These developments are of tremendous practical as well as theoretical importance in their potential for furthering the understanding of the processes of career adjustment in adulthood.

To summarize, career maturity can be generally defined as the extent to which the individual has mastered the vocational development tasks, including both knowledge and attitudinal components, appropriate to his or her stage of career development. Maturity is assumed to be an underlying psychological construct reflecting this developmental level, just as intellectual, moral, and social development are assumed to be psychological constructs. Accordingly, issues of reliability and content, criterion-related, and construct validity as detailed in the *Standards for educational and psychological testing* (AERA, APA, & NCME, 1985) must be addressed.

Major New Books and Articles

Although advances specific to each instrument will be covered as part of its discussion, a number of important new books and/or major reviews of the concept of career maturity have appeared in recent years. Readers interested in a comprehensive view of recent work should give special attention to the following.

Major recent books on the topic of career development include Brown and Brooks' (1984) *Career choice and development,* the third (1983) edition of Osipow's *Theories of career development,* and the Walsh and Osipow (1983) *Handbook of vocational psychology.* New books on counseling applications have included Kapes and Mastie's (1982) *Counselor's guide to vocational guidance instruments*, Crites's (1981a) *Career counseling*, and Zunker's *Career counseling* (1981) and *Using assessment results in career counseling* (1982). Major review chapters by Westbrook have appeared in Walsh and Osipow (1983) and Krumboltz and Hamel (1982). Finally, the Mental Measurements Yearbook Series, the test reviews in *Measurement and evaluation in counseling and development*, and the annual reviews of the literature in vocational behavior in the *Journal of vocational behavior* (e.g., Borgen, Layton, Veenhuizen, & Johnson, 1985; Greenhaus & Parasuraman, 1986; Tinsley & Heesacker, 1984) also facilitate currency of knowledge in this area. Thus, although the subsequent review attempts to be as comprehensive and as balanced as possible, readers should not overlook these other excellent resources for thorough knowledge of this area.

MEASURES OF CAREER MATURITY

In the following sections, available measures of career maturity will be reviewed. The review will begin with the traditional measures of career maturity, the Career Maturity Inventory, the Career Development Inventory, and the Cognitive Vocational Maturity Test, all developed between 1965 and 1974, and will then proceed with a discussion of more recently developed measures or measures which differ from the traditional measures, either in targeted population or the extent of emphasis on the construct of career maturity itself.

Career Maturity Inventory: The Model

The Career Maturity Inventory (Crites, 1978a) is both the most widely studied measure of career maturity and the measure most closely tied to a well-developed theory of the component parts of the construct of career maturity. Accordingly, the following discussion will include a review of Crites's theory, as well as describe the instrument in some detail.

Originally known as the Vocational Development Inventory (Crites, 1965), the first version of the Career Maturity Inventory itself appeared in 1973; the revised edition appeared in 1978. The recent edition (Crites, 1978a), like the original (1973) edition, is published by CTB/McGraw-Hill in Monterey, CA. The Inventory is accompanied by a *Theory and research handbook* (Crites, 1978c) detailing the model and rationale for inventory construction and evidence for reliability and validity, and an *Administration and use manual* (Crites, 1978b) designed for counseling and research uses. A manual for the Career Maturity Inventory for Adults (Crites, 1978d) is also available.

The Career Maturity Inventory is based on Crites's model of career maturity in adolescence. The model, shown in Fig. 3.1, is a hierarchical and multidimensional model of career development. At the top or most general level is overall

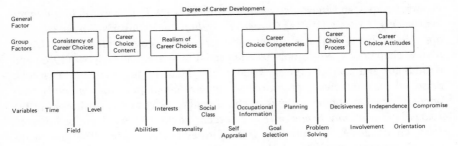

Fig. 3.1.   Crites's (1978) model of career maturity in adolescence.

degree of career development, analogous to the general intelligence of "g" factor found to characterize mental ability. The second level of generality is defined by four major group factors, two of which describe the content of career choice and two of which describe the process of career choice. These group factors may be considered analogous to the verbal-educational (v:ed) and practical-mechanical (k:m) group factors in Vernon's (1960) hierarchical model of intelligence or to Cattell's (1963) "fluid" and "crystallized" intelligence.

Within each of the major group factors are more specific factors of career maturity—these might be thought of as analogous to group factors such as verbal and quantitative abilities. The maturity of career choice *content* (the "what" of career choice, as operationalized by the individual's current occupational preferences or choices) includes the two more specific factors of "consistency of career choices" and "realism of career choices." Consistency refers to how consistent the individual's preferences are over time (such as from one month to the next) and across field (for example, science versus art) and level (for example, professional level versus unskilled work). Realism refers to the match between the characteristics of the individual and those of the work environment(s) chosen or preferred. It is with the dimension of realism that Crites incorporates models of career choice and satisfaction, for example, the original trait-factor model of Parsons (1909), Williamson (1939), and others of the Minnesota school, to more recent versions such as Holland's (1973, 1985) theory and the theory of work adjustment (Dawis & Lofquist, 1984; Lofquist & Dawis, 1969). Thus, Crites's fundamental assumptions are that the content of mature career choice behavior demonstrates some consistency across time and context and that is culminates in choices which fit or are congruent with one's individual attributes.

In addition to defining career maturity in terms of what the individual chooses, Crites defined career maturity in terms of how the choices are made. The "how" or the "process" of career decision making is the crux of the concept of career maturity, and is the section of the model incorporating Super's concept of career development tasks. Crites's model includes two major sets of process variables, career choice competencies and career choice attitudes (See Fig. 3.1).

Crites's Career Maturity Inventory measures the process variables which are said to constitute career maturity. Like the model, the inventory is divided into two major sections, the Competencies Test and the Attitudes Scale. It should be noted that the word "test" in psychometric theory refers to a domain where there are correct and incorrect answers; this domain includes intelligence, ability, and achievement tests, or in Cronbach's terms, tests of "maximum" performance (1984, pp. 28–29). The term is also appropriate for the measurement of career-choice competencies because the item content is assumed to have correct and incorrect answers. The term "scale" on the other hand, has a more general meaning but in psychometric theory refers to measuring "typical performance" [Cronbach, 1984, pp. 28–29]. where there are no right or wrong answers, only individual differences in personality and attitudes. Thus, the Attitude *Scale* in the CMI is differentiated from the Competence *Tests*. The subscales of the CMI are as shown in the figure and will be discussed further.

The CMI Competence Test

Description.   In general, the CMI Competence Test is designed to measure the degree to which the individual possesses the career information and the planning and decision-making skills to make realistic, wise educational and career decisions. More specifically, the Competence Test measures five components of effective career decision making. For each component, a technical title and a title by which the test is described to examinees in lay terms is provided. In the descriptions to follow, the first title is the technical name, while the title in parentheses is that provided to examinees.

The first competence test is self-appraisal ("knowing yourself"), designed to assess the extent to which the individual has knowledge of his or her own abilities, vocational interests, vocationally relevant needs and values, and self-concept. The assumption is, of course, that more vocationally mature individuals possess greater self-knowledge and understanding. Operationally, this test requires the examinee to assess accurately the career-relevant capabilities of *others*.

The second subtest measures occupational information ("knowing about jobs"). In addition to knowledge about oneself, the extent of knowledge about the world of work is thought to differentiate the more from the less career mature. Operationally, this test measures the examinee's knowledge of the content of jobs, for example the duties and tasks of various occupations. The CMI Goal Selection Test ("choosing a job") measures the ability to match individual attributes to the characteristics of jobs. As stated by Crites (1964), "The more vocationally mature person . . . attempts to 'bridge the gap' between himself [or herself] and the world of work, to achieve a "synthesis," as Super (1957) puts it, of the major factors involved in occupational choice (Crites, 1964, p. 329). Thus, the Goal Selection Test assesses the examinee's ability to "match" individuals and work environments.

The fourth test is Planning ("looking ahead"). Once a career decision is made, it must be implemented. As stated by Crites, the concept of planning refers to "the tendency of the individual to think about the means which are necessary to attain a desired end" [Crites, 1964, p. 328]. Crites defined the major criteria of good planning as: (1) the time spent in planning, (2) the specificity of planning, (3) the relevance of means to ends in planning, and (4) the ordering of steps in planning. The CMI Planning Test assesses the latter aspect, that is, the ability to order properly the steps in implementing a career decision. Generally it is assumed that these steps include obtaining the appropriate education and/or training, finding employment in the field, and gaining necessary credentials, such as licensing or certification, in the field.

The final competencies test is Problem Solving ("what should they do?"). Based on the reality that the processes of making and implementing career decisions are almost never problem-free, this test is designed to assess problem-solving or coping abilities in the face of problems or obstacles which occur in the career decision-making process. Obviously, the more career mature person is defined as one who can cope with the inevitable problems which arise in the career-choice process. The items in this subtest present various problematic situations related to making and implementing career decisions, for example, conflicts with parents, insufficient aptitude for a preferred occupation, and career indecision and unrealism. The multiple-choice alternatives present several possible solutions to the problem, with one being defined as more versus less effective, based on its ability to address and solve rather than deny or distort the problem situation.

Each Competencies subtest contains 20 items for each of which there is a correct response, three distractors, and the response "don't know." Correct responses were determined based on occupational information and expert judgment. The CMI competencies tests are, therefore, similar in conception and purpose to academic achievement tests, because they attempt to sample knowledge of a domain of content for which correct or effective responses can be specified. Although the specification of the correct responses is not as straightforward as is that, for example, in American history or chemistry, the underlying rationales are similar. And, as in an achievement test, the number correct represents the extent to which the individual has mastered the body of content, in this case defined as "knowledge of self and occupational environments and career decision making, implementation, and problem solving skills."

In addition to being correct as defined by experts in career decision making, the keyed responses for the CMI were also required to fulfill the requirements of a developmental variable, that is, systematic change (in this case increases in number correct) with increasing grade or age level. Thus, the items selected in the initial construction of the test were those which were not only related theoretically to the concept they were designed to measure (thus following rational procedures of test construction) but which also showed systematic improvements in performance from earlier grades to later grades and from younger to older ages (thus employing empirical methods of test construction).

Psychometric Quality. The manual provides information regarding the internal consistency reliability of the tests. Values of KR–20 have ranged from .72 to .90 in samples of 6th through 12th graders, although the reliability of the Problem Solving Scale at the 6th- and 7th-grade levels is somewhat lower, that is, .58 and .63 respectively. Alvi and Khan (1983) have reported even lower reliabilities for some of the tests, especially Goal Selection (values of .50 to .57 across grades 9–11) up to .70 to .76 for Problem-Solving. Reliabilities in grade-12 students were disconcertingly low, including several values below .50. Although restriction in range of scores may have depressed these values somewhat, it cannot account for the overall poor levels of internal consistency.

There is evidence for the convergent validity of CMI Competence Test scores. Correlations with Westbrook's CVMT range from .55 to .65 between the analogous subscores of each and .62 to .77 between the CMI and CVMT total scores. Intercorrelations among the Competence Test scores are also relatively strong, with average values ranging from .53 to .68, depending on the test pair and grade level.

Evidence for criterion-related validity as provided in the manual is based on the increase in scores with increasing grade level, but since this criterion was used to select items its true value is reduced. However, this pattern was replicated by Alvi and Khan (1983) for grades 9 through 12.

In terms of construct validity, Crites (1978c) summarizes evidence that Competence Test scores increase for students receiving career education, and Alvi and Khan (1982) found that Competence Tests scores were related to satisfaction and performance in a work-study program for students in grades 9–12. Also relevant to construct validity, although eliciting different interpretations from researchers, are the relatively high correlations between the CMI Competence Test scores and measures of academic aptitude and performance (e.g., Chodzinski & Randhawa, 1983; Crites, 1978c; Westbrook, Cutts, Madison, & Arcia, 1980).

The CMI Attitude Scale

Description. The CMI Attitude Scale measures five aspects of the maturity of the individual's attitudes toward careers and career choices. These aspects of career maturity, shown in the model depicted in Fig. 3.1, are further defined and illustrated in Table 3.1. Given the definitions provided in the table it may be noted that maturity in career-choice attitudes is defined by Crites as: (1) greater

TABLE 3.1
Variables in the Attitude Scale of the Career Maturity Inventory

Dimension	Definition	Sample Item
Decisiveness in career decision making	Extent to which an individual	"I keep changing my occupational choice."
Involvement in career decision making	Extent to which individual is actively participating in the process of making a choice	"I'm not going to worry about choosing an occupation until I'm out of school."
Independence in career decision making	Extent to which individual relies upon others in the choice of an occupation	"I plan to follow the line of work my parents suggest."
Orientation to career decision making	Extent to which individual is task- or pleasure-oriented in his or her attitudes toward work and the values he or she places upon work	"I have little or no idea of what working will be like."
Compromise in career decision making	Extent to which individual is willing to compromise between needs and reality	"I spent a lot of time wishing I could do work I know I can never do."

Note: This table is a reproduction of Table 1 (p.10) in J. O. Crites's Career maturity inventory: Theory and research handbook (2nd ed.). Copyright (1978) by McGraw Hill.

decisiveness in making a career choice; (2) more active involvement in the process; (3) independence in decision making as opposed to reliance on others; (4) a realistic orientation toward work, for example, acceptance of the reality that work isn't always alot of fun; and (5) the ability to compromise between one's own needs and reality. For each attitudinal dimension, a sample item to which examinees give a True or False answer is provided.

There have been three forms of the CMI Attitude Scale. The original form, known as A–1, is the form on which most of the research is based. Form A–1 was revised in the 1978 revision and is now a 50-item Screening Form (Form A–2). The 75-item Counseling Form (Form B–1) is the first to provide subscores for the five dimensions of attitudinal career maturity as well as a total attitudinal career maturity score. Unfortunately, since most research was done using the 1973 Screening Form (A–1), less is known about the revised versions.

Like the Competence Test, the Attitude scales are scored by counting the number of "keyed" or correct responses. Determination of the direction of item scoring, that is, the response indicative of more-versus-less career mature attitudes, was made in accordance with the responses of a majority of grade 12 students in the standardization sample. Thus, if 51% or more of the 12th-grade students answered "True" to a given attitudinal statement, then "True" would be designated as the correct or keyed response. The problem with this method of keying is its assumption that 12th graders are sufficiently "career mature" as a group to know the correct response; since career maturity is a developmental concept extending throughout the life span, this assumption seems tenuous at best. The problematical nature of this assumption is illustrated by data indicating a lack of agreement on many items between the "keyed" response and expert judgments. In the study of Hall (1962; cf. Crites, 1978c), 10 counseling psychologists failed to agree with Crites's keying on 26 of 100 items.

Psychometric Qualities. More reliability data have been obtained for the original Screening Form (A–1) of the CMI than for the Counseling Form (B–1) or the revised screening form (A–2). The manual indicates that the reliability (KR–20) of Form A–1 of the Attitude Scale averaged .74 across grade levels. Since the total score combines scores from five related but not identical attitudes, a high level of internal consistency reliability is not expected. However, the subscale scores do not appear to be particularly reliable either, ranging from .50 (Compromise) to .72 (Orientation) with intermediate values for Involvement (.62), Decisiveness (.67), and Independence (.71). For Form A–2, Alvi and Khan (1983) reported reliabilities of .56 to .69 across grades 9–12. Test-retest reliability would be expected to be somewhat lower than that for traits postulated to be stable over time, yet high enough to indicate some consistency of measurement; the value reported for Form A–1, $r = .71$ over a 1-year interval, is in this range.

Evidence for the content validity of the CMI Attitude Scale comes primarily from the fact that the item content was derived from the central concepts and ideas in the career development literature. However, the problems of concluding that 12th-grade students will give the most career mature response need to be addressed in this regard. Crites (J. O. Crites, personal communication, September 15, 1986) is currently addressing this issue with work on a second-generation CMI, to be called the Career Readiness Inventory. The latter inventory is designed to extend from 7th grade to later adulthood and will thus be revising methods of determining the criteria from which to infer career maturity in item responses.

In terms of convergent validity, correlations with other measures of career maturity are in the expected range. For example, Jepsen and Prediger (1981) reported correlations of .41 (CSAP) and .22 to .37 (CDI scales). The CMI Attitude scale-CDS correlation was .51. Evidence for the criterion-related validity of the scale is discussed in the *Theory and research handbook* for the CMI (Crites, 1978c). In brief, the maturity of attitudes has been shown to be related to such variables as the realism of occupational aspirations (Bathory, 1967; Hollender, 1964; cf. Crites, 1978c), career decisiveness (Carek, 1965; cf. Crites, 1978c), certainty about and commitment to a career choice (Graves, 1974; cf. Crites, 1978c) and congruence of Holland code and students' career choices (Capehart, 1973; Crites, 1978c; Walsh & Osipow, 1973). It should be noted that most of the correlations found in these studies are small in magnitude.

In terms of construct validity, scores on the CMI Attitude Scale seem to be related to general intellectual ability or scholastic aptitude. Correlations of the CMI Attitude Scale with intellectual ability average about .40 in high school samples (Crites, 1978c). Correlations reported by Jepsen and Prediger (1981) were .31 and .37 with the ITED Quantitative and Reading subtests, respectively. Thus, verbally expressed career attitudes are related to more general verbal ability.

Scores on the CMI Attitude scale also appear to be related to better general personality adjustment. For example, Crites (1978c) summarizes research in which career maturity was found to be related to greater assertiveness, persistence, goal orientation and independence (Bartlett, 1968, Crites, 1978c), and better vocational adjustment as represented by such variables as persistence in college, success in vocational training, and educational achievement. Alvi and Khan (1983) found relationships of the CMI Attitude scale to self-esteem, internal locus of control, and intrinsic-versus-extrinsic work values. Finally, Crites cites research suggesting a positive effect on career maturity of career counseling and education programs, but others (e.g., Westbrook, 1982) suggest that such evidence is weak at best.

The Adult CMI

Although the major uses of the CMI have been with high school students, an adult version is also available (Crites, 1978d). Designed for use with post-high school men and women, the inventory uses the same items as the regular CMI; adult examinees are asked to respond "as if" the items described their situations, even though the items may not appear to have direct relevance. The major difference between the Adult CMI and the regular version of the Inventory is that the former is designed to be self-administered—the test and instructions are simply provided to the adult respondent.

Recent Advances in Theory and Research

The CMI is the most widely used measure of career maturity, and it has also received more attention from researchers than has any other career maturity inventory. Not surprisingly, not all of the attention has been positive. A series of criticisms of the CMI have been raised by Westbrook and his colleagues (Westbrook et al., 1980; Westbrook, 1985), and largely negative reviews of the 1973 CMI have appeared in the *Eighth mental measurements yearbook* (Katz, 1978; Zytowski, 1978). Katz's (1982) review of the revised (1978) CMI was also largely negative. Most critics have addressed the instrument's inadequate levels of or evidence for reliability and validity and/or the adequacy of the underlying theory.

In response to the criticism, Crites and his colleagues have provided both logical (Crites, Wallbrown, & Blaha, 1985) and data-based arguments, including the provision of some much-needed new data (Wallbrown, Silling, & Crites, 1986). Alvi and Khan's program of research (Alvi & Kahn, 1982, 1983; Khan & Alvi, 1983) has generally supported the validity of the CMI, although it has strengthened concerns about the reliability of the subscales. Unfortunately, no review of the CMI was included in the *Ninth mental measurements yearbook* (Mitchell, 1985), preventing analysis and integration in that landmark series of the considerable amount of recent research and dialogue concerning the instrument.

Although readers are encouraged to examine and evaluate the dialogue in detail via the original articles (see especially Crites et al., 1985; Wallbrown et al., 1986; Westbrook, 1985; and Westbrook et al., 1980), some of the major criticisms of the CMI will be summarized herein. Many of the issues raised by Westbrook and others in critique of the CMI, while valid, are characteristic of all or almost all measures of career maturity. The CMI, because of its popularity and visibility, has received probably more than its share of criticisms that in reality apply to the overall state of the art in the conceptualization and measurement of career maturity, for example, low reliabilities and inadequate evidence for all types of validity. These common problems will be discussed in a subsequent section entitled "Issues in Career Maturity Assessment."

Specific to the CMI, however, is Westbrook's skepticism regarding the validity of Crites's hierarchical, multidimensional model of career maturity. Basing their arguments on results from a study of 312 rural, disadvantaged ninth graders and 200 technical, vocational, and general education students enrolled at a public technical school, Westbrook et al. (1980) suggested that CMI Attitudes and Competencies were more highly related to each other than postulated in Crites's initial model. A correlation of .59 between the (1973) Attitudes scale and the Competencies Total score was higher than the values in the .30s to .40s predicted by Crites, and the difference was even greater if the correlations were corrected for attenuation.

Among other points, Crites's rejoinder (Crites et al. 1985) noted the fact that the Attitudes–Competencies correlation in Westbrook et al.'s technical school sample, .47 and thus closer to expectation, was not mentioned by Westbrook in his critical remarks. Crites also cited several statisticians who disagree with the use of the correction for attenuation in theory testing (e.g., Guilford, 1954; Mehrens & Lehman, 1978). It is also worth noting that other studies have reported much smaller correlations between Attitudes and Competencies (Alvi & Kahn, 1983; Jepsen & Prediger, 1981).

A more significant theoretical argument is that relatively good-sized correlations between Attitudes and Competencies, if replicated across samples, would not necessarily disprove Crites's model, because they could be interpreted as indicating the presence of the large general factor, the "g" of career maturity, postulated by Crites. Simple bivariate correlational analysis is probably inadequate to a comprehensive examination of the question of the dimensionality of Crites's model and measures—factor and cluster analyses would seem to be more effective ways to address the question.

Thus, it is not surprising that the debate over the dimensionality and nature of the Crites model also received factor analytical attention. Westbrook et al. (1980) began with a factor analysis of the data described herein and reported one general factor in the entire CMI. Crites et al. (1985) criticized this finding because only one Attitude score was used (the total score from the CMI Attitude scale Form A–1), thus mitigating against the formation of an ''attitudes'' factor. Further, they criticized Westbrook et al.'s use of the principal-axis method of extracting factors. This method tends to yield all general factors rather than group factors and, further, assumes that factors are orthogonal (Rummel, 1970).

Crites et al. (1985) reanalyzed the Westbrook et al. data, using a hierarchical model of factor analysis, corresponding to the postulated nature of the trait. Although the appearance of an attitudes factor was still precluded by the presence of only one attitude score, versus the five subscale scores now available, the analysis yielded two major factors in the ninth grade and three factors in the technical school sample. In both samples, the major factors also loaded on a large general factor. The two factors in the ninth-grade group were a Competencies factor and an academic achievement factor. The technical school sample yielded the above two factors and a third factor consisting of the Attitude Scale and Osipow's (1980) Career Decision Scale.

Westbrook (1985) viewed the Crites et al. response as weak and called for additional research. A study reported subsequently (Wallbrown et al., 1986) employed hierarchical factor analytical techniques to investigate the dimensionality of the entire CMI as administered to 1567 6th through 11th graders. The analysis yielded strong support for the hierarchical model with a large general career maturity factor on which all 10 career maturity scales (the 5 competencies and the 5 attitudes) loaded significantly across all 6 grade levels. The size of the loadings was higher for competencies than for attitudes, although all were statistically significant.

In addition to a general factor, a clear-cut competencies factor and a clear attitudes factor also emerged. The patterns of loadings corresponded to Thurstone's (1947) criteria for simple structure, that is, a factor structure where variables load highly on one but only one major group factor. The loadings of the Competencies scales on what was named the ''Competencies'' factor averaged .41 to .54 across grade levels, while the loadings of the Attitudes scales on that factor ranged from a high of .20 (Involvement) to a low of -.30 (Decisiveness) and averaged -.01. On the Attitudes factor, the Attitudes scales loaded .20 to .58, while the loadings of the Competencies scales were .04 to .09.

Although these findings supported the validity of the Crites model of career maturity, Westbrook (B. W. Westbrook, personal communication, June 15, 1986) noted that inadequate information about several aspects of the study (for example, the sample) made interpretation of the data somewhat difficult. In any case, it seems clear that further research is needed.

This debate and the completely contrasting sets of factor analytical results illustrate the susceptibility of data to both differences in the samples and the analytical methods used. For example, although factor analysis is not the only statistical method requiring decisions which significantly influence the outcome of the analysis, the researchers' decisions concerning the method of extracting factors, the number of factors extracted, and whether or not and how factors are rotated put clear constraints on the nature of the factor structure that can emerge (see Weiss, 1970, 1971). Most writers would agree that the nature of the *theory* guiding the research can legitimately be used to guide these decisions (e.g., Rummel, 1977), thus legitimizing Crites's use of hierarchical factor analysis. On the other hand, the ability to replicate findings across samples and analytical methods provides assurance regarding the generalizability and robustness of the theory, and thus more research replicating the factor structure reported by Wallbrown et al. would contribute to our confidence in the Crites model.

Westbrook et al. (1980) also questioned the construct validity of the CMI on the basis of its relatively high correlations with ability variables and with Osipow's Career Decision Scale. The consistent relationship of cognitive career maturity to measures of intellectual ability is not unique to the CMI and, in fact, is characteristic of Westbrook's CVMT as well as the CDI and the CSAP. The relationship is most certainly of theoretical import and will be discussed in the section titled "State of the Art." As far as a correlation with the CDS, this criticism may now lack validity since Westbrook's newly developed model of career maturity (Westbrook et al., 1985) includes a measure called "Career Decisions," which appears to be similar in intent to the CDS. Like intellective factors, decidedness (or its opposite "indecision") needs to be included in a nomological network of the construct of career maturity, most likely as a criterion variable. Thus, correlations between the two characteristics would be expected rather than contrary to expectation.

Although these are the major points raised by Westbrook et al., others are contained in the article. Overall, this is a case where all parties to the dispute have made important arguments. Westbrook and others critical of the CMI have hopefully stimulated some much-needed research designed to explicate both the nature of the construct and the quality of the individual scales. The psychometric qualities of the CMI, particularly its reliability, could use some attention. On the other hand, the CMI has its areas of inadequacy but, as will be discussed, so do the other measures currently available. It is hoped that dialogues of this nature will stimulate continued efforts to advance our knowledge of the construct and to contribute to the refinement of the instruments used in its measurement.

CAREER DEVELOPMENT INVENTORY

General Description and Model of Career Maturity

Both the Career Development Inventory (CDI) and the newer Adult Career Concerns Inventory (ACCI) are based on Super's model of career maturity, which in its most recent form (Super, 1983), is as shown in Table 3.2. The principal dimensions—planfulness, exploration, information, decision making, and reality orientation—are those which have emerged over the years of research

TABLE 3.2
Basic Assessment of Career Maturity

I. Planfulness
   A. Autonomy
   B. Time perspective
      1. Reflection upon experience
      2. Anticipation of the Future
   C. Self-esteem

II. Exploration
   A. Querying
   B. Use of resources
   C. Participation

III. Information
   A. The world of work
      1. Career stages
      2. Coping behaviors
      3. Occupational structure
      4. Typical occupations (see B)
      5. Access and means of entry
      6. Outcomes
      7. Economic trends and change
   B. The preferred Occupational group
      1. Education and training
      2. Entry requirements
      3. Duties, methods, materials, tools
      4. Advancement, transfer, stability
      5. Working conditions and rewards
      6. Life-style
      7. Future prospects
   C. Occupational and other life-career roles
      1. Relative importance of work
      2. Role relationships and interactions
         a. Supplementary
         b. complementary
         c. Competitive or conflicting

IV. Decision making
   A. Principles
   B. Applications
   C. Style

V. Reality orientation
   A. Self-knowledge
   B. Realism as to outlets
   C. Consistency of preferences
   D. Crystallization of values, interests, and
      objectives
   E. Work experience

---

represented by the Career Pattern Study. The updated version of the model also includes the concept of work salience, the relative importance of work, and the interaction of work roles with other life roles (see Super, 1980 for the concept of a "life career," and Super & Nevill, 1984, and Nevill & Super, 1986, for discussion of the concept and measurement of work salience). Within each dimension of Table 3.2 a more detailed list of the elements and tasks of that dimension is provided.

Based on the model shown in the table, the Career Development Inventory (CDI) was developed by Donald Super and his colleagues at Teachers College of Columbia University; the instrument and accompanying materials are published by Consulting Psychologists Press. There are two forms of the CDI, the School Form (Form S; Super, Thompson, Lindeman, Jordaan & Myers, 1979) and the College and University Form (Form CU; Super, Thompson, Lindeman, Jordaan, & Myers, 1981). A *User's manual,* primarily emphasizing Form S (Thompson, Lindeman, Super, Jordaan, & Myers, 1981), and a supplement to the manual, emphasizing Form CU (Thompson, Lindeman, Super, Jordaan, & Myers, 1982) are now accompanied by the long-awaited *Technical manual* (Thompson, Lindeman, Super, Jordaan, & Myers, 1984).

The CDI is designed to achieve the same general purposes as the Career Maturity Inventory. Like the CMI, the CDI scales are organized into a cognitive or knowledge component (from the Information and Decision-making dimensions in Table 3.2) and an attitudes component, from the Planfulness and Exploration dimensions in the table. More specifically, the scales of the CDI are as follows:

1. Career Planning (CP) assesses the degree to which the student has engaged in career planning and also contains questions concerning students' knowledge of the kind of work they would like to do. The scale contains 20 items; Table 3.3 provides an example of the types of items contained in the scale.

2. Career Exploration (CE) attempts to measure the quality of exploratory attitudes by asking the student to rate the quality of various possible sources of occupational information, for example, from friends, professors, counselors, books, TV shows, etc., and to indicate how much useful information he or she has obtained from each of these sources. The CE scales contain 20 items, an example of which is provided in the table.

3. Decision-Making (DM) measures the ability to apply knowledge and insight to the problems of career planning and decision making. The 20 items involve hypothetical persons making career decisions or needing to solve some career-related problem (see Table 3.3). The scale is viewed as primarily a cognitive rather than attitudinal component of career maturity.

4. World of Work Information (WW) assesses knowledge of the tasks of Super's Exploratory and Early Establishment stages and knowledge of specific occupations. The WW scale contains 20 items of the type shown in Table 3.3.

TABLE 3.3
Sample Items from the First 4 Scales of the Career Development Inventory

A. Career Planning
How much thinking and planning have you done in the following areas?
For each question below choose the answer that best tells what you
have done so far.

  1. Finding out about educational and occupational possibilities by
     going to the library, sending away for information, or talking
     to somebody who knows.

     A. I have not yet given any thought to this.
     B. I have given some thought to his, but haven't made any
        plans yet.
     C. I have made definite plans, but don't know yet how to carry
        them out.
     D. I have some plans, but I am still not sure of them.
     E. I have made definite plans, and know what to do to carry
        them out.

B. Career Exploration
Questions 21 throuth 30 have four possible answers. Choose the
one best answer for each question to show whether or not you would go
to the following sources for information or help in making your plans
for work or further education.

    21. Friends

        A. Definitely not
        B. Probably not
        C. Probably
        D. Definitely

    22. Dormitory or residence hall counselors

        A. Definitely not
        B. Probably not
        C. Probably
        D. Definitely

C. Decision Making
What should each of the following students do? Choose the one best
answer for each case.

    41. E. R. took some tests that suggest some promise for
        accounting work. This student says, "I just can't see
        myself sitting behind a desk for the rest of my life.
        I'm the kind of person who likes variety. I think a
        traveling job would suit me fine."

        A. Disregard the tests and do what he or she wants to do.
        B. Do what the tests say since they know best.
        C. Look for a job that requires accounting ability but
           does not pin one to a desk.
        D. Ask to be tested with another test since the results
           of the first one are probably wrong.

D. World of Work Information
Choose the one best answer to each of the following questions about
career development and the world of work.

    52. Lawyers usually learn their jobs in:

        A. On-the-job training
        B. Community colleges
        C. Four-Year colleges and universities
        D. Graduate or professional schools.

5. Knowledge of Preferred Occupational Group (PO) presents 20 occupational groups on the back of the CDI answer sheet; groups include, for example, Biological and Medical Science, Social Science: Research, and Social Science: Teaching/Social Service. Students are asked to select a preferred occupational group and then to answer 40 multiple-choice questions about that group of occupations, for example, duties, abilities and interests best suited to the occupational group.

In scoring the latter scale, the amount of knowledge about one's preferred occupation is assumed to be a direct indicant of career maturity. In addition to the five specific scale scores, the CDI provides three combined scores: (1) Career Development Attitudes (CDA) is the sum of the CP and CE scores; (2) Career Development Knowledge and Skills (CDK) combines DM and WW; and (3) Career Orientation Total (COT) combines CP, CD, DM, and WW and is thus a composite measure of several important aspects of career maturity. For several reasons, including its specificity to one occupational group rather than to a more general characteristic of career maturity, the PO scale is not included in the total scores.

The School Form (Form S) is designed for use in junior and senior high schools, and the College and University Form (Form CU) for use in higher education. The forms are similar in rationale and structure, but the item content differs in order to ensure its appropriateness for younger versus older students. The CDI scores are provided as standard scores having a mean of 100 and a standard deviation of 20. The manual contains norms based on 5,039 students in grades 9 through 12 (Form S) and 1,345 college and university students, including community college students (Form CU).

Psychometric Qualities

Reliability.   Internal consistency reliability data presented in the manual for grades 9 through 12 indicate that the (coefficient alpha) reliabilities of the combined scores (CDA, CDK, and COT) and the CP, CE, and WW subscales are moderate but sufficient, ranging from medians of .78 (CE) to .84 (WW) to .89 (CP) for the subscales across grades. The median reliability coefficients for DM and PO, however, are only .67 and .60, respectively. Thus, as individual scales, neither DM and PO possesses adequate reliability for applied or research purposes beyond further instrument development and explication. On Form CU, the average values of alpha range from .75 to .90 for the combined scores and from .61 to .91 for the subscales; the reliabilities of DM (.62), WW (.67), and PO (.61) are insufficient, again suggesting great caution for counseling and research uses (see also Hansen, 1985).

The longstanding and often mentioned problem of lack of stability data has been addressed in the 1984 *Technical manual*. Stability coefficients obtained over a 3-week interval are in the .70s and .80s for the combined scores and for scale CP. For the other scales they are lower, in the .60s and .70s. Medians for PO (.61 and .63 in two schools), WW (.67 and .68) and Dm (.70 and .69) are probably inadequate to ensure consistency of measurement over a time interval. (It may be noted that PO and DM were also low in internal consistency reliability, thus casting more doubt on their quality as separate scales.) Stability coefficients for Form CU were quite low for WW (.43) and CDK (.57) but high for CP (.89), with DM (.65) and CE (.79) intermediate in value. The manual states that these low values may be due to small standard deviations of scores, particularly on Test 1, but this explanation simply substitutes one problem (low variability) for another one (inadequate stability), as well as introducing the question of why variability would be greater on the retest than on the initial testing.

Results from a canonical correlation analysis of a linear composite of Time 1 scores with a linear composite of Time 2 scores are used as further evidence of stability. Such linear composites were justified, based on the assumption of a single, underlying dimension of career maturity. There are, however, several problems with the use of canonical correlation in this way. First, the authors themselves omit PO from the calculation of total scores because it is a specific rather than a general measure, and their factor analytical data (presented later in the manual) suggest that the cognitive and attitudinal scales "clearly represent different aspects of career maturity" [Thompson et al., 1984]. There is really no good evidence that the CDI reflects one unitary dimension of career maturity. Also, canonical correlation is a maximization procedure which capitalizes on sample-specific error in the derivation of scoring weights—the correlation Rc would provide an upper-bound estimate of score stability only if the canonical weights were part of the standard scoring system, which they aren't. If our interest is in the extent to which scores as calculated for the individual examinee are stable over time, canonical correlation is an inappropriate method of addressing this question. The fact that this manual provides traditional stability coefficients should be sufficient.

Although the test authors are to be commended for the addition of much new data regarding the stability of the CDI scales, the relatively poor reliability and stability of scales such as PO and DM continues to be of concern. It may be that, until improved through refinement of the item content, these should either not be used or should be used only as part of total composite scores rather than as separate scales. Based on its performance to date, the decision of the test authors to omit the PO subscale from the calculation of the total score appears to have been wise.

Validity.   Assumptions regarding the content validity of the scale derive from the fact that the test construction was based on prior work on the nature and assessment of career maturity and from the use of experts in the field to develop test items related to each of the dimensions being assessed. Evidence for construct validity originally provided in the *User's manual* is based on the score differences between younger and older students, on score differences across high school curricula (e.g., students in college preparatory and business programs tend to obtain higher means on the cognitive scales than do students in general and those in vocational programs), and on the correspondence of the obtained factor structure to theoretical prediction. Specifically, the manual describes the derivation of a two-factor structure clearly differentiating the attitudinal from the cognitive subscales. Similar support for the validity of Form CU is provided in the supplement to the *User's manual,* and again a two-factor structure emerges in factor analyses.

Additional evidence for validity is presented in the new manual, including discriminant analyses of scores across grades, genders, and within academic programs. Discriminant analyses by sex indicated that the overall female superiority on the CDI scales was particularly prominent on the cognitive, versus the attitudinal, scales. Althoug the results from the discriminant analyses are interesting, their importance to the establishment of construct validity would have been improved by the formulation of a priori hypotheses with which the data were found to agree.

The major new validity data concern the relationships of CDI scores to themselves and to other variables. Canonical correlations between the attitudinal and cognitive variables, although statistically significant, are relatively low, ranging from .20 to .30 in grades 9–12 (Form S) and from .10 to .30 for college students on Form CU. The authors conclude the existence of two clearly separable dimensions of career maturity, which is consistent with both the factor analytical results and the fact that correlations between .10 and .30 indicate as little as 1% to a maximum of 9% shared variance.

Consistent with other findings in the career maturity literature are statistically significant and moderately sized correlations of the cognitive scales, but not the attitudinal scales, with ability measures such as the ITED and the DAT. In Jepsen and Prediger's (1981) study of convergent validity with other similar measures, cited in the CDI technical manual, the CP scales correlated more highly with the CMI Attitude Scale than with Goal Selection, while the CDI, DM, and WW cognitive scales correlated more highly with GS than with the CMI Attitude Scale. In research by Super and Nevill (1984), commitment to a career, as measured by the Salience Inventory, was related to attitudinal career maturity, at least in high school females. In college samples, commitment to a career was related to higher scores on CE and DM. Since Super has suggested that the concept of career maturity is relevant only for students with some degree of career commitment, the findings of a relationship between the two are consistent with his hypothesis.

Although these studies shed further light on the constructs measured by the CDI, there continues to be a lack of traditional criterion-related validity evidence. The need for concurrent validation, that is, with respect to immediate behavioral indicators of career mature behavior, and predictive validation, that is, with respect to later outcomes such as realistic educational and career choices and satisfying and reasonably successful occupational outcomes, is apparent.

Recent Advances

Probably most noteworthy are the recent appearances of the Form CU Supplement in 1982 and the *Technical manual* in 1984. The lack of these materials caused difficulty for test reviewers, particularly those operating under deadlines such as that for the Mental Measurements Yearbook Series. For example, Pinkney's (1985) review in the *Ninth mental measurements yearbook* and Hansen's (1985) review in *Measurement and evaluation in counseling and development* were done without benefit of the updated technical information. Such reviews are often more negative and always less useful than they might have been without updated information. In the present case, the fact that the technical manual was delayed considerably past original publication of the test is partly to blame, but test authors may also feel that their case was judged prematurely and/or inadequately (D. E. Super, personal communication, August 1, 1985). For these reasons, the appearance of the technical manual is particularly welcome.

A very different area of recent attention has been the adaptations of the CDI for use in several other countries, for example, Australia, Canada, Austria, Portugal, and Spain. The Australian revision, referred to as CDI–A (Lokan, 1983), was particularly extensive and is accompanied by a comprehensive technical and user's manual. Specifically, the Australian form eliminated the PO scale altogether and shortened the remaining scales (the CDI–A total is 72 items, in contrast to the CDI's 120) without loss in their reliability. Like the CDI, factor analyses of the CDI–A yield two clear factors, one cognitive and accounting for 41% to 45% of the variance and the other attitudinal and accounting for 25% of the variance.

More generally, cross-cultural research reviewed by Lokan (1984) provides evidence for the generalizability of findings from work on the CDI, for example, that a general cognitive factor and at least one attitudinal factor underlie the scales and that the former but not the latter are related to measures of intelligence and ability. Patterns regarding age, grade, and sex differences have not held up so consistently, possibly because of vast differences in the educational systems and cultural expectations of other countries.

The adaptation of the CDI for use in other nations is particularly noteworthy for many reasons, for example, making it possible for others to benefit from both knowledge of the concept of career maturity and from access to a measure of that construct. And cross-cultural research is a very useful approach to explicating the nature of a construct and the validity and utility of its measures. Certainly those findings which are found to be replicated in other countries, for example, the cognitive career maturity–intelligence relationship and the factor structure, are of considerable theoretical importance.

COGNITIVE VOCATIONAL MATURITY TEST

General Description

The Cognitive Vocational Maturity Test (Westbrook & Parry–Hill, 1973) differs from the CMI and the CDI in its emphasis on only the cognitive, rather than on both the cognitive and attitudinal, dimension of career maturity and on its appropriateness for somewhat younger students, those in grades 6 through 9.

The underlying assumption guiding the construction of the CVMT is the central importance of occupational information in making good career choices. According to Westbrook and Mastie (1974), knowledge of the world of work is as crucial as is self-knowledge to the process of finding occupations likely to lead to success and satisfaction. Thus, the CVMT is designed to assess the degree to which students know and can use occupational information. The six subtests of the CVMT are as follows (sample items are shown in Table 3.4):

1. *Fields of Work:* Knowledge of the occupations that are available in various fields of work.
2. *Job Selection:* The ability to choose the most realistic occupation for a hypothetical student who is described in terms of his/her abilities, interests, and values.
3. *Work Conditions:* Knowledge of work schedules, income level, physical conditions, job locations, etc.
4. *Education Required:* Knowledge of the amount of education generally required for a wide range of occupations.
5. *Attributes Required:* Knowledge of the abilities, interests, and values generally required for various occupations.
6. *Duties:* Knowledge of the principal duties performed in a wide range of occupations.

The entire CVMT contains 120 items. With the exception of Job Selection, containing 15 items, and Duties, containing 25 items, the scales contain 20 items each. The CVMT was standardized in a sample of more than 7,000 sixth through ninth graders enrolled in a North Carolina career exploration program. Scores are provided as a simple "number correct" for each subscale and for the total, having a possible maximum of 120.

TABLE 3.4
Sample Items From the Cognitive Vocational Maturity Test

Subtest	Sample Item
Fields of work	Which of the following is not in the field of construction? (a) surveyor, (b) architect, (c) carpenter, (d) lawyer (e) I don't know.
Job selection	Mike had some vocational training in high school and worked hard to graduate. He is physically strong and prefers outdoor work. He is good at doing things with his hands, is dependable and cooperative. He likes to be around other people and has a cheerful personality. Which one seems to be the most likely one for him to be in? (a) payroll clerk, (b) truck driver, (c) Bricksman, (d) night watchman, (e) I don't know.
Word conditions	Which one of the following does not have to work with tools? (a) barber, (b) mechanic, (c) carpenter, (d) milkman, (e) I don't know.
Education required	A college education is not required to be a : (a) chemist, (b) architect, (c) agronomist, (d) mechanic, (e) I don't know.
Attributes required	Imagination is most important in which occupation? (a) advertising artist, (b) electrician, (c) social worker, (d) librarian, (e) I don't know.
Duties	Which one fills prescriptions for drugs and medicines? (a) chemist, (b) physicist, (c) pharmacist, (d) pharmacologist, (e) I don't know.

Psychometric Characteristics

Reliability data for the CVMT indicate values of the KR–20 coefficient in the .80s, except for the Job Selection scale, where reliability coefficients ranged from .67 to .71. In a study by Westbrook (1976a) CVMT scores were shown to be strongly related to scores on the CMI Attitude Scale (.55 to .64), and to the CDI DM scale (.51 to .61). The CVMT subscores are themselves intercorrelated, with values of r between subscales ranging from .60 (Work Conditions with Duties) to .84 (Attributes Required with Duties). Scores are unrelated to the CDI Attitude Scales. In a factor analysis of CVMT scales with CMI Attitude and CDI scales, the CVMT scales, along with the CDI DM and the CMI Attitude, loaded on the first, general factor, accounting for 77% of the variance. The CDI Attitude scales loaded on a different factor from the cognitive scales and the CMI.

Although these studies suggest that the CVMT possesses convergent validity relative to other cognitive career maturity measures, data regarding criterion-related validity are inadequate. One criterion-related validity study cited in Westbrook and Mastie (1974) indicated that ninth-grade students currently making career choices consistent with their aptitudes and interests obtained higher CVMT scores than did students making unrealistic choices. In this study, however, only 26 of 249 students in the criterion sample were making choices consistent with both their aptitudes and their interests, while the choices of 117 students were incongruent with both. Thus, the significant findings of greater career maturity were based on an *n* of 26. Further, there is no evidence that these 26 were representative in IQ to the group as a whole. Given the strong relationship of cognitive career maturity measures, including the CVMT, to intelligence and academic aptitude (correlations of CVMT scores with the California Test of Mental Maturity range from .53 to .69 across scales), the possibility that these 26 were among the most able of the students would account for the relationship between congruence and the CVMT. In general, further evidence for the validity of the CVMT is needed, and researchers should more consistently use IQ or academic achievement covariates in the study of the relationships of career maturity measures to other measures.

In addition to more evidence regarding criterion-related validity, evidence for the necessity of six separate dimensions as measured by the CVMT subscales is needed. As with other measures of career maturity, factor analytical research is essential to the clarifying of both the number and nature of dimensions reflected in the inventory.

Recent Developments

The CVMT has not been commercially published and although it is still available from Westbrook's project, many of the ideas behind it were incorporated into the large-scale testing programs, such as American College Testing's Assessment of Career Development (ACD) and the College Entrance Examination Board's Career Skills Assessment Program (CSAP). Although the ACD is no longer available (see the section on Other Measures), the CSAP will be described subsequently.

ADDITIONAL MEASURES OF CAREER MATURITY

The next group of measures differ from the three traditional measures in being less specifically construct-oriented and more strongly oriented toward the assessment of the outcomes of career education programs. They may also be characterized by differences in their targeted population or by their relative newness to the field.

Career Skills Assessment Program

General Description. The Career Skills Assessment Program (CSAP) was developed in 1977 by researchers at the College Entrance Examination Board (CEEB, 1978). The battery is designed to measure "proficiency in skills the-

oretically considered useful for achieving a personally satisfying career''
[Westbrook & Rogers, 1980, p. 107] for purposes of individual or group assessment, fostering skill development, and evaluating career education programs.

The CSAP consists of six separate tests, or "exercises" as they are called by
the publisher. The six are as follows: (1) Self-evaluation and Developmental
Skills, (2) Career Awareness Skills, (3) Career Decision Making Skills, (4)
Employment Seeking Skills, (5) Work Effectiveness Skills, and (6) Personal
Economics Skills. Each test (consisting of 60 items except for Employment
Seeking Skills, which is based on 70 items) provides subscores as well as a total
score—the number of subscores provided ranges from 4 to 7 for the six tests.
Although it may be noted that some of the CSAP's emphases are similar to those
of other measures of career maturity, (for example, the emphases on self-knowledge, occupational information, and decision-making skills), the CSAP also
contains some additional areas not commonly assessed by measures of career
maturity. Specifically, the Employment Seeking Skills test seems to reflect the
developmental tasks of Super's Implementation substage of the Exploration
stage, and the Work Effectiveness Skills test assesses tasks of the Establishment
stage of career development. Personal Economics Skills seems somewhat out of
place, being more a general, life skill than a career development task.

Psychometric Qualities

Several features of the CSAP demonstrate the emphasis of its developers on
instructional aims. First, the answer sheet may be machine- or self-scored, and
the test booklet is accompanied by a follow-up self-instructional guide. Second,
the CEEB recommends that the tests be used only if they are consistent with local
educational objectives and, thus, local standards regarding both the nature and
the extent of knowledge of career education objectives. For this reason, no
national norms are available; users are encouraged to develop and use their own
local norms.

Although stating that final judgments regarding the appropriateness of content
should be made by local career education specialists, the CSAP manual (CEEB,
1978) does state that test construction was oriented toward comprehensive sampling of the objectives of career education programs. Procedures were carefully
designed to ensure content validity with respect to those objectives, rather than to
measure any particular underlying construct such as career "maturity." Thus,
the CSAP can be assumed to possess a reasonable degree of content validity
based on careful, explicitly formulated methods of test construction.

Evidence for concurrent validity is provided by relatively large correlations of
CSAP scores with similar scales of other inventories, for example, .74 with CDI
Decision Making and .75 with CDI World of Work Information (Jepsen &
Prediger, 1981). However, the high correlations of both the CSAP and the CDI
with general intelligence and with reading ability strongly suggest the possibility

that their interrelationship is artificially inflated due to the shared ability variance. Evidence for the criterion-related and construct, validity of the CSAP is lacking, and this constitutes one of the instrument's most serious flaws.

There is evidence that the CSAP scales are internally consistent; KR–20 coefficients range from .85 to .93, with a median of .91. (Note that although these are impressive values, they are also based on relatively long, i.e., 60- to 70-item, tests). There is, however, no evidence regarding test–retest stability. The publishers say that they cannot evaluate stability because of the effects of practice on the second testing, but use of the test to evaluate career education programs for either individuals or groups requires the ability to distinguish change due to treatment from that due to readministration of the test. Thus, the lack of stability data mitigates against one of the major recommended uses of the scales (see Westbrook & Rogers, 1980).

Thus, like other measures of career maturity, lack of psychometric data is a serious limitation of the CSAP. However, the developers of the CSAP have made no claim to be assessing underlying psychological constructs, such as career maturity. Instead, it is assumed that the behaviors assessed can be readily understood and the scores used without the need for deeper inference—thus the instruments rely on face validity for their appeal to users. Although these assumptions are both legitimate and appropriate, the lack of construct-based or more generalizable interpretive frameworks (such as national norms) seriously limits the broader utility of the instrument and will probably prevent its full integration into the career maturity literature.

For further information about the CSAP, see the review by Westbrook and Rogers (1980), Abernathy's (1980) response to Westbrook and Rogers, and the reviews by Greenhaus (1985) and Wiggins (1985) in the *Ninth mental measurement yearbook* (Mitchell, 1985).

Career Awareness Inventory

General Description.   Like the CVMT, the emphasis of Fadale's (1974, 1980) Career Awareness Inventory (CAI) is on knowledge of occupational information. Originally recommended for use with students in grades 4 through 8, the CAI is now available in an Elementary version for students in grades 3 through 6 and an Advanced (1980) version for grades 7–12.

The 125-item Elementary level consists of seven parts: (1) Identifying types of work and specific jobs (63 items); (2) Identifying levels of training necessary for specific kinds of work (6 items); (3) Familiarity with people in specific occupations (32 items), (4) Distinguishing between product and service occupations (4 items), (5) Awareness of prestige and status of one job over another (5 items), (6) Identifying the job that doesn't belong in a specific cluster (10 items), and (7) Knowledge of characteristics associated with particular jobs (7 items). The 133-item Advanced level is divided into scores for Related Occupations,

Grouping in Occupations, Work Locations, and Self-Assessment of Career Awareness; scales vary from 10 to 24 items in length.

Psychometric Qualities. The CAI is accompanied by a teacher's manual rather than a technical manual, and, overall, evidence regarding its quality is sparse. It is stated that the test was based on a model of career education, but no details of the process of test construction or its relationship to the theoretical base are given. The only evidence for content validity is the statement that the DOT was a source of items, but the wide variations in numbers of items per subtest (ranging from 4 to 63) shed doubt on the underlying rationale for test construction.

Evidence for other types of reliability and validity is also lacking. The subscales of both the Elementary and Advanced levels are poorly correlated—a substantial number of zero or negative correlations between subparts casts grave doubt on the extent to which either level measures a construct of "career awareness." Positive correlations among different career maturity measures or scales are almost always found, even across the cognitive versus attitudinal domains. Even the smaller values, for example, those in the .30s, are statistically significant, and their frequent absence here causes considerable concern. The limited number of items in four of the scales on the Elementary scale (7 or fewer items) and the great variations in number of items distorts statistical analyses and severely limits reliability. The total test reliabilities are in the low .80s, not impressive values for 125- and 133-item tests in the cognitive domain.

Like other measures of career maturity, scores are highly correlated with general intelligence. However, the CAI uses words that are probably well beyond the reading level of many if not most of the students for whom the test is intended—words such as "osteopath," "choreographer," and "meterorologist" are certainly too difficult for third graders. Thus, evidence that the CAI measures a factor other than reading ability is not provided (Sink, 1980). The pictorial material and occupational titles in the Elementary level show both sex and race bias in the examples and pictures (Cole, 1982b). For example, women are shown only in female sterotypical occupations such as nurse, secretary, and waitress, and men are protrayed as judges, doctors, and lawyers. There are no blacks in the pictorial material (Sink, 1980). Finally, the problems in defining and measuring career maturity in children as young as the third grade are not addressed. This is clearly a different population than that for which traditional theories and measures of career maturity have been developed. Although there may be merit in considering this problem, the CAI does not contribute significantly to addressing it.

Based on these problems, reviewers of the CAI (e.g., Cole, 1978, 1982b; Smith, 1978) suggest that it be viewed as an experimental instrument rather than one providing accurate individual assessment. At most it might be used with groups, but even this use should await clarification of the meaning and implications of career maturity in third through sixth as well as junior high and high school students.

New Mexico Career Education Test

The New Mexico Career Education Test (NMCET) was developed by Healy and Klein (1973) to assess objectives "thought to be significantly involved in career success and frequently incorporated into career education programs [p. 1]." The series measures the following objectives: (1) Attitude Toward Work (25 items) assessing the degree to which the individual appreciates the personal and social significance of work; (2) Career Planning (20 items), including occupational information items and items such as those in Crites's problem-solving subtest; (3) Career-oriented Activities (25 items), designed to assess the degree to which the individual has taken the important steps to make occupational decisions; (4) Knowledge of occupations (25 items); (5) Job Application Procedures (20 items); and (6) Career Development (25 items), assessing the degree to which the individual knows what is required to hold a job and advance in an occupation.

The authors of the NMCET intended it for use in the assessment of specific career objectives relevant to students in grades 9 through 12. However, several reviewers (Bodden, 1978; Prediger, 1976; Westbrook, 1976b) note that the rationale for its construction is not provided in the test manual, and that norms are available for 9th and 12th graders but not for the 10th and 11th graders for whom the test is also intended. Thus, there is insufficient information on either the nature or interpretation of test scores.

Like other measures of career maturity, evidence for psychometric quality is inadequate. Reliabilities of subtest scores are .52 to .87, with an average of .66—not an impressive set of values. No stability data are available. Evidence for validity is based on the finding of higher scores by 12th graders, compared with 9th graders (Healy & Klein, 1973) and on findings that junior college students having work experience scored higher on the Job Application Procedures and Career Development scales than did those without work experience (Yen & Healy, 1977).

Healy (1976), in a response to the critical reviews, noted that funds for further development of the instrument were not available. Thus, although the NMCET may have some potential, it should not be used for applied purposes until information regarding its construction and psychometric quality and a more complete and generalizable set of norms are made available.

Career Planning Questionnaire

Description. Based on his longstanding concerns about both the psychometric quality of career maturity measures and their correlations with intellective measures, Westbrook and his colleagues (Westbrook, Sanford, O'Neal, Horne, Fleenor, & Garren, 1985) have recently taken a rather different approach to the conceptualization and assessment of career maturity. Specifically, they postulate that the construct of career maturity includes different elements, traits, aspects, or factors, all of which have something in common with each other and with the process of making an "appropriate" career choice. As stated by Westbrook et al.,

An individual will more likely make an appropriate career choice if he or she (a) has made certain career decisions and career-related decisions; (b) has engaged in career-related activities; (c) views a career as an important aspect of his or her life; (d) knows his/her own personal characteristics/attributes; (e) has demonstrated the ability to solve career problems; and (f) knows his/her own career values. [p. 340]

Suggesting that available measures of some of these constructs were inadequate in psychometric quality or in appropriateness to the population of interest, that is, 11th graders, Westbrook (1982) developed new measures of these aspects of career maturity. The measures developed, which were designed specifically for use with 11th graders and which were collectively denoted the Career Planning Questionnaire (CPQ), consist of: (1) Career Decisions, similar to the aims of Osipow's (1980) Career Decision Scale; (2) Career Activities, similar to other measures of extent of career exploratory activities; (3) Career Salience, similar in conception to Greenhaus's (1971) Career Salience Scale and Nevill and Super's (1986) Salience Inventory; (4) Self-Knowledge, similar to the Self-Appraisal test of the CMI Competencies Test; (5) Career Concerns, similar to the Problem-Solving Test of the CMI Competencies Test and also in some respects to the CDS or Holland, Daiger, and Power's (1980) My Vocational Situation; and (6) Knowledge of Career Values, similar to other self-knowledge tests. A seventh test, Knowledge of Preferred Occupation, is like the CDI Preferred Occupational Group (PO) scale.

The first five scales listed have 20 items, while Career Values contains 30 and Knowledge of Preferred Occupation has 17. Note that those scales, similar in content to other measures of career maturity, include Career Activities, Self-Knowledge, Career Concerns, Knowledge of Career Values, and Knowledge of Preferred Occupation.

Psychometric Qualities.   In a first study of the new scales, Westbrook et al. (1985) reported KR–20 reliability coefficients ranging from .74 to .91, with Career Decisions the most reliable and Career Salience and Self-Knowledge the least reliable. Intercorrelations indicated that Career Decisions, Career Activities, Self-Knowledge, and Career Concerns formed a cluster. Career Salience was unrelated to any other scales, and Career Values was inconsistently related to the others. Note that with the exception of Career Decisions, the clustered scales were in the traditional content domain of career maturity measures.

Interpreted as a very positive sign by Westbrook was the absence of correlations with grades, one index of academic accomplishment. But since ability scores (PSATs) were available only for about 50 subjects, the correlations with a measure of academic aptitude could not be assessed.

In terms of construct validity, Westbrook collected several validity indexes 1 year later. The criterion variables were: (1) Frequency of discussion of plans for after high school; (2) Self-report of knowledge of duties required in a preferred occupation; (3) Level of certainty about entering a preferred occupation; (4) Agreement between career choice and career values, and (5) Satisfaction with plans for the next 6 months. The Career Activities score was significantly related to extent of discussion of plans, knowledge of duties of preferred occupation, and, to a lesser extent, career choice-values agreement and satisfaction with career plans. Self-knowledge was related to certainty of career choice, values agreement, and satisfaction. Career concerns was related to satisfaction. Thus, there was some evidence for criterion-related validity, but the fact that the large number of both predictors and criteria would lead to some statistically significant correlations through chance alone needs to be considered in interpreting the findings.

Although needing further refinement, Westbrook's conceptualization and measure offer a broader view of career maturity than has characterized previous work. This has the advantage of breadth of conception but the disadvantage of complicating, through heterogeneity and multidimensionality, conceptualization of a construct the nature of which even in unidimensional form cannot be agreed upon. In other words, although there is no real reason why the definition of career maturity cannot be expanded to include a variety of variables related to career decision making, the scientific and practical utility of this view, versus an approach which conceptualizes separate variables, such as maturity, indecision, and salience, need to be established.

If, as is usually the case in the literature, intercorrelation is a basis upon which to consider variables as part of the same underlying construct, then Westbrook et al.'s (1985) findings with the CPQ suggest that there may be some validity in the postulation of a relationship between career decisions status (measured herein by the CDS) and traditional career maturity measures—in the Jepsen and Prediger (1981) study the CDS was related to other indexes of the ability to conceptualize career decisions in a cluster analysis but to decisional stage in the factor analysis. Westbrook's data do not support the validity of including career salience and career values measures in the definition of career maturity, although it may be useful to include the former variables in a broader nomological network explicating the theory of the construct of career maturity. Further theoretical development and, particularly, extensive factor analytical research capable of addressing some of these definitional, dimensional questions is essential if our understanding is to progress.

Other Measures

Finally, note should be made of several other instruments associated in one way or another with the assessment of career development. First, a relatively well-known instrument now unavailable is ACT's Assessment of Career Development (ACT, 1973). The ACD is no longer published by ACT, and the firm has focused its attention on the comprehensive self-assessment and career-planning programs of VIESA (Vocational Interest, Experience, and Skill Development) and CPP (Career Planning Program). In actuality, the ACD was never intended as a measure of an underlying construct of career maturity but was directed at needs assessment in the context of career education. The measures described herein share this atheoretical basis.

More specifically, there are available numerous measures which appear similar to some of those of career maturity but which do not use that term in either their title or description. The two major types of such instruments are tests of job or occupational knowledge and tests of career education objectives. These are given brief mention here for the sake of completeness rather than theoretical import.

Mitchell (1982), in the Appendix to Krumboltz and Hamel's (1982) *Assessing career development,* notes several tests of job knowledge, for example, the Occupational Awareness Inventory (Marshall, 1980), the Short Occupational Knowledge Tests (Campbell & Johnson, 1970), the Orientation to Career Concepts (Fulton & Tolsma, 1974), and the Occupations and Career Information BOXSCORE (Feingold, Swerdloff, & Barber, 1978). In addition, Loesch, Rucker, and Shub (1978) describe the evaluation of the Job Knowledge Survey, a 48-item test of occupational knowledge. These tests are viewed as achievement tests in the domain of occupational knowledge, and though authors may describe such knowledge as a component of career maturity, no attempt to generalize to constructs deeper than knowledge is made.

Mitchell (1982) also details several batteries that are specifically designed for the evaluation of career education programs but which, again, make no pretense of deeper conceptual relevance. Examples include the Texas Career Education Measurement Tests, the Wisconsin Career Education Needs Assessment, and Project MATCH Career Education Program Tests. These instruments are designed to be isomorphic with the objectives of the career education program which they are designed to evaluate.

The fact that so much assessment in this area is atheoretical is interesting and will receive discussion in the subsequent section on issues. Suffice it to say at this point, though, that assessment without an underlying theoretical basis lacks scientific and heuristic, although not necessarily practical, utility.

The next section will review the applications of the concept of career maturity to the stages of career development on adulthood, that is, Establishment, Maintenance, and Retirement. Following this, general issues regarding the measurement of career maturity will be discussed.

CAREER MATURITY AND ADJUSTMENT

One of the most important recent advances in the assessment of career development has been the movement into the adult stages of that development. Most research attention and measures have focused on the career development of adolescents and young adults, individuals in Super's Exploration stage of career development, who have not yet made and implemented a career choice. Although a career choice represents an important end point of the *first* major stage of career development, it is only the *beginning* of one's work or career life. Super's subsequent career stages, those of Establishment, Maintenance, and Disengagement are also of great theoretical and practical interest. Although the *nature* of vocational developmental tasks changes with age and career stage, the concept has utility throughout the life span, as does the capability of assessing degree of mastery of the tasks important in one's career stage.

Before proceeding, a description of terms used in this area of research is needed. In extensions of the idea of career maturity to the adult population, the terms "career adaptability" [Super, 1983], career adjustment and development" [Crites, 1976, 1979a], and "vocational adaptation" [Heath, 1976] have been utilized. Although the terms are not interchangeable either in definition or operationally, they share an emphasis on describing characteristics which enable the worker to achieve occupational success and satisfaction over the career/life span.

Although the terms "adaptability" and "adaptation" are relatively new to the discussion of vocational processes in adulthood, the term "adjustment" and the criterion variables of success and satisfaction are nearly as old as vocational psychology itself. In his landmark text *Vocational psychology,* Crites (1969) organizes the career life into the stages of vocational choice and vocational adjustment and devotes several chapters to the discussion of various conceptualizations of vocational adjustment, as well as to its criterion indicators, vocational success and satisfaction. He further cites as a general theory of vocational adjustment the theory of work adjustment of Dawis, Lofquist, England, and Weiss (Dawis, England, & Lofquist, 1964; Dawis, Lofquist, & Weiss, 1968; see also Dawis & Lofquist, 1984 for an extensive recent review of research on the theory). In the latter theory, "work adjustment," of which the major indicator is tenure on the job, is postulated to be a function of the conditions of satisfaction and satisfactoriness (similar to success or level of performance). These in turn are postulated to be a function of the correspondence between characteristics of the individual and the reinforcers and requirements of the work environment.

Tenure as an indicator of "adjustment" bears some similarities to the description of career patterns differing in stability and security (Miller & Form, 1947; 1951; Super, 1957).

In contrast to theories of adjustment focusing on its outcomes, that is, success and satisfaction, the extensions of career maturity to adults continue to focus on the developmental tasks to be completed and/or the career stages to be negotiated. In the following section the two major measures extending the measurement of career maturity or development to the adult years will be reviewed. As with the major models of career maturity in adolescence, the models on which the instruments are based will also be described. The following sections will describe the Adult Career Concerns Inventory (Super, Thompson, Lindeman, Myers, & Jordaan, 1985) and the Career Adjustment and Development Inventory (Crites, 1979a). Although both of these instruments are relatively new, their availability offers exciting possibilities for research and theoretical advancement concerning the career development of adults.

The Adult Career Concerns Inventory

The development of the Adult Career Concerns Inventory stemmed directly from Super's (1977) model of vocational maturity in midcareer. The model postulated the same basic dimensions as does Super's theory of career development in adolescence, that is, Planfulness or Time Perspective, Exploration, Information, Decision-Making, and Reality Orientation. Super's (1977) model has now been subsumed by his more general (1983) model of career maturity, as shown in Table 3.2 in conjunction with the discussion of the Career Development Inventory. Thus, the model shown in Table 3.2 is equally applicable as an organizing framework for the assessment of career development in adulthood.

Originally Super and his group attempted to develop a measure of adult career maturity that would tap the same dimensions assessed by the CDI–School and College Forms, that is, Planfulness, Exploration, Information, and Decision-Making. However, it became clear to the test developers that writing items for use with adults was considerably more difficult than doing so with adolescents because of differences across occupational groups and the fact that options become closed to adults as time goes on. Thus, only the Planfulness dimension was assessed in the resulting instrument, known as the the CDI–Adult Form. Recently, the CDI–Adult form was revised and renamed the Adult Career Concerns Inventory.

Both the Adult Career Concerns Inventory (Super, Thompson, Lindeman, Myers, & Jordaan, 1985) and its predecessor, the Career Development Inventory, Adult Form, are published by Consulting Psychologists Press. The ACCI contains 60 items associated with the four major adult stages in Super's theory of career development. Each of the four stages, that is, Exploration, Establishment, Maintenance, and Disengagement (formerly Decline) is measured by 15 items; 5 items are used to assess each of the three major substages in each stage. Thus, 5 items are used to assess each of the following: (1) the Crystallization, Specification, and Implementation substages of the Exploration stage; (2) the Stabilizing, Consolidating, and Advancing stages of the Establishment stage; (3) the Holding, Updating, and Innovating substages of Maintenance; and (4) the Deceleration, Retirement Planning, and Retirement Living stages of the Disengagement stage.

The item format asks the respondent to indicate the degree of concern he or she has about the tasks associated with each stage. For example, a task in the Implementation substage of Exploration is "Making specific plans to achieve my current career goals," while a task representing the Consolidating substage of establishment is "Developing a reputation in my line of work." Similarly, a task in the Holding substage of Maintenance is "Holding my own against the competition of new people entering the field," and a task in the Deceleration substage of Disengagement is "Cutting down on my working hours."

Degree of concern is indicated on a 5-point Likert scale ranging from No Concern (1) to Great Concern (5). The instrument is self-scoring—the respondent totals his or her own scores for each substage and for the total of 15 items referring to each major stage. A 61st item asks the respondents about their "career change" status, where response options range from considering no career change to having just completed a career change.

After total scores are calculated, the respondent may plot his or her means (1 to 5, reflecting the original response continuum) on the "Career Stage Profile" Sheet provided. Thus, a profile showing degree of concern for each substage and each major stage is visually portrayed to the respondent. A section of the profile for the highlighting of substages and stages receiving ratings of 4 or 5 (indicating considerable or great concern) is also provided. It is assumed that there will be some correspondence between an individual's actual career stage and the nature of one's concerns, with lower degrees of concern for tasks in those stages already completed and those not yet encountered.

The ACCI manual is still being completed and will be available from the publisher, Consulting Psychologists Press. Research data (D. E. Super, personal communication, March 15, 1985) indicate that both the stage and the substage scores are highly reliable (Cronbach alphas in the .80s and .90s). Support for validity includes Morrison's (1977) findings with the CDI-Adult that adaptive managers (as assessed by evidence of fulfillment of a varied set of managerial career roles over time) had completed more tasks in the Exploration stage than had nonadaptive managers, although no differences in the other three stages were found.

John Slocum and his colleagues have examined the validity of the ACCI as a secondary purpose to studying the relationships between career stage and other job-related attitudes and behaviors (Slocum & Cron, 1985; Slocum, Cron, Hansen, & Rawlings, 1985). Slocum and Cron (1985) studied 675 salespersons in seven companies. Age was used to define stage (with under 30 in the "trial" stage, 31 to 44 in "stabilization," and 45 or over in "maintenance").

Results indicated that people in the trial stage were significantly more concerned (as indicated by the ACCI) with issues of crystallization, specification, implementation, and stabilization than were people in the stabilization or maintenance stages. People in stabilization were most concerned with updating and with doing something different, and people in Maintenance were most concerned with holding, updating, and innovating. Few people in any stage reported considerable concern with deceleration, retirement planning, or retirement living, as hypothesized for subjects in the Maintenance stage. In addition to these findings, Slocum and Cron reported a number of stage-related differences in job-related attitudes and behaviors.

Slocum et al. (1985) used the ACCI to measure career stage, rather than using age as the criterion as Slocum and Cron (1985) had done. The sample consisted of 499 salespersons in two companies. Results (among many) indicated that although career stage did vary by age (salespersons in the Exploration stage were significantly younger than were those in the Disengagement stage), age accounted for only 12% and 16% of the variance in career stage in the two companies. Thus, it is clear that using the ACCI to define career stage will result in different classifications than will using age for that purpose.

Although the ACCI is an interesting and potentially useful measure, a number of questions regarding its construct validity and the suggested interpretations and theoretical implications of resulting scores remain to be addressed. (It should be noted that the appearance of the manual and other advertised interpretive guides, such as the *Guide for ACCI analysis* to be published by Consulting Psychologists Press, will hopefully address many or most of these questions.)

A first major question concerns the construct the ACCI is intended to measure. At the level of fact validity, the ACCI assesses the stage(s) at which the individual has concerns. While an important issue, especially for use in counseling, the underlying construct reflected by stages of concerns is not clear. Super has used the term "career adaptability" with reference to optimal or adaptive career development in adulthood, but its definition and connection to the ACCI are not clear. The original model for the measure and its use of developmental tasks characterizing career stages suggest that the ACCI is related to the construct of career maturity, but this is also not clear.

Related to the question of the construct measured is that of score interpretation. First, because the ACCI assesses concern with, rather than reported mastery of the tasks of each stage, it is not possible to interpret low scores unambiguously. In other words, although high scores are interpretable as indicative of concerns at that developmental stage, a low score could mean that the individual has encountered and mastered the tasks of the stage (which would logically seem to be interpreted as adding to overall career maturity). Alternatively, a low score could be interpreted as indicating a legitimate lack of concern because the stage hasn't yet been confronted or as immaturity because the individual lacks awareness of necessary tasks either at or preceding his or her current actual or age-related stage.

Further, although it is probably realistic to expect concerns appropriate to one's developmental stage, is it desirable or necessary? In other words, are there conditions under which having no concerns is indicative of greater adaptability than having some concerns?

Another issue, raised in particular by the work of Phillips (1982a,b), concerns the extent to which an adult should complete the tasks of an earlier stage. Phillips (1982a, 1982b) has studied the role of exploratory versus commitment-related behaviors in adulthood and has contended that exploration may be important well beyond the ages typically associated with Super's Exploration stage (usually thought to end by the mid-20s, if not earlier). Phillips (1982b) finding that individuals with patterns of increasing occupational commitment did not experience higher levels of desirable career outcomes (such as success, satisfaction, attained status, and systematic career progression) than those following other patterns calls into question the assumption that Exploratory activities should decrease in frequency to be replaced by a state of increasing degree of commitment. Questions regarding the role of exploratory activities are also important in the important and rapidly growing area of research on career transitions, for example, job loss (DeFrank & Ivancevich, 1986), job change, the "midcareer crisis," work re-entry, and retirement (see Hill, Miller & Lowther, 1981) for a series of papers covering these topics.

While considerably more evidence for the reliability and validity, particularly the construct validity, of the ACCI is needed, the availability of the instrument offers some intriguing directions for further research and theory explication. The availability of the manual and other supporting materials should facilitate the extent to which researchers, as well as practitioners, can begin to more fully examine and utilize the instrument.

Career Adjustment and Development Inventory

Background.   Development of the Career Adjustment and Development Inventory (Crites, 1979a) can be said to have begun with Crites's (1976) Model of Career Adjustment in Early Adulthood. As mentioned previously, in developing his model, Crites defined problems in career adjustment as the failure to accomplish the career development tasks of a life stage. Elaborating, Crites (1976) postulated the existence of "thwarting conditions," that is, internal and/or external barriers or conflicts preventing the individual from reaching goals of occupational success and satisfaction. These thwarting conditions require coping responses from the worker; to the extent that the worker copes effectively, developmental tasks will be mastered, leading to career adjustment and maturity.

Following Crites's theoretical lead was a group of vocational researchers organized under the auspices of the National Center for Research in Vocational Education and led by Robert E. Campbell. Following an exhaustive literature review covering theories of adult career development and research on adult career problems from the literature in vocational, industrial, and organizational psychology, occupational sociology, and labor relations, an updated and elaborated list of developmental tasks applicable to Super's adult career stages was developed (Campbell, Cellini, Shaltry, Long, Pinkos, & Crites, 1979). Specifically, the four career stages, preparation (used instead of the term "exploration" as more applicable to adults), establishment, maintenance, and retirement (used instead of Super's "decline") were defined by 17 tasks and 80 subtasks. For example, tasks of the preparation stage range from that of assessing personal attributes and the world of work in anticipation of work entry/re-entry to obtaining a position in the chosen occupation.

In addition, it was found that four common themes characterized tasks recurring across stages. In other words, regardless of developmental stage the tasks likely to be required included decision making, implementing plans, organizational/institutional performance, and organizational/institutional adaptation. Using these four themes as the organizing structure, a "Diagnostic Taxonomy of Adult Career Problems" was developed (Campbell et al., 1979; Campbell & Cellini, 1981). Career development problems were postulated as occurring "When an individual experiences difficulty in coping with a career development task, when a task is only partially mastered, or when a task is not even attempted" [Campbell & Cellini, 1981, p. 177]. Examples of career development problems corresponding to each of the four themes are as follows: (1) Problems in career decision making—"Failure to generate sufficient career options due to personal limitations such as health, resources, ability, and education"; (2) Problems in implementing career plans—"Failure of the individual to take the steps necessary to implement his/her career plans"; (3) Problems in organizational/institutional performance—"Deficiencies in skills, abilities, and/or knowledge upon position entry"; and (4) Problems in organizational/institutional adaptation—"Lack of knowledge of organizational rules and procedures" and "Interpersonal conflicts arising from differences of opinion" [Campbell & Cellini, 1981, pp. 179–180].

The first instrument designed for the assessment of career adjustment as defined in the taxonomy was Crites's (1979a) Career ADI, intended to assess the extent to which the tasks/problems of the Establishment stage have been successfully addressed by the individual worker.

The Career ADI.   The Career Adjustment and Development Inventory (Crites, 1979a) assesses mastery of six developmental tasks postulated to be important in the Establishment stage of career development. The scale and the tasks assessed were based on Crites's theory and the subsequently developed Diagnostic Taxonomy of adult career problems.

The six career developmental tasks are as follows:

1. Organizational adaptability, involving the processes of becoming socialized in the organization, "learning the ropes," etc. A sample item is "I don't know what's expected of me socially on the job" (negatively scored).

2. Position Performance, involving learning the content of the job, its duties and responsibilities. A sample item is "I feel confident most of the time about how well I can do my job."

3. Work Habits and Attitudes, involving being dependable, having a positive attitude, and being receptive to supervision. An illustrative item is "Doing a good job is very important to me."

4. Coworker relationships, involving getting along well with others on the job and dealing effectively with interpersonal conflicts as they arise. A sample item is "I seldom talk with others at work" (negatively scored).

5. Advancement, involving moving up the organizational ladder. An item representative of this scale is "I have a plan for where I want to be in my job 5 years from now."

6. Career Choice and Plans, involving longer-range planning, identifying career pathways, etc. An item in this stage is "I seldom think about what I'll be doing in 5 years" (negatively scored).

The development of the Career ADI is detailed in Crites (1979b) and Crites (1982). The Career ADI consists of 90 items to which the respondent indicated agreement ("True") or disagreement ("False"). Scores for each subscale and a total score indicative of overall career adjustment or maturity in the Establishment stage of career development are calculated. In addition to the 90 items assessing degree of mastery of each of the career development tasks are 20 open-ended items used to assess the coping methods postulated in Crites's model. More specifically, keys are used to hand-score responses to such open-ended questions as: "Darlene was the only woman in her unit and found herself isolated from the men with whom she worked. She . . ." and "At mid-life, after 20 years in the same job, Bill found that he was increasingly dissatisfied with his work. He . . ." Integrative responses remove the thwarting conditions and reduce associated tension and anxiety, Adjustive responses remove anxiety but not the thwarting conditions, and Nonadjustive responses remove neither the anxiety nor the thwarting conditions. (It should be noted that although the concept of coping mechanisms is an interesting and important addition to vocational theory and is related to career maturity, detailed discussion is beyond the scope of this chapter.) Interested readers, however, are urged to consult not only Crites's work but the excellent recent work of Osipow and Spokane (1983, 1984) in their theory of occupational stress, strain, and coping and their development of the Occupational Environment scales, which provide separate measures of occupational stressors, strains, and coping skills.

Initial psychometric data describing the Career ADI revealed serious problems with the scale. First, sample means were relatively high (Fitzgerald, 1984), averaging 12 on a 15-point scale (Crites, 1979b). However, the age of the workers sampled (mean age 34.7) led to the possibility that some of them were beyond the Establishment stage and into the Maintenance stage and, thus, had successfully completed all of the Establishment stage tasks. A further problem with the Career ADI was discouragingly low reliabilities; KR–20 coefficients for the 15-item scales were as follows (Crites, 1979b:) .70, Advancement; .59, Work Habits and attitudes; .49, Position Performance; .52, Coworker relationship; .55, Organizational Adaptability; and .60, Career Choice and plans. These are generally insufficient even for research purposes. And although the reliability of the 90-item total scale was .84, this is not spectacular for a 90-item scale. Crites, however, contends that internal consistency reliability is not necessarily to be expected if scales are heterogeneous in item content—he views validity as the more important criterion for evaluating the adequacy of the instrument (J.O. Crites, personal communication, September, 15, 1986). This issue will be discussed further in the subsequent section on the reliability of measures of career maturity.

More encouraging than evidence for reliability was evidence for the construct validity of the scale. Crites's theory suggests that the means should decrease from the first task to the last, that is, from early to later in the establishment stage. In accordance with prediction, the highest means were found for organizational adaptability (13.9) and position performance (13.3), followed by those for Work Habits and Attitudes (12.6) and Coworker relationships (12.4), with lowest means for Advancement (11.5) and Career Choices and Plans (10.6). Correlations of scores with Hoppock's (1935) Job Satisfaction Blank (JSB) were also encouraging, ranging from .25 to .40 across scales and .50 with the total score.

As an approach to increasing the reliability of the Career ADI, a number of new items were written and the response format was changed from True–False to a 5-point Likert scale (to increase reliability by increasing score variance, where 1 = Strongly Disagree and 5 = Strongly Agree). Fitzgerald (1984) tested three age cohorts, that is, individuals who had graduated from college either 1, 3, or 5 years prior to the study. A sample of 328 subjects employed in a variety of occupations and organizations was utilized; 44% were male, 56% female. The mean age of the subjects was 26.8 and that, along with the fact that they were at most 5 years out of college, was assumed to ensure their presence in the Establishment stage and thereby address one of the problems in Crites's (1979b) original work.

In spite of the changes in both the instrument and the sample, Fitzgerald (1984) reported results similar to those of Crites's earlier study. Specifically, means were still uncomfortably high, ranging from 10.2 to 12.2, as opposed to from 10.6 to 13.9. Reliability coefficients were still low as well, ranging from .55 (Career Choice and Plans) to .80 (Coworker relationships) with a median of .64. On the positive side, means again arranged themselves in expected order except for the reversal of Work Habits and Attitudes and Position Performance, and a correlation of .60 between the total score and the Hoppock JSB was found.

In response to these problems, Crites and his colleagues are continuing to investigate possible bases for the apparent score ceiling and to consider issues surrounding the internal consistency reliability and validity of the instrument (Crites, personal communication, September 15, 1986). Thus, the Career ADI, while showing great promise, is still in an experimental stage of development.

Summary

Given the importance of understanding adult career development, it is surprising that the measurement of adult career stage and concepts related to maturity/development/adaptability have received comparatively little attention. A particularly serious lack is a reliable and generally agreed-upon method of classifying individuals into career stages (Greenhaus & Parasuraman, 1986). A growing body of research has investigated behavioral and attitudinal correlates of career stage (London & Stumpf, 1982; Rabinowitz & Hall, 1981; Slocum & Cron, 1985; Slocum et al., 1985; Stumpf & Rabinowitz, 1981), yet as pointed out by Slocum and Cron (1985) it is difficult to integrate findings across studies when different researchers operationalize career stage in different ways. Slocum et al. (1985) showed that age and stage as defined by the ACCI do not share significant amounts of variance, so studies using one versus the other to define career stage will not be comparable. The problem was further illustrated in Crites's and Fitzgerald's development of the Career ADI, where questions concerning the definition of subjects appropriate for a measure of task completion in the Establishment stage complicate the interpretation of resulting data.

It seems clear that further work on both the definition of career stages and the conceptualization and measurement of the tasks or behaviors which enable an individual to negotiate successfully both successive career stages within a single career and major, minor, expected and unexpected career transitions would contribute greatly to the field of vocational psychology and career development.

ISSUES IN CAREER MATURITY ASSESSMENT

There are several current issues regarding the assessment of career maturity. In the sections to follow, these issues will be discussed: (1) The relatively poor reliability and validity of career maturity measures as a group; (2) The lack of agreement concerning the criteria of career maturity; and (3) Lack of agreement concerning the nature of the construct of career maturity and the relationship of career maturity to intellective measures. The chapter will end with a summary and with a number of recommendations concerning needed directions for further research and theoretical explication.

Psychometric Quality: Reliability

As a group, measures of career maturity have not been shown to demonstrate a high degree of psychometric quality. For many instruments, there is insufficient evidence regarding reliability and validity. And what evidence there is in many cases indicates inadequate levels of these characteristics. The issue of the reliability of career maturity measures will be discussed in this section, and the next sections will cover their validity or, more generally, their *meaning*.

Internal Consistency Reliability. Overall, measures of career maturity could be improved in the areas of both internal consistency reliability (homogeneity) and test-retest reliability (stability). Internal consistency reliability refers to the extent to which all of the items in a test or scale measure the same underlying concept; common indices include coefficient alpha, KR–20, and split-half correlations corrected by the Spearman Brown formula. When a test is postulated to measure one underlying construct, relatively low internal reliability coefficients cause one to question whether or not the test is measuring the construct that the test developer intended to measure. In other words, when items are not highly related to each other, at least some of them are not measuring the intended unidimensional construct.

Although there are different points of view on what constitutes an acceptable level of internal consistency, most coefficients are in the .80s and .90s (Anastasi, 1982). Westbrook et al. (1980; Westbrook, 1985) suggest that values above .90 should characterize measures of career maturity, but others argue that coefficients above .90, while always desirable, are absolutely necessary primarily for cases in which tests are used to make admissions or selection decisions; tests like the SAT or the GRE fall into this category (Nunnally, 1978; Walsh & Betz, 1985). There is general agreement, however, that for applied purposes values below .80 are inadequate, while values below .70 are inadequate even for research other than further development of that test (Nunnally, 1978). Values this low shed doubt on the ability of the test to measure anything in a consistent, accurate manner.

Given these guidelines, the data provide cause for concern. In his discussion of studies done by or before 1981, Westbrook (1983) provides the range and median internal consistency reliability coefficients found in each of several studies. Median coefficients ranged from .61 (Moore & McClean's 1977 study of the CMI Attitude Scale, Form A–1) to .91 (the sole study of the CSAP, at least as reported by Westbrook). Medians for the CVMT (.84), CMI Competence subtests (.83), and the ACD (.80) indicate adequate reliability, but each median reflects the results of only one study. Other studies reported coefficients below .80 for the CDI and for the CMI Competence Tests and Attitude Scale (Forms A–1 and A–2). In a subsequent report, Westbrook (1985) provided additional low, internal consistency coefficients, applying primarily to the CMI,

118

the CDI, the ACD, and the CVMT. (Note that the absence of negative evidence does not necessarily imply that the measure is reliable but, rather, that it just hasn't received as much research attention as the others.)

Although there is no doubt that research suggests inadequate internal consistency reliability, other studies of the same measures suggest adequate degrees of reliability. The lack of consistency in the evidence is most likely due to differences in the nature and quality of the studies which produced them. It is well known in psychometrics that the nature of the sample has a strong influence on the obtained reliability coefficient (see e.g., Anastasi, 1982; Nunnally, 1978). Specifically, use of more homogeneous samples has a depressing effect on reliability coefficients—a sample heterogeneous on the trait of interest will maximize the obtained reliability coefficient. Also, to the extent that a study is characterized by flaws in design and/or analysis, any result will tend to be more questionable than in a high quality study. In other words, the reliability coefficient obtained from a poorly designed study could be essentially randomly determined, falling anywhere between 0 and 1.0. Thus, one low reliability coefficient (or one high one for that matter) should be generalized only with caution. The overall pattern of findings from several or many studies is more generalizable. Although Westbrook's summaries are helpful and his efforts in this regard commendable, they do not evaluate the quality of the studies from which the findings are distilled.

Arguing against the necessity for internal consistency in measures of career maturity is Crites (1978c). Crites contends that low internal consistency in these measures may be an advantage in terms of predictive validity—a factorially complex measure may be a better predictor of factorially complex criteria, such as job satisfaction. Although there is some merit to this argument, the frequent use of separate subscales, rather than one heterogeneous total score, suggests that test authors are postulating unidimensional, logically meaningful dimensions within the broader constructs of career maturity or career adjustment in adulthood. When this is the case, internal consistency reliability is one essential basis for the justification of both separate scales and logically meaningful scale names.

Low reliability coefficients not only cast doubt on the extent to which some unidimensional construct is being measured as intended, they have devastating effects on the reliability of difference scores necessary to profile interpretation (Westbrook et al., 1980). Low reliability also restricts the extent to which measure will correlate with anything else, thus reducing validity. Westbrook argues that a correction for attenuation should be applied to less reliable instruments when estimating validity coefficients; there is considerable disagreement in the literature about this practice, with some (Nunnally, 1978) supporting it and others (e.g., Guilford, 1954; Mehrens & Lehman, 1978) arguing against it.

Regardless of one's point of view on the use of a correction for attenuation, Westbrook's plea does serve to illustrate the far-reaching effects of measures which possess inadequate internal consistency reliability. This is not the first review to call for greater attention to reliability by researchers and test developers and for considerable caution on the part of test users when using measures of relatively low reliability. If heterogeneity in item content is expected, that expectation should be integrated into the published definition of the construct to be measured. In this case, other types of reliability evidence, for example, alternate forms reliability or stability, should be provided. Also helpful in such cases would be factor analytical data.

Stability.   Stability, or test-retest reliability, indicates the degree to which the test scores are stable over time. In evaluating the size of stability coefficients, most would agree that they will probably be lower than the analogous internal consistency coefficients, particularly as the time interval from test to retest increases. Also, the nature of the trait, that is, its postulated fixity versus modifiability, must be considered; traits subject to maturation or intervention will probably be less stable over time than will traits thought to be relatively fixed.

Generally, there is insufficient evidence for the stability of neasures of career maturity. As of 1981, Westbrook (1983) provided median stability coefficients as follows: CDI scales Form 1 (.82 for 2–4 weeks and .67 for 6 months); CMI Attitude Scale Form A–1 (.78 over a 3-month interval, .71 over 12 months; .67 for 5 months, .60 for 4 months); the CMI Competence Subtests (.55 over 4 months); and ACD (.76 and .71 for 9 weeks). For comparative purposes it may be noted that the 1985 Occupational Scales of the SCII have been shown to have test-retest reliabilities of .92, .89, and .87 over 2-week, 30-day, and 3-year periods, respectively. The comparable values for the 1981 form were .91, .89, and .87 (Hansen & Campbell, 1985). These values, along with a general lack of evidence for many instruments, suggest that more attention to stability is needed. Zytowski (1978) recommends particular caution in the use of relatively unstable instruments to evaluate the effectiveness of interventions, because if scores vary this much without systematic intervention, our conclusions concerning interventions are cast in doubt.

Construct Validity: What Do the Measures Measure?

One of the most challenging yet inherently interesting current issues pertains to the question of the nature of the construct(s) measured by measures of career maturity. The nature of what is measured is the question of construct validity, and the types of evidence used in the analysis of construct validity include (but are not limited to) traditional validity considerations, such as content and criterion-related validity. We can *name* a scale anything we wish to, but a more sophisticated analysis is required to make hypotheses about what is actually measured versus what we *desire* to measure.

A number of writers have expressed concern about the pervasive lack of scientific agreement concerning what is career maturity and how it should be measured. Westbrook (1983) has stated that there is little consensus regarding the number, names, or organization of dimensions of career maturity, on the relative degree of emphasis of scales on cognitive, affective, and psychomotor behavior, on whether dimensions postulated should be covered using single- or multi-item scales, or in the range of emphasis on occupational information. When to this lack of rational or substantive agreement is added a lack of convergent validity among career maturity measures as a group, there is cause for concern (Westbrook, 1983). There are several ways of attempting to address these issues in a way which may clarify the nature of the concept and its measures; these include attempts to understand its dimensionality, either by rational or factor and cluster analytical means, and by attempts to understand its external validity or meaning, through analysis of information regarding correlations of career maturity scales with other variables. It is often helpful to construct a nomological network (Cronbach & Meehl, 1955) to assist in the interpretation of a construct and its measure(s).

Dimensionality: Rational Formulations. As mentioned previously, both Super and Crites formulated theories of vocational or career maturity and used these theories as at least a partial basis for developing their measures of career maturity. Both differentiated cognitive and affective career maturity, and both postulated and developed measures of subtypes of each. There is logical and, as will be seen, empirical support for this differentiation, so it seems conceptually helpful to at least begin with the assumption that career maturity includes two separate but related components, one cognitive and the other attitudinal. Westbrook's (1974) content analysis of six career development tests resulted in the formulation of a category for psychomotor behavior in addition to the cognitive and affective categories. Other rational attempts to define or distinguish components of career maturity are described herein.

Jepsen (1984) searched the literature for recurring themes of age-related behavioral changes and clustered the themes based on theoretical and empirical similarity. The 10 clusters of themes included several that related to career maturity concepts or measures: vocational-choice realism, vocational choice rationale, vocational-choice attitudes (the CMI Attitude scale), vocational decision-making processes (actually the ACDM), occupational knowledge, and vocational exploratory behavior, including scales of the ACD and the CDI. Note that the categories of attitudes, cognitive (occupational knowledge), and psychomotor (exploratory behavior) are all represented, as are several categories not directly associated with existing measures of career maturity.

Savickas (1984) also addressed the meaning of the construct of career maturity. Using the classic Stimulus–Organism–Response (S–O–R) paradigm (e.g., Crites, 1969), Savickas defined the Stimulus as consisting of vocational developmental tasks (as originally defined by Super), the Responses as coping behavior in relation to these tasks (for example, vocational exploratory behavior), and the

Organism variables as individual characteristics that mediate one's ability to cope with the tasks salient at that life stage. As an example, the task of crystallization (of a vocational preference or choice) requires the coping or response behaviors of information gathering and making educational plans. The O here might be the attitudes and competencies that mediate the degree to which the individual engages in adaptive responses. Savickas's paper shows how some of the major career maturity inventories fit into this system, but one of the particularly helpful features of Savickas's conceptualization is its differentiation of the cognitive/affective realm from the behavioral realm (the R). This model is also helpful in addressing the vexing question of what are the appropriate criterion measures in the validation of career maturity scales—in this model, coping responses and exploratory and planning behaviors would constitute the criteria (but see also the subsequent section on this topic).

Dimensionality: Cluster and Factor Analytical Studies.   Other investigators have cluster or factor analyzed career maturity instruments to attempt to discern their fundamental elements.

One of the earliest studies was that of Super and Overstreet (1960), who factor analyzed 27 indexes of career maturity as derived from psychometric and interview data. Subjects were the 140 ninth-grade boys in the Career Pattern Study. Five factors, accounting for 38% of the variance, were extracted: Planning Orientation, Independence of Work Experience, Long View Ahead (specificity of high school plans), and Intermediate View Ahead (Awareness of factors in choice). With the exception of the Independence of Work Experience, which may be in the behavioral category, and Short View Ahead, which may be a stage or certainty variable (see the Jepsen & Prediger study which will be described), the other factors appear to resemble the general cognitive career maturity factor.

Westbrook (1976a) factor analyzed 10 career maturity measures administered to 90 ninth-grade students. Before discussion of the findings it should be noted that the sample of 90 subjects provides fewer than the absolute minimum of 10 subjects per variable recommended for factor analytical studies. Given this serious problem, the major factor extracted included seven knowledge scales, including the scales of the CVMT, the CDI Information and Decision Making scale, and the CMI Attitude Scale (the Competence scales were not administered). The second factor consisted of CDI Planning Orientation and CDI Resources for Exploration, the two scales that asked the subject to provide a self-report of the things they have done or would do about their career development. Although Super calls these Affective scales, they seem more appropriately viewed as behavioral in nature. Thus, it appears that a cognitive/affective and a behavioral factor were yielded.

A major study by Jepsen and Prediger (1981) involved the administration of 10 career maturity and decision-making instruments to 237 high school students. In an examination of correlations between pairs of scale scores, clusters were formed such that cluster intercorrelations exceeded .45 and at least two instruments were represented in a cluster.

The first cluster consisted of the ACDM Exploration, Crystallization, and Choice stages, the ACD Certainty of Choice, and the CDS; all five assess certainty of choice. The second cluster, the CDI World of Work, CDI Career Decision Making, the CSAP Career Decision Making, and the ACD Career Planning seemed to assess ability to conceptualize career decisions; although the CMI Goal Selection scale (the only CMI Competencies subtest included in the study) did not meet the requirements of cluster membership, it was highly correlated with most of these scales. The cluster, also strongly related to reading achievement, seems to be similar to what other authors have called cognitive career maturity.

The third cluster included the CDI Extent of Planning and the ACD Career Planning Involvement scales, reflecting frequency of planning and information seeking. The CMI Attitude Scale, while belonging to no single cluster, correlated significantly with 11 of the 18 other scales; Jepsen and Prediger (1981) suggest that the CMI attitude scale is, therefore, the most broadly representative of the career maturity scales.

Although these findings were intuitively logical, Jepsen and Prediger make the very interesting observation that cluster membership was also strongly associated with item type. Specifically, Cluster 1 scales used mostly True–False or Agree–Disagree item formats, Cluster 2 scales were multiple-choice items, and Cluster 3 scales were Likert response formats. Thus, method variance (see Campbell & Fiske, 1959) may be playing a part in the strong cluster intercorrelations. Ideally, a study using a multitrait, multimethod matrix where each dimension would be measured using each format would help to separate the effects of method variance from the meaningful substantive variance.

Jepsen and Prediger also factor analyzed their data. They called the first factor that was derived ''Cognitive Resources for Decision Making''; the scales loading highly on the factor were the CMI (both the Attitude scale and the Goal Selection scale), the CSAP, the CDI, the ACD, and the Iowa Tests of Educational Development (a standardized academic achievement test). As in their cluster analysis, this seems to be the cognitive maturity factor, and it is again strongly related to academic achievement.

The second factor was career decision style, represented by Harren's ACDM. Jepsen and Prediger (1981) note that style has yet to be incorporated within the traditional theories of career maturity, that is, those of Super and Crites, but is part of Harren's model.

The third factor was called ''Systematic Involvement in Career Decision Making.'' This factor represented experience as opposed to knowledge, as the first factor did. The fourth factor was exploration as opposed to certainty/commitment, like the analogous clusters of status or stage in the career decision-making process. Of the major instruments, the CMI Attitude scales correlated with the first and fourth factor but not the second and third, which would logically be expected for the Involvement, Independence, and Orientation subscales. Super's CDI cognitive scales loaded, as predicted, on Factor 1; his noncognitive scales loaded on Factor 3, as expected, although Extent of Planning loaded more highly on factor 4 than 3.

Finally, there have been several studies factor analyzing the scales within one career maturity instrument; some of these suggest the clear existence of both an effective and a cognitive factor (Super & Thompson, 1979; Wallbrown et al., 1986), but Westbrook et al. (1980) found only one factor in their analyses of the CMI.

Although the nature and extent of the attitudinal dimension needs further clarification, there seems to be no doubt that a significant component of career maturity, both the concept and the measures, is the cognitive component. Consisting of occupational information and knowledge of decision-making processes, this component is consistently and strongly related to academic achievement; thus cognitive career maturity appears analogous in some to any other type of achievement, for example, in American history, chemistry, etc.

There also seems to be a basis to conclude the existence of a behavioral component, for example, active exploratory behavior, measured by some of the available scales. In postulating a behavioral component, however, particular care needs to be taken that antecedents and consequents of career maturity are differentiated from career maturity as a psychological construct. It may well be, for example, that exploratory behavior and career-related experience are important antecedents of cognitive and/or attitudinal career maturity. Further, a psychological construct of career maturity cannot continue to justify its existence without evidence for its influence on subsequent, important behavioral outcomes. Perhaps adaptive and coping behaviors are among the outcomes of a state of career maturity. Thus, the degree to which behavioral indexes are antecedents, consequents, or the trait itself (or in Savickas's 1984 terms, the S, the O, or the R) has tremendous impact on our understanding of the construct. It is with respect to this issue that nomological networks or path models specifying not only the important variables but the extent and *direction* of the interrelationships are essential if further progress in understanding is to occur.

And finally, there are theoretical, intuitive, and empirical grounds to support the existence of attitudinal components of career maturity, but further validation of a separate attitudinal dimension requires more research where the use of more than one attitudinal scale, as well as multiple cognitive and behavioral scales, allows the emergence of a separate attitudinal factor. The recent study of Wallbrown et al., using all five CMI Attitude Scales, is a good beginning, and more work extending and replicating these findings would lend credence to the existence of attitudinal career maturity.

Obviously, the cognitive, attitudinal, behavioral/psychomotor distinction has major practical importance, but it is also essential in interpreting validity data.

For example, in evaluating convergent validity data, it is valid only to interpret the values of correlations between scales measuring similar constructs. Interpreting a low correlation between a cognitive and behavioral measure or a cognitive and affective measure as indicative of a lack of concurrent validity is not appropriate, even if a more general overall factor is also postulated. It is imperative that the relationships among cognitive, attitudinal, and behavioral career maturity be hypothesized and studied empirically; until this receives more attention, a crucial aspect of the construct of career maturity will remain murky.

The Criterion Problem: What are the Consequences of Career Maturity?   Overall, there is a lack of evidence regarding the criterion-related validity of measures of career maturity. Criterion-related validity, a component of construct validity, involves our hypotheses concerning the consequences of possessing various levels of the trait in question. In other words, to what outcomes do we hypothesize that high, moderate, or low levels of career maturity will lead? Unless a measure can be shown to be related to subsequent behavioral or attitudinal outcomes having some real-world importance, its existence and the need for the construct are difficult to justify. Thus, inadequate evidence for criterion-related validity could prove to be a fatal flaw for the survival of both constructs and instruments.

Related to the lack of criterion-related validity data is disagreement concerning the appropriate criteria, or outcomes, of career mature behavior. Criteria have varied markedly across studies, but have included the following: (1) educational criteria such as GPA, educational achievement, persistence in college, and success and satisfaction in vocational training; (2) career-choice content criteria, such as the realism of choice, level of educational and occupational aspiration; and (3) career-choice status, that is, decidedness or certainty versus indecision and uncertainty, and commitment to a career choice. However, some of these criteria may be inappropriate.

For example, vocational decidedness is not necessarily a "good" outcome if the decision was reached hastily or for reasons in conflict with one's personal characteristics and "wants"—thus, use of decidedness alone without assessment of the quality of the decision may not be a good indicator of career mature behavior. Similarly, level of aspiration, by itself, is not necessarily "good" if the level is unrealistically high. And educational achievement criteria seem generally inappropriate since there is already concern about the independence of career maturity measures from intellective measures. To use a measure of which a large portion of variance is ability variance to predict a criterion which is also largely ability variance is neither informative nor a fair test of criterion-related validity. Use of criteria reflecting *vocational* outcomes and, to the extent possible, criteria which are not largely ability related is vital.

Other suggestions regarding the selection of criteria are as follows (see also Fretz, 1981, and Oliver, 1979, for further discussion of the use of outcome criteria in career interventions). First and foremost there should be a clearly formulated theory which postulates the behavioral outcomes, both short- and long-term, of career maturity. As an example, Crites's original model of career maturity in adolescence, by postulating outcomes related to the content of career choice, that is, realism and consistency, illustrates the kind of theory needed to provide a rationale for the selection of criterion measures.

Second, multiple rather than single criteria should be used. Also, the use of varied criteria, a combination of behavioral and attitudinal measures, will enhance generalizability of resulting validity evidence. When using multiple criteria, analytical methods which consider criteria as well as predictors simultaneously, for example, canonical correlation, should be used. Only when statistical methods control for collinearity among criteria as well as among predictors can the true nature and extent of the interrelationships be discerned.

Another vital and usually neglected issue concerns the reliability and validity of the criterion measures themselves. Researchers should either use measures of known quality or should investigate the psychometric characteristics of the criteria in a pilot study or, at the least, as part of the validation study. A correlation between two measures is only informative to the extent to which both are of adequate quality—attempting to validate a test, no matter how carefully constructed, against a poor criterion is a wasteful and hopeless endeavor. Generally, the use of multi-item, objective measures will offer more potential of reliable and valid criterion assessment than will single-item questions and/or subjective, self-report questions regarding the same behavior the measure of career maturity is designed to measure.

Finally, as pointed out by Fretz (1981), more emphasis on actual job-related behaviors, for example, job-hunting activity and success and subsequent vocational success and satisfaction is necessary to demonstrate that the concept of carrer maturity has relevance beyond the educational realm. And now that the measures have been extended into the adult years, this recommendation is even more important.

Validity: The Need for Structural or Path Models.   The current state of the art in the understanding of career maturity would be greatly facilitated by the development and evaluation of structural or path models, also known as nomological networks (Cronbach & Meehl, 1955) specifying the system of variables within which the construct of career maturity occurs. Based on logical analysis and empirical evidence, a preliminary model was developed and is presented for illustrative purposes in Fig. 3.2. This model is not meant to summarize the research comprehensively but rather to give the reader an idea of how such a model might be constructed. In the figure, circles represent hypothetical constructs. In a path analysis, each circle would be measured by one instrument, and if the more general statistical and theory-testing method of structural equation modeling were used, each circle would be represented by at least two measures.

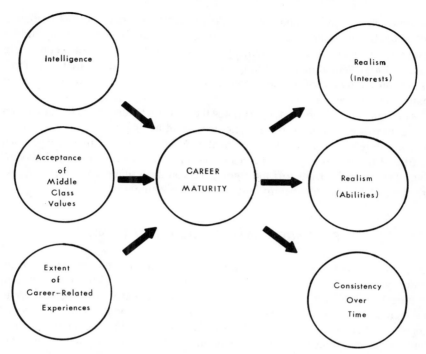

Fig. 3.2. A hypothetical path model illustrating possible antecedents to (the left side) and consequences of (the right side) of a psychological construct of career maturity.

For the sake of simplicity, no actual measures are depicted in the figure, but it should be obvious that a construct and its interrelationships can only be studied if they are operationalized in some observable way, such as a test score.

In this model, a psychological construct of career maturity is postulated to have both antecedents (the variables to the left) and consequents (those to the right). It is herein postulated that one of the antecedents to career maturity is higher versus lower intelligence, which positively influences school performance as well as career maturity. Other antecedents postulated are a construct called "acceptance of middle class values," which Crites (1978c) postulates is the explanation for race and SES differences in career maturity, and "extent of career-related experiences during childhood and adolescence," for example, a variety of occupational role models, the opportunity to learn about a variety of careers, and work experience. (Remember that this model is hypothetical and illustrative only.)

Note that use of intelligence as an antecedent allows the theoretical integration of evidence regarding moderate to high career maturity–intelligence correlations without necessarily rendering unnecessary the former construct. As long as there are other antecedents to and consequents of career maturity after the partialing out of intelligence, the construct can be meaningful and important. Only further research can answer these questions, but a model such as that shown could help guide efforts. A final note regarding the left side of the model is that it attempts to explain the nature of the development of career maturity by constructs other than simply advancing age.

The right side of the model postulates the constructs thought to be influenced *by* career maturity. For example, the outcomes of having made a realistic career decision in terms of interest/environment and abilities/environment congruence or fit and the consistency of choices over time are based on the Crites model. Even farther to the right (off the figure) we could postulate vocational success and satisfaction as longer-term outcomes of career maturity.

SUMMARY AND RECOMMENDATIONS

In summary, there is considerable current attention to the measurement of career maturity and career development. Several new measures, the appearance of technical manuals for several existing instruments, extensions of the concept to the measurement of career adaptability or adjustment in adults, and a number of major new books and articles, including dialogues regarding the quality of measures of career maturity, point to a continuing high level of interest in the concept and its measurement.

However, there are several serious problems which research should address more systematically and in more depth. Probably the most serious problem is the lack of agreement among researchers concerning the nature and definition of the concept of career maturity, either in adolescence or adulthood. Although few would disagree that career maturity contains both cognitive and attitudinal components, the definition and relative importance of these varies widely across researchers. Further, theoretical integration of the concepts and measures as applied to adolescents versus adults is also largely lacking. And understanding of the constructs of career maturity and development is further hampered by the problems with both internal consistency reliability and test-retest stability and the use of single-versus-multiple criteria and criteria which are poorly conceptualized and defined and of questionable reliability and validity.

A number of recommendations for further research are possible. First, the practical popularity of measures of career maturity, for example, for use in career counseling and for the evaluation of the effectiveness of career education programs, has very likely drawn the efforts of researchers away from theoretical issues. Yet the science of vocational psychology cannot progress unless theory development and explication and the development of reliable and valid measures of important constructs receive high priority. We seem to be on a path of theoretical divergence as different researchers pursue different definitions and instruments—while different points of view are, of course, essential in science there is also a periodic need for integrative work, for a search for theoretical convergence rather than divergence. The work of Savikas (1984) and Jepsen and Prediger (1981), among others, serves as an excellent start on the integrative process but more such work is necessary.

Second, this area of research has not fully utilized the rich variety of new multivariate statistical techniques and methods for theory development and testing using nonexperimental as well as experimental designs. Multivariate techniques which could probably be used profitably more often than they are now include canonical correlation in analyses of the relationships between multiple predictors (e.g., measures of career maturity) and multiple criteria of career maturity. Multivariate techniques, such as factor analysis, have received considerable use, but their use in the analysis of criterion measures as well as career maturity measures could prove useful.

Most importantly, as was discussed and illustrated in the previous section, the field would benefit from increased use of methods of construct validation and theory testing. First, Campbell and Fiske's (1959) multitrait, multimethod, matrix methodology in which several different instruments are used to measure several different constructs should receive more use. The method allows the separation of trait from method variance and could thus help elucidate the nature of correlations between different measures of the same construct—in this vein it is recommended that cognitive and attitudinal career maturity be considered as separate but related constructs since one is a measure of maximum and the other a measure of typical performance. For example, several cognitive scales could be included in an MTMM study with several attitudinal scales and, perhaps, several measures of career decidedness. Such a design would allow the examination of convergent validity (the extent to which measures of the same construct measure the same thing), discriminant validity (the extent to which theoretically different constructs are measuring similar or different things), and trait-versus-method variance, that is, the extent to which measures using the same method are correlated by virtue of shared method variance versus shared trait variance.

To examine theories of career maturity, methods of path analysis, confirmatory factor analysis, and more general structural equation modeling are recommended. The process of developing a path or structural model, such as that shown in Fig. 3.2, requires the researchers to formulate carefully both the important variables in a theory, in this case of theory of career maturity, and the nature and direction of their influences upon each other. Once such a model is formulated, it can be tested statistically using SEM; even better, alternative models can be compared with each other for "goodness of fit" with the data and/or they can be tested for differential quality of fit across populations. Even when the data do not support the theory as formulated they provide information which can be used to revise the theory. Thus, over time, the researcher should be able to progress toward sounder theories, using better measures of the central constructs.

Although these recommendations would require significant time and effort from researchers, it should be noted that the concept of career development and maturity are among those for which the field of vocational psychology has received considerable attention and recognition in other fields, for example, career education, organizational behavior/management sciences, etc. Thus, such efforts would be most worthwhile for theoretical as well as applied purposes. It is hoped that this chapter will serve to reinvigorate those who have been engaged in research on career maturity, as well as stimulate interest in researchers who have not heretofore been involved in this area. The efforts are much needed and have the potential of significant contribution to the understanding of career development and decision-making processes throughout the life span.

REFERENCES

Abernathy, L. J. (1980). A response to the review of the Career Skills Assessment Program. *Measurement & Evaluation in Guidance, 13,* 116–119.

Alvi, S. A., & Khan, S. B. (1982). A study of the criterion-related validity of Crites' CMI. *Educational & Psychological Measurement, 42,* 1285–1288.

Alvi, S. A., & Khan, S. B. (1983). An investigation into the construct validity of Crites' CMI. *Journal of Vocational Behavior, 22,* 174–181.

American College Testing (1973). *The ACT assessment of career development.* Iowa City: Author.

American Educational Research Association, American Psychological Association, National Council on Measurement in Education. (1985). *Standards for educational and psychological testing.* Washington, DC: American Psychological Association.

Anastasi, A. (1982). *Psychological testing* (5th ed.). New York: Macmillan.

Bartlett, W. E. (1968). Vocational maturity and personality variables of manpower trainees. *Vocational Guidance Quarterly, 17,* 104–108.

Bodden, J. L. (1978). Review of the New Mexico career education test series. In O. K. Buros (Ed.), *Eighth mental measurements yearbook.* Highland Park, NJ: Gryphon Press.

Borgen, F. H., Layton, W. L., Veenhuizen, D. L., & Johnson, D. J. (1985). Vocational behavior and career development, 1984: A review. *Journal of Vocational Behavior, 27,* 218–269.

Brown, D., & Brooks, L. (1984). *Career choice and development.* San Francisco: Jossey Bass.

Buehler, C. (1933). *Der Menschliche Lebenslauf als psychologisches problem.* Leipzig: Hirzel.

Campbell, R. E. & Cellini, J. V. (1981). A diagnostic taxonomy of adult career problems. *Journal of Vocational Behavior, 19,* 175–190.

Campbell, R. E., Cellini, J. V., Shaltry, P. E., Long, A. E., Pinkos, D., & Crites, J. O. (1979). *A diagnostic taxonomy of adult career problems.* Columbus, OH: National Center for Research in Vocational Education.

Campbell, D. T., & Fiske, D. W. (1959). Convergent and discriminant validation by the multitrait-multimethod matrix. *Psychological Bulletin, 56,* 81–105.

Campbell, B. A. & Johnson, S. O. (1970). *Short occupational knowledge tests.* Chicago: Science Research Associates.

Capehart, R. (1965). *The relationship of vocational maturity to Holland's theory of vocational choice.* Unpublished doctoral dissertation, University of North Carolina.

Carek, R. (1965). *The interrelations between social desirability, vocational maturity, vocational realism, and vocational decision,* unpublished master's thesis, University of Iowa.

Cattell, R. B. (1963). Theory of fluid and crystallized intelligence: A critical experiment. *Journal of Educational Psychology, 54,* 1–22.

Chodzinski, R. T., & Randhawa, B. S. (1983). Validity of the career maturity inventory. *Educational & Psychological Measurement, 43,* 1163–1173.

College Entrance Examination Board. (1978). *Handbook for the career skills assessment program.* New York: Author.

Cole, N. S. (1978). Review of the Career Awareness Inventory. In O. K. Buros (Ed.), *Eighth mental measurement yearbook.* Highland Park, NJ: Gryphon Press.

Cole, N. S. (1982a). Establishing reliability and validity for measures of career maturity. In J. D. Krumboltz & D. A. Hamel (Eds.), *Assessing career development.* Palo Alto, CA: Mayfield.

Cole, N. S. (1982b). Review of the Career Awareness Inventory. In J. T. Kapes & M. M. Mastie (Eds.), *A counselor's guide to vocational guidance instruments.* Falls Church, VA: National Vocational Guidance Association.

Crites, J. O. (1961). A model for the measurement of vocational maturity. *Journal of Counseling Psychology, 8,* 255–259.

Crites, J. O. (1964). Proposals for a new criterion measure and research design. In H. Borow (Ed.), *Man in a world at work.* Boston: Houghton Mifflin.

Crites, J. O. (1965). Measurement of vocational maturity in adolescence. I. Attitude test of the Vocational Development Inventory. *Psychological Monographs, 79*(2), (Whole No. 595).

Crites, J. O. (1969). *Vocational psychology.* New York: McGraw–Hill.

Crites, J. O. (1973). *Career Maturity Inventory.* Monterey, CA: CTB/McGraw–Hill.

Crites, J. O. (1976). A comprehensive model of career development in early adulthood. *Journal of Vocational Behavior, 9,* 105–118.

Crites, J. O. (1978a). *Career maturity inventory.* Monterey, CA: CTB/McGraw–Hill.

Crites, J. O. (1978b). *Career maturity inventory: Administration and use manual.* Monterey, CA: CTB/McGraw–Hill.

Crites, J. O. (1978c). *Career maturity inventory: Theory and research handbook.* Monterey, CA: CTB/McGraw–Hill.

Crites, J. O. (1978d). *Manual for the career maturity inventory for adults.* Monterey, CA: CTB/McGraw–Hill.

Crites, J. O. (1979a). *The career adjustment and development inventory.* College Park, MD: Crites Career Consultants, Inc.

Crites, J. O. (1979b). Validation of the diagnostic taxonomy of adult career problems: A pilot study. In Campbell et al. (Eds.), *A diagnostic taxonomy of adult career problems.* Columbus, OH: National Center for Research in Vocational Education.

Crites, J. O. (1981a). *Career counseling: Models, methods, and materials.* New York: McGraw–Hill.

Crites, J. O. (1981b). *Career maturity inventory: Theory and research handbook* (2nd ed.). Monterey, CA: CTB/McGraw–Hill.

Crites, J. O. (1982). Testing for career adjustment and development. *Training & Development Journal,* February, 20–24.

Crites, J. O., Wallbrown, F. H., & Blaha, J. (1985). The career maturity inventory: Myths and realities. A rejoinder to Westbrook, Cutts, Madison, & Arcia. *Journal of Vocational Behavior, 26,* 221–238.

Cronbach, L. J. (1984). *Essentials of psychological testing.* (4th ed.). New York: Harper & Row.

Cronbach, L. J., & Meehl, P. E. (1955). Construct validity in psychological tests. *Psychological Bulletin, 52,* 281–302.

Dawis, R. V., England, G. W., & Lofquist, L. H. (1964). A theory of work adjustment. *Minnesota Studies in Vocational Rehabilitation, V.*

Dawis, R. V., & Lofqist, L. H. (1984). *A psychological theory of work adjustment.* Minneapolis, MN: University of Minnesota Press.

Dawis, R. V., Lofquist, L. H., & Weiss, D. J. (1968). A theory of work adjustment (a revision). *Minnesota Studies in Vocational Rehabilitation, XXIII*.

DeFrank, R. S., & Ivancevich, J. M. (1986). Job loss: An individual level review and model. *Journal of Vocational Behavior, 28*, 1–20.

Fadale, L. M. (1974). *Career Awareness Inventory (Elementary)*. Bensenville, IL: Scholastic Testing Service.

Fadale, L. M. (1980). *Career Awareness Inventory (Advanced)*. Bensenville, IL: Scholastic Testing Service.

Feingold, S. N., Swerdloff, S., & Barber, J. E. (1978). *Occupations and Careers Information BOXSCORE, Series A*. Moravia, NY: Chronicle Guidance Publications.

Fitzgerald, L. F. (1984). *The developmental process of career adjustment during the establishment stage*. Paper presented at the annual convention of the American Psychological Association, Toronto.

Fretz, B. R. (1981). Evaluating career interventions. *Journal of Counseling Psychology, 28*, 77–90.

Fulton, B., & Tolsma, R. (1974). *Orientation to career concepts series*. St. Louis: Evaluative Research Associates.

Ginzberg, E., Ginsburg, S., Axelrad, J., & Herma, J. (1951). *Occupational choice*. New York: Columbia University Press.

Graves, T. D. (1974). *A study of vocational maturity and college students' certainty and commitment to career choice*. Unpublished doctoral dissertation, University of Northern Colorado.

Greenhaus, J. H. (1971). An investigation of the role of career salience in vocational behavior. *Journal of Vocational Behavior, 1*, 209–216.

Greenhaus, J. H. (1985). Review of the career skills assessment program. In J. V. Mitchell, Jr. (Ed.), *Ninth mental measurements yearbook*. Lincoln, NB: Buros Institute of Mental Measurements.

Greenhaus, J. H., & Parasuraman, S. (1986). Vocational and organizational behavior, 1985: A review. *Journal of Vocational Behavior, 29*, 115–176.

Guilford, J. P. (1954). *Psychometric theory*. New York: McGraw–Hill.

Hall, D. W. (1962). *Vocational development in adolescence: The measurement of vocational maturity*. Unpublished master's thesis, University of Iowa.

Hanna, G. S. & Neely, M. A. (1978). Reliability of the CMI Attitude Scale. *Measurement & Evaluation in Guidance, 11*, 114–116.

Hansen, J. C. (1985). Test review: Career development inventory. *Measurement & Evaluation in Counseling & Development, 17*, 220–223.

Hansen, J. C., & Campbell, D. P. (1985). *Manual for the Strong–Campbell Interest Inventory (4th ed.)*. Palo Alto, CA: Consulting Psychologists' Press.

Healy, C. C. (1976). Author's reply to Prediger and Westbrook reviews of the NMCET. *Measurement & Evaluation in Guidance, 8*, 266–268.

Healy, C. C., & Klein, S. P. (1973). *Manual for the New Mexico career education test series*. Hollywood, CA: Monitor.

Heath, D. H. (1976). Adolescent and adult predictors of vocational adaptation. *Journal of Vocational Behavior, 9*, 1–20.

Hill, R. E., Miller, E. L., & Lowther, M. A. (Eds.) (1981). *Adult career transitions*. Ann Arbor: University of Michigan.

Holland, J. L. (1973). *Making vocational choices*. Englewood Cliffs, NJ: Prentice–Hall.

Holland, J. L. (1985). *Making vocational choices: A theory of vocational personalities and work environments* (2nd ed.). Englewood Cliffs, NJ: Prentice–Hall.

Holland, J. L., Daiger, D., & Power, P. G. (1980). *My vocational situation*. Palo Alto, CA: Consulting Psychologists Press.

Hollender, J. W. (1964). Interrelationships of *vocational maturity, consistency and realism of vocational choice, school grade, and age in adolescence.* Unpublished master's thesis, University of Iowa.

Hoppock, R. (1935). *Job satisfaction.* New York: Harper & Row.

Jepsen, D. A. (1984). The developmental perspective on vocational behavior: A review of theory and research. In S. D. Brown & R. W. Lent (Eds.), *Handbook of counseling psychology* (pp. 178–215). New York: Wiley.

Jepsen, D. A. & Prediger, D. P. (1981). Dimensions of adolescent career development:A multi-instrument analysis. *Journal of Vocational Behavior, 19,* 350–368.

Johnson, R. P. (1982). Assessing retirement maturity. *Measurement & Evaluation in Guidance, 15,* 221–227. Kapes, J. T., & Mastie, M. M. (1982). *A counselor's guide to vocational guidance instruments.* Falls Church, VA: NVGA.

Katz, M. R. (1978). Review of the career maturity inventory. In O. K. Buros (Ed.), *Eighth mental measurements yearbook.* Highland Park, NJ: Gryphon Press.

Katz, M. R. (1982). Review of the career maturity inventory. In J. Kapes & M. Mastie (Eds.), *A counselor's guide to vocational guidance instruments.* (pp. 122–125). Falls Church, VA: NVGA.

Khan, S. B., & Alvi, S. A. (1983). Educational, social, and psychological correlates of vocational maturity. *Journal of Vocational Behavior, 22,* 357–364.

Krumboltz, J. D., & Hamel, D. A. (1982). *Assessing career development.* Palo Alto, CA: Mayfield.

Loesch, L. C., Rucker, B. B., & Shub, P. A. (1978). A field test of an instrument for assessing job knowledge. *Measurement & Evaluation in Guidance, 11,* 26–33.

Lofquist, L. H., & Dawis, R. V. (1969). *Adjustment to work.* New York: Appleton–Century–Crofts.

Lokan, J. (1983). *Career Development Inventory: Australia.* Hawthorn, Victoria, Australia: Australian Council for Educational Research.

Lokan, J. (1984). *Manual for the Career Development Inventory: Australia.* Hawthorn, Victoria, Australia: Australian Council for Educational Research.

London, M., & Stumpf, S. (1982). *Managing careers.* Reading, MA: Addison–Wesley.

Marshall, J. C. (1980). *Occupational awareness inventory.* St. Louis: Evaluative Research Associates.

Mehrens, W. A., & Lehman, I.J. (1978). *Measurement and evaluation in education and psychology.* New York: Holt, Rinehart, & Winston.

Miller, D. C., & Form, W. H. (1947). Measuring patterns of occupational security. *Sociometry, 10,* 362–375.

Mitchell, J. V., Jr. (1985). *Ninth mental measurements yearbook.* Lincoln, NB: Buros Institute of Mental Measurements.

Mitchell, L. K. (1982). Career education measures. In J. D. Krumboltz & D. A. Hamel (Eds.), *Assessing career development.* Palo Alto, CA: Mayfield.

Moore, T. L., & McLean, J.E. (1977). A validation study of the CMI Attitude Scale. *Measurement & Evaluation in Guidance, 10,* 113–116.

Morrison, R. F. (1977). Career adaptivity: The effective adaptation of managers to changing role demands. *Journal of Applied Psychology, 62,* 549–558.

Nevill, D. E., & Super, D. E. (1986). *Manual for the Salience Inventory: Theory, application, and research.* Palo Alto, CA: Consulting Psychologists Press.

Nunnally, J. (1978). *Psychometric theory* (2nd Ed.). New York: McGraw–Hill.

Oliver, L. W. (1979). Outcome measurement in career counseling research. *Journal of Counseling Psychology, 3,* 217–226.

Osipow, S. H. (1980). *Manual for the Career Decision Scale.* Odessa, FL: Psychological Assessment Resources.

Osipow, S. E. (1983). *Theories of career development* (3rd ed.). Englewood Cliffs, NJ: Prentice–Hall.

Osipow, S. H., & Spokane, A. R. (1983). *A manual for measures of occupational stress, strain, and coping.* Columbus, OH: Marathon Consulting & Press.

Osipow, S. H. (1984). Measuring occupational stress, strain, and coping. In S. Oskamp (ed.), *Applied Social Psychology Annual, 5,* 67–87.

Parsons, F. (1909). *Choosing a vocation.* Boston: Houghton Mifflin.

Phillips, S. D. (1982a). Career exploration in adulthood. *Journal of Vocational Behavior, 20,* 129–140.

Phillips, S. D. (1982b). The development of career choices: The relationship between patterns of commitment and career outcomes in adulthood. *Journal of Vocational Behavior, 20,* 141–152.

Pinkney, J. W. (1985). Review of the career development inventory. In J. V. Mitchell, Jr. (Ed.), *Ninth mental measurements yearbook.* Lincoln, NB: Buros Institute of Mental Measurements.

Prediger, D. P. (1976). Review of the New Mexico Career Education Test. *Measurement & Evaluation in Guidance, 8,* 260–262.

Rabinowitz, S., & Hall, T. (1981). Changing correlates of job involvement in three career stages. *Journal of Vocational Behavior, 18,* 138–144.

Rummel, R. J. (1970). *Applied factor analysis.* Evanston, IL: Northwestern University Press.

Savickas, M. L. (1984). Measuring career maturity: The construct and its measurement. *Vocational Guidance Quarterly, 32,* 222–231.

Sink, C. (1980). Review of the career awareness inventory. *Measurement & Evaluation in Guidance, 13,* 120–122.

Slocum, J. W., Jr., & Cron, W. L. (1985). Job attitudes and performance during three career stages. *Journal of Vocational Behavior, 26,* 126–145.

Slocum, J. W., Jr., Cron, W. L., Hansen, R. W., & Rawlings, S. (1985). Business strategy and the management of plateaued employees. *Academy of Management Journal, 28,* 133–152.

Smith, M. L. (1978). Review of the career awareness inventory. In O. K. Buros (Ed.), *Eighth mental measurements yearbook.* Highland Park, NJ: Gryphon Press.

Stumpf, S., & Rabinowitz, S. (1981). Career stage as a moderator of performance relationships with facets of job satisfaction and role perceptions. *Journal of Vocational Behavior, 18,* 202–218.

Super, D. E. (1955). The dimensions and measurements of vocational maturity. *Teachers College Record, 57,* 151–163.

Super, D. E. (1957). *The psychology of careers.* New York: Harper & Row.

Super, D. E. (Ed.) (1974). *Measuring vocational maturity for counseling and evaluation.* Washington, DC: NVGA.

Super, D. E. (1977). Vocational maturity in midcareer. *Vocational Guidance Quarterly, 25,* 294–302.

Super, D. E. (1980). A life-span, life-space approach to career development. *Journal of Vocational Behavior, 16,* 282–298.

Super, D. E. (1983). Assessment in career guidance: Toward truly developmental counseling. *Personnel & Guidance Journal,* May, 555–562.

Super, D. E. (1985). Coming of age in Middletown: Careers in the making. *American Psychologist, 40,* 405–414.

Super, D. E., Crites, J. O., Hummel, R. C., Moser, H. P., Overstreet, P. L., & Warnath, C. F. (1957). *Vocational development: A Framework for research.* New York: Teachers College Press.

Super, D. E. & Forrest, D. H. (1972). *Preliminary manual for the Career Development Inventory.* New York: Teachers College, Columbia University.

Super, D. E., & Nevill, D. D. (1984). Work role salience as a determinant of career maturity in high school students. *Journal of Vocational Behavior, 25*, 30–44.

Super, D. E., & Overstreet, P. L. (1960). *The vocational maturity of ninth grade boys.* New York: Teachers College Press.

Super, D. E., & Thompson, A. S. (1979). A six-scale, two-factor test of vocational maturity. *Vocational Guidance Quarterly, 27*, 6–15.

Super, D. E., Thompson, A. S., Lindeman, R. H., Jordaan, J. P., & Myers, R. A. (1979). *Career development inventory: School form.* Palo Alto, CA: Consulting Psychologists Press.

Super, D. E., Thompson, A. S., Lindeman, R. H., Jordaan, J. P., & Myers, R. A. (1981). *Career development inventory: College form.* Palo Alto, CA: Consulting Psychologists Press.

Super, D. E., Thompson, A. S., Lindeman, R. H., Myers, R. A., & Jordaan, J. P. (1985). *Adult career concerns inventory.* Palo Alto, CA: Consulting Psychologists Press.

Thompson, A. S., Lindeman, R. H., Super, D. E., Jordaan, J. P., & Myers, R. A. (1981). *Career development inventory. Vol 1: User's Manual.* Palo Alto, CA: Consulting Psychologists Press.

Thompson, A. S., Lindeman, R. H., Super, D. E., Jordaan, J. P., & Myers, R. A. (1982). *Career development inventory. College and university form. Supplement to user's manual.* Palo Alto, CA: Consulting Psychologists Press.

Thompson, A. S., Lindeman, R. H., Super, D. E., Jordaan, J. P. (1984). *Career Development Inventory: Volume 2: Technical manual.* Palo Alto: Consulting Psychologists Press.

Thurstone, L. L. (1947). *Multiple factor analysis.* Chicago: University of Chicago Press.

Tiedeman, D. V., & O'Hara, R. P. (1963). *Career development: Choice and adjustment.* New York: College Entrance Examination Board.

Tinsley, H. E. A., & Heesacker, M. (1984). Vocational behavior and career development, 1983: A review. *Journal of Vocational Behavior, 25*, 139–190.

Vernon, P. E. (1960). *The structure of human abilities.* London: Methuen.

Wallbrown, F. H., Silling, S. M., & Crites, J. O. (1986). Testing Crites' model of career maturity: A hierarchical strategy. *Journal of Vocational Behavior, 28*, 183–190.

Walsh, W. B., & Betz, N. E. (1985). *Tests and assessment.* Englewood Cliffs, NJ: Prentice–Hall.

Walsh, W. B. & Osipow, S. H. (1973). Career preferences, self-concept, and career maturity. *Research in Higher Education, 1*, 287–295.

Walsh, W. B. & Osipow, S. H. (1983). (Eds.) *Handbook of vocational psychology: Volumes I, II.* Hillsdale, NJ: Lawrence Erlbaum Associates.

Weiss, D. J. (1970). Factor analysis and counseling psychology research. *Journal of Counseling Psychology, 17*, 477–485.

Weiss, D. J. (1971). Further considerations in applications of factor analysis. *Journel of Counseling Psychology, 18*, 85–92.

Westbrook, B. W. (1974). Content analysis of six career development tests. *Measurement & Evaluation in Guidance, 7*, 172–180.

Westbrook, B. W. (1976a). Interrelationship of career choice competencies and career choice attitudes of ninth grade pupils: Testing hypotheses derived from Crites' theory of career maturity. *Journal of Vocational Behavior, 8*, 1–12.

Westbrook, B. W. (1976b). Review of the New Mexico Career Education Test Series. *Measurement & Evaluation in Guidance, 8*, 263–266.

Westbrook, B. W. (1982). Construct validation of career maturity measures. In J. Krumboltz & D. Hamel (Eds.), *Assessing career development* (pp. 66–112). Palo Alto, CA: Mayfield.

Westbrook, B. W. (1983). Career maturity: The concept, the instrument, and the research. In W. B. Walsh & S. H. Osipow (Eds.), *Handbook of vocational psychology* (pp. 261–303). Hillsdale, NJ: Lawrence Erlbaum Associates.

Westbrook, B. W. (1985). What research says about career maturity: A response to Crites, Wallbrown, & Blaha (1985). *Journal of Vocational Behavior, 26*, 239–250.

Westbrook, B. W., Cutts, C. C., Madison, S. S., & Arcia, M. A. (1980). The validity of the Crites' model of career maturity. *Journal of Vocational Behavior, 16*, 249–281.

Westbrook, B. W., & Mastie, M. M. (1973). Three measures of career maturity: A beginning to know about. *Measurement & Evaluation in Guidance, 6*, 8–16.

Westbrook, B. W., & Mastie, M. M. (1974). The Cognitive Vocational Maturity Test. In D. E. Super (Ed.), *Measuring vocational maturity for counseling and evaluation* (pp. 41–50). Washington, D.C.: APGA.

Westbrook, B. W., & Parry–Hill, J. W., Jr. (1973). The measurement of cognitive vocational maturity. *Journal of Vocational Behavior, 3*, 239–252.

Westbrook, B. W., & Rogers, B. (1980). Review of the career skills assessment program. *Measurement & Evaluation in Guidance, 13*, 107–115.

Westbrook, B. W., Sanford, E. E., O'Neal, P., Horne, D. F., Fleenor, J., & Garren, R. (1985). Predictive and construct validity of six experimental measures of career maturity. *Journal of Vocational Behavior, 27*, 338–355.

Wiggins, J. D. (1985). Review of the career skills assessment program. In J. V. Mitchell, Jr. (Ed.), *Ninth mental measurements yearbook*. Lincoln, NB: Buros Institute of Mental Measurements.

Williamson, E. G. (1939). *How to counsel students*. New York: McGraw–Hill.

Yen, F. B., & Healy, C. C. (1977). The effects of work experience on two scales of career development. *Measurement & Evaluation in Guidance, 10*, 175–177.

Zunker, V. G. (1981). *Career counseling: Applied concepts of life planning*. Monterey, CA: Brooks/Cole.

Zunker, V. G. (1982). *Using assessment results in career counseling*. Monterey, CA: Brooks/Cole.

Zytowski, D. G. (1978). Review of the Career Maturity Inventory. In O. K. Buros (Ed.), *Eighth mental measurements yearbook*. Highland Park, NJ: Gryphon Press.

4 Advances in Career-planning Systems

Karen M. Taylor
Ohio State University

INTRODUCTION

This chapter summarizes the most recent information available on another major type of career assessment, Career Planning Systems (CPSs). CPSs are designed to not only *measure* but *facilitate* an individual's career development. A CPS is an integrated and interactive package of materials designed to help an individual further his or her career planning.

CPSs are sophisticated vocational assessment methods designed to facilitate further growth by an individual with regard to career planning and decision-making issues and thereby facilitate the individual's career development. CPSs are theoretically based on a Parsonian approach to career development and guidance wherein you have the world of the individual and the occupational world and the relationship between the two. This matching model approach to career development is certainly not new to the career-testing domain and, in fact, is probably the cornerstone of most assessment methods in vocational psychology. Most of the CPSs evolved from the assessment tradition, focusing on a single aspect of the career-planning process, such as interest or aptitude measurement, or occupational information. In fact, many of these systems, especially the paper-pencil type, have as a central core of the program one of the widely used traditional vocational assessment tools, such as the SCII, SDS, or similar measures. Career planning systems can be viewed as the expanded and extended 1980s edition of our initial assessment tools.

A CPS has both content and process dimensions which constitute the definitional parameters of these systems. As far as content is concerned, a CPS is composed of at least two of the following components designed to help individuals:

1. Discover important career-related information about themselves, e.g., interests, values;
2. Learn information about occupational alternatives;
3. Connect the information about themselves with occupational information;
4. Focus on decision making, by facilitating the narrowing of occupational options or in some cases the expanding of occupational options if only a few are under consideration;
5. Determine the next steps necessary to take in their career-planning process [Bowlsbey, personal communication, 1986].

As Item 1 implies, discovering self-information involves self-assessment. The degree of actual assessment that occurs in a CPS varies from a simple self-description of some career-relevant attribute to the use of sophisticated psychometrically sound instruments which are an integral component of the CPS. The emphasis on decision making is another aspect of a CPS that involves a range of content across different systems. Some systems are elaborate and have a separate decision-making component while in others the focus on decision making is quite simple, for example, having a user rank order a list of occupations he or she is considering. Regardless of the level of complexity, these decision-making components help the user narrow or expand occupational alternatives.

The second dimension by which a CPS is defined is the process dimension. A career program is defined as a CPS if it:

1. Integrates the information in the program for the user,
2. Is interactive between and/or among the separate parts of the system,
3. Is commercially available.

This third criterion is important as programs not commercially available were excluded from consideration for review in this chapter. The emphasis is on CPSs accessible to the general counseling and guidance community rather than on programs developed and used only locally by a particular school district or community agency.

These assessment, self-exploration, and occupational information materials can be delivered to a client via a variety of methods. The method involves both the form and the structure of the delivery. The three main forms of delivery of career-planning systems are paper-pencil, computer-assisted, and curricular. It is often the *form* of delivery by which these systems are distinguished. This chapter also uses this convention and therefore, will examine three *types* of CPSs: standardized paper-pencil programs, computer-assisted programs and, to a lesser extent, curricular programs. A fourth type of career assessment and intervention that is related to organized CPSs is the burgeoning arena of self-help career materials. Given the scope of this chapter this growing area will not be reviewed.

A second aspect of CPSs' delivery methods is the *structure* of the delivery which includes: one-to-one, group, and computerized methods of delivery. The typical settings for the delivery of CPSs are the classroom, the counselor's office, and/or a career resource center or career-planning and placement office. Career interventions have typically assumed the presence of a counselor but with the advent of computers in career guidance materials this requirement is no longer necessary. The exact role of the counselor is an issue briefly discussed later in this chapter. Due to the tremendous growth in the use of computers in career assessment and career interventions, this chapter will use the term Computer Assisted Guidance System (CAGS) (Katz & Shatkin, 1980) to differentiate full-fledged CAGSs from CPSs or other career interventions that are available in a microcomputer format in addition to a paper-pencil version. Many companies which publish standardized paper-pencil instruments are moving toward or already have available microcomputer versions. These typically include scoring capabilities. The essential difference is that CAGSs were exclusively designed as interactive computer programs, never as stand-alone paper-pencil instruments adapted to include a computerized application. Regardless of the exact method of delivery in terms of form and structure—whether delivered one-to-one or in a group, in the classroom, at the computer terminal, or with a counselor interpreter—CPSs are one of the fastest growing areas in career assessment.

Career-planning systems have been described by others as multidimensional (Miller, 1982) and as assessment methods embedded within a larger educational/career guidance program (Walsh & Betz, 1985). Miller (1982) notes that CPSs or ''multidimensional instruments'' are a recent development in career guidance [p. 143]. A multidimensional instrument is described as an inventory combined of several tests that measures important aspects about an individual relevant to career planning. Miller (1982) further states that ''these instruments measure several characteristics, provide reports that organize test results for use in career planning, and in most cases suggest appropriate career options and further career planning activities'' [pp. 143–144].

Miller notes two obvious disadvantages to the more traditional use of separate and distinct tests (e.g., interests, aptitudes) compared with these newer, more innovative multidimensional instruments. First, the administration of a series of separate instruments does not provide an integrated picture of the information for the client who could benefit from a more comprehensive treatment of their career development. Further, the connection to occupational information and occupational options is often not readily available when using diverse tests nor is it always an easy task to relate diverse test results to each other.

Using an adapted Webster definition, Walz and Benjamin (1984) define career guidance systems as approaches composed of interacting or interdependent parts which form a unified whole and use a variety of strategies to serve a common purpose. Although valuable, Walz and Benmamin (1984) point out that a major disadvantage of these systems is that they will not have much long-term impact unless they are an integrated part of a larger, more comprehensive program of career guidance which involves a planned sequential series of career activities and is guided by professionals. These larger career programs are called systematic career guidance programs and are well described in a chapter by this same title (Walz & Benjamin, 1984). Herr (1982) believes that multidimensional instruments are a direct result of a change in emphasis in career counseling and guidance—a move from an almost exclusive focus on career choice *content* to acknowledging and incorporating the importance of the *process* of career choice. Herr believes that development of CPSs are, in part, a response to this recent trend and that the future holds even further development of this type of assessment.

One of the primary reasons for including a chapter on career-planning systems in this text is that these systems represent state-of-the-art career assessment tools on which 1980s and 1990s career-planning programs will be built. Miller (1982) saw the development of CPSs as one of the major achievements of career counseling, education, and guidance in the 1970s. It is my contention that further development and refinement of these systems will be an accomplishment of the 1980s and 1990s. Examination of the psychometric properties of these systems as well as further investigation regarding the outcome of these career-planning tools for the users will also be a major focus of career research. Not only are CPSs one of the newest developments in career psychology, they are also radically changing the look of vocational measurement and the scope of career guidance.

Miller (1984) has observed that as the definition of career guidance has expanded so have the number, diversity, and kind of career programs and strategies. According to Miller (1984), the significant developments in career guidance strategies in the last decade are in four main areas: career development curriculum, assessment and testing, career information systems, and career guidance for special populations. Excluding the fourth area, career guidance for special populations, this chapter attempts to address some of the content of the other three areas defined as depicting the forefront of career counseling, guidance, and education for the 1980s.

The title of this chapter, "Advances in CPSs," seems fitting. Advances in this area of career assessment and intervention have been both progressive and extremely fast-paced, especially with the advent of CAGSs and the application of computer technology to many of the paper-pencil systems. The changes are so rapid in this field that recent developments somewhat outdate this chapter as soon as it is published. The critical importance is, therefore, not an up-to-the-minute report of what is commercially available but a review of the most recent systems. In addition, some organizing schema in this area of career assessment and a ready reference will be provided for career professionals as they make their way through the ever growing, increasingly complicated world of career assessment and intervention.

The specific scope of this chapter is to define, identify, and describe the CPSs that are currently commercially available in the United States. Written from a descriptive point of view, this chapter is not intended to serve as a specific review or evaluation of the measurement qualities of each system but as an overall description. Test reviews of most of these systems can be found elsewhere (Buros, 1978; Kapes & Mastie, 1982; Mitchell, 1985). As mentioned, this chapter reviews three main types of CPSs: paper-pencil, computer-assisted, and to a lesser extent curricular systems. The paper-pencil and computer-assisted sections begin with an overview of the scope of these systems, followed by a list of the systems and a review of each particular system. The individual, paper-pencil CPS reviews include: a description of the program, typical users, brief psychometric information, and the strengths and weaknesses of the system. Each review answers these four basic questions: What is the CPS intended to do? Who is the CPS designed for? What are the measurement properties of the system? What are the main strengths and weaknesses of the CPS? The individual CAGS reviews describe the content of the specific system and specify the population for whom the system was developed. Given the nature of CAGSs and the lack of research and psychometric information available, the last two questions remain unanswered. Due to space restrictions, only an introductory summary of curricular CPSs is provided.

This chapter is intended to give readers an overview of CPSs and provide an initial examination of which systems may be most appropriate for the settings and the clientele represented by the readers of this text. Comparison of one system with another can only be thoroughly and well done by professionals in their individual settings with the persons who will be typical users of a system they may implement. This chapter, therefore, *does not* compare or contrast in an evaluative sense one CPS against another. In addition, there is such rapid change in this area that it is difficult to state with certainty that what is described here is all there is available. A program may be excluded for a variety of reasons: (1) such fast-paced development that the author could have missed it; (2) not fitting definitional criteria; (3) overlapping extensively with a CPS that is reviewed.

The importance of CPSs for special populations, for example, deserves more attention that would be adequately provided in this chapter; however, an excellent resource, *A counselor's guide to vocational guidance instruments* (Kapes & Mastie, 1982), has a section on vocational instruments for special populations which reviews instruments designed to assess interests, performance, abilities, work readiness, and other salient vocational characteristics. These instruments are designed for a wide range of special populations, including the hearing impaired, learning disabled, physically challenged, developmentally disabled, and economically disadvantaged. For a thorough and recent review, readers are referred to this National Vocational Guidance Association publication.

The method by which the CPSs were chosen for review was both formal and informal. A search of ERIC documents over the past 3 years and a review of journal articles in vocational publications over the last 5 years constituted the formal search process. Informally, the author spoke with nationally known career guidance, counseling, and education experts and spoke with publishers at national professional conventions. Numerous phone conversations with the publishing companies were initiated as commercial availability is one of the main definitional criteria a CPS had to meet to be included in this chapter.

The final section of this chapter addresses issues identified in this review. Brief mention is given to important implications which have arisen in career psychology as a result of the advances made in career assessment by career planning systems.

PAPER-PENCIL PROGRAMS

Paper-pencil career planning systems naturally emerged from traditional vocational assessment tools as an extension of the scope of these tools in terms of assessment, content, and outcome. Many current CPSs are elaborated versions of an original instrument or are the original instrument enhanced by new assessment devices offered in the same package of materials under the same title.

In addition to the ERIC search and contact with publishers, two recent reference books on paper-pencil CPSs served as excellent resources. The already-mentioned work by Kapes and Mastie (1982) reviews 40 instruments chosen on the basis of which instruments were the most used and the most important vocational guidance instruments. In addition, a list of more than 70 other instruments considered useful in vocational guidance was compiled as an appendium. The following are the categories of the instruments reviewed: (1) multiple aptitude batteries, (2) interest inventories, (3) measures of work values, (4) career development/maturity instruments, (5) combined assessment programs, (6) card sorts, (7) instruments for special populations.

The second and most recent text by Vetter, Hall, Putzstuck, and Dean (1986), *Adult career counseling: Resources for program planning and development,* has a major section on assessment instruments. Criteria for the choice of the 76 programs and instruments reviewed in the assessment section included (1) If the program or instruments had been used in adult career programs, and (2) If the program was known through the literature or through talking with professionals at national conventions. The authors hoped to include only instruments which actually provide norms for adult users but given the paucity of such norms some of the programs included do not.

It is apparent from the review of these two excellent resources that different writers do not always categorize instruments in the same way. There is, however, substantial overlap in the programs reviewed.

The 15 paper-pencil CPSs reviewed in this manuscript are listed in Table 4.1. The CPSs are reviewed in alphabetical order.

CAREER OCCUPATIONAL PREFERENCE SYSTEM
(COPSystem)

The Career Occupational Preference System (COPSystem), previously titled the California Occupational Preference System, is a three-part program designed to provide comprehensive career-related information that will assist individuals with their career decision-making process. The program contains three separate but related components which measure interests (Career Occupational Preference System Interest Inventory, COPS Interest Inventory), abilities (Career Ability Placement Survey, CAPS), and values (Career Orientation Placement and Evaluation Survey, COPES). The program assumes that the career-planning process "begins by assisting individuals in defining areas for occupational investigation which are specific and appropriate to their individual interests" [Knapp & Knapp, 1982, p. 2]. This CPS is based on the work of Thurstone, Guilford, and the career classification system of Roe (Knapp & Knapp, 1982). Building directly on Roe's occupational classification, the COPSystem provides 14 scores which represent five clusters of occupations (arts, service, science, technology, and business) at two levels (professional and skilled) plus four other occupational areas (consumer economics, outdoor, clerical, and communication).

The COPSystem is designed to be administered as a single, integrated career unit or as three separate career inventories. The authors favor the combined administration approach and suggest the following order if administering all three instruments: (1) COPS, (2) CAPS, (3) COPES. If administered as a single unit, the Comprehensive Career Planning Guide is the interpretive profile tool used to integrate the results for the client. Self-Interpretation Guides that correspond to each survey are used if the instruments are administered separately. In this case, a Summary Guide is used to compile information from all three instruments. Both machine and self-scoring forms are available.

COPS

The COPS interest inventory is a 168-item inventory available in four forms: (1) COPS Interest Inventory-Junior High, High School, Adult, (2) COPS Inventory R for sixth-grade reading level, grades 6–12, (3) COPS II Intermediate Inventory for fourth-fifth-grade reading level or for learning disabled persons, grades 6–12, and (4) COPS Inventory–P for professional occupational options only, college and adult. All forms of the COPS Interest Inventory are composed of item statements describing work-related activities, which require a response choice along a 4-point scale: L (Like very much), l (Like moderately), d (Dis-

TABLE 4.1

Paper-Pencil Instruments

Title	Content	Publishing Company	Author(s)	User Population	Theoretical Base
California Occupational System - COPS	COPS (interests) CAPS (abilities) COPES (values)	EDITS - Educational and Industrial Testing Service	Knapp, R.R. Knapp, L.	Intermediate (Grades 6-8) High School (Grades 9-12) College Adult	Roe
Career Decision Making System - CDM	120-item interest inventory 5 self-report short "scales" measuring occupational preferences, school subject preferences, future plans, abilities and values	AGS - American Guidance Service	Harrington, T.F. O'Shea, A.J.	Grades 7-12 Adults	Holland
Career Planning Program - CPP I & II (ACT)	UNIACT 92-item experience measure ability measures	ACT - American College Testing	ACT Staff Munday, L. Prediger, D. Lamb, D.	Grades 8-10 Grades 11-Adults	Roe Holland
Career Planning Program CPP (DAT)	DAT Career Planning Questionnaire Career Planning Report	The Psychological Corporation	DAT Bennett, G.K. Seashore, H.G. Wesman, A.G. CPP-Super, D.E.	Grades 8-12	Parson Super
CareerWise	CAI (interests) TVI (values) WNAI (skills)	NCS - National Computer Systems	CAI Johansson, C.B. TVI Johansson, C.B. Webber, P.L. WNAI Johansson, J.C. Kellogg, L.L. Johansson, C.B.	Grades 9-Adults	Holland

(continued...)

(Continued)

Title	Content	Publishing Company	Author(s)	User Population	Theoretical Base
Experience Exploration	Activity Experience Inventory Student Experience Sheet Job Chart	Chronical Guidance	Ewens, W.P.	Grades 9-14	A behavioristic theory of career development
GuidePak	SCII CPI GuidePak Workbook	Behaviordyne	Behaviordyne Staff Pick, D.J. Tondow, M. Grycz, A.	Not specified	Holland
Individual Career Exploration - ICE	One survey booklet with 5 sections: Interests, Experiences, Occupations, Skills and Abilities, Decision Level	Scholastic Testing Service	Miller-Tiedeman, A.	Grades 8-12	Roe
Ohio Vocational Interest Survey II - OVIS II	OVIS II Career Planner	The Psychological Corporation	D'Costa, A. Winefordner, D. Odgers, J.G. Koons, Jr., P.B.	Grades 7-12 College Adults	Cubist model of data-people-things
Personal Career Development Profile - PCDP Self Motivated Career Planning - SMPC	PCDP - 16 PF SMCP - PCD Questionnaire Personal Orientation Survey Education Summary Career Experience Summary Personal Career Life Summary	IPAT - Institute for Personality and Ability Testing	PCDP-Walter, V. SMCP-Walter, V. Wallace, M.	Age 16-Adults	Porter, 1976 Relationship awareness theory

Holland |
| Planning Career Goals - PCG | Life and Career Plans Inventory Ability Measures Interest Inventory Information Measures | CTB/McGraw-Hill | American Institutes for Research Staff Project Director - Flanagan, J.C. | Grades 8-12 | Developmental Theory: Career as a life-long process fitting life-style with career |

(continued...)

(continued...)

Title	Content	Publishing Company	Author(s)	User Population	Theoretical Base
Vocational Exploration and Insight Kit - VEIK	Vocational Card Sort - VCS SDS Action Plan Workbook	CPP - Consulting Psychologist Press	Holland, J. & Associates	High School College Adults	Holland
Vocational Interest Experience and Skill Assessment Program - VIESA	UNIACT - Short form Skills Assessment Work-related Experiences	ACT - American College Testing	ACT Staff Project Director - Prediger, D.	Grades 8-10 Grades 11-Adults	Roe Holland
Vocational Information Profile - VIP	USES (interests) GATB (abilities)	NCS - National Computer System	NCS Staff U.S. Employment Service Staff	Grades 9-12 Adults	United States Employment Service Occupational System (e.g., Worker Trait Groups)
World of Work Inventory - WOWI	Career interests Job Satisfaction Vocational Training Potential	World of Work, Inc.	Ripley, R.E. Hudson, J.W. Hudson, K.S.	Grades 8-12 College Adults	Not specified

like), and D (Dislike very much). Testing time for this self-administering, untimed inventory is approximately 20–30 minutes. Scores reflecting the degree of interest in the 14 occupational clusters are presented to the client in a profile format that plots the raw scores converted to percentile ranks comparing individual scores with scores of others at a comparable educational level.

Psychometric Information

Norms. "Norms for the COPS Interest Inventory are based on a national sampling of intermediate high school and community college students" [Knapp & Knapp, 1984a, p. 51]. Separate norms are presented for males and females with both sets of norms printed on the inventory profile. The high school norm group is composed of a sample of 6,834 intermediate and high school students (grade 8–12). No information (sample size, mean scores, standard deviations) is reported for the college samples. Hansen (1982) notes an overall lack of clarity and completeness in the information on norms presented in the COPS technical manual.

Reliability and Validity. The technical manual reports the following reliability coefficients for the 14 occupational clusters.

1. Internal consistency (N = 1110, .86 − .91)
2. Test-retest (1 week, N = 97, .80 − .91)
3. Test-retest (1 year, N = 497, .62 − .80)
4. Parallel forms (N = 43, .77 − .90)

From a psychometric point of view, the most consistent criticism of this instrument is the lack of predictive and concurrent validity studies (Hansen, 1982; Layton, 1978a). The 1984 version of the technical manual acknowledges the importance of good predictive validity studies while also acknowledging the length of time necessary to run longitudinal studies. The most recent manual does report initial work in this area but cautions the reader about the relatively short time between initial and follow-up testing.

Two other instrument-related issues raised by published reviews of the instrument are the fakability of this instrument and the potential for scoring inaccuracies in the self-scored forms. In response to the first concern, Bauernfeind (1972) suggested the instrument should not be used in personnel work. As to the second concern, the 1982 manual reports a study of 305 high school students of whom 92% were correct in their self-scoring. As the manual states, this result compares favorably with other scoring accuracy studies.

CAPS

Designed to provide a brief measure of abilities related to occupations, CAPS, the second assessment in the COPSystem, consists of eight 5-minute ability tests:

Mechanical Reasoning (MR), Spatial Relations (SR), Verbal Reasoning (VR), Numerical Ability (NA), Language Usage (LU), Word Knowledge (WK), Perceptual Speed and Accuracy (PSA), and Manual Speed and Dexterity (MSD). Each subtest is presented on a separate form with instructions on one side and test items on the other. Administration of the instrument can be provided in the typical manner or by using cassette-recorded instructions. The battery takes 51 minutes to complete under the recorded condition. Two methods of interpreting the results of CAPS reveal relevant information for the tester. The first method begins with the raw scores reflecting an individual's ability in the eight dimensions measured and compares these scores to the appropriate norm group for the test taker's age and educational level. In this method of interpretation, raw scores are converted to stanine scores and are presented in a profile format.

The second method of interpretation links the ability scores to the 14 occupational clusters by grouping various combinations of the eight ability measures and assigning them to correspond with one of the occupational clusters. This method is designed to help a test taker "identify occupational clusters for which their abilities most closely match the requirements of jobs in that cluster" [Knapp & Knapp, 1984b, p. 18].

Psychometric Information

Norms.   As with COPS, three norm groups (intermediate, grade 8–9; high school, grade 9–12; community college) provide the comparison for an individual's scores.

Reliability and Validity.   The technical manual discusses reliability and validity information although this information is far from complete. Reliability data are provided for a group of 11th graders $N = 200$; split-half reliability coefficients .76–.95 and 2-week, test-retest reliability data on 90 10th graders ranged from .70–.95 while alternate forms yielded reliability coefficients of .70–.89. No other reliability data are presented. Validity data are a bit more extensive with respect to concurrent validity but predictive validity data are relatively weak to nonexistent. No longitudinal data are yet available; however, a promising study is currently in progress (Knapp & Knapp, 1984b). The biggest caution for counselors in using CAPS is that the relationship between the ability scores and the occupational clusters has not been thoroughly investigated. Statements should be made with great caution to clients and students regarding their measured abilities and the relationship of these scores to the entry-level requirements of the occupations listed in the clusters.

COPES

The third component of the COPSystem is the measure of values, COPES. This instrument measures eight values in a 160-item forced-choice scale. If the self-scoring form is used, the instrument contains 128 items. The eight bipolar pairs of work values are: investigative versus accepting, practical versus carefree, independence versus conformity, leadership versus supportive, orderliness versus noncompulsive, recognition versus privacy, aesthetic versus realistic, and social versus self-concern. The instrument is easily completed in approximately 30 minutes. Scores on the eight values scales are keyed to the 14 occupational clusters, thus linking the COPES to the entire COPSystem.

Psychometric Information

Norms. The COPES continues the factor analytical tradition of all the instruments in the COPSystem. Norms are based on a national sample of intermediate, high school, and community college students. Due to the homogeneity of responses among groups, the norms were combined to create a composite norm group.

Reliability and Validity. Of the three COPSystem measures, the least amount of psychometric information is provided on the COPES. Reliability data in the form of internal consistency alpha coefficients are presented for high school and college samples on both the long and short form ranging from .67 to .97. One concurrent validity study comparing COPES with the Allport–Vernon scale is presented. A predictive validity study is in progress.

In addition to the integrated profile information presented in the Comprehensive Career Guide or the specific profile presented in the self-interpretation for each instrument, the COPSystem has a rich variety of supplemental supporting materials. These materials directly correspond to the occupational classification system upon which the COPSystem is based and is also keyed to the *Dictionary of occupational titles* (DOT) and the *Occupational outlook handbook* (OOH). These materials include a Career Briefs Kit, Career Clusters Booklets and the COPSystem Occupational Cluster Charts. The Career Briefs Kit is a card system describing more than 400 occupations. The 14 Career Cluster Booklets correspond to the occupational clusters and contain a detailed description of the cluster as well as information on more than 50 occupations per cluster. An informative wall poster designed to clarify the relationships among each cluster and occupations is also available for each of the 14 areas.

In summary, the COPSystem provides an integrated and multidimensional career-planning program linking individual personal factors (interests, abilities, and values) to occupational clusters. It is a time-efficient system inasmuch as all three instruments can be taken in less than 2 hours. The options available for self- or machine scoring provide flexibility for the teacher/counselor and the potential of immediate feedback for the test taker. However, scoring accuracy may need to be stressed with users. The greatest weakness of the system is the lack of predictive validity studies for both the interest and ability measures and lack of studies measuring COPsystem responses on persons actually employed in the occupational clusters. The greatest strengths include the degree of integration from one instrument to the others, the relationship of all occupational information to the DOT and the COH, and the helpful supplemental materials. Overall, the COPSystem can be a helpful career exploration tool as long as the scope of predicting a test taker's future is kept to a minimum.

Career Decision-Making System (CDM)

Harrington and O'Shea describe the Career Decision-Making System (CDM) as a sound, theoretically based interest inventory that goes beyond a reliable assessment of career interest. "The comprehensive CDM system surveys not only interests, but also values, training plans, and abilities" [Harrington & O'Shea, 1982a, p. 1] to help persons choose a course of educational study, a job, or a career path. The system is based on Holland's theory of vocational development. A central organizing schema for the CDM system is the 18 Career Clusters, which the authors obtained by applying Holland's six-theme classification scheme (Realistic, Investigate, Artistic, Social, Enterprising, and Conventional) to the Worker Trait Group System in the DOT and, more recently, to the occupational classification of another U.S. Department of Labor Publication, *The guide for occupational exploration*. The resulting 18 occupational clusters are: Skilled Crafts, Technical, Legal Work, Manual Work, Math-Science, Data Analysis, Art Work, Literary Work, Musical Work, Management, Clerical Work, Medical-Dental, Personal Service, Sales Work, Entertainment, Customer Services, Social Services, and Education.

The instrument is composed of six sections titled: Occupations, Subjects, Future Plans, Values, Abilities, and Interests. Test takers are instructed to read the 18 descriptions of the career clusters and list their first and second choices by determining which of the clusters best describes the kind of work they would like to do. For the 14 school subjects, first and second most-liked subjects are chosen. The future plans section consists of one question, "What kind of further education or training are you planning?" [Harrington & O'Shea, 1982b, p. 3], to which there are nine possible responses ranging from "graduate and professional school" to "no additional training or education." Fourteen job value titles and brief descriptions are listed in the next section of the system from which four values are to be chosen based on perceived importance of the particular value to the test taker. Similarly, 14 "abilities or talents" are listed in the Abilities section. A respondent chooses the 4 abilities or talents which they think are the most reflective of their strongest abilities based on their school and job performance, previous test scores, and hobby and leisure experiences. The main component of the CDM is the 120-item interest inventory of jobs and job-related activities directly based on Holland's theory of occupational choice. Response choices for each item are: "Like the activity . . . Can't make up your mind . . . Dislike the activity." The six Holland interest areas are relabeled with terms the authors believe are more descriptive of the job in each area: Crafts, Scientific, the Arts, Social, Business, Clerical. Totaled responses to the 120 items result in scores for each of these six occupational areas that lead to a Career Code based on the highest and second highest areas of interest. This Career Code in turn determines the Career Clusters which the test taker is directed to investigate.

Obviously embedded in the CDM system is the capacity for users to make comparisons of their stated occupational interests with their measured occupational interests. Once the Career Code is determined the test taker can examine the comprehensive Career Clusters chart printed in the Interpretive Folder. This tool helps the client further examine occupations and allows for comparison of the school subjects, job values, abilities, and amount of education and training they stated in the CDM system and those which relate to various occupations. Both machine and self-scored versions contain the same information in the Interpretive Folders. The Interpretive Folder takes the user step by step through the use of the information contained within the folder and shows the connection between their scores and the folder, and the next steps in the career planning process that the user can take.

The CDM can be administered individually or in a group setting. Three scoring options are available: self-scored, which provides immediate feedback and has easy-to-follow instructions; machine scored, which results in one of three reporting options (profile, narrative, and group reports), and a new micro-computer version which includes both the assets of immediate feedback and reduced mailing costs. Total testing time is approximately 30–40 minutes. A self-scored Spanish version is also available. The CDM system is designed for use with persons in grades 7–12 and for adult populations.

Psychometric Information

Norms. CDM scores are reported in the form of raw scores although the option of using norm group data is available. Norms are available for grades 7–13, adults, and adult CETA participants. The manual contains a rationale for the use of raw versus normed scores.

Reliability and Validity. Alpha coefficients measuring the internal consistency of the six CDM interest scales range from .89 to .95. For a 30-day, test-retest period, reliability coefficients ranged .75–.94. The manual also reports stability of CDM scores over a 5-month period but cautions the reader to expect some changes in scores, due to the nature of the CDM.

Most of the validity information presented in the manual focuses on construct and concurrent validity, comparing the CDM to other measures of the Holland's occupational classification system, which support a high level of agreement between the CDM summary codes and Holland codes as measured by other instruments. Previous reviews of the CDM have noted the lack of predictive validity (Vetter et al., 1986; Willis, 1978). A preliminary study is reported in the 1982 manual of a 5-year follow-up of 217 11th and 12th graders. A 46% return rate resulted in a total of 95 usable subjects, for which a 58% agreement between measured CDM scores and current job or educational status was found for females and a 51% agreement was found for males. The authors discuss the issue of predictive validity from the viewpoint that one of the purposes of the CDM is to provide a career self-exploration tool, not to predict the job an individual will eventually enter. Establishing strong predictive validity is not viewed as a main objective of the CDM; Harrington and O'Shea (1982a) therefore establish a rationale for focusing on construct and concurrent rather than predictive validity.

One of the earlier concerns raised by previous reviews of the CDM was the list of uses for the CDM which was reported but not supported in the manual (Westbrook, Rogers, & Covington, 1980). This problem seems to be rectified in the most recent manual. A related issue of overstating the scope of the instrument's empirical base was made by Westbrook et al. (1980), who noted that one of the statements made in the interpretive folder used in the self-scoring version states that the more items a person has circled in a career cluster the more likely they will be to find satisfaction in the cluster. This statement has no data base and as such is an example of an overstatement. Another concern raised by Westbrook (1980) is the classification of job titles into the 18 career clusters, e.g., should computer programmer be placed under the math-science or data analysis career cluster? As with most self-scoring systems the concern for scoring accuracy is an issue with the CDM. Close attention to this concern is warranted; however, the authors present some recent studies which mark a great improvement in scorer reliability from the earliest version of the interest inventory.

The greatest concern about the CDM for this review is whether or not the CDM fits the criteria for a Career Planning System. As noted by others (Westbrook et al., 1980; Willis, 1982) the CDM is actually *one* measure—the 120-item interest inventory—the other components of values, future plans, abilities, school subject preferences are just self-descriptions provided in a self-report format. These parts of the CDM cannot be considered scales because there is no psychometric information available on them. The CDM is included as a CPS because it does meet the basic requirements of addressing more than one aspect of a person's career-planning process. From this perspective it is more than *just* an interest inventory; however, from a psychometric point of view, these other aspects need to be developed further to allow the test taker and counselor to have more confidence regarding their inclusion in the career development process. Further integration of these components into the provided career codes would enhance the utility of this career-planning system. A final issue mentioned by Willis (1978, 1982) is the similarity of the CDM to the World of Work Inventory and the VPI. The question in a complex, career materials market becomes: Is this instrument anything new?

In response to this last question and to provide a balanced view of this CPS the following summarizes the strengths of the CDM. Westbrook et al. (1980) and Willis (1982) provide a more extensive review of the CDM. Although not formalized psychometric scales, the CDM does integrate the four aspects of an effective career decision-making program as outlined by the National Institute of Education's Career Awareness Division (Harrington & O'Shea, 1982a). These four aspects are: knowledge, values, preferences, and self-concepts. These four aspects of an effective program are reflected in the six sections of the CDM. As mentioned, it is exactly this comprehensive picture of the self that distinguishes the CDM from a single-aspect career measure. The CDM is presented in an exploratory-versus-definitive style so that a user is encouraged to explore career options instead of making a single one point in time career decision. The authors have made a commitment to avoid sex role stereotypes throughout this instrument. In addition, the excellent machine scored narrative interpretation is very thorough although expensive. And finally, the CDM does provide a more comprehensive extension into career information than does the VPI or the SDS and updates the included career information every 2 years.

In summary, the CDM is a career-planning system which offers an interpreted approach to helping individuals explore themselves in relation to the world of occupations. As long as Harrington, O'Shea, and their students or colleagues continue to refine the psychometric properties of the instrument and address some of the concerns that have been described this may become one of the mainstay career-planning tools.

Career Planning Program (CPP)

The ACT Career Planning Program (CPP) is a comprehensive career assessment and guidance program designed to assess interests, abilities, prior work-related experiences, and self-rated abilities. These data, integrated with occupational information, lead to suggestions for educational/career exploration. The CPP was first developed in 1969–1971 under the direction of Leo Munday with Dale Prediger as project director. The current version of the CPP is the third edition, published in 1983 under the direction of Prediger and Dick Lamb. The two levels of the CPP, I (grades 8–10) and II (grade 11–adult), include: (1) the Unisex Edition of the ACT Interest Inventory (UNIACT), (2) six ability scales, (3) an experience section, (4) a self-rated abilities unit, and (5) a background and plans unit.

The UNIACT is a 90-item interest scale based on the occupational classification schema of Holland, which results in interest scores in six areas: technical, science, arts, social services, business contact, and business operations. The six ability measures are: Mechanical Reasoning, Space Relations, Clerical Speed and Accuracy, Numerical Skills, Reading Skills, and Language Usage. The level of experience a user has had in the six interest areas forms the content for the work-related experiences scale. This section contains 90 items to which a respondent marks the frequency of experience (never, only once or twice, or several times). The self-ratings of ability section include a respondent's choice of "high," "medium," or "low," compared with others their age on the following abilities: scientific, creative/artistic, creative/literary, helping others, meeting people, sales, leadership/management, organization, and manual dexterity. The demographic background and future plans section includes 17 questions for which results are displayed on the profile report, "Your Career Planning Report." Included in this section are the respondent's stated occupational and educational plans.

For each level a CPP Career Guidebook (Level I: Exploring Your Career; Level II: Planning Your Future) contains 24 pages of information designed to help interpret the integrated self and occupational information presented in the CPP profile, "Your Career Planning Report." The latter is a 2-page profile which integrates all scores from all measures and organizes the scores according to Job Clusters. The report presents stanine and percentile scores for the interest and ability measures. The labels "highest," "middle," and "lowest" indicate the stanine score representing the experience level of the respondent in comparison with the same age norm group. Designed to help students relate this assessed information to occupational information and options, the "World of Work Map" is provided on the back side of the Career Planning Report.

The "World of Work Map" is a career exploration tool based on integration of the theoretical occupational clustering ideas of Roe and Holland and the DOT resulting in 23 job families. These job family groupings are based on similarity of work tasks and similarity of emphasis on the bipolar dimensions of data/ideas and people/things. Job families are organized around six Job Clusters, which correspond to the six interest and experience labels: Technical, Science, Arts, Social Services, Business Contact, and Business Operations.

Psychometric Information

Norms.   The 1983 norms for the third edition of the CPP are based on a nationally representative sample of approximately 15,400 students in grades 8, 10, and 12 in 115 schools. Norms for grades 9 and 11 were established by interpolation. No adult norms are presented in the most recent psychometric manual, *Interim psychometric handbook for the 3rd edition of the ACT Career Planning Program (Levels 1 and 2), (ACT, 1985)*. This handbook provides talbes of normative data for both sexes separately and as a combined total. The previous CPP edition used combined sex norms for ability measures and separate sex norms for the interest and experience scales. As Mehrens (1982) notes, this is a controversial topic, in light of the exact opposite choice in norming procedures by other major standardized tests. The presentation of both combined and separate sex norms seems a positive step; however, as noted subsequently, reliability data are presented only for the total sample.

Reliability.   Reliability data provided for the CPP are based on approximately half of the CPP norming sample. Internal consistency estimates of reliability for the UNIACT range from .81 to .92 for the three grade levels, 8, 10, and 12. In contrast to the earlier edition, separate reliability coefficients are not presented for each sex.

Stability test-retest coefficients for a 3-week interval were .77 to .89 for a sample of approximately 100 12th-grade students. Combined sex data are presented for the six ability scales by grade. Kuder–Richardson–20 reliability coefficients ranged from a low of .70 (eighth graders, Mechanical Reasoning) to a high of .92 (Grade 10, Space Relations). The mean reliability coefficient was .87. Due to the fact that the Clerical Skills scale is a speeded test, no reliability coefficients were given. Stability coefficients based on a 2-week test-retest ranged from .73 to .87. For the work-related experience scales, the internal consistency coefficients ranged from .71 to .92. Three-week test-retest correlation coefficients for grade 8 and 12 ranged from .72 to .86 and .66 to .85 respectively. With respect to the self-ratings of the abilities section of the CPP, the same sample of 8th and 12th graders were tested to provide stability data. Sixty-four percent of the sample did not change their self-ratings of the nine abilities. Self-rating stability varied across abilities with a range of 52% to 70% for grade 8 and 56% to 70% for grade 12.

Although the handbook states "the ratings appear to have sufficient stability for use in self/career exploration" [ACT, 1985, p. 29], this author would caution overinterpretation of these self-ratings, as approximately one-third of the sample did change their ratings in only a 3-week period. If used only for exploratory purposes, however, these self-ratings may be helpful.

Validity. The handbook summarizes validity studies performed on previous editions of the CPP and refers the reader to the technical report on the UNIACT for more information. As noted in the handbook, both divergent and convergent validity studies which examine the intercorrelations among the CPP scales by males and females and provide "strong support for the convergent and divergent validity of the CPP measures" [ACT, 1985, p. 35] have been executed. Two predictive validity studies measuring the degree of relationship between ACT CPP ability measures and subsequent academic course grades for both Levels I and II suggest a reasonably strong relationship, which supports the predictive validity of the CPP. In addition, the handbook includes validity information on the extent to which CPP measures differentiate among students in diverse academic programs and among persons employed in various occupations and the relationship between interest scores and job satisfaction. As is apparent, most of the validity work has focused on the interest and ability measures of the CPP.

Overall, the ACT CPP is a comprehensive career-planning system which does help integrate knowledge of self with occupational information. The organization of the "World of Work Map" visually presents occupational information in a useful and organized manner. In addition to providing information useful in individual career guidance, the CPP is helpful in administrative planning as group composite data are available for a school system or college. Another strength of this program is a 50-page pamphlet, *Action guide,* which provides methods to prepare students, teachers, and parents in the use of the CPP. This pamphlet is clearly designed for grade 8–12 students. Another advantage of the CPP is flexibility. The CPP can be used with an individual, as part of a comprehensive school-wide career guidance program or curricularly as a specific career-planning course.

The most cited criticism of the CPP is twofold. According to Walsh and Betz (1985) the ability measures are not sufficiently internally consistent to be used to make individual career decisions. This critique of inadequate psychometric properties was also cited by Johnson (1978) as reason to use the CPP as an exploratory career planning tool as opposed to a method to verify educational and occupational choices. Secondly, Johnson (1978) notes that although well designed to promote career exploration in its users, the effectiveness of the CPP in doing just this has not been empirically demonstrated.

Differential Aptitude Tests with Career Planning Program (DAT-CPP)

The DAT CPP (2nd ed.), first introduced by The Psychological Corporation in 1973, is a CPS that integrates aptitude information as measured by the DAT with user's responses to a Career Planning Questionnaire. Designed to extend the DAT to aid in the career counseling of students, the DAT CPP program consists of three parts: (1) Career Planning Questionnaire (CPQ), (2) DAT, and (3) Career Planning Report. The Career Planning Questionnaire measures demographic data (e.g., sex, grade, age), interests, educational plans, and self-reported school grades. More specifically, the CPQ measures interest in 94 school subjects, activities, and sports and in 100 occupations. Interests are initially assessed singly and then as a function of groups; school subjects, activities, and sports comprise 18 groups while the 100 occupations are categorized into 20 groups. Educational plans and academic grades are each measured by a single item. The educational plans item asks respondents to determine the level of education they expect to achieve while the academic grades item has respondents place themselves in one of the four quartiles of class standing. The CPQ constitutes the first two pages of the four-page Answer Document with DAT test responses recorded on the last two pages.

The DAT battery consists of eight subtests: Verbal Reasoning (VR), Numerical Ability (NA), Abstract Reasoning (AR), Clerical Speed and Accuracy (CSA), Mechanical Reasoning (MR), Space Relations (SR), Spelling (Sp), and Language Usage (LU). Separate scores are provided for each test. In addition, a ninth score combines the VR and NA scores. The 1980 version of the DAT (Forms V and W) is the third revision of the instrument. All versions of the DAT

The third part of the DAT CPP is the Career Planning Report, which integrates CPQ responses with the results of the eight aptitude tests. The report "either confirms the appropriateness of the student's occupational choices in the light of his or her abilities and expressed interests, or suggests alternative occupational areas to explore if the choices are inappropriate" [The Psychological Corporation, 1986, p. 163]. The report is presented in a two-page profile with DAT information provided in a profile on the first page and a narrative report based on the Questionnaire responses integrated with the DAT Results presented on the second page. For each DAT test the report provides: raw scores, same-sex percentile ranks, opposite-sex percentile ranks, the norm groups with which the student is compared, and a horizontal bar graph depicting the student's percentile ranks. The narrative section summarizes the user's actual responses to the questionnaire, then states the occupational area selected by the respondent and comments as to the appropriateness of this choice with regard to the student's stated educational plans, school subject preferences, and aptitude scores. If the first or second occupational choice did not match the aptitude scores, school subject preferences, and educational plans then alternative occupational suggestions are made. If a match was achieved, no further career suggestions are given.

The questionnaire is generally administered prior to the DAT. Total testing time is approximately 3½ hours, of which a half-hour is usually sufficient for the CPQ. The aptitude battery tests range in length from 6 to 30 minutes. All subtests are suggested when using the CPP and seven *must* be administered for results on the report to be generated. Machine scoring is the only available option.

The DAT CPP was developed under the leadership of D. E. Super for use with students in grades 8–12. The primary purpose is to assess the level of congruence between educational plans and career preferences and aptitudes and to encourage realistic educational/career choices. The program was designed to serve as a confirmatory tool as well as an exploratory career-planning tool. The counselor's manual lists a variety of uses for the program, including individual counseling, group counseling, curriculum planning, and evaluation research (Super, 1982).

Psychometric Information

Norms. The norming sample for Forms V and W of the DAT was drawn from 64 school districts in 32 states and results in male and female norms for grades 8–12 ($N = 61,722$). The use of opposite-sex norms is discussed in the Administrator's Handbook. No norm information is provided for the Career Planning Questionnaire.

Reliability and Validity. Using subsamples of the standardization sample, split-half reliability coefficients for each of the DAT subtests except CSA for males and females in grades 8–12 ranged from .86 to .96 (males) and .84–.96 (females). Due to the speeded nature of CSA alternative-form reliability coefficients were calculated which ranged from .93 to .97.

have equivalent parallel forms: Form A and B, 1947; Form L and M, 1962; Form S and T, 1972.

Validity information, primarily predictive and concurrent, is presented in a new publication, the Technical Supplement [The Psychological Corporation, 1984). Again, information concerns only the DAT, not the CPQ.

One of the most consistent criticisms of the DAT found in various reviews is the lack of differential validity (Bouchard, 1978; Linn, 1982). This becomes even more critical in examining the potential impact of the combined DAT with the Career Planning Program. The results of the DAT CPP as presented in the Career Planning Report differentially suggest occupational options to students based in part on their aptitude performance. There is not only relatively little validity data based on occupational criteria (Linn, 1982) but also there is no psychometric information provided on the CPQ. Given that the CPQ contains two interest inventories, the lack of reliability and validity information is disappointing at the least and potentially misleading.

Adding to this disappointment is the length of time which has passed since the CPP was introduced. Seemingly some of this work could have been completed in the past 14 years. In addition, there is no documentation of empirical evidence for the computer-based interpretive comments on the Career Planning Report. The concern being raised here is that results from the DAT CPP are not empirically based and could prematurely restrict potential career options or offer unrealistic options. Unless a very careful interpretation is done by the counselor, a student and his/her parents could overinterpret the results. In addition, although the testing materials do suggest that tests are not to be used prescriptively, some of the statements used in the test report are not quite as tentative. For example, the Career Planning Report provided in the test catalog states that a certain career choice is a *good* choice for the test taker. Although this statement may not intend to reinforce a dualistic view of occupational choice it seems possible that it and others like it may in fact do just that.

Another drawback to the report is that occupational alternatives are only suggested for students who do not make a "match" between their expressed interests and aptitudes. Especially for young students, this may prematurely narrow examination of viable career possibilities. This same issue can, however, be viewed from a more positive perspective as summarized by Walsh and Betz (1985) who note the DAT CPP results could help students whose occupational choices are discrepant from their measured aptitudes make more realistic career decisions.

Although the issue of same-versus-opposite sex norms is still under discussion, some of the earlier sex bias criticisms of the DAT have been resolved. Specifically, Mastie (1976) noted the heavy male orientation in the language used in the LU subtest and the lack of females pictured, except for one in a wheelchair, in the MR subtest. Both of these subtests have been revised in response to these criticisms.

An advantage of the DAT CPP as a career exploration tool is that a battery of aptitudes can help a student differentiate among various abilities instead of receiving a single global ability score which does not directly translate into specific abilities important for different occupations (Mastie, 1976). The supplemental materials provided for the DAT are well written and organized. A helpful brochure, the Orientation Booklet can be used to help prepare students for the administration of the DAT CPP. A useful glossary of terms is also available. *Your aptitudes* is a pamphlet for users which provides an excellent discussion of what an aptitude is and describes the aptitudes measured by the program.

In summary, the DAT CPP provides an excellent marriage of a multiple aptitude test battery with a career-planning emphasis. However, empirical work is necessary in order to use the program confidently for career planning of young people.

CareerWise

Published by National Computer System, CareerWise is a comprehensive battery of instruments which measure interests, personal characteristics, work-related values, and skills. Designed for cost-effective career guidance, this CPS includes three assessment instruments: the Career Assessment Inventory (CAI), the Temperament and Values Inventory (TVI), and the Word and Number Assessment Inventory (WNAI). The counselor has a choice of using all three instruments or choosing either the TVI or WNAI as an adjunct to the interest inventory. Obviously, another dimension of the career-planning process is included with the addition of each inventory. According to the workbook, which serves as a tool to integrate information from the three instruments, the purpose of the CareerWise program is to help a user examine interests, values, and skills and to use this information to choose a future career. The program is based on a developmental lifelong process view of career planning and encourages users to expand instead of restrict their occupational options. From this perspective it is clear that the CareerWise developers intended its use to be exploratory rather than confirmatory.

The testing time for the battery depends on the number of instruments included. Testing times are approximately: CAI–30 minutes; TVI–30 minutes; WNAI–1 hour. The test developers suggest that all instruments be completed in one administration. The target population for this CPS are individuals in grades eight or nine, to adults. The CAI in particular was developed with a specific population in mind: persons who are not pursuing postsecondary baccalaureate degrees, but plan to enter occupations requiring a 4-year degree or less. Interestingly, the most recent NCS catalog notes that the CAI will be expanded to include 20 professional scales. Machine scoring of these instruments results in either a profile or an interpretive report in narrative form. A profile report is not available for the WNAI. One report is provided for each instrument.

CareerWise is actually two or three separate assessment instruments integrated only by the test taker using the materials provided in the CareerWise Workbook and Blending Chart. These materials will be further explained following a closer look at each of the three instruments.

CAI

The CAI is a 305-item interest inventory similar to the SCII. Responses to items on three major categories (activities, school subjects, and occupational titles) range on a 5-point Likert scale from "Like very much" to "Dislike very much." Scores are provided on the following five scales: (1) six general themes (GT) measured by Holland codes, (2) 22 basic interest scales (BIS), (3) 91 occupational scales, (4) administrative indexes, and (5) special scales (Fine Arts-Mechanical, Occupational extroversion–introversion, Educational orientation, and Variability of interests).

Psychometric Information

Norms.   CAI norms for the GT and the BIS were generated from a sample of 750 females and 750 males. Occupational Scale norms were based on 70 or more persons in each occupational group.

Reliability and Validity.   Test-retest reliabilities for periods of 1 week, 2 weeks, 30 days, 4–5 years, and 6–7 years range from .72 to .92 for the GT, from .60 to .97 for the BIS and from .66 to .97 for Occupational Scales. The CAI Manual presents results of content, construct, and concurrent validity studies; however, as noted by Lohnes (1982), a serious problem is posed by the total lack of predictive validity studies in light of the stated purpose of the instrument which is to aid a student in defining *future* career plans.

TVI

A total of 230 items comprise the TVI, designed to measure work-related values and personal characteristics, labeled temperaments. The untimed inventory is divided into three sections. Parts I and II comprise the values part of the instrument to which responses range from "very important" to "very unimportant" and from "very pleasant" to "very unpleasant." Part III, The Temperaments section, has a true–false response format. Two sets of scales result from the item responses: a Personal Characteristics scale and a Reward Values scale. The Personal Characteristics scale reflects the temperaments section in a bipolar fashion, which includes the individual's scores on these scales: routine–flexible, quiet–active, attentive–distractable, serious–cheerful, consistent–changeable, reserved–sociable, and reticent–persuasive. Reward values include: social recognition, managerial/sales benefits, leadership, social service, task specificity, philosophical curiosity, and work independence.

Psychometric Information

Norms.   Three age groups by sex comprise the norm group. Age groups are 15–19, 20–25, and 26–55.

Reliability and Validity.   Median internal consistency coefficients for the scales by each norm group ranged from .79 to .85. Test-retest reliability coefficients for 1-week- and 2-week periods were .82–.93 (temperament scales) and .79–.93 (values scales). The manual includes content, construct, and concurrent validity statistics but no predictive validity data are presented.

WNAI

The third instrument of the CareerWise program is the WNAI, a verbal and numerical skills instrument. Eighty multiple-choice items (50 synonyms and 30 math problems) comprise the instrument. Raw scores on both the word and number sections are given and compared with the average score of persons with varying educational levels and in a variety of occupations. The narrative report includes a listing of all the word items with both the correct response and the user's response indicated and a list of the math problems which were answered incorrectly now corrected. This is a rather unique aspect of a standardized instrument.

Psychometric Information

Norms.   Six combined sex samples which comprise the norm groups for the WNAI are: (1) students in high school, (2) students in college, (3) adults with no college, (4) adults with some business or technical school, (5) adults with some college, and (6) adults with 4 or more years of college.

Reliability and Validity.   The internal consistency coefficients arrived at by the Kuder–Richardson–20 formula are .93 (Word Section), .90 (Number Section), and .94 (Total Scale).

The manual documents high content, construct, and concurrent validity coefficients. Validity studies have examined the WNAI with the SCII, CAI, and the MBTI.

As has been mentioned, the only integrative aspect of CareerWise is the notebook, which includes a Blending Chart. The chart is designed to be the receptacle of information from all three instruments and is organized according to the six Holland themes, which are called Job Families in this program. The integration of the WNAI scores is done by comparing the educational level most consistent with the word and number scores to the educational levels of approximately 260 occupations. The chart also contains a self-report skills section in which three skills are listed for each Holland job family. The user checks those that they now have or would like to acquire. All this information is distilled into a 3-point Career Code from which further occupational exploration is encouraged. Although this effort at integration is certainly commendable, the real task of integrating the scores from all three instruments into a comprehensive planning program has yet to be achieved. This CPS would certainly be enhanced by a truly integrated report and, according to NCS personnel, it is currently being developed.

In summary, CareerWise presents a comprehensive package of career-planning tools designed to assess interests, values, and skills and to integrate these results with educational and occupational suggestions. These materials do exactly that and seem to provide a promising package of materials. As has been mentioned of other systems, one of the criticisms of this system is the lack of predictive validity. The system seems most promising as an exploratory tool. Although the publishers list a wide range of applications for CareerWise, including helping adults make midcareer changes or re-enter the workforce, much of the written material seems to address high school students. If indeed the materials are to have a broader application, they should be rewritten to be more inclusive of other populations. An additional positive feature of the system is the tentative manner in which the material is presented to the test taker. This allows room for the individual to change and develop and for their career decision making truly to reflect a developmental process.

Experience Exploration

This CPS is included in this chapter with some caution as the criteria for a complete CPS are barely met. Experience Exploration is included primarily because it offers an approach to career exploration and planning that most other systems do not.

Developed by W. P. Ewens and published by Chronicle Guidance, Experience Exploration is a career decision-making system based on an examination of a user's experiences. The actual exercises and inventories of Experience Exploration follow directly from the theory upon which the system is built. One of the unique aspects of this CPS is its theory base. Ewens (1981) describes the theoretical postulates of the "behavioristic theory of career development." The theory maintains that success activities develop interests and people accumulate large amounts of experience in their interest areas which in turn lead to the development of skills needed for success in these activities. Interaction between the environment which is the source of experience, opportunities, and a person's self-perception of their interests, experiences, abilities, and needs create a life-long career development process.

Experience Exploration is a self-scored and self-interpreted system which includes the following six sections: (1) an experience instrument, (2) experience in school subjects, (3) perceived abilities, (4) a work values inventory, (5) experience with data, people, and things, and (6) expected educational level. Designed to facilitate the career exploration of students in grades 9–14 the program is organized in a seven-step process which corresponds to exploring the content of the aforementioned six sections and includes a seventh step of relating the results of the experience exercises to jobs. Completing and scoring the Activity Experience Inventory (AEI) is the first step of the system.

The AEI is a 200-item inventory to which a user responds by indicating the level of prior experience with the activity listed from "0—No experience in the activity" to "4—A large amount of experience in the activity." Scored inventories result in the three highest Manifest Interests, which are possible from a group of 10 interest areas: Outdoor, Mechanical, Computational, Scientific, Persuasive, Artistic, Literary, Musical, Social Service, and Clerical. Step 2 asks respondents to choose 3 school subjects from a list of 12 that they found most satisfying. To complete Step 3, students choose the 3 types of activity from a list of activities identical to the 10 interest areas in which they have the highest ability. Step 4 involves the completion of the Work Values Inventory, which is a 19-item, bipolar instrument from which users select the 3 values most important to them. Selection of whether experiences with data, people, and things—or a combination—are the most satisfying completes the single item comprising Step 5. Expected level of education is asked in Step 6. The final part of this CPS is the integration of the self-assessed information with occupational information.

A Job Chart, which provides occupational titles and corresponding DOT numbers, is organized by the 10 interest areas and the 12 school subjects. After listing occupational titles that matched a student's satisfying school courses, perceived abilities and manifest interests, the Student Experience Sheet provides a work space in which to organize the occupational information, including job description, training/education requirements, employment outlook, earnings/working conditions, and places of employment.

Psychometric Information

Norms.   Consistent with the phenomenological basis of the theory no norms are presented because all the data gathered are meaningful only as self-referenced information.

Reliability and Validity.   Split-half reliability coefficients for the AEI range from .77 to .97 with a median of .92 for the 10 interest scales. No test-retest reliability information is provided for the AIE in the manual. Test-retest information indicate that 44% of high school seniors choose the same three school subjects as satisfying after a 10-week interval and 44% choose two of the three school subjects as satisfying. The psychometric data presented on the Work

Values Inventory are test-retest data for 18 graduate students and 54 high school seniors for which the percentage of change on *each* individual item is listed but no summary statistics are given.

One concurrent validity study has been performed, using the AEI and examining the level of relationship between manifest interest scores and the major chosen by 1,300 college freshman. The results of this study are reported in tabular form only with no written summary accompanying the table. There is no indication as to the meaingfulness of the scores.

In summary, the unique aspect of this CPS is that experiences are central to the career-planning activities in the system. Although this chapter is not designed to be evaluative nor to compare one system with others, there is such a difference between Experience Exploration and the other CPSs reviewed here that a comment seemed necessary. The system is just not as sophisticated or extensive as others, especially in the amount and complexity of investigations of the psychometric properties of the system. In addition, the inferred target population for the program is students. This terminology is used throughout the printed materials. While not a criticism of the system, it does limit the use of Experience Exploration with other populations. It would certainly not fit to have adult career changers using a workbook entitled the Student Experience Sheet. Another concern about this CPS is similar to one voiced about the CDM and that is that the system has only one inventory, the AEI. The rest of the inventoried information does not qualify as actual assessment. Other issues which have been raised about other CPSs include the question of scoring accuracy in a self-scored program and the issue of user honesty in response. This second issue is important in a system that is entirely based on self-report.

One final comment is that the rationale for the choice of 10 activity interest areas and 12 school subjects is never offered. This system was almost excluded because it is similar in structure and purpose to the SDS, which is not reviewed here as a separate system. The decision to include Experience Exploration was made because the program does offer an examination of both experience activities and work values, thus meeting the criteria of measuring two aspects of the career-planning process.

GuidePak

GuidePak offers an interesting combination of a psychological assessment program and a self-help approach to career planning. Users complete the Strong–Campbell Interest Inventory (SCII) and the California Personality Inventory (CPI) and are provided with a workbook which helps them interpret the two inventories and relate results to their career plans. The system can also be used in ongoing individual and/or group career counseling or as part of a course in career development. Behaviordyne, Inc. developed and markets GuidePak, which is titled *The professional GuidePak* when a counselor or other trained professional is the mediator of information to the respondent. The main difference in the two forms is the length and complexity of the narrative report, which summarizes the CPI and the supplemental material—a GuidePak Workbook for the test taker and a pamphlet entitled "Professional's Procedural Outline" for the counselor.

Three types of CPI narrative reports are available: a report for the person who completed the inventory, a report for personnel administrators, and a report for counselors. The level of technical complexity increases with each report. Promotional materials for GuidePak suggest that the program is an appropriate self-help or career-counseling tool for a wide range of users, including high school and college students, individuals who are changing careers, and persons re-entering the labor force.

The untimed administration of inventories usually is completed within 2 hours. In the self-administered GuidePak instructions, test takers are told to complete the CPI first, take a break, and then complete the SCII. Instructions list the necessary materials and specify how to return the inventories for processing.

Given the popularity of the SCII and the CPI with professionals, this review will assume a working knowledge of both instruments and only briefly summarize them. As one of the most widely used and researched interest inventories, the SCII has a solid reputation. The 325-item inventory yields three types of interest information: General Occupational Theme scores which reflect the degree of interest in the six Holland themes; Basic Interest Scale scores which report level of interest in 23 general interest areas; and Occupational Scale scores, which reflect the degree of interest similarity between the test taker and persons in 207 occupational groups. The CPI is also a widely regarded and researched psychometric tool measuring personality variables in adolescent and adult populations. The 480-item instrument assesses personality traits, such as dominance, leadership, social maturity, and responsibility.

In both the self-help and counselor-assisted versions, the test taker receives an SCII profile, a CPI narrative report, and a GuidePak Workbook. The SCII report is the standard profile format scored by Consulting Psychologists Press. Written in the second person, the CPI report is approximately three pages in length and simply describes in everyday language the measured personality traits in terms of strengths and weaknesses.

The final section of the CPI narrative is entitled "World of Work" and describes the relationship between an individual's strong and weak points and work tasks. An example of a typical statement in this section is "You can do very well in a job in which you are called on to do precise, accurate, well-controlled work with careful attention to detail."

The workbook is actually the only integrative component in GuidePak and as such qualifies this program as a Career Planning System. The workbook is divided into the following three sections: Part 1: The Inventory Results, Part 2: Selecting the Job, and Part 3: Getting the Job. Part 1 provides an understandable explanation of the SCII and provides worksheets to be used by the individual to integrate the SCII and CPI results. The self-help nature of these materials is quite apparent in this section as the user first matches strong and weak CPI personality characteristics to the six Holland themes, which have been previously described in the explanation of the SCII. Part 2 focuses on helping the individual relate personal and/or work experiences to Holland theme qualities and CPI results. This section also includes a discussion of occupational information. Part 3 focuses on the job search strategies of resume writing and interviewing skills. A two-page bibliography of career reference material is listed at the end of the workbook.

The counselor-assisted GuidePak differs only in the clinical report available to the counselor and the procedural outline which presents a step-by-step process of interpreting the inventory results and reviewing the client's work in the Guidebook.

Psychometric Information

Norms.   CPI norms are based on a sample of 2,000 normal women and men collected by J. C. Finney. SCII norm groups include a Women in General ($N = 300$) and a Men in General ($N = 300$) sample, which together comprise the General Reference sample. Occupational Scale scores are based on comparisons of a test taker's response to an occupational sample comprised of approximately 200 persons employed in the occupation who are satisfied, successful, have been in the field for at least 3 years, and are between the ages of 25–60.

Reliability and Validity.   Because of widespread use and familiarity of the SCII and CPI, readers are referred to the test manuals for a thorough psychometric report on the reliability and validity of both instruments. This author believes both have proven to be sound psychometric instruments.

One of the most readily apparent strengths of GuidePak is the use of such respected psychometric tools. In addition, combining interest and personality data can serve as powerful information for the individual desiring career guidance. Another strength of the system is the wider applicability of these instruments and materials to populations other than high school students.

A disappointing aspect of GuidePak is the relative lack of psychometrically sound integration. The only true integration that occurs in the system is done by the user after receiving the results of the CPI and SCII so essentially the system itself does not integrate the material for the user. Using the data base available to Behaviordyne a truly impressive integrated report could be generated. Another disappointment is the content of Parts 2 and 3 of the workbook. Both are very superficial. More specifically, only three broad sources of occupational information are listed in Part 2, which include "libraries, guidance counselor, and employment services (private, state, federal)" [Pick, 1981, p. 29] and only one specific source of information, the DOT, is given. In addition, included in the short paragraph on guidance counselors is the following statement with which this author disagrees: "If you look in the yellow pages of your telephone directory, you can find private agencies which can be of service to you. They are listed under "Vocational Consultants" [p. 29]. This obviously overlooks individuals and agencies differently titled, for example, career counselor, psychologist, and career-planning office. Part 3 which addresses the job search presents three examples of resumes that range in quality from mediocre to poor.

A final disquieting aspect of these materials is a response in part to the marketing of the system which notes that the system brings the benefits of psychological assessment directly to the consumer. As attractive as this might seem, some caution needs to be presented. Psychological instrumentation in the hands of untrained persons can result in faulty ideas about oneself and support poor career and life decisions. The attempt here is not to sound alarming or turf protective but to air a caution that is supported by one of the documents included in the marketing materials received with the GuidePak program. It is an enthusiastic article published in the Boston *Globe* that is a fairly simplistic and at one point erroneous presentation. The article's author, with total journalistic license, states that she "should have been, it turns out, a female lawyer." [Foreman, 1981], and later in the article confuses interests and skills. In defense, the workbook does make a statement emphasizing that the SCII measures interests not abilities.

This conclusion may be less likely to occur if the system was supervised by a professional. Possible misinterpretation raises the issue of what the appropriate role of the counselor should be with a program that promotes itself as a self-help system. For many users no professional input will be involved, thus decreasing the potential power of this career-planning tool.

Individual Career Exploration

The Individual Career Exploration (ICE) is a self-report, self-administered, and self-scored CPS. Designed to measure the career-related activity interests, experiences, occupational interests, skills/abilities, and ambitions of students in grades 8 through 12, the ICE can be completed in about 2 hours. Each test taker receives a Student Inventory Booklet, a Classification of Occupations by Group and Level Booklet and several copies of a two-page pamphlet titled "Job Information Checklist." The survey booklet contains five sections (Interests, Experience, Occupations, Skills and Abilities, and Decisions Level), a one-page values checklist and a Summary Record Sheet. The first few pages of the survey booklet introduce the user to Roe's theory of occupations, upon which the ICE is based. The classification of occupations into the eight groups of service, business contact, organization, technology, outdoor, science, general culture, arts and entertainment and the six decision levels which range from professional and managerial personnel making independent decisions to unskilled labor personnel without specific skills are described to the student.

Following this description the student begins the actual inventories, which are contained within the survey booklet. Completion of the inventories yields data on two Roe occupational groups and the decision levels most reflective of the user's interests. The next step is the search for occupational information, which is promoted by referring students to the Classification of Occupations pamphlet and to their ACT interest inventory results. Further emphasis on occupational information gathering is made in the Manual of Directions written for the counselor. Two additional sources of occupational information are suggested in the manual: *The occupational outlook handbook* and the Computerized Vocational Information System (CVIS), a computer-assisted career-planning program also based on Roe's theory. The manual suggests counselors encourage students to complete the Job Information Checklist for at least three occupations. Also included in the manual are some ideas for using the ICE results in a group setting.

Psychometric Information

No psychometric or technical information concerning norms, reliability, and validity are available for the ICE.

One of the advantages emphasized by the creator of ICE is that the self-administered and self-scored nature of this career-planning program provides immediate feedback to the student and facilitates the potential for counselor intervention while student's interest is high (Miller–Tiedeman, 1976). This advantage has also been raised by others when promoting self-scored measurements. A strength of this system is the referral to other career-planning materials, such as the ACT Interest Inventory and the CVIS, which is made in both the student survey booklet and the professional manual. This is an integrative strength, which obviously could help a student connect these two sources of career-planning information. The ICE was created to serve students in grades 8–12. Materials seem to be appropriate for these students. Use of the ICE with populations other than students would be difficult as all the materials use the term "student" to refer to the person completing the materials. Another helpful aspect of the ICE is the Job Information Checklist, which makes a direct connection between inventoried results and occupational information. The only drawback is that no sources of occupational information are given to the user. This is an example of how important the counselor is even when using a self-administered and scored instrument. To assume that a self-scored CPS is merely a self-help program would be a mistake.

As was true with Experience Exploration, this CPS is included with some hesitancy due to its limitations. The lack of psychometric information is quite clearly a major weakness. To what extent should a student, counselor, or parent base educational/vocational decisions on a series of "instruments" which have no psychometric base? Further, the system is quite transparent. The author does note that sections of the inventory are not labeled with Roe titles but the descriptions of the career classifications precede the inventories and could obviously bias the test taker. Although described in a forgoing passage as a strength, referral of users to the CVIS is now antiquated as the computerized system is no longer available. The most pervasive concern is whether the system truly qualifies as a CPS. The conclusion drawn from the above analysis is that the ICE is a marginal CPS and due to lack of psychometric data may not be chosen by many professionals over a similar instrument, such as the SDS. The ICE is included in this chapter as it does integrate more than occupational interests by including experiences and values.

Ohio Vocational Interest Survey with the Career Planner

The OVIS II, a career interest inventory, is presented in this review of CPSs because it includes the Career Planner (The Psychological Corporation, 1981), which extends the traditional interest inventory. Following a brief description of the OVIS II, focus will be on integration of the Career Planner with the OVIS II's career exploration system. For a more extensive discussion of the OVIS II the reader is referred to three recent reviews (Domino, 1985; Hoyt, 1986; Sorenson, 1982).

The OVIS II is an untimed, 253-item interest inventory based on the data–people–things occupational classification system used in the DOT and the Guide to Occupational Exploration (GOE). Responses to the 253 job activity items, which range on a 5-point scale from "like very much" to "dislike very much," result in interest scores in 23 career clusters (11 items for each cluster with each item pertaining to a single occupation in the career cluster). A second method of presenting results of the OVIS II is the Work Characteristics Analysis section, which is based on the items to which the test taker responded "like" or "like very much." Test takers are described in terms of the degree of association between the activities they like and the following seven characteristics: data, people, things; vocational preparation; aptitude; work preferences; work environments; physical demands; and work settings. The instrument can be completed in approximately 45 minutes and three scoring options are available (machine, microcomputer, and hand scoring). Machine scored results are presented in a two-page profile, entitled the Student Report.

As described in the manual, the OVIS II was designed as a central part of a comprehensive career exploration system which consists of the following steps: orientation, assessment, exploration, interpretation, and educational planning. Program materials have been designed to help implement this career exploration system. The other central components of the system are the Career Planner, two filmstrips (Your Interests, Interpreting OVIS, II), and the *Handbook for exploring career*. The 16-page Career Planner designed to help users explore the world of work within the context of their interests consists of five parts: (1) Career Planning Questionnaire, (2) Preference Questionnaire, (3) Exploring Clusters, (4) Exploring Occupations, and (5) Making Educational Plans.

The Career Planning Questionnaire asks test takers to describe themselves in terms of school subject interest, high school program in which currently enrolled, educational or training plans after high school, and the two career areas which most interest them. These results correspond with OVIS II results and can be used to compare test taker's measured interests with those expressed. The Preference Questionnaire designed to measure self-reported personal preferences, aptitudes, and characteristics corresponds to the seven aspects of the Work Characteristic Analysis included in narrative form on the Student Report.

The next two sections focus on the use of OVIS II results to identify which career cluster to consider and on the use of the *Handbook for exploring careers* as a source of occupational information vital to exploration of the job clusters and specific occupations identified in Step 3. Making Educational Plans is a section which aids the user in analyzing the skills, abilities, and education or training necessary for the occupations identified in previous steps of the Career Planner. The final part of this section is a worksheet designed to help a student plan an educational curriculum to meet their career goals. The manual delineates the specific sequence of the career exploration system and suggests appropriate uses for the program materials. Although presented with a group or classroom design and with high school students in mind, the system can certainly be adapted to a variety of settings and individuals. In addition, a self-directed version of the career exploration program is presented in the manual.

Psychometric Information

As the Career Planner is actually a structured series of exercises no psychometric information is provided. Psychometric information however, is available for the OVIS II as it is a measurement tool.

Norms. The norm group of approximately 16,000 students in grades 7–12 from 17 states were tested in the spring of 1980 and the data from a group of college students ($N = 2800$ first- and second-year students) were collected in the fall of 1980. This group is extensive, but one reviewer noted that it is not representative (Domino, 1985). Norms are provided for the 23 scales for males and females in the following age groups (grades 7–9, grades 10–12, first and second years in college).

Reliability and Validity. Internal consistency reliability coefficients range from .83 to .95 for the 23 OVIS scales with medians of .88–.90. Test-retest reliability coefficients for a group of 564 8th graders and 318 10th graders over a 4-week period ranged from .69 to .88 for males and .72 to .91 for females.

The manual summarizes the content and construct validity studies for the OVIS II. Content validity is examined by investigating whether the sample of OVIS occupations and the sample of work activities are representative. According to the manual, the pool of occupations from which the final sample was chosen represents 90% of the workforce. The teachers and counselors who evaluated the research edition of OVIS II concluded that the work activity items were representative. Winefordner (1983), the manual author, believes these data support the content validity of the OVIS II. The construct validity section lists, but does not describe, a number of research studies which are purported to support construct validity of the OVIS II. No comparisons of the OVIS with other vocational interest measures or predictive validity data is reported.

One of the strengths of the OVIS II with the Career Planner is integration of the interest inventory within a systematic career exploration system. The system is reasonably explained in the manual and supporting materials. Another strength of this CPS is the excellent interface with up-to-date occupational information. This benefit follows naturally from a system built upon the occupational classifications of the DOT and GOE. Users are taken step by step through the process of identifying their interests then exploring them via occupational information. Many other systems merely list sources of information without providing any guidance regarding effective use of these materials.

One glaring problem of the OVIS II is the lack of validity for the instrument. In referring to the support for content validity given in the OVIS II manual, Domino (1985) states "such evidence seems shaky at best, and is akin to arguing that test X has content validity because the words used come from the dictionary" [p. 1091], and concludes that the OVIS II shows little evidence of validity. Given the number of years the OVIS has existed it is especially disappointing that validity studies relating the OVIS scales to other vocational measures have either not been done or were not reported in the manual. This information is vital for professionals in choosing an appropriate CPS for a clientele.

Overall, the OVIS II career exploration system certainly shows some promise but as is true of other CPS, more psychometric work is necessary.

Personal Career Development Profile and the Self-Motivated Career Planning System

The Personal Career Development Profile (PCDP) and the supplemental Self-Motivated Career Planning System (SMCP) constitute a CPS based on the Sixteen Personality Factor Questionnaire (16 PF). This paper-pencil personality inventory measures 16 personality traits in a bipolar fashion, such as reserved–outgoing, less intelligent–more intelligent, and relaxed–tense. The 187-item questionnaire requires 45–60 minutes to complete. The PCDP is a computer-generated report of the 16 PF designed for use in career exploration and planning. The narrative PCDP report contains nine sections, comprised of (1) Orientation, (2) Problem-solving Patterns, (3) Patterns for Coping with Stressful Conditions, (4) Patterns of Interpersonal Interactions, (5) Organizational Role and Work-Setting Patterns, (6) Patterns for Career Activity Interests, (7) Personal Career, Life Style Effectiveness Considerations, (8) Occupational Comparisons, and (9) a graphic profile of the test data. The last two sections are intended for use only by qualified professionals.

A revision of the PCDP currently in process will most likely result in dropping the orientation section. The PCDP narrative report runs seven pages and delegates from one to several paragraphs in describing the user's personality and career interests. Narrative comments for sections 3, 4, 5, and 7 are based on "interaction motivational orientation" scores (Walter, 1985) derived from regression equations using the 16 PF primary factors as predictor variables of these scores. The concept of interactional motivational orientation scores is based on the work of Porter (1976) and is operationally defined in the Strength Deployment Inventory (Porter & Maloney, 1977). Three basic patterns of motivation are serving/supporting, competing/directing, and autonomizing/thinking. Six scores are possible representing the three patterns in two interactional conditions: when things are going well (harmony) and when things are in conflict.

Results for the Career Activity Interests (6) and the Occupational Comparisons (8) sections are derived from scores on the six PCDP Occupational Interest Themes of Venturous-Influential (V), Nurturing-Altruistic (N), Creative-Self-Expressive (C), Procedural-Systematic (P), Analytic-Scientific (A), and Mechanical-Operative (M). These interest themes were generated in part by regression equations using the 16 PF primary factors as predictor variables of the six Holland Themes as measured by the SCII. In addition to a description of the highest interest themes, Section 6 lists occupations in which the user may be interested. The Occupational Comparisons section lists a test taker's scores on the six interest themes, and displays the career activity interest scores for the interest profiles of persons working in about 50 different occupations.

Two supplemental programs, the PCDP-Plus and the SMCP, are available to augment the PCDP. The PCDP-Plus allows for a self-directed, self-help approach including a thorough step-by-step analysis of the PCDP results whereas the SMCP is an extensive workbook of career-planning exercises which the user begins by completing the 16 PF. The eight SMCP paper-pencil exercises are organized into four career planning steps: (1) Getting to Know Oneself, (2) Developing a Career Plan, (3) Putting the Career Plan into Action, and (4) Regularly Reviewing Career Progress.

The seven exercises following the completing of the 16 PF include: (1) the Personal Orientation Survey, which measures attitudes, sources of pressure, stress, challenge and gratification, growth needs, and career and personal goals (50 minutes), (2) the Educational Summary, which helps test takers summarize their educational goals and expectations, interests and skills, growth experiences and needs, and accomplishments (60 minutes), (3) the Career Experience Summary, which reviews the same content areas as the previous section while focusing on career experiences (60 minutes), (4) the Personal Career Life Summary, which reviews and integrates the above exercises (120 minutes), (5) the Personal Career Strengths and Interests section, which uses PCDP results as a basis for personal reflection on skills and interests (90 minutes), (6) the Identify Your Next Career Steps exercise (60 minutes) and (7) the Compose Your Personal Development Summary, in which participants list their educational, career, and personal plans (90 minutes).

The final step involves putting the plan into action, with the remainder of the SMCP program focusing on job search techniques such as resume writing and interviewing skills. Dolliver (1985) summarized the SMCP as consisting of 12 steps (7 assessment and 5 review or planning steps) and described the SMCP as a programmed learning package helpful in career planning.

Psychometric Information

Norms. No psychometric information is available for the SMCP. The norms used for the PCDP are those developed for the 16 PF which are provided in the 16 PF Handbook and Supplemental materials. Norm tables are presented in these materials for different ages, educational levels, and sex, with samples sizes ranging from 468 to 3,322.

Reliability and Validity. Test-retest reliability coefficients range from .61 to .92 for a short time interval and .21 to .88 for a long time interval (Vetter, et al.). The validity data presented in the PCDP manual are derived from construct validity studies, such as those investigating the relationship between the PCDP and the SCII Holland themes, and to certain Jackson Vocational Interest Survey scales. Validity coefficients ranged from .35 to .94.

One of the overall strengths of the PCDP as supplemented by the SMCP is that the system does integrate information about an individual with specific career development issues, such as career interests and occupational options. In addition, if the two systems are used jointly, the participant can experience the advantages of using both a professionally developed, scored, and interpreted system and a self-directed, self-interpreted career-planning tool.

In his recent review of the PCDP, Mossholder (1985) observed that one of the original objectives of this system was to free counselors from routine, time-consuming report writing. By using a computer-generated narrative report format, this objective has been met. This very advantage, however, is also the basis of the strongest criticism of this system. The manual does not provide an adequate explanation of how the 16 PF scores translate into PCDP narrative. In addition, this reviewer found it was difficult to discern how certain scores were derived. For example, the manual was not clear about how the occupations listed for consideration by the test taker in Section 6 and the sten scores listed for occupational groups in the Occupational Comparisons section were derived. As these sections may be of particular interest to a person who is trying to define potential career options, the lack of clarity in the professional materials is viewed as a major weakness of the program. Another aspect of the system, which presents both a strength and a weakness, is inclusion in the development of the PCDP a wide range of theoretical ideas and data such as Holland themes, JVIS scores, and relationship awareness theory. The inclusion of theory in instrumentation is, of course, a strength; however, the explanation of how these elements relate to PCDP narrative and scores is inadequate.

In summary, the system would be greatly strengthened by a well-conceived and well-written technical manual. Walter (1985) does refer the professional to three publications which seem crucial for use with the PCDP: *Handbook for the 16 PF; Interpreting the 16 PF profile patterns,* and *A guide to the clinical use of the 16 PF.* Overall this CPS is, as Mossholder (1985) noted, "a relatively new instrument that has potential in overall career planning" but due to the lack of validity studies is recommended with caution and as a supplement to more extensively researched instruments, such as the SCII. If one uses the PCDP from the perspective of exploration, rather than validation, the program would seem to be a potential aid in the career-planning process. One of the strongest advantages of the PCDP is inclusion of behavioral motivational variables. Unfortunately, no empirical work has been cited which confirms the theoretical connection of these concepts to actual career choice, satisfaction, and success; therefore this aspect of the program remains a *potential* strength.

Planning Career Goals

Another comprehensive, multidimensional CPS is Planning Career Goals (PCG), developed by the American Institutes for Research under the leadership of J. C. Flanagan and published by CTB/McGraw-Hill. The purpose of the PCG program is to help students in grades 8–12 develop and determine appropriate career plans. An assumption underlying the PCG system is that there may be *many* careers suitable for an individual and the goal of the program is to facilitate individuals' "understanding of themselves in relation to life styles and career opportunities" [American Institutes for Research, 1975, p. 7], rather than to help them choose the *one* career which is best fitted for them, given their interests and abilities. PCG is a CPS based on a national longitudinal study, Project TALENT, conducted by the American Institutes for Research and the University of Pittsburgh in 1960.

The original sample of approximately 400,000 high school students in grades 9–12 were administered interest, information, ability, and demographic measures. Follow-up testing was scheduled at 1-, 5-, 10-, and 20-year intervals and according to PCG materials, has actually been conducted at 1, 5, and 11 years. The most recent date of publication of these materials is 1977. Therefore, the 20-year follow-up had not yet been conducted. Not only did Project TALENT provide the basis for the inventories and measures of PCG, the follow-up data, primarily from the 11-year interval, provides comparison information which a current high school student can use to contrast their PCG results to those of persons who have entered various careers. This comparison ideally results in more informed and realistic educational and career plans.

The testing component of PCG system includes three test booklets entitled: (1) Ability Measures, (2) Interest Inventory, and (3) Information Measures and a Life and Career Plans inventory which is printed on the PCG answer sheet. The first step in the PCG program is completion of the Life and Career Plans Inventory, which includes a 15-item values inventory and can be completed in approximately 10 minutes. The ability instrument includes the following timed measures: Reading Comprehension, Mathematics, Abstract Reasoning, Creativity, Mechanical Reasoning, English, Quantitative Reasoning, Vocabulary, Visualization, and Computation. These 10 measures were selected from the Project TALENT group of 19 ability measures because they resulted in the greatest amount of differentiation among individuals who later entered different occupations. Total testing time for all the ability measures is about 2½ hours.

The Interest Inventory consists of 300 items, can be completed in about 30–45 minutes, and is divided into three parts: Occupations, Occupational Activities, and Current Activities. Responses based on a 5-point Likert scale, ranging from "I think I would *like* this *very much*" to "I think I would *dislike* this *very much*," produce 12 interest scores in 12 career groups. The career groups, determined by and refined by organizing occupations into clusters according to the homogeneous interests and abilities of the Project TALENT participants, are: Engineering, Physical Sciences, Mathematics, Architecture; Medical, Biological Sciences; Business Administration; General Teaching, Social Service; Humanities, Law, Social and Behavioral Science; Fine Arts, Performing Arts; Technical Jobs; Proprietors, Sales Workers; Mechanics, Industrial Trades; Construction Trades; Secretarial-Clerical, Office Workers; and General Labor, Public, and Community Service. The first six career groups typically require at least four years of college while the remaining six clusters do not require college training.

The third measurement booklet contains the Information Measures, which are designed to assess the level of accurate information that the test taker actually possesses about the 12 career groups. A total of 240 items (20 items for each career cluster) comprise this measure. The assumption underlying the construction of this instrument is that individuals who express interest in an occupational area would expose themselves to that interest area and gather occupationally relevant information. The test taker can complete this instrument in approximately 80 minutes. Total testing time for the values, ability, interest, and information measures is about 4½ to 5 hours.

In addition to the assessment aspect of PCG, the system also involves facilitation of a user's career planning. This aspect of PCG includes three basic components: (1) Planning Your Career; (2) PCG Career Planning Report; and (3) the PCG Career Handbook. Planning Your Career is a student guide which prepares the individual for the program and should be read before the PCG results are received. The five sections included in this guide are: (1) An introduction to planning life and career goals, (2) The first step: Finding out about yourself, (3) The second step: Learning about careers, (4) Thumbnail sketches, and (5) The third step: comparing yourself with people who have entered various jobs. The final section details a PCG Career Planning Report and describes the three main parts of this report: (1) Narrative Report, (2) Responses, and (3) Comparisons. Although both hand and machine scoring options are available, the Career Planning Report can only be received if PCG is machine scored.

The narrative section of the report summarizes the results of the PCG measures while the Responses section provides a graphic display of the student's interests in the 12 career areas and presents results of the ability measures. The comparisons section of the report compares the degree of similarity between a student's values, interests, abilities and information with persons who entered each of the 12 career areas. The Career Handbook describes occupational information about 151 jobs and presents PCG profiles for persons in those occupations.

Psychometric Information

Norms.   Separate sex norms are used for the Ability measures and Information measures for which an individual's scores are converted to percentile ranks. For the Interest Inventory, raw scores only are reported. Norms are provided for males and females in grades 8–12 and were updated from the original Project TALENT data pool in 1975, creating a norm group of more than 6,100 students from 28 schools.

Reliability and Validity.   Reliability coefficients for the PCG inventories are presented in the PCG Technical Bulletin No. 1. The split-half reliability coefficients for grades 8–12 range from .84 to 1.0 for the Interest Inventory, from .63 to .89 for the Information measures and from .68 to .94 for the Ability measures. The Validity information provided refers to the predictive validity data resulting from the 5- and 11-year follow-up studies of Project TALENT subjects.

One of the positive features of PCG is the integration of the assessment aspects of the system with the career-planning sections of the program. The national data base from which the assessment measures were drawn and/or refined is also impressive. For example, the 15-item values inventory was the result of a national sample of more than 6,500 critical incidents that individuals stated made their lives significantly better or worse. Another strength of this CPS is the integration of this system within a larger context of career development interventions contained in the McGraw-Hill career choice system, such as the Career Maturity Inventory. The supplemental materials, such as the Examiner's Manual are well written and organized.

One of the most major drawbacks of PCG is the age of the materials. Most of the work was published in 1975–1977 and is now 10 or more years old. In addition, no recent validity studies have been done nor are there any studies comparing PCG results with other career planning measures. Another potential drawback is the amount of testing time required to complete the program. On the other hand the system could easily be incorporated into a curriculum on career planning and would not require extensive out of classroom time.

Vocational Exploration and Insight Kit

The Vocational Exploration and Insight Kit (VEIK) was developed in response to research studies suggesting that diverse types of interest inventories are helpful to clients and a combination of such treatments may be even more helpful. The VEIK was designed to "encourage self-exploration and self-understanding, to resolve vocational indecision, to clarify the advantages of one vocational alternative over another, and to increase the range of vocational options" [Holland & Associates, 1980, p. 1].

The VEIK involves a 15-step, self-directed process in career exploration that includes three main parts: (1) the Vocational Card Sort (VCS), (2) the Self-Directed Search (SDS), and (3) the Action Plan. The first 10 steps involve the use of the VCS. The VCS is a card sort of 84 occupational titles taken from the seventh edition of the Vocational Preference Inventory (VPI). The occupations are equally divided among the six Holland themes and represent a range of education required for occupational entrance: 26%—high school diploma or less, 49%—college degree, and 24%—postgraduate education. The occupations are sorted in three categories: "Would Not Choose," "In Question," and "Might Choose." Following the steps outlined in the Action Plan Workbook, the user first sorts the occupations into the three general categories, then groups the occupations within each category according to similar reasons for placing the occupation in a particular group. Subsequent steps result in test takers using the Occupations Finder of the SDS to define the Holland three-letter code most frequent in the occupations they have selected.

The next four steps of the VEIK involve the completion and use of the SDS which includes the following sections: Occupational Daydreams, Activities, Competencies, Occupations, Self-estimates of Abilities, and Summary Code. For excellent and extensive descriptions of the SDS, the reader is referred to previous reviews (Holland & Rayman, 1986; Walsh & Betz, 1985). Not only does the VEIK incorporate the SDS as an assessment tool but it includes the use of the SDS supplemental materials of the Occupations Finder and the user booklet "Understanding You and Your Career." Step 14 asks users to make a new list of occupations they are still considering after completing both the VCS and the SDS. The final step, entitled Action Plan, requires the test taker to list the strengths and weaknesses of the occupations under consideration and to describe the kinds of information still necessary to make a final selection. The entire VEIK can be completed in 3 to 4 hours.

The Workbook is designed to encourage the user to complete the program in sections rather than in one sitting. Reviews of the system suggest that the program can be effectively used with high school, college, and adult populations (Daniels, 1985; Tittle, 1985) although the VEIK materials do not directly specify the appropriate user populations.

Psychometric Information

No reliability, validity, or normative information is provided for the VEIK; however, such data are available for the SDS.

Norms.   The norm groups for the SDS consist of a high school ($N = 4,675$) and a college ($N = 3,355$) sample. Norms are presented separately for males and females converting raw scores to percentile scores.

Reliability and Validity.   Median test-retest reliability coefficients for high school students were .81 for males and .83 for females over a 3–4 week interval and .92 for college students over a 7–10-month interval. A 1-year, test-retest study was conducted for adults resulting in correlation coefficients of .63–.95 for males ($N = 27$) and .59–.89 for females ($N = 52$). Most of the validity work reported in the SDS manual (Holland, 1985) concerns predictive validity studies of high point codes. Approximately 43% of male subjects and 66% of female subjects retain the same high point code after a 3-year period.

One of the potential disadvantages of the VEIK is the high level of motivation required from a user. Even the Counselor's Guide to the system states that to complete the VEIK without counselor assistance, clients "must have a compelling motive to finish all fifteen steps" [p. 1]. Of course, the system can be utilized in forms of intervention other than self-directed, such as one-to-one counseling or group counseling. Treatment delivery flexibility is one of the strengths of this system. The level of education required by the VCS occupations (73% college or above) is another factor which may restrict the populations for which the VEIK is most useful. The potential for scoring errors is also a possible drawback with a self-directed, self-scored CPS such as VEIK. Another potential drawback of the self-directed aspect of the VEIK is the potential problem of a user who after completing the VCS does not generate a consistent or clear three-letter Holland code. The instructions assume this code can be easily generated; however, there is probably a group of persons for whom this aspect of the program could be frustrating. A final criticism, raised by Tittle (1985), is that no empirical work has been done to support the sequence and the activities of VEIK.

In addition to intervention flexibility, a strength of the VEIK is the number and diversity of reflective questions which are asked of the user as the VCS steps are completed (Dolliver, 1981). In summary, the VEIK offers a CPS that has integrated two different career development tools in a single career-planning program.

Vocational Interest Experience and Skill Assessment

The Vocational Interest, Experience, and Skill Assessment (VIESA) developed and distributed by ACT, may appear familiar as it is a companion of the ACT CPP program. In fact, VIESA is the short form of the CPP. First introduced in 1971, it was completely revised in 1983. Dale Prediger directed the ACT staff that developed VIESA, which is designed to initiate thinking about career planning. The major purpose of this program is *exploration* of self and career options in the early stages of career decision making. This self-administered and self-scored career-planning tool helps a user examine interests, work-related skills, and experiences in relationship to occupational possibilities. This exploration is supplemented by a section on job values.

The major differences from the CPP program are in the length and scope of the assessment measures, the self-rated nature of all measures, especially in contrast to the CPP ability measures, the lack of psychometric information except for the interest instrument, and the lack of options for interpretation as the program is self-scoring.

The VIESA system includes four components: (1) a 60-item interest inventory, which is actually a short form of the 90-item ACT UNIACT, (2) a skills assessment section, (3) a work-related Experiences Component, and (4) a unit on job values. In self-rating of skills, the user selects his or her best from three skill activities in each of the four areas: people, data, things, and ideas. This skill selection translates into two regions on the World of Work Map in which the 23 ACT job families are plotted. By responding with "haven't done, done once or twice, or done several times" to work-related activity items, the user receives experience scores which are also translated on the World of Work Map. In the Job Values section the three most important values are selected from a list of eight. These values are then compared to a list of previously generated job possibilities.

The total inventory can be completed and scored in approximately 40 minutes. Similar to the CPP, two forms of VIESA are available: Level I (grades 9–10) and Level II (grade 11–adult). The main tool of this career-planning system is the VIESA Career Guidebook: Charting Your Future. Separate versions exist for both levels although the length is similar (15 and 16 pages for Level I and II respectively). The main counselor or professional tool is the User's Handbook.

A revised edition was published by ACT in 1984 in which the rationale, construction, limited psychometric information, and possible uses of VIESA are discussed. Central to both ACT's career-planning programs is the occupational classification system theoretically based on Roe and Holland's work, which culminates in 23 ACT Job Families. A thorough understanding of this conceptualization is essential for informed use of both CPP and VIESA.

Psychometric Information

Norms.   An extensive study conducted in 1983 provides normative data for both the CPP and VIESA based on national samples of students in grades 8, 10, and 12. Approximately 14,400 students comprised the norming sample.

Reliability and Validity.   The User's Handbook states that recent reliability and validity information for VIESA scales are provided in the Psychometric Handbook for ACT's Career Services. This handbook is a separate publication, scheduled for publication in 1984, but as of this writing it is not yet available. An interim handbook for the ACT CPP is available but does not present VIESA information.

According to other reviewers, VIESA provides a psychometrically sound interest inventory (Krauskopf, 1978) but as far as psychometric instruments, that is all VIESA delivers. In addition, Krauskopf (1978) mentions that the reliability and validity information provided is "borrowed" from the UNIACT IV. This lack of "normal technical information" has been noted by other reviewers as well (Read, 1982; Vetter et al., 1986). VIESA authors defend this lack of technical sophistication by presenting the program as a vocational *exploration* tool as opposed to a vocational interest measure. It seems that the authors have taken extensive latitude by including the skills, experiences, and values aspects of the program in this rationale. As Walsh and Betz (1985) noted, "the problems with the programs stem from their attempt to do too much . . . with one set of measures that is probably too short, as well as insufficiently reliable and valid [p. 291]." Another controversial aspect of VIESA is the use of unisex norms.

Strengths of VIESA include the flexibility that a self-scoring system provides for use in a wide range of applications including one-to-one counseling, career-planning workshops or groups, academic advising, and academic courses. In addition, Level 1 of this program is geared to the younger student and can initiate him or her into a lifelong career development process. If used as an exploratory tool rather than a confirmatory one, VIESA can provide some excellent first steps in this career-planning process.

Vocational Information Profile

In conjunction with the U.S. Employment Service, National Computer Systems developed the Vocational Information Profile (VIP) which was designed to provide a comprehensive interest-aptitude assessment. The VIP combines the scores of the General Aptitude Test Battery (GATB) and the USES interest inventory. These instruments are two of the central assessment tools in the Counselor Assessment/Occupational Exploration System developed by the U.S. Employment Service. As such, both instruments are integrally connected to the Guide for Occupational Exploration (GOE), the central component of the Counselor Assessment/Occupational Exploration system. The GOE is an extensive occupational classification system which delineates interest and aptitude information about occupations listed in the 4th edition of the DOT. The classification system organizes jobs into 66 different Work Groups which are further organized into 12 occupational interest-defined areas coinciding with the 12 areas of the USES interest inventory which, in turn, corresponds to Holland's vocational schema.

The completion of the GATB and the USES interest inventory comprise the VIP program. Results are presented in the profile report, which is approximately six pages long and combines both narrative and graphic displays of the user's scores. This report is the only truly integrative aspect of the VIP. The target population of 9th-to-12th-grade students and adults typically complete the program in about 2 hours, 45 minutes.

The GATB is a well-known multiple aptitude test battery which consists of nine subtests: General Learning Ability, Verbal Aptitude, Numerical Aptitude, Spatial Aptitude, Form Perception, Clerical Perception, Motor Coordination, Finger Dexterity, and Manual Dexterity. The GATB was developed for use in vocational counseling and job placement counseling. It helps users discover their personal aptitude strengths and weaknesses, as compared with the minimum aptitudes necessary for specific occupations (Specific Aptitude Test Batteries, SATBs) and for clusters of similar occupations (Occupational Aptitude Patterns, OAPs) (Borgen, 1982). The untimed, 162-item interest inventory yields scores on 12 interest scales which are: Artistic, Scientific, Plants and Animals, Protective, Mechanical, Industrial, Business Detail, Selling, Accommodating, Humanitarian, Leading-Influencing, and Physical Performing.

The narrative report presents results in the following sections: (1) Your Interests, which in both narrative and graphic form displays the 12 interest areas assessed in the interest inventory in rank order of expressed interest, (2) Your Aptitudes, which summarizes the GATB results according to the level of ability (high, medium, low) to perform jobs within the 66 Work Groups, and (3) Your Job Planning Profile, which presents a graphic summary of both interest and aptitude results and lists the GOE page number for the user to refer to for more occupational information. The chart also contains a section for comments which can be used by the counselor or test taker to note discrepancies and confirmations. The final two sections of the VIP report include a summary of the highest interest areas with corresponding Work Groups and a Test Record Summary displaying an overall summary of the test results.

Psychometric Information

No psychometric information is provided for the VIP although information is available for both the USES interest inventory and the GATB. Readers are referred to the manuals for both of these instruments for a thorough psychometric presentation.

Norms. The norm group for the USES interest inventory is comprised of 2,876 male and 3,654 female students and nonstudents from 28 states representing a range of ethnic and cultural backgrounds. Separate sex norms are provided for the interest inventory. GATB norms are comprised of workers in 460 occupations and are presented separately for 9th and 10th graders and adults.

Reliability and Validity. The reliability information provided in the USES interest inventory manual concerns internal consistency and item analyses. No test-retest data nor validity information is presented. Test-retest reliability for the GATB subtests range from the mid .70s to .90 and an extensive range of validity studies of more than 400 occupations are presented.

One of the most positive features of the VIP is the use of a well-established and researched instrument such as the GATB. The VIP profile does provide an integrated ability/interest report for the test taker and counselor which is another strength of this system. The User Workbook, which extends the profile integration, would seem to enhance the quality of the VIP. Another contribution which the VIP makes is the natural connection to excellent occupational information in the form of the DOT and the GOE.

One of the weaknesses of the VIP, which echoes similar statements made of other CPSs, is the absence of outcome studies to determine the effectiveness of the system. The NCS promotional materials list an extensive array of applications, from employee assessment to vocational choice counseling to use with correctional inmates for federal training program placement; however, no empirical work justifies these applications.

World of Work Inventory

The World of Work Inventory (WOWI) is a comprehensive inventory designed to assess career interests, job-related temperament factors, and aptitude/achievement levels. This self-administered CPS can be used by high school and college students and by adults to better understand themselves, their potential and the world of work. Approximate testing time is 2½ hours. The inventory consists of four parts: (1) Identifying Information, (2) Career Interest Activities, (3) Vocational Training Potentials, and (4) Job Satisfaction Indicators. Machine scoring results in an Inventory Profile, which is the integrative report of the WOWI. On the back of this profile is a narrative Guide to the World of Work Inventory.

Basic demographic data such as sex, age, education, and best liked school subjects are assessed in the Identifying Information section.

The Career Interest Activities section includes 238 job-related activity items to which a test taker responds "like," "neutral," or "dislike." Responses to the interest inventory result in overall interest scores in 17 basic occupational areas. Part 3 of the WOWI includes measures of six aptitudes: Verbal, Numerical, Mechanical-Electrical, Spatial-Form, Abstractions, and Clerical. Twelve job temperament scales result from the test taker's responses to the 180 items on the Job Satisfaction Indicators section. Both the 17 interest scales and the 12 temperament scales are keyed to the DOT. Users are provided with the Interpretation Mini Manual and Occupational Exploration Worksheets which aid their understanding of the WOWI profile and help facilitate their active participation in examining occupational information.

Psychometric Information

Norms.   Promotional materials for the WOWI state that it is normed on ages 13–65. However, this material is not completely presented in the manual. Norms are presented for Vocational Training potentials for males and females in 10 age groups.

Reliability and Validity.   Previous reviews of the WOWI have reported reliability coefficients for the Career Interest Activity Scales and the Vocational Training Potentials which ranged from .81 to .94 and from .89 to .94 respectively. This reliability information should be viewed with caution, according to Layton (1978b), due to the rather curious correction of these alpha coefficients via the Spearman Brown formula, which may have raised the actual correlation coefficients. The most recent manual (Neidert, Hudson, Ripley, & Ripley, 1984) contains no reliability information at all. The validity data presented in this manual include recent concurrent and content validity studies, comparing the WOWI scales with other related instruments such as the SCII, EPPS, and the 16 PF. No predictive validity data are available.

The strengths of the WOWI include the multidimensional nature of the instrument, which allows for both aptitude and interest assessment from a single instrument and the integration of WOWI dimensions with the DOT. Another asset is the extensive discussion of the occupational information provided in the manual. This information is organized according to the 17 career interest areas into Career Families and can serve as a useful occupational information tool.

One of the shortcomings of the system noted in previous reviews (Layton, 1978b; Locke, 1982) is the lack of validity data. This weakness has been partly overcome as the most recent WOWI manual (Neidert et al., 1984) presents the results of content and concurrent validity studies. Predictive validity data, however, are still not available, nor is reliability information. The criticism regarding the psychometric weakness of the system therefore remains viable. A wide array of uses and populations are listed as the domain of the WOWI instrument. No evidence is presented to support such claims. As with many of the CPSs reviewed here, more empirical work is necessary to support the use of the WOWI instead of the more well-researched and therefore more established vocational instruments.

Paper-Pencil Programs Summary

As is apparent from the preceding reviews, the number and range of paper-pencil CPSs is quite extensive. These programs offer a rich selection from which practicing professionals can choose a system to meet the career development needs of their clientele. As noted earlier, one of the similarities among many of these systems is reliance on a vocational assessment inventory as the central core of the system. These systems, however, offer comprehensive career-planning programs which expand the utility of the single vocational assessment inventory and provide an integrated program which enhances the career development of the users of such systems.

Overall these systems are an excellent addition to vocational psychology especially in the assessment and practice arenas; however, some problems do exist. The state of the psychometric properties for some of the systems is not adequate. One problem is the lack of predictive validity studies for many of the programs. In addition, the majority of systems lack the necessary evaluation and outcome studies which are essential for confident use of these systems. Some minor problems involve scoring accuracy in those systems which allow for users to self-score and the amount of time necessary to complete some of the systems. A final comment regards the weak attempts by some of these systems to provide a truly integrated report for the user. This issue is important because systems which do not fully integrate the material do only a partial job in aiding the user and do not live up to the potential inherent in a CPS which, by definition, should involve such integration.

COMPUTER-ASSISTED CAREER GUIDANCE SYSTEMS

Computer-assisted career guidance systems (CAGSs) are one of the fastest growing developments in counseling and guidance. Computer applications in the field have been especially successful in the career guidance arena. The discussion which follows is a descriptive overview of what is currently available in computer-assisted CPSs. This review is not exhaustive or inclusive of all the systems and issues relevant to a "state of the art" discussion of CAGSs. The reader will be referred to selected CAGS resources which are currently available.

Before the brief descriptions of specific CAG programs this chapter addresses the following salient issues in the fast-growing world of CAGSs: history of

CAGSs, types of CAGSs, selection of CAGSs, and comparisons between and among CAGSs. Following the specific CAGS reviews this section of the chapter concludes with a discussion of the evaluation of CAGSs and other relevant issues.

The history of the development of CAGSs is both interesting and informative. A number of excellent historical reviews provided by the following authors are suggested reading as the historical perspective can provide a broader understanding of CAGSs (Harris–Bowlsbey, 1984; Katz & Shatkin, 1980; Maze & Cummings, 1982; and Montross, 1984).

Many authors have lent their expertise to discerning various types of CAGSs, which can be simplistically divided into two main types of systems: information access and retrieval systems and guidance systems (Clyde, 1979; Harris–Bowlsbey, 1984; Maze, 1985; Nagy & Donald, 1981; Sampson, 1983). Clyde (1979) conceptualized a CAGS continuum on which systems ranged from an emphasis on information access and retrieval at one end of the continuum to a focus on guidance and decision making at the other end of the continuum. Sampson (1983) distinguished two forms of CAGSs, information systems and guidance systems, while Nagy and Donald (1981) added a third form and used different labels: (1) occupational information systems, (2) career development programs, and (3) combined programs. Harris–Bowlsbey (1984) provided a discussion of factors which characterize and distinguish information systems from guidance systems. Maze (1985) agreed that the main distinction between the two forms is the inclusion of on-line assessment devices in guidance systems.

The issue of selection—which CAG system to choose for which setting and with which users—is of course a very important question especially in a marketplace that continues to see such rapid development. Katz and Shatkin (1980) provided a conceptual schema by which to evaluate CAGS which includes eight major topics:

(1) scope (information and guidance, data processing, and populations and settings), (2) content (appraisal, information, decision-making, and planning), (3) structure (direct access to information; structured search for occupations, crosswalks, and recapitulation for decision-making), (4) style (interactivity, hardware, system design, and script writing), (5) procedures (what to include, sources of data, interpretation of data, and updating information), (6) costs (itemization of components and typical costs per terminal hour), (7) effects, and (8) rationales for guidance and models of career decision making (Parsons's true reasoning, trait-matching for success or membership, and freedom, understanding, competence and satisfaction). [p. i]

As Shatkin (1980) stated, the eight criteria ask these questions: How much does the system attempt to do? How well does the system address the different components of the guidance process? How are the parts of the system interconnected? How interactive is the system? How is the information selected and prepared? How much does the system cost? What outcomes are due to the system? and What theoretical model of guidance underlies the system?

Maze and Cummings (1982) and more recently Maze (1984) detailed steps to take in selecting the appropriate system. After determining institutional needs and priorities, test piloting the CAGSs of interest with potential users, gathering information on the systems from discussion with current user sites and by reading system literature and any available research, Maze and Cummings (1982) suggest a more in-depth evaluation of each CAGS. In conjunction with the previous steps, Maze and Cummings have developed a detailed checklist to use in a thorough evaluation of a CAGS program, which results in rating the overall functioning of the system, the ability of the system to meet institutional needs, and the cost of the system per user. Important advice offered by Maze (1984) is to choose software first and then determine the appropriate hardware selection.

Another recent discussion of CAGS selection defined 17 criteria to use in the evaluation process: (1) content of the system, (2) hardware, (3) cost, (4) contacts for further information, (5) designer, (6) content update, (7) reading level, (8), graphics, (9) staff requirements, (10) additional costs, (11) built-in evaluation and accountability, (12) ability to tailor the basic program, (13) theoretical orientation, (14) use of previous test scores, (15) sex fairness, (16) use by the physically disabled, and (17) ease of use (Heppner & Johnston, 1985). Depending on user and institutional needs, different criteria may be more salient for different settings.

The issue of comparisons between and among CAGSs overlaps the content of the previous section on selection as many of the authors delineating selection criteria proceeded to use these to describe, compare, and contrast one system with another. One of the most impressive, although now somewhat dated, descriptive reviews was conducted by Shatkin (1980) who reviewed 18 CAGSs on the dimensions of scope and content, structure, and procedures. For reasons of convenience and space restrictions, the reader is referred to Table 4.2, which adopts the convention used by Katz and Shatkin (1983) of listing a glossary of acronyms by which to identify CAGSs, thereby permitting the reader to forgo the redundancy of reading full CAGS titles each time they are named.

The systems described by Shatkin (1980) were: CHOICES, several state CIS systems (Nationwide, Oregon, Iowa, Colorado, Minnesota, Nebraska, Washington, and California's CIS, titled EUREKA), COIN, CVIS, DISCOVER, GIS, MOIS (Massachusetts, Michigan), OCIS, SIGI, SOICC, and WOIS. Descriptions of these CAGSs which were all on-line at the beginning of 1980 were based on a questionnaire completed by the system's director and, in most cases, on-line experience with the system. Nagy and Donald (1981) reviewed six CAGSs which they believed were some of the most well developed and most appropriate to a college or university population including SIGI, DISCOVER, GIS III, CVIS, CHOICES, and CIS. The content, cost, necessary hardware, and user population were described for each system. In addition, the advantages and

TABLE 4.2
Glossary of CAGS and Other Relevant Acronyms

CCAPP	Computerized Career Assessment and Planning
CHOICES	Computerized Heuristic Occupational Information and Career Exploration System
CIS	Career Information System
COCIS	Colorado Career Information System
COIN	Coordinated Occupational Information Network
CVIS	Computerized Vocational Information System
DOT	Dictionary of Occupational Titles
ECES	Educational and Career Exploration System
GIS	Guidance Information System
GOE	Guide for Occupational Exploration
ISVD	Information System for Vocational Decisions
MOIS	Massachusetts or Michigan Occupational Information System
OCIS	Ohio Career Information System
OOH	Occupational Outlook Handbook
SIGI	System of Interactive Guidance and Information
SOICC	State Occupational Information Coordinating Committee
WOIS	Washington Occupational Information System

disadvantages of the computer as a career guidance tool were discussed for the following criteria: cost, staff, coordination, student aversion, counselor support, time, patience, and confidentiality.

The previously mentioned work of Maze and Cummings (1982) used the selection variables they had defined to evaluate CIS, GIS, SIGI, and DISCOVER. The specific systems chosen for review were selected to represent different philosophies. Another comparative description of various systems which specifically evaluates CHOICES, DISCOVER, and GIS was conducted by Jacobson and Grabowski (1982). More recently, the College Placement Council developed a CAGS comparison form which was adapted from the work of Katz and Shatkin (1980) and is used in CPC workshops designed for the career-planning and placement professional (Montross, 1984). The adapted CAGS comparison form examines the scope and content, structure, procedure, theory, costs, and technical aspects of a CAGS. Specific systems compared in the CPC materials were: CIS, SIGI, GIS, CHOICES, and DISCOVER. Using the 17 criteria suggested as guidelines for selection of a CAGS, Heppner and Johnston (1985) compared SIGI, DISCOVER II, C-LECT, CHOICES, MicroSKILLS, GIS, and CA-REER/COLLEGE SCAN. Three of these systems are more thoroughly reviewed by Heppner (1985) in a comparison of DISCOVER II, SIGI, and MicroSKILLS. An examination of the following nine CAGSs is provided by Zunker (1986): ISVD, ECES, CVIS, SIGI, DISCOVER, GIS, COCIS, CHOICES, and INQUIRY.

It would, of course, be impossible to review any of the currently available CAGSs without overlapping with previous descriptions and comparisons. Given that such resources are available to the reader and the issue of rapid change can make any review less than current upon publication, this review provides very brief descriptions of 12 CAGSs which are currently commercially available in the United States. This discussion is intended as descriptive, not evaluative nor comparative, and will focus on the content of each system and the population for which the system was developed. Cost information will not be included as this changes too rapidly to be meaningful for this review; however, Maze (1985) estimates that software program for "the most popular guidance and information systems cost between $900 and $2,000 per year" [p. 159]. Software for some information systems may be less expensive but consumers should be informed about whether or not updates are an additional expense.

This current description does not specify the hardware appropriate to run each system because of rapid change and the belief of this writer that the choice of a CAGS should rest more with content of the system and the user population than hardware availability. The writer does acknowledge the practicality of such an issue.

The specific CAGSs described in the next section of this chapter are:

Career Finder	COIN
Career Scan IV	DISCOVER
CCAP	GIS
CHOICES	MicroSKILLS
CIS	PATHFINDER
C-LECT	SIGI & SIGI PLUS

Table 4.3 summarizes the reviews that have been done and lists the specific systems described here.

The selection strategy for the CAGSs to be included in this section was initially to follow the strict definitional criteria established earlier for selection of a CPS. The CAGSs reviewed here consistently met the process dimensions of integrating the information in the program for the user, interacting between and/or among the separate parts of the system, and being commercially available. However, as the field of possibilities was examined further, it became apparent to this writer that some degree of definitional flexibility was necessary with regard to the content dimensions in order to provide a wide diversity of CAGSs to review. Some readers may agree with Harris–Bowlsbey's (1983) description of the two roles a CAGS can play: the role of interactive data file or the role of guidance service based on decision making. If the definitional criteria for inclusion of a CAGS were set to match the second role or to include CAGSs only if both roles were provided, very few systems would be left to review. J. Harris–Bowlsbey (personal communication, February 1986) believes that the only two currently available systems which truly reflect a complete guidance system are DISCOVER and SIGI.

TABLE 4.3
Descriptive and Evaluative Reviews of CAGS

Shatkin[a] (1980)	Nagy & Donald (1981)	Maze & Cummings (1982)	Jacobson & Grabowski (1982)	Montross (1984)	Heppner & Johnston (1985)	Heppner (1985)	Zunker (1986)	Taylor (this chap.)
CHOICES	CHOICES	CHOICES	CHOICES	CHOICES	CHOICES		CHOICES	CHOICES
CIS	CIS	CIS	CIS	CIS				CIS
CVIS	CVIS						CVIS	
DISCOVER	DISCOVER	DISCOVER	DISCOVER	DISCOVER	DISCOVER	DISCOVER	DISCOVER	DISCOVER
GIS	GIS	GIS	GIS	GIS	GIS		GIS	GIS
SIGI	SIGI	SIGI	SIGI	SIGI	SIGI	SIGI	SIGI	SIGI
					Career/College Scan			Career Scan IV
					C-LECT			C-LECT
					MicroSKILLS	MicroSKILLS		MicroSKILLS
COIN							COIN	COIN
							COCIS	Career Finder
							ECES	CCAPP
							INQUIRY	PATHFINDER
							ISVD	

[a]The specific state systems which Shatkin reviewed are listed in the text.

189

Obviously, from examination of the list of CAGSs which are reviewed here, the strictest criteria were not applied. Some systems that have been reviewed by others were excluded because they are no longer in existence (such as the CVIS) or because this writer believes that the scope of some systems was too narrow, (such as the ECES), or beyond the scope of this chapter, (such as the National Center for Research in Vocational Education's Career Planning System). Table 4.3 summarizes the reviews that have been done by others and lists the specific systems described here. For a more in-depth look at these systems see Table 4.4. The last column of Table 4.4, entitled "Information to Guidance Continuum," reflects the relative emphasis of the specific system on these two roles. Like Clyde (1979), this author conceptualizes these roles as a continuum rather than as two separate, nonoverlapping categories. The comment written in this column signifies whether a system is primarily an information or a guidance system. Systems which seem to fall between the two ends of the continuum are labeled Info to Guidance.

Career Finder

Developed for junior high and high school students, the system provides a list of 20 occupations from a possible population of 390 by using the respondent's answers to a series of 18 questions about general and occupational interests. As described by Vetter et al. (1986) the system has four main components: Questions, List, Fit, and Information. A helpful aspect of the program is provided with Fit in which users receive a rating of the level of fit between the occupational requirements of specific careers and the responses they made to the questions. Occupational information compiled from the DOT, OOH, and GOE is provided in Information. Additional materials include a Career Finder Counselor's Manual (Maze & Waldren, 1985), a paper-pencil version of the questionnaire, and a list of the occupations in the system.

Career Scan IV

As an outgrowth of the career information system for the state of Wisconsin, Career Scan IV is primarily an information retrieval system. Marketed by Roger Lambert, who was instrumental in the development of the state system, Career Scan IV is one of four information systems available from National Educational Software Services. The other three systems are College Scan IV, Job Hunters' Scan IV, and Financial Aid Scan IV. The approximately 800 occupational titles included in Career Scan IV are organized by the Standard Occupational Classification Structure, which clusters the 12,000 DOT titles by function. By responding to a series of questions about life-styles, abilities, school subjects, training or education, interests, values, job characteristics, and high technology requirements, users are supplied with a list of occupational titles which correspond to

TABLE 4.4

Computer Assisted Guideance Systems (CAGS)

Title	Content	Publishing Company	Author(s)	User Population	Information to Guidance Continuum
Career Finder	4 Components: Questions List Fit Information	Eureka Corporation	Maze, M. Waldren, P.	Junior High, High School	Information
Career Scan IV	Questionnaire of 9 categories with 42 variables about life-styles, abilities, interests, education, etc. provides data for occupational title search	National Educational Software Services	Caulum, D. Lambert, R. Myren, M. Abrahams, L.	Junior High through Adults	Information
CCAPP	4 modules: Career Assessment Selecting Alternatives Career Planning Career Exploration	Jefferson Software	Systems Design Associates	High School through Adults	Guidance
CHOICES	Paper-pencil instrument of 16 self-assessment topics (GUIDE) 4 programs to access occupational information: Explore Specific Compare Related	Canada Systems Group (CSG)	Jarvis, P.	Junior High through Adults	Information to Guidance

(continued...)

(continued...)

Title	Content	Publishing Company	Author(s)	User Population	Information to Guidance Continuum
CIS	Paper-pencil 21 item self-assessment (Quest) 5 information files: DESC PREP BIB PROG SCH	Not actually commercially available (see text)	McKinlay, B.	Junior High through Adult	Information
C-LECT	4 modules: Occupation Module Education Module Financial Aids- Apprenticeship Module Report Writer Module	Chronicle Guidance Publications, Inc.	Chronicle Guidance Publications, Inc.	Junior High through Adults	Information
COIN	6 files: Occupation File School Subjects File College Major File School File Apprenticeship File Military File	Bell & Howell	Bell & Howell	Junior High through Adults	Information
DISCOVER	4 modules: Learning About Yourself Searching for Occupations Learning About Occupations Educational Information	American College Testing Program	Harris- Bowlsbey, J.	High School, College	Guidance

(continued....)

(continued....)

Title	Content	Publishing Company	Author(s)	User Population	Information to Guidance Continuum
DISCOVER for Adult Learners	6 modules: Weathering Change Assessing Self and Identifying Alternatives Gathering Occupational Information Making Decisions Drafting Educational Plans Getting a Job	American College Testing Program	Harris-Bowlsbey, J.	High School, College	Guidance
GIS	6 information files: OCCU ASOC COL2 COL4 GRADS AIDS	Time Share Corp., Div. of Houghton Mifflin	TSC	Junior High through Adults	Information
Micro-SKILLS	4 sections: SUMM RATE VIEW INFO	Eureka Corp.	Maze, M.	Adults	Guidance
PATHFINDER SCII	4 step process: Understand Identify Evaluate Action	Interactive Video Systems, Inc.	Interactive Systems, Inc.	Junior High through Adults	Guidance
SIGI	6 subsystems: Values Locate Compare Prediction Planning Strategy	Educational Testing Service	Katz, M.	High School, College	Guidance

(continued....)

(continued...)

Title	Content	Publishing Company	Author(s)	User Population	Information to Guidance Continuum
SIGI PLUS	9 modules: Introduction Self-Assessment Search Information Skills Preparing Coping Deciding Next Steps	Educational Testing Service	ETS Staff under leadership of Lila Norris	High School Through Adults	Guidance

their answers. For each occupation listed, the page numbers are supplied for information in the following publications: OOH, GOE, *Exploring careers, Health careers guidebook, Environmental protection careers guidebook,* and *Criminal justice career guidebook.* Developed for a wide range of users, from junior high school through adults, the average length of an occupational search is 15 to 30 minutes.

CCAPP

The Computerized Career Assessment and Planning Program is a four-part career guidance program predicated on the assumption that career planning is an on-going, lifelong process. The four modules, Career Assessment, Selecting Alternatives, Career Planning, and Career Exploration, were developed to teach career decision-making skills to the high school through adult users of the system. Each of the four modules requires about 30 to 40 minutes to complete. Module 1 includes four activities designed to assess general occupational, work activity, and curricular interests and aptitudes while the activities of Module 2 were designed to assess preferences for work environments and other variables relevant to actual occupational choices. Module 3 allows the user to choose one of the three tracks of vocational training, college, and job hunting to explore next steps and Module 4 provides occupational information by listing page numbers of the GOE, the OOH, the DOT and providing sections of *Lovejoy's college guide* and *Barron's profile of American colleges.*

One of the helpful aspects of this system is the excellent manual, which delineates the counseling strategies which can be used with each module and offers ideas of further activities for the user to complete following a particular module.

CHOICES

CHOICES was developed as a service of the Canadian Employment and Immigration Commission and is currently being used in a wide variety of settings in the United States and countries in Europe as well as in Canada. CHOICES is only one of the career software programs marketed by Canada Systems Group (CSG) under the overall title of Careerware. Four levels or types of CHOICES programs exist. CHOICES I is a career exploration program developed for students in the fifth through ninth grades. CHOICES II and III are essentially the same program although CHOICES III contains more occupational information. According to the promotional material, CHOICES II is more appropriate for users in the career exploration process while III is designed for persons actually making occupational decisions; thus the main difference in the programs is in the occupational data base. CHOICES Colleges/E.T. provides information on education and training programs. This review describes CHOICES II, which is the most widely used of the CHOICES systems.

Developed for users of junior high school age through adult, CHOICES combines paper-pencil self-assessment with computerized career exploration and information. Prior to interaction with the computer, users complete a workbook entitled CHOICES Guide which contains 16 self-assessment exercises on topics such as education level, work site, physical demands, temperament, earnings, aptitudes, interests, future outlook, Holland categories, career fields, and physical activities. The average length of time to complete the Guide is approximately 2 hours.

The results of these self-assessment activities are summarized in a Personal Profile, which the user and counselor are to review before the user gains access to the computer. Once the user sits down at the computer terminal, four programs or routes are available by which to access the occupational and educational data bases of the system. These routes are: Explore, Specific, Compare, and Related. Using the information determined by the self-assessment exercises, Explore allows the user to prepare and narrow lists of potential occupations as criteria are changed or deleted. Specific provides detailed occupational information on any occupation specified by the user whereas Compare enables a user to compare the characteristics of two occupations at the same time. A list of occupations is provided which have similar characteristics to an occupation specified by the user in Related.

Some of the adjunctive materials available with the CHOICES system which are very helpful to both users and counselors are the Counselor Manual, the master lists of occupations and educational and training programs, and the audiovisual orientation package designed to introduce users to the CHOICES program. The orientation program does allow for the reduction of tedius repetitions of such an introduction for each new user of the system. From the point of view that values counselor contact with users of CAGSs, another advantage of this system is that such involvement is implicitly designed into the system. In fact, the promotional material for the system states that CHOICES is designed as a tool to aid the counselor in assisting individuals in the career-planning process.

CIS

Developed initially as a state career information system for Oregon, CIS is now utilized in approximately 17 states. The Oregon CIS served as a model for these other systems which retained much of the basic program while making appropriate refinements for each state. Similar to the CHOICES program, CIS does not provide on-line assessment and thus combines a paper-pencil assessment activity with computerized occupational and educational information. Prior to going online, users complete Quest, a 21-item questionnaire which surveys work-related preferences, such as amount of income preferred and the extent to which a user would like to use different abilities on the job. Once the questionnaire is complete the user can search the occupational information, either through Quest responses or via direct access. The main information files in the CIS are: DESC, PREP, BIB, PROG, and SCH. The Description File provides occupational information while the Preparation File examines the appropriate steps a user would take to gain entrance to an occupational field. A bibliography in the next file lists relevant publications containing more information. The Program and School files deal with information about specific educational and training programs.

One potential problem for professionals who are attempting to discern which system is appropriate for the clientele they serve is confusion. Some of the state CIS systems have adopted their own name, such as "Eureka" in California. This name change may provide an interesting title for the users of that particular state system but may also confuse the professional. Another issue is that CIS does not satisfy strict CPS definitional criteria as it is not commercially available in the traditional sense but is developed and distributed by each state with assistance from the Oregon program. Given the wide use of this state-based program, however, this criterion was waived in order to include it for review.

C-LECT

The C-LECT program contains the following four modules: Occupation, Educational, Financial Aids-Apprenticeship, and Report Writer. Both the Educational and the Financial Aids-Apprenticeship modules are information retrieval programs, which the user can access by setting the desired criteria regarding these two topics. Chronical Guidance Publications, Inc., which publishes C-LECT, is quite pleased with the data base for these two systems. Included is information on about 875 college majors, 2,075 4-year colleges, 2, 640 2-year colleges, 3,740 vocational-technical schools, and more than 700 financial aid programs. Users can retrieve a report of the information they have entered into the computer while working on C-LECT by using the Report Writer Module.

The C-LECT program combines self-assessment with computerized occupational information in the Occupational module. If a user selects this module to work on, three methods of access are available. A user can input previously derived Holland codes, can complete a 100-item questionnaire which surveys interests and work temperaments either on the computer or in a paper-pencil version, or can select interests and temperaments from menus that appear on the computer screen. Once the user has completed these steps, a list of occupations compatible with responses is generated. At this point, users may explore options by examining the computer information files, which include work performed, education and training, qualifications, salary outlook, occupation outlook, related occupations and other sources of information, or by using printed occupational information which is referenced and includes the following publications: DOT, GOE, and *Chronicle occupational briefs*.

COIN

COIN is the computerized occupational information system developed by Bell and Howell for junior high through adult users. The system is composed of six files: Occupational File, School Subjects File, College Major File, School File, Apprenticeship File, and Military File. Before gaining access to these files, a user completes the COIN Occupational Interest Profile, which allows the user to respond to seven search variables which will be used by the computer to select appropriate occupations. These search variables are: interests, working conditions, career clusters, education/training requirements, physical strengths, physical demands, and salary ranges. A user may make more than one response for each of the search variables.

Typically, the more criteria the user defines the fewer occupations will meet the specifications. The total number of occupations meeting the selection criteria are noted on the computer screen. The user can choose to search the seven categories consecutively or in any order preferred. Once a list of occupational choices is defined, the Occupational File can provide information on more than 300 occupations or the School Subjects File, which contains information relating high school subjects to occupations. Academic programs and schools which offer the programs are contained in the College Major File. Information on 4- and 2-year colleges and on financial aid is presented in the the School File. National apprenticeship programs are described in the Apprenticeship File and occupations available in the military are described in the Military File. The COIN system can be delivered in three systems: microfiche, microcomputer, or on-line, interactive computer.

DISCOVER

Representing the career guidance end of the CAGSs continuum is DISCOVER, a comprehensive computerized career-planning program. Two DISCOVER systems are available: DISCOVER and DISCOVER for Adult Learners. Both systems provide self-assessment activities and occupational and educational information. The DISCOVER program developed for high school and college students and other persons in the planning phase of their career development contains four modules: Learning About Yourself, Searching for Occupations, Learning about Occupations, and Educational Information. The first module provides three on-line self-assessment measures of interests, abilities, and values.

The results of the 90-item interest inventory, the Uniact, are summarized according to the level of a user's interest in six scales: technical, science, creative arts, social service, business contact, and business detail. This information is graphically presented on a bar graph and on the World of Work Map, which allows for an introduction to the occupational classification system of ACT. A user's interests are summarized in a 3-point code which reflects the highest scores on the six interest scales. On a 5-point scale from 1 = poor (bottom 10%) to 5 = outstanding (top 10%) users rate themselves on 14 abilities compared with people their age. The abilities are: meeting people, helping others, sales, leadership/management, organization, numerical, mechanical, manual dexterity, mathematical, scientific, creating/artistic, creative/literary, reading, and language usage. A recent change in the DISCOVER program has reduced the values inventory from 16 to 9 values to which a user responds on a 4-point importance scale. Users can decide how many of the assessment measures to complete and are provided with a list of occupations which correspond to their responses. If all three measures are completed, a cumulative summary is provided.

Part II of DISCOVER provides an opportunity to search for occupations via a variety of paths, including entering results obtained from paper-pencil assessment inventories and by examining occupations according to job characteristics and academic majors or programs of study necessary to prepare for the occupation. Scores from the following interest and aptitude measures can be entered: Uniact, SDS, SCII, OVIS, Kuder E, CPP, GATB, ASVAB, and DAT.

Parts III and IV are the information retrieval sections of the DISCOVER program which contain occupational and educational information respectively. Two methods are available in the search for occupational information. The first strategy teaches the World of Work Map and provides brief explanations of job families while the second strategy provides more in-depth information on specific occupations. Information on 1,500 2-year and 1,800 4-year colleges and 1,000 graduate schools are provided in the fourth part of this program.

DISCOVER for Adult Learners was developed to address the career development needs of the returning student, the nontraditional student, and the continuing education student. All of these titles are various methods by which adult learners are identified and for whom this most recent ACT career-planning product was developed. The six modules which comprise DISCOVER for Adult Learners are highly interactive and rely on users' life experiences to be a vital part of the program. The six modules are: Weathering Change, Assessing Self and Identifying Alternatives, Gathering Occupational Information, Making Decisions, Drafting Educational Plans, and Getting a Job.

Module A presents a model of adult transitions and encourages users to examine their own lives and to set goals for desired changes. The second module focuses on self-assessment of interests, experiences, or values. Taking the Uniact is also a possible assessment activity which a user can complete in Module B. The next module teaches the World of Work Map and explains the ACT occupational classification system while also providing specific occupational information. Module D teaches a planful decision-making process and allows a user to apply the decision making process to their own career decision making. Drafting Educational Plans is an information file of 2- and 4-year colleges and graduate schools. Information on some of the special interests of the adult learner are presented, such as college credit for life experience. The final module of this program presents job search-process strategies and skills, such as resumé writing and interviewing skills. A new version of DISCOVER is currently in preparation.

GIS

GIS emerged from ISVD, one of the earliest CAGSs, developed by Tiedeman and O'Hara and colleagues at Harvard University. This widely used career information system is now available from Time Share Corp., a division of Houghton Mifflin. The basic GIS system does not provide any on-line assessment or instruction for the user but is one of the most flexible information systems currently available. Much of the flexibility of this system is a result of numerous access strategies by which to search the six information files which comprise GIS. For instance, occupations can be searched according to the following criteria: interests, aptitudes, physical demands, work conditions, salary, employment potential, education and training, and by examining the specific occupation in the context of the "world of work." Each of the six files has separate search strategies which a user can add or delete to modify the list of possibilities presented. Direct access of any file is also possible. The six files are: OCCU (Occupational Information File), ASOC (Armed Services Occupational Information File), COL2 (Two-Year College Information File), COL4 (Four-Year College Information File), GRAD (Graduate and Professional School Information File), and AIDS (Financial Aids Information File).

The most recent change in the GIS system is the addition of the Career Decision Making system of Harrington and O'Shea, which is described earlier in this chapter. This enhanced GIS also provides the capability of entering interest inventory scores derived from the CAI, SCII, SDS, and the CDM. These modifications which allow actual assessment move the GIS closer to the guidance end of the continuum at least for the enhanced version of the GIS.

MicroSKILLS

MicroSKILLS was designed to serve adults but has also been used by high school juniors and seniors and college students. The emphasis is on identification of transferrable skills developed through life experiences and the use of these skills to search for appropriate occupations to consider as career choices. Two versions of MicroSKILLS exist (I and II) with the second program being more complete. Thus MicroSKILLS II is reviewed here.

Three methods of skills assessment are available: the paper-pencil Skills Inventory, the skills card sort, and completion of the Skills Inventory on the computer. The skill assessment begins by asking users to list seven accomplishments which demonstrate different skills. Following completion of this list, users rate these activities for the skills used and have an opportunity to signify which skills would be desirable for future use. From 72 skills, users select the 5 skills which were very satisfying, the 10 moderately satisfying skills, and the 20 somewhat satisfying skills. Selected skills are divided into 12 skill areas: self-management, situational, detail, movement, operational, numerical, communication, conceptual, judgment, reasoning, interpersonal, and leadership. The 35 selected skills are then entered into the computer if the paper-pencil inventory or card sort methods of assessment has been used. Once the self-assessment section of this program has been completed, the user can access four programs: SUMM, RATE, VIEW, and INFO. The first section provides a summary of the skills assessment and displays the 35 skills, according to the level of satisfaction indicated by the user. This section provides a chance for the user to make any necessary corrections.

In the RATE program, the 30 occupations which most closely correspond to the user's skills are presented and the degree of similarity between the occupation and the user's skills is noted. Users often explore the content of VIEW if an occupation they expected to appear in RATE did not. VIEW contains the skills for each of the 371 occupations in the data file of MicroSKILLS and thus allows for comparison between a user's listed skills and the occupation. The final section, INFO, contains occupational information on the occupations in the system and reference page numbers for these occupations in the OOH. Additional materials which are helpful are the Counselor's Manual and the User Handbook.

PATHFINDER

The PATHFINDER program is included with some caution as the program is a computerized scoring system of the SCII. However, this author believes that the program does elaborate on the basic interpretation of the interest inventory and provides a four-step career-planning process which also extends the system. This program falls between a single career planning instrument and a full-blown career-planning system but is reviewed for the reasons given.

With the results of the SCII in hand, a user completes a four-step process of career exploration: Understand, Identify, Evaluate, and Action. With the use of videodisc technology, the user receives an interpretation of the six Holland themes in Step 1. In addition, a Career Guide workbook aids in the interpretation of the SCII results and corresponds to the videodisc program. In Identify the user can explore an additional 850 related occupational titles and can use the PATHFINDER Reference Library, which includes the DOT, the OOH, and the *User's guide for the SVIB–SCII*. The Evaluate step of the program takes a user's top 10 to 12 occupations and helps a user evaluate them in terms of real-world criteria, such as educational requirements, actual job duties, geographical location, and so forth. The Action step of the program involves interaction with a counselor, who can motivate the user to use the list of occupations which the program has provided to set personal career planning goals.

SIGI and SIGI PLUS

Another widely used computerized-assisted guidance system is SIGI, which was developed in 1976 by Martin Katz at ETS. The SIGI system was joined by another ETS career-planning program, SIGI PLUS in 1985. Both systems will be briefly described here.

SIGI consists of six subsystems: Values, Locate, Compare, Prediction, Planning, and Strategy. The theoretical underpinning of this system is the importance of values in educational and career planning, thus there is a values clarification exercise is the first activity which a user must complete before gaining access to the rest of the SIGI system. The values activity is a forced-choice exercise, which requires the user to rank the 10 occupational values of income, prestige, independence, helping others, security, variety, leadership, field of interest, leisure, and early entry. In Locate, the occupations which fit combinations of five values derived in the Values section are listed and the user can change the level of importance attached to a particular value and observe the possible subsequent changes in the occupations list. Compare allows for three occupations to be examined at the same time. The six general areas of questions which can be posed to gather occupational information are definitions and descriptions, education and training, income, personal satisfactions, conditions of work, and opportunities and outlook. Prediction is a subsystem which relies on local information and thus may not be available for use if the local agency does not provide the data necessary to use this subsystem. If local data are provided, Prediction can suggest how well a student will perform in a given field of study at the particular setting providing the information. The Planning section focuses on teaching the steps necessary to complete to gain occupational entry while the Strategy subsystem teaches a decision-making module and summarizes all the information gathered on the user from other subsystems in predictions for success on selected occupations.

Designed to address some of the career-planning needs of adults as well as younger users, SIGI PLUS is a nine-module program. SIGI PLUS was not initially designed to replace SIGI but, depending on market response, may do just that. The SIGI PLUS program while retaining much of the original SIGI program has expanded the values section and added assessments of interests and skills. In addition, the new model is more interactive and modules can be used in any order in contrast to the programmed SIGI system sequence which could not be changed the first time through. The nine modules are: Introduction, Self-Assessment, Search, Information, Skills, Preparing, Coping, Deciding, and

Next Steps. An overview to the SIGI PLUS system is provided in the Introduction. Module 2 involves completing values, interests, and skills inventories. Based on this self-assessed information, Search defines occupational and educational objectives for the user. Occupational information is available in the Information file. Examining the occupational skills necessary for specific careers is the task of the Skills module.

Preparing consists of information about the paths a user could take to enter an occupational field, such as programs of training, necessary coursework, and work tasks to be mastered. Coping is a module created for the adult learner and discusses practical help with relevant issues, such as child care and college credit for prior life experience. Deciding allows a user to compare three occupations simultaneously and teaches a decision-making process. Goal setting is the topic of the final module.

CAGSs Summary

The final section of this CAGSs discussion addresses some of the questions these systems pose for the professional. The issue of evaluation of CAGSs is a critical one. For the most part, evaluation and outcome studies of CAGSs are extremely rare or nonexistent. Obviously, research in this area is in its infancy, due to both their recent development and the lack of demand for proof of the program efficacy in furthering the users' career development. A possible reason for the lack of pressure on program developers to substantiate the claims of providing sound career guidance interventions may be due to the inherent appeal of many of these systems. The programs are easy-to-use systems presented on the most recent of educational teaching implements, the computer. Given the data storage capacity of computers, up-to-date occupational information is more current than in previously published works.

Another immediate advantage of these systems is the capacity for interaction among separate parts of the system. In addition, another reason evaluative research has not been completed may relate to the difficult task of deciding on the outcome criteria desirable after completing a CAGS. The criteria to be examined as dependent variables in such research may well depend on one's theoretical orientation. Attempting to find consensual agreement among various professionals may indeed be difficult. Regardless of the possible explanations for the lack of adequate evaluation studies, more work clearly needs to be done to substantiate the claims of the promotional materials and to specify for the practicing professional which program is appropriate for which type of user. It is imperative to use CAGSs within the framework they were developed and not as computer-age crystal balls. Without good research, we run such a risk.

For a somewhat dated review of research, readers are referred to Cairo (1983). In addition, research which pertains to SIGI and DISCOVER is available from the Clearinghouse for Computer-Assisted Guidance Systems at Florida

State University. The reader will find that these studies examined the effects of a single CAGS on the users of the system in a pre–post design. Some studies compare the users' scores on the dependent variables with scores obtained by the control or comparison group. Research which examines the effects between various CAGSs on relevant dependent variables and which examines the possible placebo effect of interacting with a computer will further expand the available literature.

Related to the state of research on the effectiveness of these systems is the question of the psychometric properties that characterize them. Unfortunately, this is an area of CAGSs development which is sadly lacking. Systems which use attributes as access variables versus assessment tools may not be seen as needing reliability and validity estimates; however, these attribute ''scales'' or search variables do indeed determine the list of occupations which a user considers as appropriate for potential career selection. Given such an important role in the career development of a user, this author would like to see enhanced effort to substantiate the psychometric properties of these measures. In addition, for the CAGSs which claim to offer assessment tools as part of the product provided to users, it is essential for these measures to provide psychometric information. As professionals, we expect this from other types of assessment and should therefore, require this from our most recent assessment devices whether computer-delivered or not.

Obviously, a necessary element in providing quality psychometric data is adequate time in which to conduct the necessary studies. Enough time has not yet been available for some of these systems, such as the new values inventory of SIGI PLUS. An interesting related concern which may cause some confusion about the psychometric issue is the concept of adaptive testing in which a user significantly alters the assessment device through their own unique responses. In that case, traditional psychometric data become less meaningful. More work in necessary regarding the psychometric properties of these systems.

Another relevant issue raised by the appearance of CAGSs is the role of the counselor. Initially, caution or alarm was a response to the earliest versions of today's sophisticated systems. Much of the alarm centered on the potential absence of the counselor in the career guidance process. Such fears were quieted as programs were implemented and it became apparent that there was still plenty of work for the busy professional to do. This author believes, however, that the concern should again be raised from a different perspective. The concern here is not that the counselor lacks a role in the CAGSs process but that the role is not always adequately filled, either because of users who assume the process of career planning is over once the computer bids them farewell or because of professionals who are too busy to adequately interface with users as they progress through the computer program. The first possibility is more of a concern for information access and retrieval systems while the second poses a potential threat to the most thorough use of any CAGS.

A final issue to be raised here is the ethical concern of confidentiality. Given the highly visible nature of CRTs and the placement of many CAGSs work stations in most schools or agencies, the right of privacy may be violated for some users. This author encourages professionals who design user space to take this issue into consideration so our professionalism is not damaged by the tools of our trade.

CURRICULAR CAREER PLANNING SYSTEMS

The third main type of CPS is a career development program designed in a curricular format. As mentioned in the Introduction, only a very brief look at these systems is provided here. Curricular programs incorporate the many aspects of career planning into the classroom setting. Most curricular programs are designed for a career course that is taught over an entire academic term though many of these systems could be adapted for use as career modules within other courses. Many schools and universities offer a career course for academic credit but most of these programs are not commercially available. For a review of two such programs, see Zunker (1986). In addition, Miller (1984) reviews state career guidance programs and "Career development programs in the schools" in a chapter so titled in N. C. Gysbers and Associates' *Designing careers*. The list of curricular programs provided here is not inclusive of all the currently commercially available programs.

The programs presented in Table 4.5 are in alphabetical order by the title of the program, followed by the name of the author and publishing company. All of the programs except Powell's (1981) contain both a user text or workbook and an instructor's manual. Recent changes in some of these programs have just been completed or are anticipated, such as a second edition of the Carney and Wells (1986) text and upcoming changes in the AEL program. These programs represent the third major form of career delivery systems.

SUMMARY

This chapter reviewed the most recent information on career planning systems in order to summarize exciting new developments and refinements in these comprehensive career guidance instruments and to expose the professional to an integrated presentation of this material. Too often the information available on these systems is that provided by the publisher of the program. As Willis questions, "Who should have the final word on publicity materials for a measurement instrument, the authors or the publishers?" [1982, p. 59]. Hopefully, this review written from a practice and a testing perspective provided the reader with informatin which will be useful in making a selection of the CPS which will be most

TABLE 4.5
Curricular Career Planning Systems

Title	Author(s)	Publishing Company
AEL Career Decision Making Program	Appalachia Educational Laboratory, Inc. Winefordner, D.W. Director	Bennet & McKnight Publishing Company
Career Planning: Skills to Build Your Future (2nd Ed.)	Carney, C.G. Wells, C.F.	Brooks/Cole Publishing Company
Career Planning Today	Powell, C.R.	Kendall/Hunt Publishing Company
Coming Alive from Nine to Five (2nd Ed.)	Michelozzi, B.N.	Mayfield Publishing Company
Guilded Career Exploration	Super, D.E. Harris-Bowlsbey, J.	The Psychological Corporation
Take Hold of Your Future	Harris-Bowlsbey, J. Spivack, J.D. Lisansky, R.S.	American College Testing Program

beneficial to the particular populations served in the various settings in which career interventions are provided.

The final paragraphs of this chapter review some of the issues most salient in a discussion of CPSs and summarize some of the advantages and disadvantages of these systems.

Overall, all three types of CPSs have high face validity which can aid in promoting a positive user response. In addition, these systems provide maximum flexibility in implementing a career development program in multiple settings, such as school or university career development settings, community mental health settings, and state job development agencies and in multiple forms, such as individual counseling, group or workshop interventions, or classroom designs. This flexibility can also free counselor time from some of the redundant aspects of career interventions, such as scoring a vocational instrument. Of course, every advantage has another side such as scoring inaccuracies on self-scored instruments or the more serious issue of incomplete career-planning programs if users only obtain information and do not integrate this self or occupational information within a more comprehensive career development process.

One of the advantages of using CPSs is to guard against this very concern as the programs are designed to promote this type of integration. The arrival of the computer in career guidance has prompted growth not only in the establishment and refinement of CAGSs but also in the integration of various types of CPSs with each other. This integration has involved the use of traditional paper-pencil instruments within a CAG, such as incorporating the UNIACT within DISCOVER, and the extension of paper-pencil instruments by adding a more comprehensive report made possible by a computerized format, such as the one used in the DAT CPP. Finally, one of the newest advances which will meet the needs of a fast-growing population of users is the development of systems designed for the adult.

Some of the issues which professionals should consider before choosing a system include the lack of predictive validity and of evaluation outcome studies. This is a serious problem which must be addressed before confidence can be thoroughly placed in the majority of the currently available systems. In addition, the poor to nonexistent psychometric information available on some of the systems also needs to be rectified. Another overall concern is the theoretical base on which these systems were built. Different systems have varying levels of commitment to theoretical bases. The role of the counselor also is an issue which needs thoughtful scrutiny and will most likely depend on the purpose of the program which is being offered to users.

The issue which this author finds of most concern, however, is the possibility of users' prematurely choosing a career direction without awareness of the broader context of the lifelong aspect of career development. In other words, without appropriate guidance, users could receive the three to five occupational options that correspond with the information they provided to the system and that could be the end of their career exploration. Learning any of the career development skills necessary to equip them to make later career and life decisions would be missed. Essentially, if these systems only promote a focus on career *selection* versus a focus on career *development,* this author believes these systems have not lived up to their potential and have only mirrored an earlier problem reflected in the "test and tell" tradition. Finally, the development of these systems is so rapid and the content is so sophisticated that the actual selection of a specific program has become increasingly complex. In order for a career professional to make an informed and wise choice among all the systems available, adequate training in both vocational theory and instrument design is crucial.

To conclude this discussion of the latest "state-of-the-art" career-planning interventions, a number of recommendations are offered. First of all, selection of a CPS should be a matter of careful scrutiny of the target population of users' needs as well as an assessment of the institutional or agency needs of the organization. Regardless of the type of system selected, a thorough evaluation of the psychometric properties is imperative. Beyond this recommendation is a strong suggestion to institute outcome evaluation studies of user satisfaction and other salient criteria which can help determine if the system is indeed meeting the stated goals of the institution which initiated its use or the individual who completed the program.

This type of follow-up of users is essential, not just from a cost-effective viewpoint, but from a quality career-counseling viewpoint as well. As mentioned, the potential of identity foreclosure for users is great if the user does not question or work with the educational/career options the CPS provides but merely accepts without contemplation the career options suggested. In addition, depending on the program, there may be little to no reality considerations built into the system and the user may leave the CPS in a glow of unrealistic self-discovery. One of the roles of counselors in career counseling has been to serve as a mediator of reality or at least a word of caution that some choices are more difficult than others, in part depending on one's life circumstances. Certainly, all the systems with the exception of the Career Planning System developed for special populations, assume middle class opportunities, which inherently limits their applicability.

Comparative studies of the use of the systems in different settings with different users would be enlightening. Both paper-pencil and curricular programs are in need of further research; however, the strongest emphasis should be placed on the CAGSs as their use is rapidly proliferating with little evidence as to their effectiveness.

In summary, this author highly recommends the continued use and research of CPSs. If correctly implemented, these exciting programs can only enhance the career development interventions intended to help our user populations.

REFERENCES

American College Testing Program. (1985). *Interim psychometrical handbook for the 3rd edition ACT career planning program levels 1 and 2.* Iowa City, IA: Author.

American Institutes for Research. (1975). *Planning Career Goals: Examiner's manual.* Monterey, CA: CTB/McGraw–Hill.

Appalachia Educational Laboratory, Inc. (1978). *Exploring career decision-making.* Bloomington, IL: McKnight.

Bauernfeind, R. H. (1972). Test review of the California occupational preference survey. In O. K. Buros (Ed.), *The seventh mental measurements yearbook* (pp. 1012–1013). Highland Park, NJ: Gryphon Press.

Borgen, F. H. (1982). USES general aptitude test battery. In J. T. Kapes & M. M. Mastie (Eds.), *A counselor's guide to vocational guidance instruments* (pp. 42–46). Falls Church, VA: National Vocational Guidance Association.

Bouchard, T.J. (1978). Test review of the differential aptitude tests. In O. K. Buros (Ed.), *The eighth mental measurements yearbook* (pp. 655–658). Highland Park, NJ: Gryphon Press.

Buros, O. K. (Ed.). (1978). *The eighth mental measurements yearbook.* Highland Park, NJ: Gryphon Press.

Cairo, P. C. (1983). Evaluating the effects of computer-assisted counseling systems: A selective review. *Counseling Psychologist, 11,* 55–59.

Carney, C. G., & Wells, C. F. (1986). *Career planning: Skills to build your future* (2nd ed.). Monterey, CA: Brooks/Cole.

Clyde, J. S. (1979). *Computerized career information and guidance systems.* Columbus, OH: National Center for Research in Vocational Education. (ED 179 764).

Daniels, M. H. (1985). Test review of the vocational exploration and insight kit. In J. V. Mitchell (Ed.) *The ninth mental measurements yearbook* (pp. 1675–1676). Lincoln: University of Nebraska Press.

Dolliver, R. H. (1981). Test review of the occupational/vocational card sorts. *Measurement & Evaluation in Guidance, 14,* 168–174.

Dolliver, R. H. (1985). Test review of the self-motivated career planning system. In J. V. Mitchell (Ed.), *The ninth mental measurements yearbook* (pp. 1347–1348). Lincoln: University of Nebraska Press.

Domino, G. (1985). Test review of the Ohio Vocational Interest Survey (2nd ed.). In J. V. Mitchell (Ed.), *The ninth mental measurements yearbook* (pp. 1089–1091). Lincoln: University of Nebraska Press.

Ewens, W. P. (1981). *Theory base and technical data for Experience Exploration.* Moravia, NY: Chronical Guidance Publications.

Foreman, J. (1981, October 3). Using a computer to pick a career. *Boston Globe,* p. 6.

Hansen, J. C. (1982). California occupational preference system. In J. T. Kapes & M. M. Mastie (Eds.), *A counselor's guide to vocational guidance instruments* (pp. 48–52). Falls Church, VA: National Vocational Guidance Association.

Harrington, T. F., & O'Shea, J. O. (1982a). *Career decision-making system manual.* Circle Pines, MN: American Guidance Service.

Harrington, T. F., & O'Shea, J. O. (1982b). *Career decision-making system: Survey booklet.* Circle Pines, MN: American Guidance Service.

Harris–Bowlsbey, J. (1983). The computer and the decider. *Counseling Psychologist, 11,* 9–13.

Harris–Bowlsbey, J. (1984). The computer as a tool in career guidance programs. In N. C. Gysbers & Associates (Eds.), *Designing careers* (pp. 362–383). San Francisco: Jossey–Bass.

Harris–Bowlsbey, J., Spivack, J. D., & Lisansky, R. S. (1982). *Take hold of your future.* Iowa City, IA: American College Testing Program.

Heppner, M. J. (1985). DISCOVER II, SIGI, and MicroSKILLS: A descriptive review. *Journal of Counseling & Development, 63,* 323–325.

Heppner, M. J., & Johnston, J. A. (1985). Computerized career guidance and information systems: Guidelines for selection. *Journal of College Student Personnel, 26,* 156–163.

Herr, E. L. (1982). Testing for career counseling, guidance, and education: Reactions to the symposium articles. *Measurement & Evaluation in Guidance, 15,* 159–163.

Holland, J. L. (1985). *The self-directed search professional manual—1985 edition.* Odessa, FL: Psychological Assessment Resources, Inc.

Holland, J. L., & Associates. (1980). *Counselor's guide to the vocational exploration and insight kit (VEIK).* Palo Alto, CA: Consulting Psychologists Press.

Holland, J. L., & Rayman, J. R. (1986). Self directed search. In W. B. Walsh & S. H. Osipow (Eds.), *Advances in vocational psychology, Vol. 1: The assessment of interests* (pp. 55–82). Hillsdale, NJ: Lawrence Erlbaum Associates.

Hoyt, K. B. (1986). Ohio vocational interest survey (OVIS II), microcomputer version. *Journal of Counseling & Development, 64,* 655–657.

Jacobson, M. D., & Grabowski, B. T. (1982). Computerized systems of career information and guidance: A state-of-the-art. *Journal of Educational Technology Systems, 10,* 235–255.

Johnson, R. W. (1978). Test review of the career planning program. In O. K. Buros (Ed.), *The eighth mental measurements yearbook* (pp. 1568–1570). Highland Park, NJ: Gryphon Press.

Kapes, J. T., & Mastie, M. M. (Eds.). (1982). *A counselor's guide to vocational guidance instruments.* Falls Church, VA: National Vocational Guidance Association.

Katz, M. R., & Shatkin, L. (1980). *Computer-assisted guidance: Concepts and practices.* Princeton, NJ: Educational Testing Service.

Katz, M. R., & Shatkin, L. (1983). Characteristics of computer-assisted guidance. *Counseling Psychologist, 11,* 15–31.

Knapp, L., & Knapp, R. R. (1984b). *Technical manual: CAPS.* San Diego: EdITS.

Knapp, R. R., & Knapp, L. (1982). *COPSystem Examiner's Manual.* San Diego: EdITS.

Knapp, R. R., & Knapp, L. (1984a). *Manual: COPS Interest Inventory.* San Diego: EdITS.

Krauskopf, C. J. (1978). Test review of the vocational interest, experience, and skill assessment. In O. K. Buros (Ed.), *The eighth mental measurements yearbook* (pp. 1633–1634). Highland Park, NJ: Gryphon Press.

Layton, W. L. (1978a). Test review of the California occupational preference system. In O. K. Buros (Ed.), *The eight mental measurements yearbook* (pp. 1546–1547). Highland Park, NJ: Gryphon Press.

Layton, W. L. (1978b). Test review of the world of work inventory. In O. K. Buros (Ed.), *The eighth mental measurements yearbook* (pp. 1645–1648). Highland Park, NJ: Gryphon Press.

Linn, R. L. (1982). Differential aptitude tests/DAT career planning program. In J. T. Kapes & M.

M. Mastie (Eds.), *A counselor's guide to vocational guidance instruments* (pp. 37–41). Falls Church, VA: National Vocational Guidance Association.

Locke, D. C. (1982). World of work inventory. In J. T. Kapes & M. M. Mastie (Eds.), *A counselor's guide to vocational guidance instruments* (pp. 143–146). Falls Church, VA: National Vocational Guidance Association.

Lohnes, P. R. (1982). Career assessment inventory. In J. T. Kapes & M. M. Mastie (Eds.), *A counselor's guide to vocational guidance instruments* (pp. 53–56). Falls Church, VA: National Vocational Guidance Association.

Mastie, M. M. (1976). Test review of the differential aptitude tests, forms S and T with career planning program. *Measurement & Evaluation in Guidance, 9,* 87–95.

Maze, M. (1984). How to select a computerized guidance system. *Journal of Counseling & Development, 63,* 158–161.

Maze, M. (1985). How much should a computerized guidance program cost? *Journal of Career Development, 12,* 157–165.

Maze, M., & Cummings, R. (1982). *How to select a computer assisted career guidance system.* Madison: Wisconsin Vocational Studies Center, University of Wisconsin.

Maze, M., & Waldren, P. (1985). *Career finder counselor's manual.* Richmond, CA: Eureka Corp.

Mehrens, W. A. (1982). Career planning program. In J. T. Kapes & M. M. Mastie (Eds.) *A counselor's guide to vocational guidance instruments* (pp. 131–135). Falls Church, VA: National Vocational Guidance Association.

Michelozzi, B. N. (1984). *Coming alive from nine to five.* Palo Alto, CA: Mayfield.

Miller, J. V. (1982). 1970's trends in assessing career counseling, guidance, and education. *Measurement & Evaluation in Guidance, 15*(2), 142–146.

Miller, J. V. (1984). Career development programs and practices in the schools. In N. C. Gysbers & Associates (Eds.), *Designing Careers,* (pp. 433–457). San Francisco: Jossey–Bass.

Miller–Tiedeman, A. (1976). *Manual of directions for individual career exploration.* Bensenville, IL: Scholastic Testing Service.

Mitchell, J. V. (Ed.). (1985). *The ninth mental measurements yearbook.* Lincoln: University of Nebraska Press.

Montross, D. H. (1984). *Computer-assisted guidance systems: Participant's manual.* Bethlehem, PA: College Placement Council Foundation.

Mossholder, K. M. (1985). Test review of the personal career development profile. In J. V. Mitchell (Ed.), *The ninth mental measurements yearbook* (pp. 1140–1141). Lincoln: University of Nebraska Press.

Nagy, D. R., & Donald, G. M. (1981). Computerized career guidance systems and beyond. In D. H. Montross & C. J. Shinkman (Eds.), *Career development in the 1980s,* (pp. 146–168). Springfield, IL: Charles C. Thomas.

Neidert, G. P. M., Hudson, K. S., Ripley, R. E., & Ripley, M. J. (1984). *World of work inventory interpretation manual and guide to career families.* Scottsdale, AZ: World of Work, Inc.

Pick, D. J. (1981). *GuidePak Workbook.* Palo Alto, CA: Behaviordyne, Inc.

Porter, E. H. (1976). On the development of relationship awareness theory: A personal note. *Group & Organization Studies, 1,* 302–309.

Porter, E. H., & Maloney, S. E. (1977). *Manual of administration and interpretation: Strength deployment inventory.* Pacific Palisades, CA: Personal Strength Assessment Service.

Powell, C. R. (1981). *Career planning today.* Dubuque, IA: Kendall/Hunt.

Read, R. W. (1982). Vocational interest, experience and skill assessment. In J. T. Kapes & M. M. Mastie (Eds.), *A counselor's guide to vocational guidance instruments* (pp. 83–87). Falls Church, VA: National Vocational Guidance Association.

Sampson, J. P., Jr. (1983). An integrated approach to computer applications in counseling psychology. *Counseling Psychologist, 11,* 65–74.

Shatkin, L. (1980). *Computer-assisted guidance: Description of systems.* Princeton, NJ: Educational Testing Service.

Sorenson, G. (1982). Ohio vocational interest survey (2nd ed., OVIS II). In J. T. Kapes & M. M. Mastie (Eds.), *A counselor's guide to vocational guidance instruments.* (pp. 83–87). Falls Church, VA: National Vocational Guidance Association.

Super, D. E. (1982). *DAT career planning program (2nd ed.), counselor's manual.* New York: The Psychological Corporation.

Super, D. E., & Harris–Bowlsbey, J. (1979). *Guided career exploration.* New York: The Psychological Corporation.

The Psychological Corporation. (1981). *Directions for using the career planner OVIS II.* New York: Author.

The Psychological Corporation. (1984). *Differential aptitude tests technical supplement.* New York: Harcourt Brace Jovanovich.

The Psychological Corporation. (1986). *Catalog 1986 tests and services for education.* New York: Harcourt Brace Jovanovich.

Tittle, C. K. (1985). Test review of the vocational exploration and insight kit. In J. V. Mitchell, *The ninth mental measurements yearbook* (p. 1676). Lincoln: University of Nebraska Press.

Vetter, L., Hull, W. L., Putzstuck, C., & Dean, G. J. (1986). *Adult career counseling: Resources for program planning and development.* Bloomington, IL: Meridian Education Corp.

Walsh, W. B., & Betz, N. E. (1985). *Tests and assessment.* Englewood Cliffs, NJ: Prentice–Hall.

Walter, V. (1985). *Personal career development profile.* Champaign, IL: Institute for Personality and Ability Testing.

Walz, G. R., & Benjamin, L. (1984). Systematic career guidance programs. In N. C. Gysbers & Associates (Eds.), *Designing careers* (pp. 336–361). San Francisco: Jossey–Bass.

Westbrook, B. W., Rogers, B., & Covington, J. E. (1980). Test review of the Harrington/O'Shea system for career decision making. *Measurement & Evaluation in Guidance, 13,* 185–188.

Willis, C. G. (1978). Test review of the Harrington/O'Shea system for career decision-making. In O. K. Buros (Ed.), *The eighth mental measurements yearbook* (pp. 1584–1585). Highland Park, NJ: Gryphon Press.

Willis, C. G. (1982). The Harrington/O'Shea Career decision-making system. In J. T. Kapes & M. M. Mastie (Eds.), *A counselor's guide to vocational guidance instruments* (pp. 57–60). Falls Church, VA: National Vocational Guidance Association.

Winefordner, D. W. (1983). *Ohio vocational interest survey (2nd ed.), manual for interpreting.* USA: Harcourt Brace Jovanovich.

Zunker, V. G. (1986). *Career counseling: Applied concepts of life planning* (2d ed.). Monterey, CA: Brooks/Cole.

5

An Expanded Context for the Study of Career Decision Making, Development, and Maturity

Howard E. A. Tinsley
Diane J. Tinsley
Southern Illinois University at Carbondale

Our current views about the developmental process in which career life planning occurs and career maturity is achieved are the product of a series of complex interactions among four lines of scholarly development in the history of psychology: our philosophical beliefs about work, the emergence of the discipline of differential psychology and the development of assessment techniques which was stimulated by that school, the development of theories of career development, and the development of career intervention strategies. Both the current status and future development of the field are dependent on advances in these areas. The previous chapters in this volume have focused on the second and third of these areas. This chapter proposes a point of view which encourages a reconsideration and expansion of our philosophical notions about the place of work in the life of the individual.

In order to provide a context within which to interpret our ideas, we will begin with a brief review of the historical development of the field. This is not intended as an exhaustive review; the reader is referred to Phillips's chapter for more details about some of the developments we mention. This overview is intended to give the reader a better understanding of the importance of these four lines of inquiry as influencers of our current knowledge of career decision making, development, and maturity. The major purposes of this chapter are to summarize our theory of the causes, attributes, and benefits of an experience which we have labeled ''leisure'' experience, and to review some evidence regarding the psychological benefits of this experience. The most promising assessment devices in this area will be identified briefly, and some concluding thoughts about the implications of this body of work for theory development, research and practice in career life development will be offered.

HISTORICAL FOUNDATIONS

Philosophical Beliefs About Work

Humankind's concern about the relationship between persons and their work is as old as civilization. Witness Plato's early contributions to career development theory. In *The Republic,* Plato extolled the wisdom of assigning persons to jobs in accordance with their temperament and abilities. A basic principle underlying Plato's notions about a republic was that "one man cannot practice many arts with success [Kaplan, 1950, p. 249]." Rather, there are diversities among persons which are adopted to different occupations. According to Plato, for example, the guardians of the city must be quick to see the enemy, swift to overtake the enemy, strong, brave, and possessing of an invincible and unconquerable spirit, yet so gentle in nature that they will not turn their hand against their friends.

Thus, the basic idea underlying many of our contemporary theories of career decision making (i.e., matching persons to jobs) was formulated by Plato more than 2000 years ago. At the time of Plato's writing and in the centuries immediately following, work was viewed as a curse, to be delegated exclusively to slaves if at all possible. In the Greek language, for example, the words for work and sorrow came from the same root word. Greek and Roman citizens believed that the gods hated mankind and condemned them to toil.

Examining the early Greeks' view of leisure leads to a more complete understanding of their view of work. The classical perspective, attributed to Aristotle, regarded leisure as the central goal of life, the end toward which all action is directed. According to this perspective, leisure is a condition of the soul, a state of being or form of contemplation which involves the pursuit of truth or understanding. All other forms of action are related to leisure and are defined, in essence, as the absence of leisure, which is the highest or most god-like state of being. The ancient Greeks and Romans defined leisure and work at opposite ends of a moral–ethical continuum, with leisure being a god-like existence and work a curse.

This attitude toward work persisted for centuries, but a revised view of work began to emerge in western Europe with the development of feudalism. For the serfs of medieval times, bound to the land as they were, work provided the only basis for dignity. These peasants—slaves for all intents and purposes—had no hope of ever enjoying a life other than that of a beast of burden. The gradual change in philosophy to the view that good work afforded a measure of dignity to the industrious, served the important social purpose of appeasing the serfs and making them more content with their lot. The landed gentry still preferred a life of leisure and contemplation, but for sociopolitical purposes work began to take on more positive attributes for the actual workers.

The organized religions of the time also contributed to the evolution of our views about work. Again for rather practical purposes, organized religions began to support the belief that manual labor was dignified when it was performed by a member of a religious order. This view, gave a measure of religious sanction to the monks and nuns performing the mundane but essential functions necessary for the religious order to survive: milking the cows, cooking the meals, tilling the garden. In this manner, a stratified view of work gained the official acceptance of the established religious orders. Work performed by a member of a religious order afforded a measure of dignity, but it conferred a lower order of dignity than contemplation or prayer. This allowed those persons powerful in the religious hierarchy to spend their time in contemplation and prayer while still enjoying a higher level of dignity. Work was regarded as essential and worthwhile, and therefore acceptable, but not as something which had intrinsic value in itself.

Martin Luther and John Calvin both stimulated the further evolution of our ideas regarding work. Luther argued that work was not only essential, but was carrying out God's purpose. Mere piety without work was unnatural and ungodly. Calvin advanced this belief a step further by arguing that work was required of man by God. Toil was a virtue, whether in pursuit of a religious or secular objective, and idleness was a sin. This view of work stands in opposition to the beliefs of the Greeks and Romans. While work was earlier viewed as a curse, now Luther and Calvin argued that all work was required of man by God. The Greeks and Romans viewed a life of reflection and contemplation as the highest calling, Luther and Calvin argued that idleness was unnatural, ungodly, and essentially sinful. In short, Luther and Calvin advanced the position that all work is for the advancement of the kingdom of God.

The influence of Luther and Calvin in reshaping current attitudes toward work was the driving force of the work ethic that today we call the protestant ethic. Parental admonitions to children to avoid idleness, (i.e., don't just sit around all day, do something useful), equate idleness with laziness and lack of character, and reflect our unwitting acceptance of Luther's and Calvin's beliefs that idleness is a sin. Well engrained in our society are the beliefs that there is something inherently bad about idleness, and that work for the sake of work is good.

Differential Psychology

The developments related to the emergence of the school of differential psychology also played a significant role in shaping our current views of career decision making, development, and maturity. It is to the school of differential psychology that the credit belongs for the formulation of the philosophical notions about the psychometric treatment of human characteristics and the development of assessment techniques. In the late 19th and early 20th centuries, psychologists such as Wundt, Fechner, Weber, and von Helmholtz were engaged in the search for universal laws. The Weber–Fechner law is perhaps the clearest expression of this approach to the study of human behavior. As we know today, people do not behave in the narrowly circumscribed manner dictated by such laws. Psychologists of the late 19th century and early 20th century regarded these individual differences as annoying sources of error.

The way for the statistical treatment of human variations was paved by LePlaus and Gauss in 1735 with the derivation of the mathematical equation for what is today called the normal curve. Gauss continued to study the normal curve and its applicability to such human characteristics as life expectancy and birthrate. Quatelet continued this work a century later, applying the normal curve to human measurements such as height and weight. Gauss and Quatelet concluded that the normal curve provided a reasonable approximation of the distribution of such human phenomena.

Gauss and Quatelet pioneered the use of statistical and mathematical procedures for treating human data, demonstrating that deviations in human attributes followed a natural, predictable pattern. Nevertheless, psychologists still continued to treat deviations as error, pressing forward in the search for universal laws. It was Francis Galton, widely regarded as the father of differential psychology, whose contributions set in motion the events which so influenced our views of career development and maturity. Galton, a cousin of Charles Darwin, was intrigued by Darwin's theory of evolution and believed that genetic differences explained much of the variability of human behavior. Like Darwin, Galton believed that variation was a naturally occurring and important attribute of all species.

Beginning about 1869, Galton applied the normal curve to the study of eminence by investigating phenomena such as grades in math at Cambridge. Galton divided the normal curve into categories and treated data in terms of the relative frequency with which individuals fell into each category. He demonstrated that eminence and many other human characteristics could be ordered on a continuum, and that the normal curve provided a reasonable approximation of the distribution of these characteristics. In short, human variations were reliable and predictable.

Galton's work was in many ways as revolutionary as Darwin's theory of evolution. Prior to that time, the leading scholars regarded individual and intraindividual differences as error. Galton's approach emphasized the individuality of each person and the importance of gaining an intimate understanding of the ways in which persons differ. This emphasis on the uniqueness of each individual is the philosophical foundation upon which both the school of differential psychology and the discipline of counseling psychology are built.

If the differences among individuals are important in understanding human behavior, techniques for assessing each individual's unique status on characteristics of interest are essential for the development of the science of psychology. Consequently, the school of differential psychology both encouraged and emphasized the development of assessment techniques. One of the earliest successful efforts was the development of the Binet intelligence scales. In 1895, Binet and Henri criticized the available tests as concentrating unduly on simple, highly specialized abilities. They proposed as an alternative a series of tests assessing functions such as attention, comprehension, and memory. This work led to the development in 1905 of the Binet and Simon Intelligence Scale.

Career Development Theory and Counseling Practice

The other two important influencers of our present views of career life planning and maturity are career development theory and career-counseling practice. Advances in these areas often went hand in hand, so their genesis is difficult to trace independently. Frank Parsons, widely regarded as the father of trait-and-factor theory, deserves credit for the development of one of the first theories of career development and for the advancement of career counseling practice (see Zytowski, 1985, for a brief biographical sketch of this multitalented individual). Parsons became concerned about the plight of immigrants who needed to find jobs quickly in order to establish themselves and their families in America. Parsons's concern for this situation led him to found Breadwinners College in 1905 and to become the first director of the Vocation Bureau of Boston in 1908.

Parsons's report to the executive committee of the Vocation Bureau on May 1, 1908, was prophetic. He argued that vocational guidance should become a part of the public school system in every community. He recommended that vocational guidance centers be staffed by experts, trained in the art of vocational guidance as exhaustively as an M.D. is trained. He also recommended that these experts have available to them every facility science can devise for testing the students' physical, intellectual, and emotional characteristics. Today, vocational guidance is widely available and most vocational guidance counselors have pursued graduate training. Sadly, the goal to provide these experts with every facility that science can devise is not often achieved.

Parsons outlined his theory of vocational choice in *Choosing a vocation,* published posthumously in 1909. Parsons believed that successful vocational choice requires a clear understanding of the attitudes, abilities, interests, ambitions, resources, and limitations of the worker; a knowledge of the requirement for success, advantages and disadvantages, compensation, opportunities, and prospects of different jobs; and a knowledge of the lawful relationships among these two sets of information. Modern trait-and-factor theories can be seen as embellishments of Parsons's outline, and the importance of measurement and matching is almost universally recognized in current practice.

Continued Developments

Advances in assessment techniques and practices, career development theory, and career-counseling practice have continued to occur in the three-quarters of a century since Parsons's contributions. Once these forces were set in motion, efforts in all areas occurred simultaneously. Developments have continued to the present.

These four lines of development were instrumental in shaping our current views of career decision making, development, and maturity, thereby influencing the research questions we ask and the interventions we attempt. The formulation and refinement of theories of career development have continued apace. Phillips discusses these developments in Chapter 1. The school of differential psychology emphasizes that a clear understanding of each person's individuality requires sophisticated psychometric assessment techniques. This book summarizes the most recent advances in techniques for assessing career decision making (see Chapter 2), and career development and maturity (see Chapter 3). Finally, advances in theory and refinements in assessment techniques often have stimulated the further development of career intervention strategies, a topic treated by Taylor in Chapter 4.

In contrast to the many developments and changes occurring in the other three areas, our philosophical beliefs about work remain largely unchanged from the 16th century. The way we think about work continues to influence theory building, the development of assessment devices, our approach to career counseling and, ultimately, our interaction with our clients. Many individuals continue to define work and leisure as the antithesis of each other and the attributes, causes, and psychological benefits of leisure are still poorly understood.

Because of the datedness of our beliefs about work and the limiting influences these beliefs exert on research and practice, the next sections propose a different perspective from which to understand leisure. This treatment begins with a brief coverage of definitions of leisure, followed by the exposition of our theory of leisure experience. The attributes, causes, and immediate psychological benefits of leisure experience are elucidated, and research on the immediate psychological benefits of leisure is summarized. Tests designed to measure aspects of leisure experience are identified and the implications of this line of inquiry for theory development, research, and practice are explored.

A THEORY OF LEISURE EXPERIENCE

Definitions of Leisure

In contrast to Aristotle's classical view of leisure, contemporary definitions of leisure have emphasized the residual or discretionary element of leisure. The residual time perspective advanced by Brightbill (1960) defines leisure as the time remaining to the individual after the time required for existence (e.g., eating, sleeping, meeting biological needs) and subsistence (e.g., working at a job) are subtracted. An example is Kaplan's (1975) definition of leisure as a "relatively self-determined activity experience that falls into one's economically free time roles . . . [p. 26]." A similar view is the notion of leisure as discretionary time (Dumazedier, 1967). This perspective emphasizes the freedom or discretion of the individual to choose the activity. Like the residual definition of leisure, however, the amount of discretionary or free time available to the individual is usually defined as that remaining after the existence and subsistence needs of the person have been met.

The discretionary and residual time definitions of leisure reflect the view most commonly held by the lay public. These definitions of leisure are objective, thereby facilitating research, but this advantage is outweighed by several problems inherent in the residual and discretionary definitions. First, these definitions are not as objective as might be supposed, especially when an individual is involved in more than one activity simultaneously (e.g., see Szalai's, 1972, discussion of time deepening). Second, they define leisure only in terms of the negation of other activities. Third, these definitions focus on when the activity happens and ignore information about the nature and quality of what happens. Finally, these approaches define work and leisure as mutually exclusive, just as the classical Greeks and Romans did, ignoring the possibility that work and leisure might have a similar psychological impact on the individual. For these reasons, the residual and discretionary time views do little to enhance our understanding of the nature of leisure or of the role of leisure in individual development.

Tinsley and Tinsley (1986) have recently suggested a holistic theory of leisure experience which offers a more integrated view of the work and nonwork aspects of life. Holistic approaches have often suffered from excessive zeal, with numerous writers labeling the most extreme or intensely moving form of leisure experience as "leisure" or "the" leisure experience. Use of the term "leisure" as a synonym for "leisure experience" fails to communicate clearly the focus of the writer on the personal nature of the individual's experience as opposed to the objective reality of having free time. Leisure is most commonly defined as "freedom from time consuming duties, responsibilities or activities . . . having free time [Morris, 1969, p. 747]." Tinsley and Tinsley focus on the individual's subjective experience of leisure (i.e., on leisure experience).

Before reviewing our theory of leisure experience, it is instructive to recognize how it fits into the historical context. The ancient Greeks and Romans regarded work as a curse and leisure as the central goal of life, the end toward which all action is directed. According to this perspective, all other forms of action are related to leisure and are defined, in essence, as the absence of leisure. The protestant ethic, which is more consistent with the way we think today, is the antithesis of the classical view. In this view, idleness is a sin and work for the sake of work is honorable. In contrast, we regard a balancing of work and leisure as ideal. We believe work and leisure will eventually be shown to be very similar in some of the ways they effect people. Finally, we believe both work and leisure are required for a healthy, satisfying life.

Attributes of Leisure Experience

Tinsley and Tinsley (1986) focus not on leisure per se, nor on leisure activities, but on individuals' subjective experiencing of leisure and the effects of those experiences. For example, individuals who frequently experience leisure while watching television will most likely not experience leisure when they turn on the television to see the temperature or when they are absent-mindedly watching television while waiting for a friend to arrive. Hence, it is important to understand this semantically subtle but important distinction; we have proposed a theory of leisure experience, not a theory of leisure.

We believe the determinants of leisure experience are both individual and environmental. Individuals may experience leisure: "in all aspects of life, including work and other life functions where there is objective evidence that external demands to engage in the activity have been made of the individual [Tinsley & Tinsley, 1982, p. 105]." Our emphasis on the importance of individuals' leisure experiences rather than their participation in activities is shared by writers such as Avedon (1974), Brok (1975), Csikszentmihalyi (1975), Green (1968), Iso–Ahola (1980), Mannell (1980), McDowell (1976), Neulinger (1974), and Remple (1977).

There is general agreement among theorists that there is not a single leisure experience but a continuum of leisure experiences (see Kaplan, 1975; Table 5.1). Leisure experiences vary in overall intensity from those barely perceivable by the individual to intense experiences which we designate as the leisure state. We believe a given individual will have leisure experiences which vary in overall intensity (i.e., potency) across time, depending on factors which will be explicated later. Furthermore, individuals differ in the range and average intensity of their leisure experiences.

Regardless of the intensity of the experience, leisure experiences are characterized to some degree by both cognitive (i.e., thoughts, images) and affective (i.e., feelings, sensation) attributes. These include absorption or concentration on the ongoing experience, lessening of focus on self, feelings of freedom or lack of constraint, enriched perception of objects and events, increased intensity of emotions, increased sensitivity to feelings, and decreased awareness of the passage of time. Even in less potent leisure experiences, these attributes are experienced to some degree. In the most intense leisure experience (i.e., the leisure state), these attributes are experienced as salient.

It is our belief, therefore, that the leisure state is similar in its psychological properties to mystic experiences, peak experiences, and flow experiences. This possibility has been noted previously by Mannell (1980) and Ellis and Witt (1984), but virtually no research on this issue has been forthcoming.

TABLE 5.1
Attributs of Leisure Experience

Attributes	Theorist				
	Neulinger (1974, 1976, 1981)	Csikszentmihalyi (1975, 1980)	McDowell (1976, 1981)	Mannell (1980)	Kelly (1972, 1976)
Not a unitary experience	X	X	X		X
Transitory	X	X	X	X	X
Effects on Individual					
Distortion of time perception		X	X	X	
Enjoyment (pleasure)		X	X	X	
Loss of anxiety, constraint		X	X		
Total involvement (forgetting self)		X	X		
Narrowed focus of attention		X		X	
Enriched perception		X			

From Tinsley and Tinsley (1986). Reprinted by permission.

The attributes we have postulated for the leisure experience are similar to those proposed by previous writers (Table 5.1) with one important difference. Contrary to Csikszentmihalyi (1975), Mannell (1980) and McDowell (1981), we believe leisure experience can be stressful or unpleasant at times. We agree with Kaplan (1975) that leisure experience is pleasant in anticipation and recollection, but not necessarily in the experiencing. For example, recreational runners talk about the first mile of a run as a time for "sorting out the aches and pains," and runners who want to improve their speed sometimes engage in grueling speed practice sessions called "intervals." In both instances, however, runners are cognizant that they have freely chosen to engage in this activity for personal, idiosyncratic reasons. In our view, leisure experience is characterized by increased intensity of emotions and sensitivity to feelings, both positive and negative.

We believe the individual's awareness of leisure experience is transitory, usually occurring for a short time. This notion is consistent with the scientific evidence bearing on the attentional processes. Attention varies; humans focus on one aspect of the situation, then another, then another. Consequently, the individual's experiencing of leisure will be interrupted periodically. Ellis and Witt (1984) concur, interpreting the pattern of alpha and stability coefficients on the Leisure Diagnostic Battery as suggesting that the perception of freedom in leisure is a state rather than a trait concept.

The individual's cognitions may be expected to vary from an awareness of nonleisure (i.e., involvement in an extrinsically motivated work or maintenance activity) through nonawareness of either leisure or nonleisure, to an awareness of leisure. The intensity with which individuals concentrate on themselves and the experience, however, has a curvilinear (i.e., inverted U-shaped) relationship to the quality and/or potency of leisure experience. An optimal level of attention to leisure experience is somewhat between the two extremes. Runners, for example, report experiencing an exhilarating sense of their bodies in motion and a collage of environmental sights and sounds. Focusing too intensely on self (e.g., the constant self-monitoring of the competitive runner during a marathon) interrupts this experience as surely as paying too little attention to the experience (e.g., worrying about work to be done at home).

Research Postulates.   The following propositions and corollaries represent a beginning theoretical model. We urge the development of multiple methods to measure the constructs explicated in these propositions. Space limitations and the paucity of information available about leisure experience preclude the specification of precise operational definitions of some of the terms used in the propositions. Indeed, more than one operational definition is desirable for some of the terms and we encourage readers to relate these constructs to their understanding of leisure. Nevertheless, the following propositions and their corollaries offer a conceptual framework within which research on the nature and attributes of leisure experience and the leisure state can be pursued. We anticipate that the theoretical and empirical contributions of the scientific community over the next few years will enable the refinement of this effort.

Proposition 1. Leisure experiences consist of a constellation of covarying cognitive and affective attributes experienced by an individual which can be measured by scales reflecting both qualitative and quantitative dimensions.

Corollary 1. Individuals may notice a relationship between participation in a particular activity and the experiencing of leisure. This relationship is mediated by attributes of their thoughts and feelings. Participation in a leisure activity is neither necessary nor sufficient to cause individuals to experience leisure.

Proposition 2. Leisure experiences vary in potency from those barely perceivable by individuals to intense experiences having a significant impact on individuals. (**Note:** The most potent form of leisure experience is designated the leisure state.)

Corollary 2A. The potency of individuals' leisure experiences varies across occasions.

Corollary 2B. The level and range of potency of leisure experiences vary across individuals.

Proposition 3. Individuals' awareness of leisure experience is transitory, meaning that it usually occurs for short periods of time.

Corollary 3A. Individuals may become aware of leisure experience numerous times while participating in an activity.

Corollary 3B. Individuals may fluctuate between awareness of leisure experience and awareness of nonleisure experience (i.e., involvement in an extrinsically motivated work or maintenance activity) while participating in an activity.

Proposition 4. The intensity with which individuals focus on self and/or the experience has an inverted U-shaped relationship to the quality and/or potency of leisure experience.

Corollary 4A. Increasing concentration on self and/or the experience from low to moderate causes an increase in the potency and/or quality of leisure experience.

Corollary 4B. Increasing concentration on self and/or the experience to stronger than moderate causes a decrease in the potency and/or quality of leisure experience.

Proposition 5. The leisure state is the most potent leisure experience, having psychological properties similar to those of psychic, peak (Maslow, 1968) and flow experiences (Csikszentmihalyi, 1975).

Proposition 6. Individuals experiencing leisure and/or the leisure state will report that they experienced:

a. Total absorption in (or intense concentration on) the activity at hand,

b. Lack of focus on (or forgetting of) self,

c. Feelings of freedom,

d. Enriched perception of objects and events,

e. Increased sensitivity to bodily sensations,

f. Increased sensitivity to and intensity of emotions, and

g. Decreased awareness of the passage of time.

Corollary 6A. Individuals experiencing the leisure state will rate the potency of the feelings described herein and cognitions as "high" when using an absolute rating procedure.

Corollary 6B. Individuals experiencing leisure will rate the potency of the above feelings and cognitions as moderate to low when using an absolute rating procedure.

Corollary 6C. Individuals experiencing leisure will rate the potency of their feelings and cognitions lower than individuals experiencing the leisure state when using a relative rating procedure.

Corollary 6D. Because conscious awareness of leisure experience varies, individuals may experience leisure without being consciously aware of it at the time. These feelings and cognitions will be reported, however, when they are asked subsequent to the experience to describe their feelings and thoughts during the experience.

Causes of Leisure Experience

We believe four conditions must be present for a person to experience leisure or the leisure state: perceived freedom of choice, intrinsic motivation, facilitative arousal, and commitment. Each of these factors can vary in the degree to which they are perceived as present. For example, persons can perceive themselves as having complete freedom of choice, some freedom of choice, a little freedom of choice, or no freedom of choice. Since research to date has treated these primarily as dichotomous factors by contrasting "perceived freedom of choice" to "perceived absence of freedom of choice [see Iso–Ahola, 1980, 1984]," it is not possible yet to specify the level at which these factors must be experienced to be perceived as descriptive of the individual's state. Each condition must be present to some as yet undetermined degree, however, so each is a necessary but not sufficient condition for experiencing leisure.

The most widely acknowledged prerequisite for experiencing leisure is perceived freedom of choice (Bordin, 1979; Ellis & Witt, 1984; see also Table 5.2). We believe individuals will experience leisure only when engaging in an activity they perceive to be freely chosen. Individuals will not experience leisure if they believe they are required to engage in an activity, either as a direct requirement or less directly as an expectation of their employer or colleagues. Consultants who play golf with business associates, for example, will not experience leisure

TABLE 5.2

Factors Theorized to be Necessary for an Individual to Experience Leisure

Factor	Theorist						
	Neulinger (1974, 1976, 1981)	Czikszentmihalyi (1975, 1980)	Kelly (1972, 1976)	Brok (1975)	McDowell (1976, 1981)	ISO-Ahola (1980, 1984)	Mannell (1980)
Perceived freedom (Voluntary)	X	X	X	X	X	X	X
Intrinsic motivation	X		X	X	X	X	X
Social Factors							
Culturally recognized as leisure		X					
Work relationship			X		X		
Situational and Social factors	X				X	X	
Personal Factors							
Personal experiences					X	X	
Leisure attitudes					X		X
Optimal arousal						X	
Demands effort				X			
Innate drive	X				X		
Facilitates Personal Growth				X			
Ideal Not Easily Achieved	X	X					

From Tinsley and Tinsley (1986). Reprinted by permission.

if they perceive themselves as having been required to golf. On other occasions, however, such persons may choose to golf and may experience leisure while doing so.

A point which must be underscored is that it is the person's perception of freedom of choice which is the necessary condition, not freedom of choice as it would be judged by independent observers. We believe a person's perception of his or her motivation for engaging in an activity may vary across time in the activity, a belief shared by Iso–Ahola (1980). When a woman golfs for business reasons, for example, her thoughts may initially be on business. If the match is especially interesting or she is having a good day and is close to a personal record, however, her subjective perception of why she is engaged in the activity may change from one of performing the activity for external reasons to one of doing the activity because she so chooses. When this occurs, she may then experience leisure.

In order to experience leisure, persons must also perceive themselves as motivated to experience conditions which occur as a result of factors inherent in participating in the activity (i.e., intrinsically motivated; see Table 5.2). Persons engaging in an activity for external reasons (i.e., extrinsically motivated) frequently perceive themselves as lacking in freedom of choice. Since they are not engaging in the activity to experience conditions intrinsic to the activity itself, they are less likely to perceive themselves as "doing it because I want to." Likewise, persons who perceived themselves as engaging in an activity because of some degree of external coercion are less likely to perceive themselves as intrinsically motivated. Nevertheless, it is possible to pursue an activity voluntarily for extrinsic rewards (e.g., the person who builds cabinets in order to supplement the family income), so these conditions are not completely confounded.

Conditions which are intrinsically motivating to one person may lack motivating power for another person. A woman who experiences a need for solitude is intrinsically motivated to some degree when she takes a long bicycle ride by herself in the country because experiencing solitude occurs as an integral part of the experience. A different woman who experiences a need for social relationships may be said to be extrinsically motivated when she takes a similar bicycle ride solely for the purpose of keeping physical fit for her work as a wrestler. The psychological needs of the person are influential in determining that which is intrinsically motivating.

The needs for freedom of choice and intrinsic motivation are most likely learned in the context of the person–environment interaction. It is well established, however, that the need for facilitative arousal is innate (e.g., Bronfenbrenner, 1968; Harlow & Harlow, 1962; Hunt, 1969, 1972). The need may be expressed as curiosity (Butler, 1954; Harlow, 1953; Glickman & Sroges, 1966), or as the need for environmental complexity (e.g., Cooper & Zubek,

1958), but the consequences of failure to satisfy this need may be tragic (e.g., Cooper & Zubek, 1958; Dennis, 1960).

In order to experience facilitative arousal, a moderate level of stimulation must occur. The novelty, complexity, and dissonance of the situation are important determinants of the amount of perceived stimulation which occurs. When too much stimulation occurs, persons experience sensory overload and a feeling of loss of control which can be an uncomfortable or frightening experience. At the other extreme, lack of sufficient stimulation leads to boredom, lethargy and, over long periods of time, to decline of mental and physical capacity. Schreyer, Lime, and Williams (1984) recently reported evidence which illustrates the importance of facilitative arousal in leisure behavior. Novice river recreationists reported the desire to experience new and different things was among their most important motives for taking a river trip.

Without the personal engagement which occurs as a function of facilitative arousal, the individual can experience stress and anxiety or boredom but not leisure (see Iso–Ahola, 1980, for a discussion of this point). The level of stimulation which results in facilitative arousal varies from person to person (see Farley, 1986) and, for a given person, across time. The past experiences of the person and his or her configuration of psychological needs are influential in determining what will be facilitatively arousing. The experience of rappelling from a 50-foot cliff may be too frightening or stimulating to the novice rock climber, facilitatively arousing to the person who has rappelled from a similar height on 10 previous occasions, and almost commonplace to a person with years of rappelling experience.

The final prerequisite to leisure experience is commitment to the activity in which the person is engaged (see Table 5.2). Bordin (1979) has written about the need to leaven spontaneity with disciplined effort to achieve fully satisfying play. Disciplined effort is a combination of behavioral and cognitive activity. A disciplined physical and/or mental effort may sometimes be required as in learning to play the piano or to bowl. The literature on imprinting (e.g., Gray, 1958; Hess, 1959) has documented the importance of physical effort in shaping personality and the subsequent behavior of the organism. For activities such as chess, however, the effort required may be more cognitive than physical.

Regardless of the type of effort, we believe it is the person's personal commitment of self which indicates this willingness to undertake a disciplined physical and/or mental effort. Support for this belief can be found in Schreyer et al. (1984) who found that the most important motives of veteran river recreationists for taking a river trip included developing their skills, testing their abilities, strengthening their feelings of self-worth and thinking about their personal values. Although the nature of the required effort may change as the person gains experience in the activity, some form of personal commitment is necessary in order to experience leisure.

Research Postulates.   Given the forgoing discussion, it is possible to state the following propositions:

Proposition 7. A leisure experience occurs only when an individual perceives his or her participation in an activity to be voluntary or freely chosen.

Proposition 8. The likelihood of experiencing leisure while participating in an activity varies as a function of changes in the individual's perception that his or her participation in the activity is voluntary.

Corollary 8A. The probability that an individual will begin to experience leisure during participation in an activity varies as a linear function of the strength of the individual's perception that his or her participation in the activity is voluntary.

Corollary 8B. The probability that an individual will cease to experience or not begin to experience leisure during participation in an activity varies as an inverse function of changes in the individual's perception that his or her participation in the activity is voluntary.

Proposition 9. A leisure experience occurs only when the individual perceives the benefits of participation in an activity to derive from factors intrinsic to participation in the activity.

Proposition 10. The extent to which the individual perceives the benefits of participation in an activity to derive from factors intrinsic to participation in the activity is a function of the correspondence between the psychological needs of the individual and the psychological benefits intrinsic to the activity.

Corollary 10. The probability increases than an individual will experience leisure while participating in an activity as the correspondence increases between the individual's psychological needs and the psychological benefits intrinsic to the activity.

Proposition 11. An individual will experience leisure only when he or she experiences a facilitative level of arousal during participation in the activity.

Corollary 11A. Individuals are less likely to experience leisure during their first experience in a new activity than after a few experiences in the activity.

Corollary 11B. The probability an individual will experience leisure has an inverted U-shaped relationship to the extent of the individual's participation in the activity unless changes occur in the novelty or complexity of the activity.

Corollary 11C. Individuals having a high need for variety, novelty, or stimulation will experience leisure after fewer experiences in a new activity than individuals having a low need for variety, novelty, or stimulation.

Corollary 11D. Individuals having a high need for variety, novelty, or stimulation will experience leisure for a shorter period of time (or a fewer number of participations) than individuals having a low need for variety, novelty, or stimulation unless changes occur in the novelty or complexity of the activity in which they are participating.

Proposition 12. The probability that individuals will experience leisure increases as a positive monotonic function of their psychological commitment of self to the activity in which they are participating.

Corollary 12A. The probability persons will experience leisure has a linear relationship to the consistency with which they exert a disciplined physical and/or mental effort across their history of participation in the activity.

Corollary 12B. The probability persons will experience leisure while participating in an activity has an inverted U-shaped relationship to the intensity of their physical and/or mental effort.

Corollary 12C. Individuals who make a moderately disciplined physical and/or mental effort while participating in an activity will be more likely to experience leisure than individuals who make very little or an exceedingly intense effort.

Corollary 12D. Individuals who make a moderately disciplined physical and/or mental effort will be more likely to experience a narrowing of focus on a limited stimulus field than individuals who make very little or an exceedingly intense effort.

Proposition 13. Although all persons have the potential to experience the leisure state, some persons will rarely experience the leisure state because of their failure to exert a disciplined effort or their overly intense commitment of self to the activity in which they are participating.

Proposition 14. Individuals will experience leisure only when they experience freedom of choice, intrinsic motivation, facilitative arousal and personal commitment.

Benefits of Leisure Experience

Fig. 5.1 illustrates our theory of the benefit of experiencing leisure or the leisure state. We believe that whenever an individual experiences leisure some psychological needs will be satisfied. The evidence suggests that psychological needs at all five levels of Maslow's (1970) hierarchy (i.e., physiological, safety, belongingness, self-esteem, and self-actualization needs) may be satisfied by participation in leisure activities. This includes both primary needs, defined as "a deficit or lack of something which, if present, would further the welfare of the individual or would facilitate his or her usual behavior," and secondary needs, defined as "a learned preference for a set of stimulus conditions in which responding is usually associated with satisfaction [Tinsley, 1978, p. 88]." Whether the need gratification results from leisure experience or the mere act of engaging in an activity culturally recognized as leisure has yet to be determined.

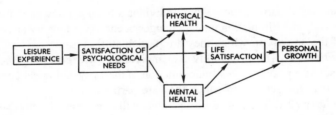

FIG. 5.1.   Causal effects of leisure experience. From Tinsley and Tinsley (1986). Reprinted by permission.

The research evidence regarding the potential need gratification which may be obtained by experiencing leisure will be described in the next section.

Although many needs can be satisfied in a variety of ways, it is our position that every individual has some needs for which leisure experience is the only source of gratification. For example, an accountant by profession may enjoy the satisfaction he or she gains from raising house plants. This activity may allow him or her to use skills and to express interests quite different from those generally associated with his or her work or maintenance activities. In addition, caring for plants may satisfy one's learned psychological (i.e., secondary) needs to express personality through creative use of talents and it may reflect the importance to the accountant of contributing to a world of beauty.

It is our prediction that the attributes of leisure experience (Proposition 6) are common to peak and flow experiences. Anecdotal evidence supporting this prediction is available from an interview with a middle-aged career woman. She related an instance in which she became so completely engrossed in tending her house plants after a difficult day at work that she forgot to pick up her daughter after a school activity. The woman reported experiencing a heightened sensitivity to the beauty and uniqueness of the individual plants, a narrowing of focus on her interaction with the plants and complete loss of awareness of the passage of time. The conditions (Proposition 14) prerequisite to experiencing these attributes (Proposition 6) are more likely to be present when the person is engaged in leisure than in other pursuits. Hence, we regard the label "leisure experience" as preferable to the alternatives which have been suggested.

The satisfaction of psychological needs has a salutary effect on mental health, physical health and satisfaction with life (Fig. 5.1), which, in turn, have a salutary effect on personal growth. Failure to satisfy one's psychological needs is detrimental to the physical and mental health of the person and results in a reduction of life satisfaction and a lack of personal growth. The benefits of need satisfaction, enhanced physical health, mental health and life satisfaction, and personal growth are referred to collectively as the psychological benefits of leisure (see Fig. 5.1). For purposes of clarity, the satisfaction of psychological needs is considered to be an immediate psychological benefit of leisure. The benefits of enhanced physical health, mental health, life satisfaction, and personal growth are considered developmental psychological benefits of leisure.

LEVEL OF NEED SATISFACTION		LEVEL OF LIFE SATISFACTION	PERSONAL GROWTH	PHYSICAL, MENTAL HEALTH
OPTIMAL	LEISURE ENRICHMENT	ABOVE AVERAGE	OPTIMAL	ENHANCEMENT
	T_G			
ADEQUATE	LEISURE SUFFICEINCY	HIGH OR AVERAGE TO LOW	MINIMAL	MAINTENENCE
	T_M			
INSUFFICIENT	LEISURE DEFICIT	LOW	NONE	DETERIORATION

FIG. 5.2. The relationship of psychological need satisfaction through leisure experience and personal growth. From Tinsley and Tinsley (1986). Reprinted by permission.

The dependence of physical health, mental health, life satisfaction, and personal growth on gratification of the individual's psychological needs is best represented by a stepwise model in which changes in need satisfaction must exceed a threshold before effects occur (see Fig. 5.2). Some minimal level of need satisfaction is a necessary but not sufficient condition for maintaining life satisfaction at or above the maintenance threshold (T_M). Whenever a person's level of need gratification falls below the maintenance threshold, the probability increases that he or she will experience leisure deficit (i.e., chronic inadequacy of leisure experience), a notion similar to Neulinger's concept of "leisure lack [1981, p. 70]." Failure to rectify this situation is postulated as resulting in a low level of life satisfaction (Fig. 5.3), a lack of personal growth (Fig. 5.4), and deterioration of the person's physical and mental health (Fig. 5.5).

Leisure sufficiency results from experiencing leisure frequently enough that the level of need gratification exceeds the maintenance threshold (T_M) but not the

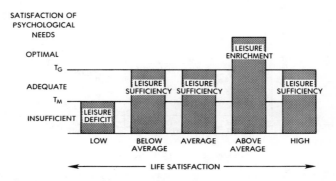

FIG. 5.3. The relationship of psychological need satisfaction to life satisfaction. From Tinsley and Tinsley (1986). Reprinted by permission.

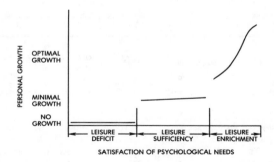

FIG. 5.4.   The relationship of psychological need satisfaction to personal growth.

growth threshold (T_G). Consequently, leisure deficit is avoided but the level of need satisfaction is not sufficient to stimulate personal growth. Leisure sufficiency may be associated with a life satisfaction level which the individual judges to be below average, average, or high (Fig. 5.3). Persons who judge their life satisfaction to be below average or average must attend to the further satisfaction of their physiological, safety, and belonginess needs in an effort to enhance life satisfaction. Consequently, little time or energy is available for personal growth. Persons who judge their life satisfaction to be high, typically are motivated to avoid making personal changes. Consequently, persons experiencing leisure sufficiency may give minimal attention to personal growth (Fig. 5.4), but the primary result is maintenance of the status quo. Under such circumstances, physical and mental health will remain largely unchanged (Fig. 5.5).

The growth threshold (T_G) is exceeded whenever need gratification is sufficient to satisfy the individual's physiological, safety, and belongingness needs. Persons experiencing this condition judge their level of life satisfaction to be above average (Fig. 5.3). This frees them from the necessity of devoting time

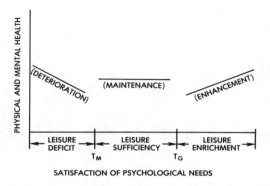

FIG. 5.5.   The relationship of psychological need satisfaction to physical and mental health.

and attention to the maintenance of physical and mental health and allows them to attend to their self-esteem and self-actualization needs. The resulting increase in self-awareness leads to the identification of aspects of self the person would like to change. Consequently, leisure enrichment stimulates personal growth (Fig. 5.4) and enhanced physical and mental health (Fig. 5.5).

Consider the following example which illustrates this point. An individual's job as an auto mechanic may satisfy his or her needs to work with his or her hands, see tangible results from the efforts, and have financial security. On the other hand, needs for self-fulfillment (i.e., self-esteem and self-actualization) may not be satisfied by the job. Such a person might be expected to report an average level of life satisfaction and mental and physical health, but psychological growth and enhancement of physical health, mental health, and life satisfaction are unlikely. Suppose, however, that this person's grandmother was an avid photographer who had taught her grandchild to appreciate the beauty and complexity of the world by introducing the child to photography as a leisure activity. The decision to pursue photography as a leisure activity may result in leisure experiences which provide opportunities for enhanced self-esteem and self-actualization. This, in turn, could be expected to result in an increase in life satisfaction and an improvement in physical and mental health.

Our belief in the growth producing effects of leisure experience is consistent with our contention that leisure experience can be stressful or unpleasant at times. We believe that growth is inherently stressful to some degree. Achieving the growth-producing benefits of leisure, therefore, implies that persons may sometimes experience stress as an aspect of leisure experience.

Research Postulates.   The preceding ideas about the benefits of leisure experience can be stated in the form of the following propositions:

> *Proposition 15.* Experiencing leisure results in the satisfaction of some psychological needs of the individual.
>
> *Proposition 16.* All individuals have some needs which can be satisfied only by experiencing leisure.
>
> *Proposition 17.* There exists a level of need satisfaction (i.e., the maintenance threshold; T_M) which is the minimum sufficient to allow maintenance of physical health, mental health, and life satisfaction.
>
> *Proposition 18.* Need satisfaction by experiencing leisure is a necessary but not sufficient condition for need satisfaction to exceed the maintenance threshold.
>
>> *Corollary 18.* Need satisfaction by experiencing leisure is a necessary but not sufficient condition for the maintenance of physical and mental health.
>
> *Proposition 19.* The probability that need satisfaction will fall below the maintenance threshold is an inverse linear function of leisure deficit.

Corollary 19A. The probability that a person's physical health will deteriorate is an inverse linear function of leisure deficit.

Corollary 19B. The probability that a person's mental health will deteriorate is an inverse linear function of leisure deficit.

Proposition 20. Need satisfaction by experiencing leisure is a necessary but not sufficient condition for need satisfaction to exceed the growth threshold (T_G).

Corollary 20. Need satisfaction by experiencing leisure is a necessary but not sufficient condition for the stimulation of personal growth.

Proposition 21. The probability that need satisfaction will exceed the growth threshold (T_G) increases as a linear function of the potency and quantity of leisure experience.

Corollary 21A. The probability that leisure experience may contribute to the formation of temporary feelings of dissatisfaction with self increases as a linear function of the potency and quantity of leisure experience.

Corollary 21B. The probability that leisure experience may be perceived as stressful at the time of its experiencing increases as a linear function of the potency and quantity of leisure experience.

Corollary 21C. The probability that leisure experience may stimulate negative or unhappy moods, feelings, or thoughts at the time of its experiencing increases as a linear function of the potency and quantity of leisure experience.

Corollary 21D. The probability that personal growth will occur increases as a linear function of the potency and quantity of leisure experience.

RESEARCH ON NEED-SATISFYING PROPERTIES OF LEISURE ACTIVITIES

Psychological Benefit Factors

The development of assessment instruments provided career counselors with tools which could be used to further their understanding of the unique characteristics of the individuals with whom they work. In a similar manner, research on the immediate psychological benefits of participation in specific leisure activities can help counselors to understand the potential benefits these individuals might obtain by participation in various leisure activities.

Investigations of the psychological benefits of leisure experience are relatively new. Tinsley and Tinsley (1986) provide a comprehensive summary of the literature bearing on the relationships among leisure participation and need gratification, mental health, and life satisfaction. This section reviews the findings accruing from the research program of Tinsley (1978, 1984) and his associates (Tinsley, Barrett, & Kass, 1977; Tinsley & Johnson, 1984; Tinsley & Kass,

1978, 1979; Tinsley, Teaff, Colbs, & Kaufman, 1985), a program which has focused for the past 10 years on the need-satisfying properties of leisure.

Tinsley and Kass (1979) identified eight need gratification dimensions in a factor analysis of the 27 leisure activity specific scales of the Paragraphs About Leisure (PAL). Table 5.3 describes the factors identified and indicates the split-group reliability of each factor. Of equal concern is the adequacy of these factors in representing the plethora of immediate psychological benefits which have been postulated. Numerous writers have suggested psychological benefit dimensions on the basis of factor analyses, cluster analyses, or theoretical considera-

TABLE 5.3

Psychological Benefits of Leisure: Reliability and Description of
Factors Derived from Analysis of 27 Leisure-Specific Need Satisfier Scales

Factor (Reliability)

I. Self-expression[1] (.92)
   A complex benefit reflecting, in order of prominence: (1) satisfaction of the individual's need to express one-self successfully throuth creative use of one's talents, (2) to untertake novel activities, often of benefit to others, and (3) to enjoy recognition and power for these efforts.

II. Companionship (.93)
    Satisfies the person's need to engage in playful but supportive relationships with others in which feelings are valued, self-expression is accepted and one's feelings about self are enhanced.

III. Power (.97)
     Satisfies the individual's needs to be in control of the social situation and enjoy the center of attention, often at the expense of others.

IV. Compensation (.80)
    Satisfies the person's need to experience something new, fresh, or unusual; to satisfy needs not satisfied by their job or daily routine.

V. Security (.80)
   Satisfies the individual's need to be able to make a safe and secure, long-term commitment free of bothersome change, in which they will be rewarded for their efforts and receive a measure of recognition.

VI. Service (.87)
    Satisfies the person's need to be of assistance to others.

VII. Intellectual Aestheticism (.94)
     Satisfies the need of the individual for intellectual stim-ulation and aesthetic experiences. Note: This factor appears to be bipolar with low scores reflecting satisfac-tion of the individual's need for physical activity.

VIII. Solitude[2] (.93)
      Satisfies the person's need to do things alone without feeling threatened.

[1]Originally named self-actualization
[2]Originally named autonomy
From Tinsley (1984). Reprinted by permission.

tions. Tinsley (1984) compared the results of Tinsley and Kass with those of other writers to provide a basis for judging the adequacy or comprehensiveness of the eight psychological benefit dimensions.

Table 5.4 identifies the works reviewed and provides some details about their methodology and findings. Table 5.5 summarizes the relationship between the eight psychological benefits reported by Tinsley and Kass (1979) and the dimensions postulated or observed by the authors reviewed. In drawing the conclusions reported in Table 5.5, an effort was made to consider all of the data available (i.e., scale names, item wordings, factor loadings) rather than just the labels given the dimensions by their authors. Nevertheless, the elements of subjectivity and uncertainty which influenced this analysis require that these conclusions be regarded as illustrative rather than definitive.

Despite the need for caution in interpreting the data in Table 5.5, there appears to be a consensus that the psychological benefits of leisure include self-expression, companionship, and compensation. The psychological benefits of self-expression and companionship have been so universally recognized that no further comment seems necessary. The corroboration of the compensation dimension serves as partial validation of the notion that some persons engage in leisure activities which differ markedly from their work in order to compensate for factors they find missing in their work. The compensation factor accounted for less of the variance in psychological benefits (3.4%), however, than any other factor (Tinsley & Kass, 1979). This result is consistent with Staines's (1980) conclusion than seeking leisure activities which will provide compensation for factors lacking in work is a less frequently used strategy than seeking leisure activities which will provide satisfactions similar to those found on the job. Accordingly, research from several substantive areas offers a consistent view of this immediate psychological benefit.

Review of Table 5.5 also reveals agreement regarding the existence of intellectual aestheticism and solitude as psychological benefits of leisure and some agreement about the existence of the power benefit. Psychological benefits classified as unrelated may also reflect aspects of these benefits. For example, Pierce's (1980b) destructiveness factor may reflect the aggression which is an aspect of the power benefit. Brown and Haas's (1980) reflection on personal values factor seems related to the philosophical contemplation that is an element of the intellectual aestheticism benefit. Rossman's (1981) physical fitness factor and Beard and Ragheb's (1980) physiological factor clearly touch upon an aspect of the physical activity benefit which is the other pole of the bipolar intellectual aestheticism factor. These factors were classified as unrelated because the radically differing methodologies and item pools or scales used in these investigations make it difficult to judge them as corresponding to one of Tinsley and Kass's factors with certainty. Nevertheless, the consensual validation for these three psychological benefits seems more than adequate and a potentially important area to pursue in future research.

TABLE 5.4
Methodologies Used in Identifying Psychological Dimensions

Author	N	Method	Findings
Havighurst (1961)	--	Asked respondents why they participate in particular activiites	8 meanings of leisure activities
Goodman (1969)	45	Time utilization rated from taped interviews	2 meanings of freetime activity
Neulinger (1974)	335	Factor analysis of leisure attitudes	5 leisure attitude factors
Brok (1975)	--	Primarily theoretical	Suggested relevance of Erikson's developmental stages
Kelly (1976)	215	Surveyed reasons for choosing 90 leisure activities	4 (groups of) reasons
Csikszentmihalyi (1979)	--	Theoretical	4 restorative and 4 growth benefits of leisure
Beard & Ragheb (1980)	603	Factor analysis of leisure satisfaction items	6 factors
Brown & Haas (1980)	264	Cluster analysis of 71 psychological outcome statements appearing on REPS	8 clusters
Pierce (1980a)	250	Cluster analyzed 68 satisfactions of work and leisure	6 factors that replicated across two studies
Pierce (1980b)	250	Cluster analyzed 80 adjectives evaluating work and leisure	10 clusters
Pierce (1980c)	250	Cluster analyzed 36 characteristics of work and leisure	6 clusters
Rossman (1981)	725	Factor analyzed 40 Leisure need-satisfier items	7 scales
Grey (1981)	75	Themes identified in college student essays on most significant and memorable recreation experiences	26 components of recreation experience
Allen (1982)	212	Canonical analysis of 20 needs from Personality Research Form	4 canonical variates
Iso-Ahola & Allen (1982)	438	Factor analyzed 40 need-satisfaction items administered to intermural basketball players	7 factors
Iso-Ahola (1982)	--	Theoretical	Postulated an approach and an avoidance motive
Beard & Ragheb (1983)	1205	Factor analyzed 48 items measuring reasons for engaging in leisure activities	4 factors

From Tinsley and Tinsley (1986). Reprinted by permission.

237

TABLE 5.5

Correspondence Between Leisure Activity Dimensions Postulated or Reported and the
Psychological Benefit Dimensions Identified by Tinsley and Kass (1979)

Author	Unrelated Dimensions	Self-Expression	Companionship	Power	Compensation	Security	Service	Intellectual Aestheticism	Solitude
Havighurst	Pass time, Pleasure	Achievement, Creativity	Contact with friends		Change from work, New experience		Benefits society		
Goodman		Accomplishment & Self-expression			Change, pleasure, & relaxation				
Neulinger[a]		Self-definition							
Brok	Industry, Integrity	Identity, Initiative	Trust, Intimacy				Generativity		Autonomy
Kelly	Role determined	Intrinsic	Relational		Compensatory-Recuperative				
Csikszentmihalyi[a]	Homeostasis	Develops personal potential	Social solidarity		Enjoyment				
Beard & Ragheb	Relaxation, Physiological	Psychological	Social					Educational, Aesthetic	
Brown & Haas	Risk taking, Reflection on personal values	Achievement	Sharing/Recollection, Meeting/Observing people		Escape pressure			Relationships with nature	Autonomy
Pierce-A	Time filling, Relaxation	Achievement	Intimacy	Power				Intellection	

(continued)

(Continued...)

Author	Unrelated Dimensions	Self-Expression	Companionship	Power	Compensation	Security	Service	Intellectual Aestheticism	Solitude
Pierce-B	Destructiveness, Humor, Instinctiveness, Importance	Fulfillment	Affection	Flamboyance				Cerebration, Rationality	Solitude
Pierce-C	Risk	Sociability	Autonomy vs. Sociability		Stimulation			Sensuality, Mental Challenge, Physical Challenge	Autonomy vs. Sociability
Rossman	Risk, Physical Fitness	Achievement	Social enjoyment		Environment				Autonomy, Family escape
Gray[a]	Relaxation. Insight, Challenge, Risk	Self-Testing Improved self-discovery, Culmination, Personal development	Communion Positive feedback, Sharing		Escape, Novelty, Renewal	Order & regularity		Aesthetics	Introspection
Allen	Canonical Variate I			Canonical Variate III				Canonical Variate II	Canonical Variate IV
Iso-Ahola & Allen	Diversion, Interpersonal competence	Personal competence	Interpersonal development, Meet opposite sex	Interpersonal Diversion & control	Escape daily routine				
Iso-Ahola		Intrinsic Rewards			Escape				
Beard & Ragheb		Intellectual	Social					Competency/Mastery	Stimulus Avoidance

[a]These dimensions do not reflect psychological benefits, but other aspects of leisure. The dimensions identified by Neulinger are social influences on leisure, amount of leisure, amount of work, or vacation desired and affinity for leisure. Csikszentmihalyi suggested dimensions such as relief or pressure on the environment and development of cultural values. Gray suggested dimensions such as time distortion and anticipation. From Tinsley (1984). Reprinted by permission.

One immediate psychological benefit identified by Tinsley and Kass (1979), the benefit accruing from one's need to be of service, has yet to be reported with any consistency by other investigators. Havighurst (1961) did identify a service benefit and Brok (1975) postulated the existence of such a benefit, but corroboration has not yet been forthcoming. This is somewhat surprising, given the many leisure activities in which satisfaction of the need to be of service seems assured. Most likely, the service benefit has been confounded with the companionship benefit in many previous investigations. Review of the specific items used by previous investigators reveals service items loading on the companionship dimensions reported by Kelly (1976) and Beard and Ragheb (1980). Moreover, the occupation of nurse scored at the social end of Pierce's (1980c) autonomy-sociability factor, suggesting an element of service in this dimension. It is our belief that service is an important psychological benefit of leisure, distinct from the benefit of companionship.

To our knowledge, Tinsley and Kass (1979) and Gray (1981) are the only writers who have suggested security as a psychological benefit of leisure. Other writers have suggested psychological benefits, such as risk (Brown & Haas, 1980; Gray, 1981; Pierce, 1980c; Rossman, 1981) which may be the reverse of the security factor. It is possible that a sample which included activities in which security and risk were important psychological benefits would reveal a bipolar security–risk factor.

Psychological benefits not included in the eight benefits identified by Tinsley and Kass have been suggested by some writers. Some of these reflect benefits which might be expected to be true of leisure activities in general. Certainly, benefits, such as passing the time (Havighurst, 1961; Pierce, 1980a; Iso–Ahola & Allen, 1982), and pleasure (Havighurst, 1961) are likely to be generally true of leisure. As such, there is no advantage to considering these benefits when our purpose is to consider differences among leisure activities. Thorough review of the literature suggests, therefore, that the eight factors identified by Tinsley and Kass (1979) offer an adequate representation of the psychological benefits available from leisure activities.

Comparison of Leisure and Work

Proposition 15 of our theory states: Experiencing leisure results in the satisfaction of some psychological needs of the individual. The eight psychological benefits that we have reviewed were extracted from respondents' descriptions of the satisfactions they gained from leisure activities. These and the research evidence summarized by Tinsley and Tinsley (1986) on the relationships between leisure participation and need satisfaction provide substantial support for Proposition 15. Before studying in greater detail the immediate psychological benefits of specific leisure activities, it is instructive to examine how these benefits correspond to previously identified need-satisfying properties of occupational environments. We have stated previously our belief that individuals may experience leisure in all aspects of life, including while engaged in work and maintenance activities. If this is accurate, some correspondence between the need gratification gained from leisure and work is to be expected.

Axis II of the Minnesota Occupational Classification System II (MOCS-II) classifies occupations in term of the needs satisfied by that occupation (Dawis, Lofquist, Henly, & Rounds, 1979). Ratings of occupations on 21 reinforcer dimensions were analyzed and 6 need-satisfying dimensions were identified: achievement, status, safety, altruism, autonomy, and comfort. Holland (1985) has developed a system which classifies occupations as realistic, investigative, artistic, social, enterprising, and conventional. A salient feature of these environments is the types of rewards received by persons working in each. Comparison of these 12 dimensions upon which occupations have been classified with the eight immediate psychological benefits of leisure described above reveals areas of substantial agreement (Table 5.6).

Good correspondence is apparent between leisure and work on the power, security, and self-expression factors. The elements of control, authority over others, and status, which are the essence of the power benefit of leisure, are clearly reflected in the status and enterprising dimensions identified in work. The psychological benefit of security seems to be clearly mirrored in the safety and conventional dimensions identified in analyses of occupational environments. The self-expression factor is more complex than the others, so it included elements which correspond to the artistic (expressing self through creative use of

TABLE 5.6

Correspondence of the MOCS-II Axis II Dimensions and Holland's Environmental Models to the Need Satisfier Dimensions Identified by Tinsley and Kass (1979)

Tinsley & Kass	MOCS-II	Holland
Power	Status	Enterprising
Security	Safety	Conventional
Self-expression	Achievement[1] Autonomy[1]	Artistic Enterprising
Companionship	Altruism[1]	Social
Service	Altruism	Social[1] Conventional
Intellectual aestheticism		Realistic Investigative
Solitude	Autonomy	Realistic Investigative Artistic
Compensation	--	
Unrelated dimensions	Comfort	--

[1]Although classified elsewhere, elements of this dimension seem to correspond to this need satisfier dimension of leisure.

one's talents, undertake novel activities), enterprising (enjoyment of recognition and power), and achievement (utilizing one's abilities to achieve personal objectives) reinforcers identified in work. In addition, elements of the autonomy reinforcer (creativity) corresponded to the self-expression dimension.

The leisure benefits of companionship, service, intellectual aestheticism, and solitude were also identified as benefits of work in at least one of the two occupational classification schemes. The leisure benefits of companionship and service distinguish between the needs persons satisfy by being with others and the needs they satisfy by doing things for others. The classification systems of Dawis et al. and Holland each contain a dimension focusing primarily on one of those aspects, although some elements of the other are also apparent. In addition, some elements of Holland's conventional theme seem to be included in the service benefit found in leisure.

The bipolar intellectual aestheticism factor seems to reflect the inquisitive, intellectual characteristics of Holland's investigative occupations at one pole and the preference for physical activity and the asocial emphasis found in realistic occupations at the other pole. None of the dimensions used in the MOCS-II system of classifying occupations seem to correspond to the intellectual aestheticism dimension found in leisure.

The solitude and autonomy factors both reflect the characteristic of individuality although the autonomy factor also encompasses elements of self-expression, as has been noted. Moreover, the orientation away from persons toward things or ideas, which underlies Holland's realistic, investigative, and artistic occupational environments is consistent with the solitude dimension.

The compensation factor did not correspond to any dimension identified by Dawis et al. (1979) or Holland (1985). This was expected since this factor indicates the extent to which leisure activities satisfy needs not satisfied by the job or daily routine, an issue which was not examined by either investigator. The comfort dimension of Dawis et al. (1979), likewise, did not correspond to any single psychological benefit factor identified in leisure activities. In our judgment, this dimension combined elements of the self-expression (activity, variety), solitude (independence) and security (remuneration, working conditions, security) benefits of leisure.

Need-Satisfying Properties of 34 Leisure Activities

The eight factors identified by Tinsley and Kass (1979) appear to offer an adequate representation of the psychological benefits available from leisure activities. Work is now under way to measure the need satisfying properties of a large sample of leisure activities. The following preliminary report is based on an analysis of 34 leisure activities. Table 5.7 indicates the T scores of each activity on the eight factors. Reviewing each column allows identification of the leisure activities providing high and low levels of satisfaction for each need. Com-

TABLE 5.7

T Scores of Leisure Activities on Psychological Benefit Factors

Activity	Self-Expression			Psychological Benefit				
		Companionship	Power	Compensation	Security	Service	Intellectual Aestheticism	Solitude
Attending popular musical performances	44	61	65	55	44	43	55	35
Baking & cooking	54	49	54	46	48	64	58	43
Bicycling	60	53	58	61	49	39	36	52
Bowling	49	48	45	45	50	49	36	44
Camping	58	56	43	63	49	53	49	50
Canoeing	58	55	39	64	61	52	39	53
Ceramics	54	43	41	48	54	47	55	60
Collecting autographs	52	45	38	60	72	45	56	60
Collecting stamps	48	35	36	49	61	43	53	64
Drinking & socializing	38	69	73	40	36	46	57	29
Going to movies	30	45	54	55	35	42	64	52
Hiking	60	59	36	65	53	61	47	56
Jogging	54	46	42	51	61	43	37	60
Lake fishing	51	54	60	65	45	51	53	59
Painting with oils, acrylics, or water colors	58	47	40	55	56	53	56	55
Photography	56	49	51	52	51	52	59	55
Picnicking	51	65	54	62	38	61	51	39
Playing cards	39	44	55	19	32	33	48	41
Playing chess	52	39	53	41	55	42	65	47
Playing golf	53	51	58	48	58	49	50	52
Playing guitar	54	58	60	46	57	58	57	50
Playing tennis	57	51	56	52	56	44	36	44
Playing volleyball	57	61	52	52	48	52	34	30
Raising house plants	51	50	48	46	56	66	62	60
Reading fiction	34	40	46	58	46	46	68	62
Roller skating	54	56	58	49	40	46	34	46
Shooting pool	46	48	65	36	41	44	48	48
Swimming	58	55	54	43	58	54	38	54
Vegetable gardening	65	50	39	53	61	76	47	54
Visiting friends/relations	47	70	63	46	59	72	59	29
Watching basketball	49	47	60	42	46	44	33	36
Watching television	19	30	45	52	31	36	51	58
Woodworking	59	47	45	51	59	58	48	57
Working crossword puzzles	32	23	28	31	33	35	61	63

parison of selected leisure activities, on the other hand, provides a clearer understanding of the psychological benefits of those activities. In discussing these results we characterized T scores as follows: Very high, $T>65$; high, $T = 61-65$; above average, $T = 56-60$; average, $T = 55-45$; below average, $40-44$; low, $T = 35-39$; very low, $T<35$.

Self-expression.   Among the leisure activities studied, only gardening provides a high level of self-expression. Ten activities provide above-average levels of self-expression with bicycling, hiking, and woodworking having higher scores than the others. The person who has a strong need for self-expression, therefore, would be most likely to find that need satisfied by participating in one of these activities.

Watching television provides much lower levels of reinforcement of the need for self-expression than working crossword puzzles, going to movies and reading fiction, activities which also provide very low amounts of self-expression relative to the other activities for which data is available. Playing cards and, surprisingly, drinking and socializing were described as providing relatively low levels of this benefit. Persons having little need for self-expression may find these activities to be enjoyable. The individual with an above average need for self-expression, on the other hand, may experience the feeling that something is missing when participating in these activities. It seems likely that persons with a strong need for self-expression will generally not enjoy spending much time watching television, going to movies, reading fiction, and working puzzles.

Companionship.   Individuals with a strong need for companionship may be expected to enjoy visiting friends and relatives and drinking and socializing, activities which provide very high levels of this psychological benefit. A relatively high level of companionship is provided by picnicking, playing volleyball, and attending popular musical performances. In common parlance, playing volleyball is regarded as a sport and attending popular musical performances as a cultural or a popular entertainment activity. Indeed, these activities are classified in that manner by Overs, Taylor, Cassell, and Chernov (1977). The data, however, reveal companionship to be a salient psychological benefit of these activities.

Relative to the other activities under investigation, very low levels of companionship are provided by working crossword puzzles and watching television. Low levels of companionship are provided by playing chess and collecting stamps. Note that woodworking, painting, and jogging are activities which are often done alone, but that participants report an average level of companionship. On the other hand, people may watch television with others and chess requires two players, but participants do not experience companionship. When viewed from this perspective, it is clear that these data are descriptive of the individual's psychological experience when participating in the activity rather than the externally observable "reality" of the situation. In the future, it may be of interest to obtain additional information about aspects of the situation in which the person experiences leisure in order to clarify the elements of the situation which influence their psychological experiences.

Power.   Drinking and socializing provides a very high level of reinforcement of the need for power relative to the other activities studied. Given the aggressive, exploitive nature often attributed to excessive drinking and socializing, this finding is perhaps not surprising. The finding that the psychological benefit of power is high in shooting pool, attending popular musical performances, and visiting friends and relatives, however, is less expected. It appears that activities such as shooting pool and attending popular musical performances provide a more complex array of psychological benefits than has been previously realized.

Working crossword puzzles provides very low levels of the power benefit and canoeing, vegetable gardening, hiking, collecting autographs, and collecting stamps provide relatively low levels of power. The fact that some of these activities are often done alone may partly explain the low levels of power. Canoeing and hiking, however, are frequently done with others and hiking provides above average levels of companionship. Thus, the low levels of the power benefit probably reflects an element of equality or cooperation inherent in the activity while activities such as shooting pool may involve more competition between participants.

Compensation.   High levels of compensation are available in bicycling, canoeing, camping, picnicking, lake fishing, and hiking. Each of these activities might be expected to provide something different than that which the participant typically experiences on the job. Consequently, these results have substantial face validity.

Relative to the other activities under investigation, playing cards and working crossword puzzles provide very low levels of compensation and shooting pool provides a low level of compensation. These findings suggest that respondents perceived these activities as incorporating elements more highly related to their jobs than activities such as bicycling and camping. The fact that the leisure activities which are relatively low in compensation enjoy a greater general popularity than many of the activities which are relatively high in compensation is consistent with Staines's (1980) conclusion that the psychological benefit of compensation is less frequently sought in leisure than are other benefits.

Security.   Collecting autographs offers very high levels of security relative to the other activities under study, and jogging, canoeing, vegetable gardening, and collecting stamps provide relatively high levels of security. The security benefit reflects a long-term commitment, characterized by routine, ritual, or at least the absence of bothersome changes and uncertainty, for which individuals feel themselves to be rewarded and to achieve a position of some station. Collecting autographs and stamps obviously requires a long-term commitment and confer rewards and status on the faithful participant. Advocates of jogging suggest that it should be a lifelong activity; the rewards of jogging are reportedly a happier, healthier life, and being a jogger confers some status, at least among a group of health or physical fitness enthusiasts. The elements of commitment across time and rewards for one's efforts are also obvious in vegetable gardening. Sharing the fruits of one's efforts with appreciative neighbors, a thoughtful gesture which some successful gardeners seem to enjoy making, may also provide an element of status. Consequently, these findings, perhaps not predictable in advance, seem strikingly accurate and insightful in retrospect.

Playing cards, working crossword puzzles, watching television, picnicking, going to movies, and drinking and socializing are all low to very low in security, relative to the other activities studied. These activities may be engaged in for brief periods of time and even the decision to engage in them can be "spur of the moment." The person will experience little status from participating in these activities, but other benefits are available which accounts for the popularity of these activities.

Service.   Several surprises occur when looking at the activities which provide very high (raising house plants, vegetable gardening, visiting friends and relatives) and high (picnicking, hiking, baking and cooking) levels of service. When we think of service as doing things for others, the finding that persons experience a satisfaction of their need to be of service when vegetable gardening and baking and cooking is predictable. Although we typically think of visiting friends and relatives as satisfying the need to experience conpanionship, it is apparent that we also experience the psychological benefit of service. Somewhat unexpected was the finding that raising house plants, picnicking, and hiking also bestow the benefit of service. This seems to imply that these activities typically are not done exclusively for oneself, but with the additional intention of meeting the needs of others.

Relatively low levels of service are experienced by persons while bicycling, watching television, or working crossword puzzles and very low levels of service are experienced while playing cards. These findings are consistent with what is already known about these activities.

Intellectual Aestheticism.   This is a bipolar factor named for the positive pole. High scores on this factor represent satisfaction of the person's need for intellectual and aesthetic stimulation and to avoid or abstain from vigorous physical exercise. Reading provides very high levels of this benefit. Playing chess, working crossword puzzles, and going to movies provide high levels, relative to the other activities under study. Reading may be regarded as the epitome of the intellectually stimulating leisure activity while raising house plants is a classic example of the aesthetically stimulating activity. To some extent, however, these activities possess both the intellectual and aesthetic elements. That this benefit is weighted in favor of intellectual stimulation is illustrated by the finding that chess and working crossword puzzles provide high levels of this benefit while painting with oils, acrylics, or watercolors just barely provides an above average level.

The negative pole of this factor reflects satisfaction of the need to engage in vigorous physical activity. Activities having low scores on this dimension might be described as having low levels of intellectual aestheticism, but such scores also indicate the presence of high levels of vigorous physical exercise. Although we will interpret these scores as reflecting the presence of the psychological benefit of exercise, the absence of intellectual and aesthetic stimulation must also be remembered to comprehend the results fully.

Roller skating, playing volleyball, and watching basketball provide very high levels of the exercise benefit. Relative to the other activities under investigation, high levels of the exercise benefit are present in canoeing, bicycling, jogging, swimming, bowling, and tennis. Why watching basketball is experienced by participants in this manner is uncertain. Undoubtedly, the low levels of intellectual and aesthetic stimulation serve as partial explanation, but there must be other factors which contribute. This puzzle can only be resolved by future research.

The relatively lower levels of exercise in jogging, bicycling and canoeing, when compared with roller skating and volleyball, no doubt reflects the presence of higher levels of aesthetic stimulation in these activities. Running magazines, for example, tout the experience of communing with nature while jogging. Canoeing and bicycling frequently takes place in scenic locals. The relative placement of bowling, on the other hand, probably reflects the fact that bowling is a less vigorous physical activity than roller skating and playing volleyball.

Solitude.   Collecting stamps, reading fiction, and working crossword puzzles provided relatively high levels of solitude. Very low levels of the solitude benefit are provided by playing volleyball, drinking and socializing, and visiting friends and relatives, while low levels are available in watching basketball, picnicking, and attending popular musical performances. Several activities, however, reveal that this is not just the reverse of the companionship dimension. Watching basketball is low on solitude and jogging, raising house plants, collecting autographs, and ceramics are above average on solitude, but all are average on companionship. Chess is low on companionship and roller skating and playing guitar are above average on companionship, but all are average on solitude. It appears from Table 5.7 that high or very high levels on one benefit cannot be achieved without low levels on the other benefit, but that between the extremes the solitude and companionship benefits operate somewhat independently.

Illustrative Activities.   Review of each row of Table 5.7 provides information on the pattern of psychological benefits available from individual activities.

We have selected two comparisons and a single activity to illustrate the types of insights which can be gained.

Raising house plants and vegetable gardening may be thought of as highly similar activities. Both activities involve caring for plants, and might be supposed to require the same skills and interests on the part of participants. Review of Table 5.7, however, reveals a markedly different pattern of benefits. Both provide average levels of companionship and compensation, and both provide very high levels of service. Raising house plants, however, provides higher levels of power and solitude than vegetable gardening and a substantially higher level of intellectual aestheticism. Gardening, on the other hand, provides a higher level of security and a substantially higher level of self-expression. Although the two activities may appear similar, they are significantly different when the psychological benefits of participation in each is considered.

Jogging, bicycling, and swimming would all be classified as sports by sociologists. Cooper (1968) has further demonstrated that these activities have high aerobic point values. Consequently, these three activities have been demonstrated to have similar physical benefits; what about their immediate psychological benefits? The differences are less pronounced than in the previous example. All three activities provide high levels of exercise (i.e., low levels of intellectual aestheticism) and average levels of companionship. Moreover, they differ only modestly on self-expression and solitude. But they range from below average (jogging) to above average (bicycling) on power, from low (bicycling) to average (swimming) on service, from below average (swimming) to high (bicycling) on compensation and from average (bicycling) to high (jogging) on security.

Finally, the data in Table 5.7 cast some light on the age-old question, "Why do you watch television?" When asked in a casual manner, most respondents will reply that it is relaxing, that it kills time and/or that they have nothing better to do. Table 5.7, however, reveals that watching television provides an above average level of satisfaction of the need for solitude. Watching television is also an excellent leisure activity for the person who wants to avoid self-expression and the necessity of a long-term commitment. Findings such as these underscore a basic assumption underlying this research, that every leisure activity satisfies some need of the participants. We believe such information can be helpful to individuals engaging in career/life-style planning, and counseling.

MEASUREMENT OF LEISURE CONSTRUCTS

Largely unknown to counseling psychologists are the tests and scales that have been developed to measure constructs such as leisure interests, satisfaction, attitudes, and identity. Most of these instruments have been developed by an author or agency pursuant to some specific research or service objective without apparent consideration of more general research issues or service considerations of concern to the discipline. Only one of these tests is published by a commercial publishing company, the rest being available only from their authors. Although many of these instruments have been used in applied settings, without exception these instruments are in an early stage of development and do not meet APA standards (Novick, 1985) for such applications.

Table 5.8 identifies those instruments we were able to identify. Although an effort was made to be reasonably thorough, the result is not exhaustive. The frequency with which instruments have been developed and used in specific contexts with little discussion in the literature makes it likely that some instruments were overlooked. Because all of these instruments fall short of APA standards for use in applied settings, a detailed description and evaluation of each is contraindicated. Instead, specific instruments of each type are described for illustrative purposes. More information about these tests is available from their authors. Some of these tests have been described in reviews by Howe (1984), Loesch and Wheeler (1982), and Walshe (1977).

Leisure Interests

Eleven leisure interest inventories were identified, most of which have apparently had limited usage. A brief summary of two of these tests will provide a good understanding of the level of psychometric sophistication currently achieved by leisure interest inventories. The only instrument published by a major publishing company is the Leisure Activity Blank (McKechnie, 1975). The LAB contains 120 items which consist of leisure activities that have high participation rates in the United States. Respondents are required to rate each item twice, once on a 4-point scale indicating their frequency of participation and a second time on a three-step scale indicating their intended future involvement. Separate scales for scoring the past and future responses were developed by factor analyzing data from 288 residents of Marin County, California, an affluent suburb of San Francisco. Six factors were extracted from the past participation data, mechanics, crafts, intellectual, slow living, sports, and glamour sports. The parallel of the mechanics, crafts, and intellectual factors to Holland's (1985) realistic, artistic, and intellectual personality types is readily apparent. Pursual of the descriptions of the high and low scorers on the slow living and sports factors reveals their similarity to Holland's conventional and enterprising personality types, respectively. The factor analysis of the future data yielded eight scales: the mechanics, crafts, intellectual and slow living factors, and factors labeled adventure, easy living, ego recognition, and clean living. Two validity scales are also included to determine whether the respondent answered accurately and purposefully.

The manual (McKechnie, 1975) advises the user repeatedly that use of the LAB is presently restricted to research; this restriction should be scrupulously

TABLE 5.8

Instrumentation Developed to Measure Leisure Constructs

Construct	Instrument	Developer/Reference
Leisure Interests	Avocational Activities Interest Index	D'Agostini (1972)
	Avocational Activities Inventory	Overs, Taylor, Adkins (1977)
	Constructive Leisure Activities Survey	Edwards (1970)
	Leisure Activities Balnk	McKechnie (1975)
	Leisure Interest Inventory	Hubert (1969)
	Mirenda Leisure Interest Finder	Mirenda & Wilson (1975)
	Preference Survey	Tinsley (1986)
	Recreation Activity Inventory	McEwen & Malley (1977)
	Recreation Interest Finder	McEwen & Malley (1977)
	Self-Leisure Interest Profile	McDowell (1973)
	State Technical Institute Leisure Activities Project	Navar (1979)
Leisure Attitudes	Beliefs About Work	Buchholz (1978)
	Leisure Attitude Scale	Ragheb (1980)
	Leisure Ethic	Bryan & Alsikafi (1975)
	Leisure Ethic Scale	Slivken (1978)
	Leisure Orientation Scale	Burdge (1961)
	A Study of Leisure	Neulinger (1974)
	Survey of Leisure Values	Loesch & Wheeler (1982)
Leisure Satisfaction	Leisure Satisfaction Inventory	Rimmer (1979)
	Leisure Satisfaction Scale	Beard & Ragheb (1980)
	Milwaukee Avocational Satisfaction Questionnaire	Overs, Taylor, Adkins (1974)
Leisure Behavior	Comprehensive Evaluation in Recreation Therapy Scale	Parker, Ellison, Kirby, & Short (1975)
	Joswiak's Leisure Counseling Assessment Instruments	Joswiak (1979)
	Mundy Recreation Inventory of the Mentally Retarded	Mundy (1981)
	Recreation Behavioral Inventory	Berryman & Lefebvre (1979)
	What Am I Doing?	Neulinger (1981)
	Your Lifeline	Neulinger (1986)
Leisure Personality	Leisure Diagnostic Battery	Ellis & Witt (1984)
	Leisure Well-Being Inventory	McDowell (1979)
	Walshe Temperament Survey	Walshe (1977)
Leisure Activity Attributes	Leisure Activities Questionnaire	Tinsley & Kass (1980a)
	Paragraphs About Leisure	Tinsley & Kass (1980a)
	Recreation Experience Preference Scales	Driver (1976)

observed. The manual contains no normative data beyond that available on the developmental sample and no information to document the validity of the instrument. The personality assessments suggested in the LAB manual are speculative, based on a sample of only 50 adults. Test-retest reliabilities range from .71 to .92 for the past scales and from .63 to .93 for the future scales. Internal consistency reliabilities range from .76 to .94.

The inventory which has had the greatest impact on research is the Avocational Activities Inventory (Overs, Taylor, & Adkins, 1977). Patterned after the Dictionary of Occupational Titles, the AAI lists more than 800 leisure activities. Intended primarily as a classification scheme for leisure activities, the AAI served as the basis for the development of instruments such as the Inventory of Avocational Activity Participation, Avocational Title Card Sort, Avocational Picture Card Sort, and Avocational Plaque Sort. Although these instruments were used extensively in the research conducted by the Curative Workshop of Milwaukee (Overs, Taylor, & Adkins, 1974; Overs et al., 1977), validity data have not been published and little normative data are available. Although the research cited, still represents the most extensive and systematic investigation of avocational counseling reported in the literature, the use of these instruments in counseling cannot be recommended without further development.

Leisure Attitudes

Seven instruments measuring leisure attitudes were identified in our review. Neulinger's (1974) Study of Leisure (SOL), designed for use in survey research, is one of the earliest leisure attitude instruments. The initial questionnaire of 150 items was reduced to 32 during a series of investigations (see Neulinger, 1974, for details about the development of the SOL).

Factor analysis revealed five leisure attitude dimensions defined by 28 items. Affinity for leisure (7 items) measures the extent to which persons like liesure. Neulinger speculates that scores on this factor may be inversely related to the extent to which persons are enmeshed in the protestant ethic, indicating the extent to which they believe that leisure must be earned to be enjoyed. Also reflected by this factor is the person's capacity for leisure (i.e., how much leisure individuals believe they can handle). Society's role in leisure planning (5 items) measures the individual's general attitude toward societal control and support of leisure. Self-definition through leisure and work (6 items) concerns the relative importance of work and leisure in a person's life, and particularly the degree to which individuals define themselves in terms of their work or their leisure. The amount of leisure perceived scale (6 items) measures the extent to which persons believe they have enough leisure and their satisfaction with their leisure status. Scores on the amount of work or vacation desired scale (4 items) reflect the individual's attitudes regarding how much of their life should be spent at work or on vacation.

Neulinger (1974, 1981) does not report reliability or validity data for the SOL. The survey of leisure has been used some by investigators so it seems likely that some reliability or validity data might exist. Nevertheless, we found no published evidence to support Loesch and Wheeler's (1982) conclusion that the SOL "does appear to be sufficiently reliable for at least research purposes and perhaps for individual evaluations [p. 115]."

The 10-item Leisure Ethic Scale (LES) was developed as a master's degree thesis project by Slivken (1978) and Crandall (her adviser). The LES has a much narrower focus than the SOL, concentrating on affinity for leisure. Unlike previous such scales, the LES items contain no reference to work. This allows respondents to indicate their attitudes toward leisure without forcing them to define leisure as antithetical to work.

Extensive data regarding the development, reliability, and validity of the LES are available in Slivken's thesis. Test-retest reliability coefficients have ranged from .59 to .87 with a median of .84 for intervals of 1 to 5 weeks. Significant and substantial correlations are reported between the LES and peer ratings, background variables, and other leisure attitude scales (e.g., $r = .45$ and $.58$ with the affinity factor of the SOL). The LES has also shown evidence of discriminant validity, discriminating between business and leisure majors, and correlating significantly with wilderness attitudes, leisure satisfaction and number of hours desired in the workweek. On balance, the LES shows good reliability and some evidence of face, content, and construct validity.

Leisure Satisfaction

Only three leisure satisfaction instruments were identified. The Milwaukee Avocational Satisfaction Questionnaire (Overs et al., 1974), the pioneer in the field, was adopted from the Minnesota Satisfaction Questionnaire to yield a global leisure satisfaction measure. The 24-item MASQ uses a 5-point rating scale format with response alternatives ranging from not satisfied to extremely satisfied. Minimal information is available about the reliability and validity of the MASQ. Trafton and Tinsley (1980) reported an internal consistency (coefficient alpha) reliability of .89 for the MASQ and a convergent validity correlation of .32 with a global leisure satisfaction item. Although their multitrait-multimethod analysis revealed significant convergent and discriminant validity for the MASQ, the evidence for the validity of the MASQ was weaker than the evidence for the job satisfaction, life satisfaction, and dyadic satisfaction instruments included in the same analysis.

Beard and Ragheb's (1980) Leisure Satisfaction Scale (LSS) was developed from a 57-item, forced-choice instrument, the Leisure Satisfaction Index (LSI), designed to measure the extent to which the respondent's personal needs are met through leisure activities. Six subscales of 4 items each were extracted from the LSI through factor analysis to compose the LSS. The psychological satisfaction scale measures the extent to which respondents perceive a sense of freedom, enjoyment, and intellectual challenge. The educational satisfaction scale indicates the extent to which respondents report satisfaction with the intellectual stimulation and opportunity to learn about themselves and their surroundings. Persons who score high on the social satisfaction scale report the presence of rewarding relationships with other people. Individuals having high scores on the relaxation scale generally report their leisure activities provide relief from the stresses and strains of life. High scores on the physiological satisfaction subscale indicate respondents perceive their leisure activities as a means to develop physical fitness, control their weight, and promote well-being. Finally, persons scoring high on the aesthetic satisfaction scale generally view their leisure activities as occurring in areas which are pleasing, beautiful, and well designed. Alpha reliabilities for the LSI, based on a sample of 347 respondents, ranged from .85 to .92.

Ragheb and Beard (1980) reported that scores on the six LSS scales correlate substantially, despite the use of the varimax (orthogonal) rotation procedure. The pair-wise correlations among scales range from .38 to .66 with a median of .52. Three of the subscales correlate .60 or higher and all but three of the 15 subscale correlations are .50 or higher.

Thus far, little information about the validity of the LSS has appeared in the literature. Unlike McKechnie (1975), who repeatedly cautions against the use of the LAB for any purpose other than research, Beard and Raghed (1980) discuss ways in which the LSS could be used in counseling. Furthermore, Loesch and Wheeler (1982) appear to approve of its use in counseling. They state,

> The LSS should prove to be a valuable assessment instrument, both for researchers and leisure counselors. It's psychometric qualities allow it to be used validly and with confidence in a variety of situations . . . it assesses dimensions of leisure satisfaction which should be amenable to leisure counseling intervention [Loesch & Wheeler, 1982, p. 125].

We disagree. No information about the validity of the LSS is provided in Beard and Ragheb (1980) and only primitive comparisons of demographic groups on the LSS are summarized. Although the LSS may ultimately be shown to possess sufficient validity to justify its use in counseling, it is premature to use it for purposes other than research at the present time.

Leisure Behavior

Six subscales were located which measure some aspect of leisure behavior. Neulinger's What Am I Doing? (WAID) is "designed to enable you to measure the quality of your life, your unique sense of well-being or lack thereof [Neulinger, 1986, p. 1]." Using a log book approach, the WAID instructs users to begin with the hour they wake up and record their primary activity (i.e., the most important thing they did) for each hour of the day. For each activity, respondents are also instructed to indicate where the activity occurred and with how many persons the activity was done. Also asked is who chose to do the activity (totally my choice—not my choice at all), why the activity was chosen (for its own sake—for payoff only) and how the respondent felt while engaged in the activity (extremely good–extremely bad). Responses to these questions are recorded for each activity using a rating scale which varies from zero to 100. Frequency distributions of the "where" and "with how many" responses are tallied at the end of the day, as are means for the choice, reason, and feeling scales.

The WAID is intended as an aid in self-exploration. Neulinger describes what he labels an impressionistic approach to using the instrument which focuses on the experience of completing the WAID. A statistical approach is also explained in which users complete six WAID logs using a Monday, Wednesday, Friday, Sunday, Tuesday, Thursday pattern. This procedure provides the data to establish a baseline for analysis of present behavior and for comparison to future data. Several tips are provided for analyzing these baseline data to identify the individual's comfort zone.

Neulinger (1986) cautions users against uncritical acceptance of their own data and an uncritical sharing of their personal data with others. This caution must be underscored since reliability and validity data have not been published for the WAID. Neulinger seems ambivalent about the necessity of such data, however, stating "While you remain the final judge of whether your data are valid, you also must accept the possibility that they are not [Neulinger, 1986, p. 27]." Further evaluation of the WAID is needed before its use for purposes other than research can be advocated.

Leisure Personality

The three scales classified as measures of leisure personality share little in common. The Walshe Temperament Survey (Walshe, 1977) assesses an individual's personality temperament into one of four dominant categories: the melancholic, phlegmatic, sanguine, or choleric. McDowell's (1979) Leisure Well-Being Inventory (LWBI) measures four aspects of psychological health; coping, awareness/understanding, knowledge, and assertion. From this information, inferences are made about how well prepared and able the respondent is to maintain leisure well-being. Neither Walshe nor McDowell report any normative, reliability, or validity data for their instruments.

The Leisure Diagnostic Battery (Ellis & Witt, 1984) shows more promise as a usable instrument at this point in its development. The LDB was developed to measure perceived freedom in leisure. The instrument yields scores on five subscales and a total perceived freedom score, obtainable by summing the subscale scores. The perceived leisure control scale (20 items) measures respondents' perceptions of the degree of personal competence they perceive themselves as having in recreation and leisure endeavors. Items are included on this scale to assess perceived cognitive, social, physical, and general competence. The internal consistency reliability of this scale was reported to be .89, using coefficient alpha, for a sample of 200 junior high school students. The test-retest reliability for a sample of 84 junior high school students using a 2-week intertest interval was .82. The perceived leisure control scale (18 items) measures the extent to which individuals perceive themselves as controlling events and outcomes (i.e., degree of internality) in their leisure experience. The alpha and test retest reliabilities for this scale were .88 and .82, respectively.

Two scales measure aspects of perceived intrinsic motivation. The leisure needs scale (20 items) measures the extent to which individuals are able to satisfy 10 different personal and intrinsic needs through their leisure behavior. The depth of involvement in leisure scale (18 items) assesses the extent to which individuals achieve a "flow" experience (see Csikszentmihalyi, 1975) during their leisure activities. Five aspects of the "flow" concept are reflected in the item content of this scale. The coefficient alpha reliabilities of these two scales are .90 and .88, respectively, and their test-retest reliabilities are .75 and .77.

Finally, the existence of a behavioral component of perceived freedom was hypothesized, leading to the development of the playfulness scale (20 items). Four aspects of individuals' degree of playfulness are assessed, cognitive, physical, and social spontaneity, and manifest joy. The alpha and test-retest reliabilities of the playfulness scale were .90 and .77, respectively.

Ellis and Witt (1984) report preliminary evidence of the convergent and discriminant validity of the LDB. As intended, the LDB measures a single, perceived freedom factor, which accounts for 60.9% of the variance in scores on the five subscales. Factor scores on this perceived freedom factor evidenced a theoretically meaningful pattern of correlations with variables such as perceived barriers to leisure involvement (−.64), knowledge of leisure involvement (−.01), age (.08), and gender (−.20).

Leisure Activity Attributes

Three instruments are available which provide information about the needs satisfied by participation in leisure activities. The Recreation Experience Preference scales (Driver, 1976) provide an indirect measure of the need gratification derived from leisure activities, asking respondents to indicate how important each potential immediate psychological benefit was to them at the time they decided to engage in the activity. In contrast, the Leisure Activities Questionnaire (LAQ) and the Paragraphs About Leisure (Tinsley & Kass, 1980a) ask about the need gratification obtained by participants engaged in a designated leisure activity. Since the PAL requires 20–30 minutes to complete while the LAQ requires about an hour longer, the PAL has been used more frequently than the LAQ. The information presented earlier in this chapter on psychological benefit factors and the psychological benefits of participation in 34 leisure activities was obtained through administration of the PAL.

The PAL contains 44 paragraphs, each of which begins with the phrase, "Participants in this activity," and continues by describing the gratification of a single psychological need. Respondents are instructed to indicate the extent to which each paragraph accurately describes their experiences while participating in a designated leisure activity, using a rating scale with response alternatives ranging from not true (1) to definitely true (5). Split-group reliabilities have been reported for the 34 leisure activities described earlier. These were obtained by dividing the total sample of respondents who described a given leisure activity into two samples, using an odd/even split. Then the mean score assigned the activity on each of the 44 scales was calculated independently for the two split groups and the two sets of scale scores were correlated. The split-group reliabilities of the 34 leisure activities described in this chapter ranged from .86 to .98, with a median of .96. This provides convincing evidence of the stability of the results obtained by the PAL across independent samples.

Although the evidence for the validity of the PAL still must be regarded as preliminary, more validity information is available for the PAL than for most of the other instruments identified in Table 5.8. Tinsley and Kass (1980a) reported a multitrait-multimethod analysis of the PAL and LAQ based on a sample of 10 leisure activities. Convergent validity coefficients for the activities ranged from .68 to .88, with a median of .81. Both analysis of variance and factor analysis procedures revealed substantial evidence of discriminant validity for the PAL. Tinsley and Kass (1980b) reported a discriminant analysis in which the PAL was administered to one of two cross-validation groups. The developmental sample and the other cross-validation sample had completed the LAQ. The cross-validation hit rates for the PAL were higher than those for the LAQ, and the cross-validation hit rates of both instruments exceeded the expected chance rate by a ratio of 4.2 to 1. Tinsley and Bowman (1986) reported significant differences in the ratings of stamp collecting obtained from experienced stamp collectors and naïve respondents, providing further evidence of the discriminant validity of the PAL.

THOUGHTS ABOUT FUTURE PRIORITIES

As noted at the outset, the place which work occupies in our society is still heavily influenced by the protestant ethic, a moral-ethical philosophical system which values work for the sake of work and regards idleness as sinful. Formulated to serve sociopolitical purposes of the 16th century, this philosophical belief system influences counseling psychologists and the discipline of counseling psychology in limiting ways. A major portion of the time and effort of

counseling psychologists is devoted to studying and attempting to facilitate career development, career maturity, and career decision making, while leisure and
the role that leisure experiences play in the life of the individual are often
ignored.

Some recognition of the importance of leisure is apparent in earlier publications of a few counseling psychologists. Super's (1940) treatise on appraising
avocational interests and Williamson, Layton, and Snoke's (1954) investigation
of the leisure activities of college students represent two of the earliest examples.
Super's (1980) life-span, life-space approach to career development continued
this emphasis. He identified nine life roles of the individual, two being those of
the leisurite and the worker. Super suggested that individuals devote attention to
these roles across the life span. In all of these efforts, however, leisure was
examined from the limiting perspective afforded by the residual time definition
of leisure.

Lofquist and Dawis's (1969) discussion of the applicability of their Theory of
Work Adjustment to retirement and to leisure environments stands as one of the
earliest suggestions that leisure should be analyzed using the same perspective
applied to work. The theory we propose suggests another step in this process of
developing an integrated view of work and leisure. This holistic view disposes
with the artificial dichotomy between work and leisure and postulates an experience (i.e., leisure experience) which can occur during leisure or work. This view
suggests the possibility that many of the earlier effects ascribed to work may be
due to the individual's experiencing of leisure while engaged in work, rather than
to work per se. Evidence supporting this theory has been summarized elsewhere
(Tinsley & Tinsley, 1986).

These efforts represent a beginning. Additional work is needed to refine this
theory and to integrate it with the larger bodies of theory pertaining to human
development, in general, and to career development and maturity, in particular.
A systematic investigation of the issues raised in this theory will be helpful in
evaluating the current theory, in stimulating further theorizing, and in identifying
efficacious modifications in career-counseling practice. The following sections
identify areas in which theory development, research, and practical application
should receive early attention.

Theory

We view overall maturity as a function of career maturity and leisure maturity.
For this reason, we believe attention should be given to developing a more
complete and formal statement of the construct of leisure maturity. Some aspects
of leisure maturity are clear. An early task in the development of leisure maturity
is to move toward balance (see Super, 1980). Children are primarily focused on
leisure to the exclusion of work. Parents are aware of the need to educate their
children to the importance of work, and they attempt to accomplish this through

various means, such as assigning chores. Because overall maturity requires that leisure exists in balance with other activities, this may be viewed as a part of the process of developing leisure maturity.

Another aspect of leisure maturity is a growing awareness and effective utilization of leisure. This develops through several stages. Children are likely to emphasize leisure as the primary source of enjoyment in their lives. The young adult may place greater emphasis on work as valuable and regard leisure as only for children or the retired. The workaholic adult may be fearful and disdainful of leisure. In contrast, the leisure mature individual recognizes leisure as an important aspect of life which must be maintained in balance with other aspects of life.

We believe that leisure maturity has both a content and a process component. The process elements may be similar for all individuals although we believe that the rate of progress through the process will vary from person to person. The content component is more closely associated with the leisure identity of the individual. We expect this component to be highly unique to the individual and to vary substantially across most recognizable demographic groups.

We recognize the speculative nature of these ideas. Nevertheless, we believe the further development of the construct of leisure maturity will lead to a more complete understanding of the synergistic roles that leisure and work play in shaping the adjustment of the normal individual.

Research

Lewko and Crandall (1980) surveyed leisure researchers regarding future research directions they believed were important in the field. The research issues most frequently mentioned concerned the antecedents and consequences of leisure behavior, i.e., the factors that predispose a given individual to participate in a designated leisure activity, and the consequences of that participation. The model we have outlined provides a conceptual framework for this research, distinguishing as it does between the attributes, causes, and benefits of leisure experience. As we noted previously, some of the propositions and corollaries in this theory are presented at a conceptual level, and in some instances more than one operational definition of a construct or relationship is desirable. Nevertheless, this model provides an organizational scheme within which a systematic program of research can be conducted.

We believe Propositions 5 and 6 concerning the attributes of leisure experience deserve high priority for investigation. Proposition 6 and its corollaries describe the constellation of attributes which define leisure experience. Proposition 5 postulates a relationship between leisure experience and other psychological experiences. We recommend that research on the causes of leisure experience be directed to investigating the four postulated causal conditions specified in Propositions 8, 9, 11, and 12 and their corollaries. In addition, Proposition 10 provides one of the more clearly specified operational definitions in the theory and as such deserves a high priority for investigation.

The propositions specifying the benefits of leisure experience are stated at a more conceptual level than those concerning the causes and attributes of leisure experience. Nevertheless, the anticipated relationships among need gratification, psychological health, mental health, life satisfaction, and personal growth are clear at a general level. Investigations of the issues identified in these propositions and corollaries will advance knowledge of leisure experience.

Applications

"Don't put all of your eggs in one basket" is an admonition which all of us recognize from childhood. In a sense, counseling psychologists who focus on work to the exclusion of leisure are doing exactly that. Counseling psychologists are often called upon to assist clients with problems concerning personal identity and need gratification. In dealing with these issues, many focus too narrowly on their client's occupation. Those counseling psychologists who recognize that leisure experiences have the potential to gratify many of their clients' needs and influence their clients' sense of personal identity have a much better chance of intervening successfully in their clients' lives.

Most previous writers on the topic of leisure counseling have advocated leisure guidance models which focused rather narrowly on helping individuals to pick the right leisure activity (Tinsley & Tinsley, 1981). Although, we believe helping individuals to decide how to use their leisure may be one function of the counseling psychologist, other functions are equally or more important. Often, helping individuals to understand their leisure identify is very important. In many instances, this will lead to a focus on the leisure attitudes of the individual. Helping individuals to understand the foci of satisfaction and dissatisfaction in their lives often results in a more complete understanding of the role that leisure plays in their lives. This understanding may, in turn, lead to a focus on leisure activity choice, but it is equally or more likely to lead to the discovery that some form of change is desirable. Change can take the form of attitude change, as in modifying one's attitudes toward leisure. This form of intervention may be especially important with individuals who are overly committed to the protestant work ethic. Alternatively, some behavioral change may be desirable. Finally, leisure counseling may focus on confusion reduction. This is especially true for individuals needing to gain a clearer understanding of themselves and their identity, and of the influence of their work, leisure, and other roles on their identity.

We have discussed these ideas in more detail in an earlier work on leisure counseling (see Tinsley & Tinsley, 1982). We believe the theory we have outlined in this chapter and the model of leisure counseling published earlier provide a fruitful jumping-off place for practitioners. Careful consideration of the issues raised herein should dispel the notion that leisure counseling merely involves the transposition to leisure of the trait-and-factor approach to career counseling. Furthermore, we argue strongly against the notion that a separate specialty of leisure is needed. Explicit in our theory is the belief that leisure experience has a vital impact on the physical health, mental health, life satisfaction, and personal growth of all individuals. Given the importance of leisure experience, it is obvious that any counseling psychologist not properly prepared to deal with this aspect of the individual's life is, in fact, a counseling psychologist not properly prepared.

REFERENCES

Allen, L. R. (1982). The relationship between Murray's personality needs and leisure interests. *Journal of Leisure Research, 14,* 63–76.

Avedon, E. M. (1974). *Therapeutic recreation service.* Englewood Cliffs, NJ: Prentice–Hall.

Beard, J. G., & Ragheb, M. G. (1980). Measuring leisure satisfaction. *Journal of Leisure Research, 12,* 20–33.

Beard, J. G., & Ragheb, M. G. (1983). Measuring leisure motivation. *Journal of Leisure Research, 15,* 219–228.

Berryman, D. L., & Lefebvre, C. B. (1979). *Recreation behavioral inventory.* Unpublished instrument, (available from C. B. Lefebvre, 2225 East McKinney, Denton, TX 76201).

Bordin, E. S. (1979). Fusing work and play: A challenge to theory and research. *Academic Psychology Bulletin, 1,* 5–9.

Brightbill, C. K. (1960). *The challenge of leisure.* Englewood Cliffs, NJ: Prentice–Hall.

Brok, A. J. (1975, August). *Issues in leisure relevant to counseling and applied human development.* Symposium presented at the meeting of the American Psychological Association, Chicago.

Bronfenbrenner, U. (1968). When is infant stimulation effective. In D. C. Glass (Ed.), *Environmental influences.* New York: Rockefeller University Press and Russell Sage Foundation.

Brown, P. J., & Haas, G. E. (1980). Wilderness recreation experiences: The Rawah case. *Journal of Leisure Research, 12,* 229–241.

Bryan, H., & Alsikafi, M. (1975). *The case of university professors.* Sociological Studies No. 3, University of Alabama, Bureau of Public Administration.

Buchholz, R. A. (1978). The work ethic reconsidered. *Industrial & Labor Relations Review, 31,* 450–459.

Burdge, R. J. (1961). *The development of a leisure orientation scale.* Unpublished master's thesis, Ohio State University, Columbus.

Butler, R. A. (1954). Curiosity in monkeys. *Scientific American, 190,* 70–75.

Cooper, K. H. (1968). *Aerobics,* Philadelphia: J. B. Lippincott.

Cooper, R. M., & Zubek, J. P. (1958). Effects of enriched and restricted early environments on the learning ability of bright and dull rats. *Canadian Journal of Psychology, 12,* 159–164.

Csikszentmihalyi, M. (1975). *Before boredom and anxiety.* San Francisco: Jossey–Bass.

Csikszentmihalyi, M. (1979). *The value of leisure: Towards a systematic analysis of leisure activities.* Waterloo, Ontario: Otium Publications, Research Group on Leisure and Cultural Development, University of Waterloo.

Csikszentmihalyi, M. (1980). *Subject delineation of proposed leisure information network.* First International Leisure Information Network (LINK) Conference, Brussels.

D'Agostini, N. (1972). *Avocational activities interest index.* Unpublished manuscript (available from N. D'Agostini, Sutter Memorial Hospital, Sacramento, CA 95819).

Dawis, R. V., Lofquist, L. H., Henly, G. A., & Rounds, J. B. (1979). *Minnesota occupational classification system II.* Minneapolis: Vocational Psychology Research, Department of Psychology, University of Minnesota.

Dennis, W. (1960). Causes of retardation among institutionalized children: Iran. *Journal of Genetic Psychology, 96,* 47–59.

Driver, B. L. (1976). Quantification of outdoor recreationists' preferences. In B. Van der Smissen (Ed.), *Research camping and environmental education.* University Park, PA: Pennsylvania State University HPER Series No. 11.

Dumazedier, T. (1967). *Toward a society of leisure.* New York: Free Press.

Edwards, P. B. (1980). *Leisure counseling techniques: Individual and group counseling step-by-step* (3rd ed.). Los Angeles: Constructive Leisure.

Ellis, G., & Witt, P. A. (1984). The measurement of perceived freedom in leisure. *Journal of Leisure Research, 16,* 110–123.

Farley, F. (1986). The big T in personality. *Psychology Today, 20*(5), 44–52.

Glickman, S. E., & Sroges, R. W. (1966). Curiosity in zoo animals. *Behaviour, 26,* 151–188.

Goodman, N. C. (1969). Leisure, work and the use of time: A study of adult style of time utilization, childhood determinants, and vocational implications. *Dissertation Abstracts International, 30*(4–B), 1897.

Gray, D. E. (1981, March). *Recreation experience.* A paper presented at the meeting of the California Parks and Recreation Society, Pacific Southwest Conference, San Diego.

Gray, P. H. (1958). Theory and evidence of imprinting in human infants. *Journal of Psychology, 46,* 155–166.

Green, T. F. (1968). *Work, leisure, and the American schools.* New York: Random House.

Harlow, H. F. (1953). Mice, monkeys, men and motives. *Psychological Review, 60,* 23–32.

Harlow, H., & Harlow, M. K. (1962). Social deprivation in monkeys. *Scientific American, 207,* 136–146.

Havighurst, R. J. (1961). The nature and values of meaningful free-time activity. In R. W. Kleemeier (Ed.), *Aging and leisure.* New York: Oxford University Press.

Hess, E. H. (1959). Imprinting. *Science, 130,* 133–141.

Holland, J. L. (1966). *The psychology of vocational choice: A theory of personality types and model environments.* Waltham, MA: Ginn.

Holland, J. L. (1985). *Making vocational choices* (2nd ed.). Englewood Cliffs, NJ: Prentice–Hall.

Howe, C. Z. (1984). Leisure assessment and counseling. In E. T. Dowd (Ed.), *Leisure counseling: Concepts and applications.* Springfield, IL: C. C. Thomas.

Hubert, E. E. (1969). *The development of an inventory of leisure interests.* Unpublished doctoral dissertation, University of North Carolina at Chapel Hill.

Hunt, J. McV. (1969). *The challenge of incompetence and poverty.* Urbana: University of Illinois Press.

Hunt, J. McV. (1972). *Heredity, environment, and class of ethnic differences.* Invitational Conference on Testing Problems.

Iso-Ahola, S. E. (1980). *The social psychology of leisure and recreation.* Dubuque, IA: W. C. Brown.

Iso-Ahola, S. E. (1982). Toward a social psychological theory of tourism motivation: A rejoinder. *Annals of Tourism Research,* 256–262.

Iso-Ahola, S. E. (1984). Social psychological foundations of leisure and resultant implications for leisure counseling. In E. T. Dowd (Ed.), *Leisure counseling: Concepts and applications.* Springfield, IL: C. C. Thomas.

Iso-Ahola, S. E., & Allen, J. R. (1982). The dynamics of leisure motivation: The effects of outcome on leisure needs. *Research Quarterly for Exercise & Sport, 53,* 141–149.

Joswiak, K. F. (1979). *Leisure counseling programs materials for the developmentally disabled.* Washington, DC: Hawkins & Associates.

Kaplan, J. D. (Ed.). (1950). *Dialogues of Plato.* New York: Washington Square Press.

Kaplan, M. (1975). *Leisure: Theory and policy.* New York: Wiley.

Kelly, J. R. (1972). Work and leisure: A simplified paradigm. *Journal of Leisure Research, 4,* 50–62.

Kelly, J. R. (1976). *A revised paradigm of leisure choices.* Paper presented at the meeting of the American Sociological Association, New York.

Lewko, J., & Crandall, R. (1980). Research trends in leisure and special populations. *Journal of Leisure Research, 12,* 69–79.

Loesch, L. C., & Wheeler, P. T. (1982). *Principles of leisure counseling.* Minneapolis: Educational Media Corporation.

Lofquist, L. H., & Dawis, R. V. (1969). *Adjustment to work.* New York: Appleton–Century–Crofts.

Mannell, R. C. (1980). Social psychological techniques and strategies for studying leisure experience. In S. E. Iso–Ahola (Ed.), *Social psychological perspectives on leisure and recreation.* Springfield, IL: C. C. Thomas.

Maslow, A. H. (1968). *Toward a psychology of being* (2nd ed.). New York: Van Nostrand.

Maslow, A. H. (1970). *Motivation and personality* (2nd ed.). Harper & Row.

McDowell, C. F. (1973). *Approaching leisure counseling with the self leisure interest profile.* Unpublished master's thesis, California State University, Los Angeles.

McDowell, C. F., Jr. (1976). *Leisure counseling: Selected lifestyle processes.* Eugene, OR: Center for Leisure Studies.

McDowell, C. F. (1979). *The leisure well-being inventory.* Eugene, OR: Leisure Lifestyle Consultants.

McDowell, C. F., Jr. (1981). Leisure: Consciousness, well-being, and counseling. *Counseling Psychologist, 9,* 3–32.

McEwen, D., & Malley, F. G. (1977). Leisure counseling for the college undergraduate. In D. M. Compton & J. E. Goldstein (Eds.), *Perspectives of leisure counseling.* Washington, DC: National Recreation and Park Association.

McKechnie, G. E. (1975). *Manual for the Leisure Activities Blank.* Palo Alto, CA: Consulting Psychologists Press.

Mirenda, J. J., & Wilson, G. T. (1975). The Milwaukee leisure counseling model. *Counseling and Values, 20*(1), 42–46.

Morris, W. (Ed.). (1969). *The American heritage dictionary of the English language.* New York: American Heritage.

Mundy, C. J. (1981). *Leisure assessment instruments.* Unpublished manuscript (available from Dr. C. J. Mundy, Department of Human Services and Studies, Florida State University, Tallahassee, FL 32306).

Navar, N. (1979). *State Technical Institute Leisure Activities Project.* Champaign, IL: Department of Leisure Studies, University of Illinois.

Neulinger, J. (1974). *The psychology of leisure.* Springfield, IL: C. C. Thomas.

Neulinger, J. (1976). The need for the implications of a psychological conception of leisure. *Ontario Psychologist, 8,* 13–20.

Neulinger, J. (1981). *To leisure: An introduction.* Boston: Allyn & Bacon.

Neulinger, J. (1986). *What am I doing? The WAID.* Dolgeville, NY: Leisure Institute.

Novick, M. R. (chair). (1985). *Standards for educational and psychological testing.* Washington, DC: American Psychological Association.

Overs, R. P., Taylor, S., & Adkins, C. (1974). *Avocational counseling in Milwaukee.* Final report on project H233466, No. 5D, Curative Workshop of Milwaukee.

Overs, R. P., Taylor, S., & Adkins, C. (1977). *Avocational counseling manual: A complete guide to leisure guidance.* Washington, DC: Hawkins & Associates.

Overs, R. P., Taylor, S., Cassell, E., & Chernov, M. (1977). *Avocational counseling for the elderly*. Sussex, WI: Avocational Counseling Research.

Parker, R. A., Ellison, C. H., Kirby, T. F., & Short, M. J. (1975). Comprehensive evaluation in recreation therapy scale: A tool for patient evaluation. *Therapeutic Recreation Journal, 9*, 143–153.

Pierce, R. C. (1980a). Dimensions of leisure, I: Satisfactions. *Journal of Leisure Research, 12*, 5–19.

Pierce, R. C. (1980b). Dimensions of leisure. II: Descriptions. *Journal of Leisure Research, 12*, 150–163.

Pierce, R. C. (1980c). Dimensions of leisure. III: Characteristics. *Journal of Leisure Research, 12*, 273–284.

Ragheb, M. G. (1980). Interrelationships among leisure participation, leisure satisfaction, and leisure attitudes. *Journal of Leisure Research, 12*, 138–149.

Ragheb, M. G., & Beard, J. G. (1980). Leisure satisfaction: Concept, theory and measurement. In S. E. Iso–Ahola (Ed.), *Social psychological perspectives on leisure and recreation*. Springfield, IL: C. C. Thomas.

Remple, J. (1977). A community-based experiment in leisure counseling. In A. Epperson, P. A. Witt, & G. Hitzhusen (Eds.), *Leisure counseling: An aspect of leisure education*. Springfield, IL: C. C. Thomas.

Rimmer, S. M. (1979). *The development of an instrument to assess leisure satisfaction among secondary school students*. Unpublished doctoral dissertation, University of Florida.

Rossman, J. R. (1981, October). *Development of a leisure program evaluation instrument*. A paper presented at the SPRE Research Symposium. National Recreation and Park Association, Minneapolis.

Schreyer, R., Lime, D. W., & Williams, D. R. (1984). Characterizing the influence of past experience on recreation behavior. *Journal of Leisure Research, 16*, 34–50.

Slivken, K. E. (1978). *Development of a leisure ethic scale*. Unpublished master's thesis, University of Illinois at Urabana–Champaign.

Staines, G. L. (1980). Spillover versus compensation: A review of the literature on the relationship between work and nonwork. *Human Relations, 33*, 119–129.

Super, D. E. (1940). *Avocational interest patterns*. Palo Alto, CA: Stanford University Press.

Super, D. E. (1980). A life-span, life-space approach to career development. *Journal of Vocational Behavior, 16*, 282–298.

Szalai, A. (Ed.). (1972). *The use of time: Daily activities of urban and suburban populations in twelve countries*. The Hague: Mouton.

Tinsley, H. E. A. (1978). The ubiquitous question of why. In D. J. Brademas, *New thoughts on leisure*. Champaign: University of Illinois Press.

Tinsley, H. E. A. (1984). The psychological benefits of leisure participation. *Society & Leisure, 7*, 125–140.

Tinsley, H. E. A. (chair). (1986, August). *Development of a leisure counseling infrastructure*. Symposium at the meeting of the American Psychological Association, Washington, DC.

Tinsley, H. E. A., Barrett, T. C., & Kass, R. A. (1977). Leisure activities and need satisfaction. *Journal of Leisure Research, 9*, 110–120.

Tinsley, H. E. A., & Bowman, S. L. (1986). Discriminant validity of the Paragraphs About Leisure for expert and naive respondents. *Educational & Psychological Measurement, 46*, 461–465.

Tinsley, H. E. A., & Johnson, T. L. (1984). A preliminary taxonomy of leisure activities. *Journal of Leisure Research, 16*, 234–244.

Tinsley, H. E. A., & Kass, R. A. (1978). Leisure activities and need satisfaction: A replication and extension. *Journal of Leisure Research, 10*, 191–202.

Tinsley, H. E. A., & Kass, R. A. (1979). The latent structure of the need satisfying properties of leisure activities. *Journal of Leisure Research, 11*, 278–291.

Tinsley, H. E. A., & Kass, R. A. (1980a). The construct validity of the leisure activities questionnaire and of the paragraphs about leisure. *Educational & Psychological Measurement, 40,* 219–226.

Tinsley, H. E. A., & Kass, R. A. (1980b). Discriminant validity of the leisure activity questionnaire and the paragraphs about leisure. *Educational & Psychological Measurement, 40,* 227–233.

Tinsley, H. E. A., Teaff, J. D., Colbs, S. L., & Kaufman, N. (1985). A system of classifying leisure activities in terms of the psychological benefits of participation reported by older persons. *Journal of Gerontology, 40,* 172–178.

Tinsley, H. E. A., & Tinsley, D. J. (1981). An analysis of leisure counseling models. *Counseling Psychologist, 9*(3), 45–53.

Tinsley, H. E. A., & Tinsley, D. J. (1982). A holistic model of leisure counseling. *Journal of Leisure Research, 14,* 100–116.

Tinsley, H. E. A., & Tinsley, D. J. (1986). A theory of the attributes, benefits and causes of leisure experience. *Leisure Sciences, 8,* 1–45.

Trafton, R. S., & Tinsley, H. E. A. (1980). An investigation of the construct validity of measures of job, leisure, dyadic and general life satisfaction. *Journal of Leisure Research, 12,* 34–44.

Walshe, W. A. (1977). Leisure counseling instrumentation. In D. M. Compton & J. E. Goldstein (Eds.), *Perspectives of leisure counseling.* Washington, DC: National Recreation and Park Association.

Williamson, E. G., Layton, W. L., & Snoke, M. L. (1954). *A study of participation in college activities.* Minneapolis: University of Minnesota Press.

Zytowski, D. G. (1985). Frank, Frank! Where are you now that we need you? *Counseling Psychologist, 13,* 129–135.

Author Index

A

Abel, W. H., 35, *71*
Abernathy, L. J., 103, 130
Adkins, C., 251, 252, *262*
Alexander, D. E., 50, *75*
Alexander, R., 49, *75*
Allen, J. R., 240, *260, 261*
Alvi, A. S., 85, 87, 88, 89, *130, 133*
Anastasi, A., 118, 119, *130*
Anderson, H. D., 3, *28*
Arcia, M. A., 85, 88, 89, 90, 91, 118, 124,
    136
Arroba, T., 22, 23, 25, 27
Ashby, J. D., 36, *71*
Astin, A. W., 33, 35, *71*
Aubrey, R. F., 4, *27*
Avedon, E. M., 220, *260*
Axelrad, S., 4, *28,* 35, *72,* 77, *132*

B

Baird, L. L., 34, 36, *71*
Baker, R. D., 15, *30*
Bandura, A., 23, *27*
Barak, A., 25, *30,* 46, 48, 49, 66, *71, 74, 76*
Barber, J. E., 108, *132*
Barber, S., 57, *74*
Barnett, D. C., 57, *75*

Barrett, T. C., 36, *71,* 234, *263*
Bartlett, W. E., 88, *130*
Bartling, H. C., 61, *71*
Bauernfeind, R. H., 147, *208*
Beard, J. G., 236, 240, 252, 253, *260, 263*
Benjamin, L., 139, 140, *211*
Bernard, C. B., 57, *75*
Betz, N. E., 23, 25, *31,* 50, *76,* 118, *135,*
    139, 156, 158, 177, 180, *211*
Blaha, J., 89, 90, *131*
Blum, C. R., 43, 44, *72*
Bodden, J. L., 105, *130*
Bohn, M., 35, *71*
Boocock, S. S., 19, *27*
Bordin, E. S., 224, 227, *260*
Borgen, F. H., 61, *71,* 81, *130,* 181, *208*
Bouchard, T. J., 158, *208*
Bowman, S. L., 256, *263*
Bradley, R. W., 36, 39, 49, *72, 74*
Brewer, J. M., 3, *27*
Brightbill, C. K., 218, *260*
Brok, A. J., 220, 240, *260*
Bronfenbrenner, U., 226, *260*
Brooks, L., 80, *130*
Bross, I. O., 13, 15, *27*
Brown, D., 80, *130*
Brown, P. J., 236, 240, *260*
Buehler, C., 4, 5, *27,* 78, *130*
Burkey-Flanagan, R. J., 61, *71*
Buros, O. K., 141, *208*
Butler, R. A., 226, *260*

C

Cairo, P. C., 61, *71*, 203, *208*
Campbell, B. A., 108, *130*
Campbell, D. P., 120, *132*
Campbell, D. T., 123, 129, *130*
Campbell, R. E., 114, *130*
Capehart, R., 87, *130*
Carek, R., 87, *130*
Carney, C. G., 25, *30, 43*, 46, 48, 49, 61, 74, 205, *208*
Cassell, E., 244, *263*
Cattell, R. B., 82, *131*
Cellini, J. V., 114, *130*
Cesari, J. P., 50, *71*
Chenery, M. F., 58, *73*
Chernov, M., 244, *263*
Chodzinski, R. T., 85, *131*
Clarke, R. B., 18, *28*
Clyde, J. S., 185, 190, *208*
Colbs, S. L., 235, *264*
Cole, N. S., 104, *131*
Collarelli, S. M., 18, *30*
Cooper, J. F., 18, *27*
Cooper, K. H., 248, *260*
Cooper, R. M., 226, 227, *260*
Cooper, S. E., 42, 44, *71, 76*
Coscarelli, W., 24, *29*
Covington, J. E., 152, *211*
Crandall, R., 258, *262*
Crites, J. O., 5, 6, 8, 9, 10, 11, 12, 17, 25, *27, 31, 33*, 39, 40, 41, *71*, 78, 79, 81, 82, 83, 84, 85, 86, 87, 88, 89, 90, 109, 110, 113, 114, 115, 116, 117, 119, 121, 124, 127, *130, 131, 134, 135*
Cron, W. L., 111, 112, 117, *134*
Cronbach, L. J., 83, 121, 126, *131*
Csikszentmikalyi, M., 220, 222, 223, 255, *260*
Cummings, R., 185, 186, 187, *210*
Cutts, C. C., 85, 88, 89, 90, 91, 118, 124, *136*

D

Daiger, D. C., 25, *29*, 51, 52, 53, 54, 55, *73*, 106, *132*
Daniels, M. H., 178, *208*
Darley, J. G., 2, *30*
Darrow, C. N., 7, *30*

Davidson, P. E., 3, *28*
Dawis, R. V., 3, *28*, 82, 109, *131, 132, 133*, 241, 242, 257, *261, 262*
Dean, G. L., 142, 151, 173, 180, 190, *211*
DeFrank, R. S., 113, *132*
Dennis, W., 227, *261*
Dickson, R. D., 61, 63, *75*
Dilley, J. S., 13, 17, 20, *28, 29*, 65, *73*
Dinklage, L. B., 21, 22, 23, *28*
Dixon, D. N., 18, *28*
Dolliver, R. H., 61, *71*, 173, 179, *208*
Domino, G., 169, 170, 171, *208*
Donald, G. M., 185, 186, *210*
Driver, B. L., 255, *261*
Dumazedier, T., 219, *261*
D'Zurilla, T. J., 16, *28*

E

Edwards, W., 20, *28*
Ellis, G., 220, 222, 224, 254, 255, *261*
Elton, C. F., 35, 36, *71, 75*
England, G. W., 109, *131*
Erikson, E. H., 4, 6, *28*, 35, *71*
Ewens, W. P., 162, *209*

F

Fadale, L. M., 103, *132*
Farley, F., 227, *261*
Farnum, S. O., 50, *72*
Fast, S., 36, *71*
Fauble, M. L., 36, *75*
Feingold, S. N., 108, *132*
Festinger, L., 14, *28*
Fiske, D. W., 123, 129
Fitzgerald, L. F., 115, 116, *132*
Fitzgerald, P. W., 50, *74*
Fleenor, J., 91, 106, 107, *136*
Fletcher, F. M., 14, *28*
Foote, B., 35, *71*
Foreman, J., 167, *209*
Form, W. H., 4, *30*, 110, *133*
Forrest, D., 9, *28, 31*, 79
Fretz, B. R., 125, 126, *132*
Friedkes, R., 49, *71*
Fuqua, D. R., 43, 44, *71, 72*
Fukuyama, M., 50, *74*
Fulton, B., 108, *132*

G

Galinsky, D. A., 36, *71*
Garren, R., 91, 106, 107, *136*
Gati, I., 69, *71*
Gelatt, H. B., 15, 18, *28, 65, 71*
Gelso, C. J., 66, *71*
Ginsburg, S. W., 4, *28*, 35, *71*, 77, *132*
Ginzberg, E., 4, *28*, 35, *72*, 77, *132*
Glaize, D. L., 50, *72*
Glickman, S. E., 226, *261*
Goldfried, M. R., 16, *28*
Goodstein, L. D., 38, 40, *72*
Gordon, V. N., 33, 61, *72*
Gorsuch, R. L., 39, *75*
Gotkin, E. H., 9, *31*
Gottfredson, G. D., 53, 54, 55, 58, 59, *72*,
  73
Gottfredson, L. S., 69
Grabowski, B. T., 187, *209*
Graef, M. I., 49, 56, *72*
Graves, T. D., 87, *132*
Gray, P. H., 227, 240, *261*
Green, T. F., 220, 261
Greenhaus, J. H., 35, 59, *72*, 81, 103, 106,
  117, *132*
Gribbons, W. D., 11, *28*
Grotevant, H. D., 56, *72*
Guilford, J. P., 89, 119, *132*

H

Haas, G. E., 236, 240, *260*
Hall, D. W., 35, 87, *72, 132*
Hall, T., 117, *134*
Hall, W. L., 142, 151, 173, 180, 190
Hamel, D. A., 15, 20, 23, 24, 25, *30*, 67, 68,
  72, 73, 81, 108, *133*
Hansen, J. C., 95, 98, 120, *132*, 147, *209*
Hansen, R. W., 111, 112, 117, *134*
Harlow, H. F., 226, *261*
Harlow, M. K., 226, *261*
Harman, R. L., 35, 36, *72*
Harmon, L. W., 49, 50, *72*
Harren, V. A., 14, 16, 17, 19, 22, 23, 24,
  28, 59, *72, 74*
Harrington, T. F., 150, 152, 153, 209
Harris-Bowlsby, J., 185, 188, *209, 211*
Hartman, B. W., 43, 44, 50, *71, 72*
Hartman, K., 18, *30*

Hartman, P. T., 43, 44, 50, *72*
Havighurst, R. J., 6, *29*, 240, *261*
Hawkins, J. G., 36, 39, *72*
Healy, C. C., 105, *132, 136*
Heath, D. H., 109, *132*
Hecklinger, F. J., 35, 36, *72*
Heesacker, M., 81, *135*
Henkels, M. T., 57, *72*
Henly, G. A., 241, 242, *261*
Heppner, M. J., 187, *209*
Heppner, P. P., 16, 18, 23, 25, *28*, 50, 60,
  72, 73
Herma, J. L., 4, *28*, 35, *72*, 77, 132
Herman, D. O., 36, 49, *72, 74*
Herr, E. L., 140, *209*
Hesketh, B., 24, 25, *29*
Hess, E. H., 227, *261*
Heyde, M. B., 9, *29*
Hill, R. E., 113, *132*
Hilton, T. L., 14, 17, *29*
Hoffman, M. A., 57, *72*
Holland, J. E., 17, 23, 25, *29*, 41, 49, 52,
  53, 61, 62, *73*
Holland, J. L., 3, 17, 21, 23, 25, *29*, 35, 41,
  49, 51, 52, 53, 54, 55, 57, 58, 59, 61,
  62, 63, *73, 75*, 82, 106, *132*, 177, 178,
  209, 241, 242, 249, *261*
Hollender, J. W., 87, *133*
Hollingshead, A. B., 3, *29*
Hood, A. B., 61, *71*
Hoppock, R., 116, *133*
Horan, J. J., 13, *29*
Horne, D. F., 91, 106, 107, *136*
Howe, C. Z., 249, *261*
Hoyt, K. B., 169, *209*
Hudson, K. S., 183, *210*
Hummel, R. C., 5, 6, 8, 9, *31*, 78, *134*
Hunt, J. McV, 227, *261*
Hyland, A. M., 49, 56, *72*

I

Iso-Ahola, S. E., 220, 224, 226, 227, 240,
  261
Ivancevich, J. M., 113, *132*

J

Jacobson, M. D., 187, *209*
Janis, I. L., 16, 17, 18, *29*

Jepsen, D. A., 13, 20, 21, 23, 24, *29*, 65, *73*, 87, 88, 89, 97, 102, 107, 121, 122, 123, 129, *133*
Johnson, D. ., 81, *130*
Johnson, J., 24, *29*
Johnson, R. P., 80, *132*
Johnson, R. W., 21, 23, 24, *29*, 156, *209*
Johnson, S. O., 108, *130*
Johnson, T. L., 234, *263*
Johnston, J. A., 187, *209*
Jones, G. B., 15, 17, 18, *29, 30*
Jones, L. K., 58, *73*
Jordaan, J. P., 5, 6, 9, 17, *29, 31*, 56, *75*, 93, 94, 96, 110, *135*

K

Kaldor, D. B., 15, 17, *29*
Kapes, J. T., 81, 141, 142, *209*
Kaplan, J. D., 214, *262*
Kamplan, M., 218, 220, 222, *262*
Kass, R. A., 17, *29*, 234, 235, 236, 240, 242, 255, 256, *263, 264*
Katz, M. R., 15, 17, 18, 19, 20, *29*, 65, 67, *73*, 88, *133*, 139, 185, 186, 187, 202, *209*
Kaufman, N., 235, *264*
Kelly, J. R., 240, *262*
Khan, S. B., 85, 87, 88, 89, *130, 133*
Kidd, J. M., 12, *31*
Kiesler, D. J., 41, *73*
Kimes, H. G., 36, 39, *73*
Kinnier, R. T., 20, 22, 23, 24, 25, *30*, 68, *73*
Kitson, H. D., 2, 3, *30*
Klein, E. B., 7, *30*
Klein, S. P., 105, *132*
Knapp, L., 143, 147, 148, *209*
Knapp, R. R., 143, 147, 148, *209*
Koschier, M., 43, 46, 61, *74*
Kowalski, R. S., 9, *31*
Krauskopf, C. J., 180, *209*
Krumboltz, J. D., 15, 17, 18, 20, 22, 23, 24, 25, *29, 30*, 65, 67, 68, *73, 74*, 81, 108, *133*

L

Layton, W. L., 81, *130*, 147, 183, *209*, 257, *264*

Laird, I. O., 50, *71*
Larson, L. M., 50, 60, *73*
Lazarsfeld, P., 4, *30*
Lehman, I. J., 89, 119, 133
Levinson, D. J., 7, *30*
Levinson, M. H., 7, *30*
Lewin, K., 14, *30*
Lewis, E. T., 57, 64, *75*
Lewis, R. O., 36, *76*
Lewko, J., 258, *262*
Lindeman, R. H., 9, 12, 17, *31*, 56, *75*, 93, 94, 96, 110, *135*
Lime, D. W., 227, *263*
Linn, R. L., 158, *209*
LoCascio, R., 12, *30*
Locke, D. C., 183, *210*
Loesch, L. C., 108, *133*, 249, 252, 253, *262*
Lofquist, L. H., 3, *28*, 82, 109, *131, 132, 133*, 241, 242, 257, *261, 262*
Lohnes, P. R., 11, *28*, 160, 210
Lokan, J., 98, 133
London, M., 117, 133
Long, A. E., 114, 130
Lowe, B., 50, *73*
Lowther, M. A., 113, 132
Lunneborg, P. W., 17, 25, *30, 33, 35*, 56, *73, 74*
Lutz, S. W., 61, *73*
Lushene, R. E., 39, *75*

M

Mac-Kinnon-Slaney, F., 57, 61, 64, *74, 75*
Madison, S. S., 85, 88, 89, 90, 91, 118, 124, *136*
Magoon, J. M., 63, *73*
Maier, D., 36, *74*
Maloney, S. E., 172, *210*
Mann, L., 16, 17, 18, *29, 30*
Mannuell, R. C., 220, 222, *262*
Manuele, C. A., 12, *30*
Marr, E., 36, *74*
Marshall, J. C., 108, *133*
Maslow, A. H., 223, 229, *262*
Mastie, M. M., 79, 81, 99, 100, *136*, 141, 142, 158, 159, *209, 210*
Matlin, N., 5, 6, *31*
Maze, M., 185, 186, 187, 188, 190, *210*
McDowell, C. F., 220, 222, 254, *262*
McGowan, A. S., 40, *74*

McKechnie, G. E., 249, 253, *262*
McKee, B., 7, *30*
McKillip, J., 66, *74*
McLean, J. E., 118, *133*
Meehl, P. E., 121, 126, *131*
Mehrens, W. A., 89, 119, *133*, 154, *210*
Mendonca, J. D., 40, *74*
Miller, C. H., 35, *74*
Miller, D. C., 14, *30*, 110, *133*
Miller, E. L., 113, *132*
Miller, J. V., 139, 140, 205, *210*
Miller-Tiedeman, A., 168, *210*
Mitchell, A. M., 15, 17, *30*
Mitchell, J. V., Jr., 89, 103, *141*, 141, *210*
Mitchell, L. K., 20, 22, 23, 24, 25, 65, 67,
    68, *73, 74*, 108, *133*
Montrose, D. H., 185, 187, *210*
Moore, T. L., 118, *133*
Moreland, J. R., 17, *29*
Morris, W., 219, *262*
Morrison, R. F., 111, *133*
Moser, H. P., 5, 6, 8, 9, *31*, 78, *134*
Mossholder, D. H., 173, 174, *210*
Muchinsky, P. M., 49, 56, *72*
Myers, R. A., 9, 17, *31*, 56, *75*, 93, 94, 110,
    135
Myrick, R. D., 50, *72*

N

Nafziger, D. H., 53, 59, *73*
Nagy, D. R., 185, 186, *210*
Neidert, G. P. M., 183, *210*
Neimeyer, G. J., 50, *74*
Nelson, E., 35, *74*
Nelson, N., 35, *74*
Neulinger, J., 220, 231, 251, 252, 253, 254,
    262
Nevill, D. D., 50, *74*, 93, 97, 106, *133, 135*
Nichols, R. C., 35, *73*
Niece, D., 49, *74*
Norris, L., 19, 20, *29*
Novick, M. R., 249, *262*
Nunnally, J., 118, 119, *133*

O

O'Hara, R. P., 13, 16, *31*, 37, *76*, 77, *135*
Oliver, L. W., 19, *30*, 66, *74*, 125, *133*

O'Neal, P., 91, 106, 107, *136*
Osipow, S. H., 25, *30*, 33, 36, 43, 46, 48,
    49, 50, 61, *71, 74, 75*, 78, 80, 81, 87,
    90, 106, 115, *133, 134, 135*
O'Shea, J. O., 150, 152, 153, *209*
Overs, R. P., 244, 251, 252, *262, 263*
Overstreet, P. L., 5, 6, 8, 9, *31*, 78, 122,
    134, 135
Owens, W. A., 56, *74*

P

Palko-Nonemaker, D., 49, *75*
Parasuraman, S., 81, 117, *132*
Parr, F. W., 2, *30*
Parry-Hill, J. W., 11, *31*, 99, *136*
Parsons, F., 2, 13, *30*, 82, *134*
Patterson, D. G., 2, *30*
Pears, L., 19, 20, *29*
Petersen, C. H., 18, 25, *28, 29*, 60, *72*
Phillips, S. D., 113, *134*
Pick, D. J., 166, *210*
Pierce, R. C., 236, 240, *263*
Pinder, F. A., 50, *74*
Pinkney, J. W., 98, *134*
Pinkos, D., 114, *130*
Piper, K. R., 50, *71*
Pitz, G. F., 19, *30*, 65, 66, *74, 75*
Porter, E. H., 172, *210*
Powell, C. R., 205, *210*
Power, P. G., 25, *29*, 51, 52, 53, 54, 55, 58,
    73, 106, *132*
Prediger, D. P., 87, 88, 89, 97, 102, 105,
    107, 122, 123, 129, *133, 134*
Probert, B., 50, *74*
Putzstuck, C., 142, 151, 173, 180, 190, *211*

R

Rabinowitz, S., 117, *134*
Ragheb, M. G., 236, 240, 252, 253, *260, 263*
Randhawa, B. S., 85, *131*
Rawlings, S., 111, 112, 117, *134*
Rayman, J. R., 57, *75*, 177, *209*
Read, R. W., 180, *210*
Reed, R., 50, *74*
Remple, J., 220, *263*
Resnick, H., 36, *75*
Richards, L. S., 2, *30*

Ripley, M. J., 183, *210*
Ripley, R. E., 183, *210*
Rogers, B., 102, 103, *136,* 152, *211*
Rogers, C. R., 4, *30*
Rogers, W. B., 49, *75*
Ronning, R. R., 18, *28*
Rose, H. A., 35, 36, *71, 75*
Rossman, J. R., 236, 240, *263*
Rounds, J. B., 241, 242, *261*
Rucker, B. B., 108, *133*
Rude, S., 20, 22, 23, 24, 25, *30,* 68, *73*
Rummel, R. J., 90, 91, *134*
Russell, J. E. A., 49, 61, 62, *75*

S

Sacks, N. J., 65, *75*
Salomone, P. R., 42, 44, *75*
Sampson, J. P., Jr., 185, *210*
Sanford, E. E., 91, 106, 107, *136*
Savickas, M. L., 50, 56, 57, *75,* 121, 124, 129, *134*
Schein, E. H., 7, *30*
Scherba, D. S., 20, 22, 23, 24, 25, *30,* 67, *73*
Schneulle, L., 25, *31,* 61, *76*
Schreyer, R., 227, *263*
Seeman, J., 58, *75*
Selig, M. J., 61, *71*
Shaltry, P. E., 114, *130*
Shatkin, L., 139, 185, 186, 187, *209, 211*
Sheppard, D. I., 12, *30*
Shub, P. A., 108, *133*
Siess, T. F., 40, *74*
Silling, S. M., 89, 90, 124, *135*
Simon, H. A., 22, *30*
Simon, W. E., 35, 59, *72*
Sink, C., 104, *34*
Slaney, R. B., 49, 57, 61, 62, 63, 64, *74, 75*
Slivken, K. E., 252, *263*
Slocum, J. W., Jr., 111, 112, 117, *134*
Smith, M. L., 104, *134*
Snoke, M. L., 257, *264*
Sorenson, G., 169, *211*
Spielberger, C. D., 39, *75*
Spokane, A. R., 57, 63, *72, 73,* 115, *133*
Sroges, R. W., 226, *261*
Stafford, M. J., 49, 62, *75*
Staines, G. L., 236, 263
Starishevsky, R., 5, 6, *31*
Stumpf, S. A., 18, *30,* 117, 133, 134

Super, D. E., 3, 5, 6, 7, 8, 9, 12, 17, *30, 31,* 35, 36, *75,* 77, 78, 79, 80, 83, 92, 93, 94, 96, 97, 98, 106, 109, 110, 111, 122, 124, *133, 134, 135, 211,* 257, *263*
Swerdloff, S., 108, *132*
Szalai, A., 219, *263*

T

Taylor, K. M., 23, 25, *31,* 35, 36, 50, *75, 76*
Taylor, S., 244, 251, 252, *262, 263*
Teaff, J. D., 235, 264
Terman, L. M., 4, *31*
Thompson, A. S., 9, 12, 17, *28, 31, 56, 75,* 79, 93, 94, 96, 110, 124, *135*
Thompson, O., 35, *76*
Thorbecke, W. L., 56, *71*
Thurstone, L. L., 90, *135*
Tiedeman, D. V., 13, 16, 18, *31,* 35, *76,* 77, *135*
Tinsley, D. J., 219, 220, 234, 240, 257, 259, *264*
Tinsley, H. E. A., 17, *29,* 36, *56, 71, 76,* 81, *135,* 219, 220, 229, 234, 235, 236, 240, 242, 252, 255, 256, 257, 259, *263, 264*
Tittle, C. K., 178, 179, *211*
Tolsma, R., 108, *132*
Trafton, R. S., 252, *264*
Troth, W. A., 36, 39, *73*
Tversky, H., 69, *76*
Tyler, L. E., 38, *76*

U

Utz, P. W., 50, *72*

V

Van Matre, G., 42, *76*
Veenhuizen, D. L., 81, *130*
Vernon, P. E., 82, *135*
Vetter, L., 142, 151, 173, 180, 190, *211*
Vroom, V., 14, *31*

W

Waldren, P., 190, *210*
Wall, H. W., 36, *71*

Wallbrown, F. H., 89, 90, 124, *131, 135*
Walsh, W. B., 36, *76,* 80, 81, 87, 118, *135,*
    139, 156, 158, 177, 180, *211*
Walshe, W. A., 249, 254, *264*
Walter, V., 172, 174, *211*
Warnath, C. F., 5, 6, 8, 9, *31,* 78, *134*
Watley, D., 35, 36, *76*
Walz, G. R., 139, 140
Weiss, D. J., 91, 109, *132, 135*
Wells, D. L., 49, 56, *72*
Wells, C. F., 205, *208*
Westbrook, B. W., 11, *31,* 49, 56, *75,* 76,
    79, 85, 88, 89, 90, 91, 99, 100, 102,
    103, 105, 106, 107, 118, 119, 120, 121,
    122, 124, *135, 136,* 152, *211*
Wheeler, P. T., 249, 252, 253, *262*
White, G. W., 36, 39, *72*
White, R. W., 4, *31*
Wiggins, J. G., 103, *136*
Will, J. A., 61, *71*
Williams, D. R., 227, *263*
Williams-Phillips, L. J., 49, 56, 60, 62, *76*
Williamson, E. G., 34, 35, *76,* 82, *136,* 257,
    264
Willis, C. G., 151, 152, 205, *211*

Winefordner, D. W., 171, *211*
Winer, J. L., 43, 46, 50, 61, *71, 74*
Witt, P. A., 220, 222, 224, 254, 255, *261*
Wolf, F. M., 50, *75*
Woodbury, R. W., 11, *31*

Y

Yaegel, J. S., 25, *31*
Yanico, B., 43, 46, 61, *74*
Yen, F. B., 105, *136*

Z

Zakay, D., 66, *76*
Zener, T. B., 25, *31,* 61, *76*
Ziller, R. C., 36, *76*
Zubek, J. P., 226, 227, *260*
Zunker, V. G., 81, *136,* 187, 205, *211*
Zychlinski, F., 50, *71*
Zytowski, D. G., 1, 15, 17, *29, 31,* 88, 120,
    136, 217, *264*

Subject Index

A

Adult Career Concerns Inventory, 110–113

C

Career Adjustment and Development Inventory, 113–117
Career Awareness Inventory, 103–105
Career decision making, 33–70
Career decision making process, 13–20
Career decision making system, 150–153
Career Decision Scale, 46–51
Career development and maturity, 77–130
Career Development Inventory, 9–11, 92–99
Career development theory, 3–4
Career finder, 190
Career indecision, 37–65
Career information system, 196–197
Career maturity and adjustment, 109–117
Career Maturity Inventory, 81–91
Career occupational preference system, 143–150
Career planning program, 153–156
Career Planning Questionnaire, 105–108
Career planning systems, 137–208
Career scan IV, 190–195
Career skills assessment program, 101–103

Careerwise, 159–162
Cognitive Vocational Maturity Test, 11, 99–101
Computerized heuristic occupational information and career explorations system, 195–196
Coordinated occupational information network, 198
Curricular career planning systems, 205

D

Decision making theory, 13–27
Differential Aptitude Tests with career planning program, 156–159
Discover systems, 198–200

E

Experience exploration, 162–164

G

Guidance information system, 200
Guide Pak, 164–167

I

Individual career exploration, 167–169
Individual differences, 20–26

M

Measurement of leisure constructs, 248–256
Micro skills, 200–201
My Vocational Situation Scale, 51–58

N

New Mexico Career Education Test, 105

O

Ohio Vocational Interest Survey with the career planner, 169–171

P

Pathfinder, 201–202
Personal career development profile, 171–174
Planning career goals, 174–177

R

Readiness for vocational planning, 11
Research on leisure activities, 234–248

S

System of interactive guidance and information, 202–203

T

The computerized career assessment and planning program, 195
The occupational alternatives question, 60–65
The select program C-LECT, 197–198
The Vocational Decision Scale, 58–60
Theory of leisure experience, 218–234

V

Vocational development, 4–12
Vocational Exploration and Insight Kit, 177–179
Vocational interest experience and skill assessment, 179–180
Vocational information profile, 180–182

W

World of Work Inventory, 182–184